CRITICAL ACCLAIM FOR ALEXIS BESPALOFF'S COMPLETE GUIDE TO WINE

"A pleasure to recommend. It is written with clarity and understanding ... literate, knowledgeable and nonpedantic approach ... an informal, common sense dissertation with the goal of a respectable understanding of what it's all about."
—*New York Times*

"Best book in many a year ... strongly recommended." —*Bon Appetit*

"The best all-round introduction to wine yet published in the USA ... serious yet never dull, thorough, and full of good sense." —*Decanter*

"A novice cannot seek a better preceptor than Alexis Bespaloff. He is knowledgeable and thorough, a writer who values clarity and seems incapable of condescension." —*Chicago Tribune*

"A classic work, it's the best one-volume no-nonsense guide there is." —*House Beautiful*

ALEXIS BESPALOFF revised and expanded *The New Frank Schoonmaker Encyclopedia of Wines,* edited *The Fireside Book of Wine,* a literary anthology, and wrote a *Guide to Inexpensive Wines.* He is a longtime contributor to *New York* magazine, and has written about wine for many other publications.

ALEXIS BESPALOFF'S COMPLETE GUIDE TO WINE

Revised and Expanded Edition

A SIGNET BOOK

SIGNET
Published by the Penguin Group
Penguin Books USA Inc., 375 Hudson Street,
New York, New York 10014, U.S.A.
Penguin Books Ltd, 27 Wrights Lane, London W8 5TZ, England
Penguin Books Australia Ltd, Ringwood, Victoria, Australia
Penguin Books Canada Ltd, 10 Alcorn Avenue,
Toronto, Ontario, Canada M4V 3B2
Penguin Books (N.Z.) Ltd, 182–190 Wairau Road,
Auckland 10, New Zealand

Penguin Books Ltd, Registered Offices:
Harmondsworth, Middlesex, England

Published by Signet, an imprint of Dutton Signet,
a division of Penguin Books USA Inc. An earlier edition was published
under the title *Alexis Bespaloff's New Signet Book of Wine*.

First Printing, July, 1994
10 9 8 7 6 5 4 3

Maps of California and Australia drawn by Karen Holland; Italy drawn
by Betsy Welsh; other maps drawn by Elizabeth von Italie.

 REGISTERED TRADEMARK—MARCA REGISTRADA

Printed in the United States of America

CONTENTS

Introduction   1
   Reading Wine Labels   2
   How Wine Is Made   5

Wine Tasting   13

The Wines of France   24
   Bordeaux   29
   Burgundy   61
   Beaujolais   82
   The Rhône Valley   86
   The Loire Valley   90
   Alsace, Provence, and Other Regions   94

The Wines of Italy   101
   Piedmont and the Northwest   107
   Veneto and the Northeast   115
   Tuscany and Central Italy   124
   From Rome to the South   136

The Wines of Germany   140
   The German Wine Regions   158

OTHER EUROPEAN WINES 169
    Spain 169
    Portugal 178
    Switzerland 182
    Austria 183
    Hungary 185
    Greece 188
    Bulgaria 189
    Romania 189

THE WINES OF CALIFORNIA 191
    The Principal Grape Varieties 208
    Napa 216
    Sonoma 227
    Mendocino and Lake County 237
    Alameda, Santa Clara, and the
      Santa Cruz Mountains 239
    Monterey, San Luis Obispo,
      and Santa Barbara 245
    Amador and the Sierra Foothills 253
    The San Joaquin Valley 255

OTHER WINES OF THE UNITED STATES 257
    New York State 258
    The Pacific Northwest:
      Washington and Oregon 265
    Other States 270

THE WINES OF SOUTH AMERICA 273
    Chile 273
    Argentina 278

VARIOUS OTHER WINES 280
    Australia 280
    New Zealand 289
    South Africa 290
    Canada 294
    Israel 296
    Algeria 297
    Lebanon 297

CHAMPAGNE AND SPARKLING WINES   299

FORTIFIED WINES   314
    Sherry   315
    Port   319
    Madeira   324
    Vermouth and Aperitifs   326

COGNAC AND OTHER BRANDIES   327

THE ENJOYMENT OF WINE   340
    Starting a Cellar   340
    Serving Wines   343
    Wine and Food   352
    Wine in Restaurants   358

VINTAGES   362

PRONUNCIATION GUIDE   369

INDEX   375

MAPS

France   25
Bordeaux   30
Burgundy   63
Northern Italy   110
Central and Southern Italy   126
Germany   141
Spain and Portugal   170
Northern California   218
Central California   242
Australia   282

ILLUSTRATIONS

Corkscrews   346
Wineglasses   350

INTRODUCTION

The only equipment you need to enjoy wine is a cork-screw and a glass. Two glasses are better, as one of the most agreeable aspects of drinking wine is that it seems to taste better when shared. (And, come to think of it, you don't always need a corkscrew.) Yet, despite the number of people who now drink wine with their meals or as an alternative to cocktails, wine is not an everyday pleasure for most Americans. We simply lack a tradition that encourages us to take for granted a bottle of wine on the dinner table, or to regard the moderate consumption of wine as one of the most accessible of casual pleasures.

Those who do enjoy wine and would like to know more about the subject will find it encouraging that there is now a greater variety of the world's fine wines to be found in almost any large American city than in Paris, London, or Rome. It is, perhaps, that very diversity—the labels in a well-stocked wine shop, the names on a restaurant wine list—that intimidates some consumers and discourages them from expanding their knowledge beyond a few reliable brands. But then, the diversity of wine and the range of tastes it provides is what makes wine so fascinating to those who know even a little about it. And the good news about wine is that you need learn

I

only as much—or as little—as you want. Someone who drinks an inexpensive jug wine at home and orders wine by the glass in restaurants may be no less enthusiastic about wine, and its role with meals, than the enophile who assembles a few friends to compare several vintages of a leading Bordeaux château or to evaluate half-a-dozen Napa Valley Cabernet Sauvignons.

This book—which is a revised and expanded version of the *New Signet Book of Wine*—is meant to be a basic introduction to the wines of the world, but with enough detail to provide additional background where it might be useful. Of course, the only way to learn about wines is by tasting, and there is no substitute for pulling a cork. But to learn even a minimum amount about wine you must do two simple things: take a moment to really taste the wine in front of you, and look carefully at the label to determine just what it is you are drinking. An approach to tasting is described in another chapter, but here are some guidelines to understanding wine labels.

READING WINE LABELS

Labels for most of the world's wines indicate either the wine's place of origin or the name of the grape variety from which it is made. Most European wine names are place-names, so you are being told just where the wine comes from. Chablis, Sauternes, Saint-Julien, Pommard, Vouvray, and Tavel are villages in France; Soave, Bardolino, Barolo, Orvieto, and Frascati are in Italy; German villages include Bernkastel, Piesport, Johannisberg, and Nierstein; other wine villages include Tokay in Hungary, Neuchâtel in Switzerland, and Rueda and Valdepeñas in Spain. Wines whose names are those of their district of origin include Beaujolais, Anjou, Côtes du Rhône, Médoc, Chianti, and Rioja. Geography is the key to understanding wines so labeled. If you can focus on the wine's place of origin, rather than on the appearance of the label as a whole, and gradually build up a mental wine map for each country as you taste its wines, you will more easily recall the wines you enjoy.

The wine laws now in effect in many European countries (such as *Appellation Contrôlée* in France, *Denomi-*

nazione di Origine Controllata in Italy, *Denominación de Origen* in Spain, and *Região Demarcada* in Portugal) not only define the geographical limits of specific appellations of origin, but also take into account the grape varieties that are permitted, the maximum quantity produced per acre, the wine's minimum alcoholic content, and other elements of winemaking that affect its quality. The laws simply reflect certain observations about quality based on long periods of trial and error. For example, in many wine regions, specific grape varieties are best suited to certain soils and climatic conditions, and these are the ones that produce the finest wines. Some classic combinations of grape, soil, and climate include Pinot Noir and Chardonnay in Burgundy, Nebbiolo in northern Italy, and Riesling along the Rhine and Moselle. Elsewhere, the finest wines are produced from a combination of several grape varieties, but the specific varieties, and sometimes the proportions of each, are strictly defined. Chianti, Rioja, and Châteauneuf-du-Pape are three familiar examples, as is red Bordeaux, where Merlot and Cabernet Franc are planted along with the classic Cabernet Sauvignon grape.

Wine laws limit the quantity of wine that can be produced from an acre of vines because quantity and quality have traditionally been mutually exclusive, and the most fertile soils, producing the most grapes, are rarely noted for the quality of their wines. A vineyard in Bordeaux, Burgundy, or the Napa Valley may produce less than two hundred cases of fine wine per acre; fertile districts in the south of France or in central California are capable of producing up to a thousand cases of undistinguished wine per acre.

A label that reflects the geographical origin of a wine may indicate not only a region, an inner district within that region, or an individual village, but also the ultimate geographical entity, the name of a specific vineyard. Every wine comes from a vineyard, of course, but most of the world's wines are blended together from many plots within a village or from several villages within a district. There are vineyards throughout the world, however, whose wines are vinified, aged, and bottled separately from those of adjoining plots of land. The most famous individually named vineyards are in Bordeaux,

Burgundy, and along the Rhine and Moselle; some are less than five acres in size, others extend for 150 to 200 acres. Although it is standard wine humor to satirize the taster who tries to guess whether a wine comes from the right slope or the left slope, the fact is that the exact position of a plot of vines will have a recognizable effect on the quality of its wines year after year. A vineyard's exposure to the sun, its ability to absorb heavy rains without flooding or to retain moisture during a dry spell, the elements in its subsoil that nourish its vines—all these factors and more account for the astonishing fact that the wines of one vineyard plot will consistently sell for two or three times as much as those of an adjoining plot.

Although labeling wines with their place of origin is the most traditional approach, and is used throughout most of Europe, there is another approach that has become increasingly familiar to wine drinkers. That is the use of varietal names, in which wines are labeled with the name of the grape variety from which they are primarily, or entirely, made. This method is used in Alsace, in parts of Italy, in Chile and Australia, and most notably in California and other American states because the grape variety is a more useful indication of the style of a wine than is the name of the village or region from which the wine comes. Chardonnay, Sauvignon Blanc, Cabernet Sauvignon, Merlot, Pinot Noir, and Zinfandel are among the best-known varietal wines of California. Other varietal wines include Seyval Blanc, Concord, and Catawba from New York State; Riesling and Gewürztraminer from Alsace; Lambrusco, Barbera, Dolcetto, and Verdicchio from Italy; and Fendant from Switzerland. Sometimes a label will combine both the grape variety and place of origin: Bernkastel Riesling, Dolcetto d'Alba, Debröi Hárslevelü, Hunter Valley Sémillon, Alexander Valley Cabernet Sauvignon, and Willamette Valley Pinot Noir are examples from Germany, Italy, Hungary, Australia, California, and Oregon.

The names by which most of the inexpensive wines produced in this country are sold are, unfortunately, the least useful to the consumer. These are generic names—that is, specific place-names, usually European, that are so well known to the public that they have been adopted to market wines from somewhere else. California and New York State Chablis, Burgundy, Rhine Wine, and Sauterne (usually spelled without the final *s*) are the best-known examples of wines whose names have no relation to their origin, and whose characteristics may be similar only in the vaguest way to the wines whose names are being usurped. In recent years, a number of producers have turned away from generic labeling to the use of such terms as Red Table Wine, Premium Red, Vintage White, or Mountain White Wine.

Another approach to labeling wines is the use of proprietary brand names created by individual producers for their own wines. A proprietary name is likely to be better known to consumers than that of the producer or the wine's place of origin. Mouton-Cadet, Blue Nun, Lancers, Corvo, and Partager are some popular proprietary brands that are moderately priced and in wide distribution. A recent development has been the use of proprietary names for a producer's best, and most expensive, wines, usually made in limited quantities. This use of a proprietary name represents an effort to individualize such wines by going beyond the limits imposed by appellations of origin or varietal labeling. Some examples are Opus One, Dominus, Insignia, and Rubicon from California and Tignanello, Sassicaia, Le Pergole Torte, and Vintage Tunina from Italy.

HOW WINE IS MADE

Wine is commonly defined as the fermented juice of fresh grapes. This obviously leaves out such specialty products as cherry wine, dandelion wine, or a beverage made from dehydrated grapes to which water has been added.

Grape juice is transformed into wine by the process of fermentation, in which the natural sugar present in grapes is converted into almost equal parts of alcohol and carbon dioxide gas. To begin with the making of red wines, the normal sequence is for the grapes to be brought to the vinification shed or winery, stripped of their stems, and lightly crushed to release their juice. (The time-honored process of treading on the grapes by foot—which is pretty rare these days—was carried out not to press the grapes but to crush them so that the released juice could begin to ferment.) The crushed red grapes are transferred to fermentation tanks. These may be open wooden vats, large cement tanks, or stainless-steel cylinders. In recent years, many wine producers throughout the world have been replacing the traditional wooden vats with large plastic-lined, fiberglass, or stainless-steel tanks. They are much easier to keep clean, and the stainless-steel tanks in particular permit the temperature of the fermenting juice to be more carefully controlled.

The juice, also known as must, now begins to ferment as a result of various chemical transformations effected by yeast cells that were already present on the grape skins. (In many regions today, the natural yeasts are inhibited, and specially selected strains of cultured yeasts are added to the juice.) As the sugar/water solution becomes an alcohol/water solution (with carbon dioxide gas escaping into the atmosphere), coloring matter and tannin are extracted from the skins. The amount of color and tannin that is desired determines the length of time that the juice is left in contact with the skins, and this vatting, or *cuvaison*, may vary from two or three days to two or three weeks. Short vatting is traditional for wines whose principal attraction is their fruit and charm, longer vatting for wines noted for their deep color, depth of flavor and longevity. With very few exceptions, grape juice is clear and untinted. When a white wine is made from black grapes, as for champagne, the grapes are pressed immediately, before the skins can impart excessive color to the juice. Rosés are traditionally made by keeping the juice and skins together just long enough to impart the desired amount of color to the evolving wine, although cheap rosés are sometimes made by mixing red and white wines.

Fermentation normally continues until all of the sugar is converted into alcohol. The resulting wine generally varies in alcoholic content from as low as 7 or 8 percent to as high as 15 to 16 percent, depending on the wine region and the nature of the vintage. Even if the juice is especially rich in sugar, an alcoholic content of 15 to 16 percent kills the yeast cells that produced it, thus stopping fermentation. Almost all the table wines we drink, however, contain 10 to 14 percent alcohol, and in this country a natural table wine is legally defined as one that has less than 14 percent alcohol. Some, such as the white wines of Germany, may contain only 8 or 9 percent.

With very few exceptions, red table wines are fermented until they are completely dry: the minute trace of sugar that may be left in the wine cannot be perceived by the taste buds. Consequently, what sometimes makes one red wine taste "drier" than another is the amount of tannin or acids present. Some well-known red wines are slightly sweet, however: *sangría* from Spain and Lambrusco from Italy are the best-known examples. Also, a number of inexpensive California red wines are slightly sweetened before bottling, which rounds out their taste and makes them more appealing to many consumers.

There is another fermentation technique, called carbonic maceration, that is used to some extent in the Beaujolais region of France, and by some California wineries, to produce fruity, light-bodied red wines that can be consumed within months of the vintage. In conventional red-wine fermentation the grapes are in the presence of air. When carbonic maceration is practiced, the grapes, which are not crushed at all, are loaded into a closed container that is filled with carbon dioxide gas. Fermentation occurs within each grape in the absence of air, and color, but not much tannin, is extracted from the skins. Eventually, the grapes are removed from the closed container and pressed, and the must continues its fermentation in the normal way. In California, carbonic maceration is sometimes referred to as whole-berry fermentation.

After fermentation is complete, the wine is transferred to small barrels, large casks, or even larger tanks to age and to rid itself of its natural impurities. The red wine that drains freely from the fermentation tank is called free-run; that which is recovered from the remaining solids by pressing is classified as press wine. Generally speaking, press wine tends to have more color and body than free-run wine, and is harsher and more tannic as well. Sometimes a wine producer will sell off the press wine, sometimes it is blended with the free-run juice to intensify its flavor and add to its longevity.

Red wines may be aged before bottling from as little as a few weeks to three years or more. Longer aging, which usually takes place in large wood casks or small oak barrels, softens the tannic harshness of a young red wine and rounds out its taste. The use of small oak barrels, also known as *barriques*, which hold about 225 liters, or 60 gallons, is traditional in Bordeaux and Burgundy, and has been adopted by winemakers throughout the world, who debate the merits of oak from America and from different forests in France—Nevers, Allier, Tronçais, Limousin, and the Vosges—and its effect on their wines. In general, aging in *barriques* adds to the complexity of a wine's taste and introduces notes of spice, vanilla, and toast, especially if the winemaker chooses to use new oak barrels, which impart a more pronounced taste to the wine.

White wines are made by a somewhat different method. Because they do not need to pick up color from their skins, the grapes are pressed immediately, and the juice ferments away from the skins. As a result, white wines have less tannin than reds, as tannin is derived primarily from the skins. Tannin is an important constituent of fine red wines and gives young red wines an astringent, puckerish taste. Its comparative absence from white wines constitutes one of the principal taste differences between red and white wines.

Perhaps the most significant technological achievement of the past thirty years in the production of white wines in California and throughout the world has been the increasing use of temperature-controlled fermentation tanks, which permits white wines to be fermented slowly at relatively low temperatures. Slow, cool fermentation retains the fruit and freshness that are the principal attributes of most white wines. If such simple, uncomplicated wines are bottled within a few months instead of being aged in wood for a year or more, as was traditional in many wine regions, they will display a youthful appeal rather than the dull, woody, and even oxidized tastes so prevalent in the past.

Many fine white wines, especially those made from Chardonnay in Burgundy, California, and elsewhere, are fermented in small oak barrels rather than large, temperature-controlled tanks. Although barrel-fermentation requires more attention, it results in richer, more complex white wines. After fermentation is complete, barrel-fermented wines may be left *sur lie*, that is, on the lees, the sediment that consists primarily of dead yeast cells; the additional contact between the wine and its lees adds texture and flavor to the wine. Whether or not they are fermented in wood, fine white wines are often aged in small oak barrels, which impart tannin and contribute complex nuances to the aroma and taste of the wine.

There are certain naturally sweet white wines, notably Sauternes and Barsac from Bordeaux, Auslese and Beerenauslese wines of Germany, and certain late-harvest wines from California, which are produced by stopping the fermentation while residual grape sugar remains in the wine.

Because the ferments are naturally present on grape skins at harvest time, winemaking is a natural process, but it must nevertheless be controlled very carefully at every step. If the fermenting juice, or must, gets too cold (an early frost in Germany) or too hot (a late summer in Spain), fermentation will stop and is extremely difficult to start again. What's more, if the new wine were just left exposed to air in its fermentation vat, another natural process would soon take place—through the presence of the vinegar bacteria—that would transform the wine into an acetic acid solution, i.e., into *vin aigre*, or sour wine.

Besides normal alcoholic fermentation, most red wines and many whites also undergo malolactic fermentation, by which the sharper malic acid (found in apples) is transformed into the softer lactic acid (found in milk). This process is of particular interest to winemakers who produce white wines in cool regions, where grapes are usually harvested with a relatively high acid content. In addition to reducing a wine's acidity, malolactic fermentation changes the character of fine white wines, which become somewhat richer and rounder.

One element of wine making that is sometimes referred to, and that can affect the quality of wines, is chaptalization. The process is named after Chaptal, one of Napoleon's ministers, who encouraged the idea of adding sugar to the must during fermentation. After a cold or rainy summer, when grapes have not ripened sufficiently, their lack of natural sugar would result in a wine without enough alcohol to make it healthy and stable. Chaptalization is permitted in several countries, notably France and Germany, in order to raise the alcohol content of a wine to its normal level as determined by good vintages. Chaptalization can be overdone, producing unbalanced wines that are too high in alcohol, but without it many famous wine districts would be unable to produce much drinkable wine in certain years.

The wine laws of Italy and California do not permit chaptalization, but they do permit the use of concentrated grape juice. The effect is basically the same—the concentrate contains a high proportion of sugar, which is converted into alcohol—but other elements present in the juice, notably acid, are also concentrated. Consequently, many winemakers believe that chaptalization is a more effective way to compensate for a lack of natural sugar than is the use of concentrate. In some regions whose wines are particularly high in acid, notably in New York State, it is permitted to add both sugar and water to the must, the water having the effect of reducing high acidity by diluting it. Of course, the water dilutes the wine as well and permits the winemaker to produce more wine from a given amount of grapes.

At some point before a wine is bottled it is likely to be fined, or clarified, to remove any impurities that may be suspended in it. A primitive form of fining is used by campers when they throw crushed eggshells into coffee that has been made by boiling water and coffee together in a pot. Suspended coffee grounds will cling to the egg whites on the shells as they fall to the bottom of the pot; as a matter of fact, a traditional fining method that is still used is to mix beaten egg whites into red wine. Gelatin is more widely used today for red wines, and certain clays for white wines.

Just before bottling, most wines are filtered to remove any remaining impurities. Because American consumers have traditionally rejected wines that are not completely bright and clear in appearance, many American wineries favor rather severe fining and filtering, which may also diminish a wine's character and depth of flavor. Today, a number of wineries throughout the world, both large and small, bottle their finest wines without fining or filtering, or with very little, because they believe the wines will retain more character and develop greater complexity.

Historically, many inexpensive wines were pasteurized to kill any microorganisms that may spoil the wine after it is bottled. Unfortunately, pasteurization may effectively stop a wine from developing in the bottle, and the exposure to heat may also give the wine a slightly cooked taste. Today, the alternative to pasteurization is microfiltration—the use of an extremely fine membrane filter that removes most of the microorganisms that pasteurization would have killed.

Sulfur is an element that is widely and properly used in many phases of grape-growing and winemaking. In the cellar, it is a standard sterilizing agent, and empty casks and barrels are treated with sulfites (the derivative of sulfur most often used in the winery) to eliminate harmful bacteria; and because sulfur is an antioxidant and prevents microbial spoilage, sulfites are used to protect wines during bottling. Although Federal regulations permit 350 parts per million (ppm) of sulfites in wine, any wine that contains more than 10 ppm must carry the phrase "Contains Sulfites" on its label. In practice, well-equipped wineries are now able to bottle wines with only 40 to 60 ppm.

Wine continues to change after it has been bottled, as the various pigments, acids, tannins, alcohols, and other elements present in minute quantities combine and alter the characteristics of the wine. Age alone is no guarantee of quality, however, and it is only the best wines that are sturdy and complex enough to improve for several years. The life cycle of each wine is different, and some wines are at their best when they are bottled, or within six months. All rosés and most white wines are best consumed within a year or two of the vintage, as are many light red wines. Some dry white wines, such as the best Burgundies and California Chardonnays, achieve additional richness and complexity with bottle age, as do the finest sweet white wines from Sauternes, Germany, and California. The best reds from Bordeaux, Burgundy, Italy, Rioja, and California will begin to reveal their qualities only after four or five years, and it is by no means unusual to discover that a red wine from a top vineyard is coming into its own only after ten or fifteen years in the bottle.

A note about bottle sizes: fine wines develop more slowly and sometimes more completely in larger bottles. For that reason connoisseurs ideally prefer an old red wine that has been matured in a magnum, which holds two bottles. Although half-bottles provide the opportunity of experimenting at less expense, remember that wine ages more quickly in a half-bottle and that a fine red wine may never fully develop its qualities in such a small container.

As to the contents of wine bottles, both American and imported bottles now conform to metric sizes and contain the same amount of wine, which was not previously the case. The standard bottle of 750 milliliters is equivalent to 25.4 ounces; the half-bottle contains 375 milliliters, or 12.7 ounces; a 1-liter bottle contains 33.8 ounces; the metric magnum holds 1.5 liters, or 50.7 ounces; and the 3-liter jeroboam is equivalent to 101.4 ounces. The gallon and half-gallon sizes in which inexpensive jug wines were once marketed are no longer permitted, and have been replaced by the metric magnum and jeroboam. The bottles for such traditional wines as red Bordeaux, however, are named somewhat differently: magnum (two bottles), double magnum (four bottles), jeroboam (six bottles), and imperial (eight bottles). Champagne bottle sizes are described elsewhere.

WINE
TASTING

For a professional wine buyer, wine tasting is a skill
requiring a long apprenticeship and rather delicate judgment. For the person who enjoys wine with his or her
meals, tasting is a most agreeable pastime. On the simplest level, tasting wines is an inescapable part of drinking them, and there are many people who are content
merely to determine whether a wine is "good" or "not
good." Sooner or later the casual wine drinker will experiment with new wines, and at that point he or she
begins to taste wine. Unlike many other pursuits, tasting
wines is enjoyable from the very start and becomes increasingly fascinating and rewarding with experience.

The principal difference between the professional
taster and everyone else is that he (and, increasingly,
she) has a greater opportunity to taste many different
wines, and thus his perspective is wider and his palate
more developed. Furthermore, because a buyer tastes
wine soon after the vintage, and months or years before
the wine is even bottled, he has the additional opportunity of following the development of various wines from
the cradle, so to speak. This is especially important as it
is his role to judge young wines long before they are
ready to be consumed, and he can do this precisely be-

cause he has tasted wines of previous vintages at a similar stage of their evolution.

However, there is another aspect of wine tasting that is most important, and that is concentration. We can't all spend days on end going in and out of wine cellars in Burgundy, the Rheingau, or the Napa Valley, but we can at least devote ten seconds or so to a wine when we first taste it with dinner. Different wines and different occasions call for a flexible approach. A bottle of Château Lafite-Rothschild 1961 served at a formal dinner demands more attention (and appreciative remarks) than does a Valpolicella served with pasta. But in each case a few moments' attention to the wine before you is the only way to build your knowledge and increase your pleasure. Look at the label and note where the wine comes from in general terms, and if it's a special wine, note the specific district or vineyard that produced it, or the grape variety from which it is made, as well as the vintage. As you sip the wine, try to place it geographically in your mind, and compare it to other wines you've tasted from the same place or the same grape. Only in this way will you develop your palate; otherwise you will simply have tasted, in time, a blur of individual bottles that you can neither recall nor repurchase.

It's often assumed, by the way, that wine experts are people who can taste wines whose labels have been covered up and then name the vineyard and vintage. Although some members of the wine trade amuse themselves by putting their colleagues through such blind tastings, the real skill of a wine buyer is demonstrated in exactly the opposite manner. He stands in a particular cellar, tasting a specific wine, and has even noted the barrel from which it was drawn. He must now determine how good it is, how good it will be six months or six years later, and what it is worth. It is precisely this ability to concentrate on the wine at hand—in order to judge its value, not guess its origin—that is the primary attribute of his expertise.

When professional tasters are at work, they always spit out the wines they are judging—either onto the floor of a cellar or into a special receptacle in a tasting room. For one thing, it's not a pleasant experience to swallow very young red wines starting at eight or nine in the morning. For another, a taster in the vineyard region may sample fifty or seventy-five wines in a day, and if he swallowed each wine, his judgment would soon become impaired, to say the least.

Whatever our specific knowledge about wine, each of us prefers to drink what he or she likes. As you taste different wines, it's interesting to try to determine why one wine is more pleasant than another, what attributes make one cost three times as much as another, and why one wine might suit a particular dish more than another at the same price: in short, to taste a wine critically and to sort out your impressions. Wine tasters generally approach a wine in three successive steps—color, bouquet (or smell), and taste. These will be examined in some detail, but remember that when a specific wine is tasted, all of these considerations can be reviewed mentally in just a few seconds of concentration.

The first attribute of a wine is its color. Just as we anticipate a dish even more when it's attractively presented on the serving plate, so our enjoyment of a fine wine can be heightened by a look at its color. For this reason, wine is served in clear, uncut glasses. There are two aspects of a wine's color that deserve attention. The first is its appearance in the glass. Whether red or white, a healthy wine should be bright—that is, free of any cloudiness or suspension. If a wine appears dull or hazy, it may be unsound in some way, and its unattractive appearance is your first warning signal. This cloudiness is not to be confused with sediment, which is harmless and will fall to the bottom of the glass. Sediment is a natural by-product of age in older red wines, and such wines should be decanted whenever possible (as described elsewhere). Very occasionally you will come across crystals in a white wine; these are harmless (although admittedly unattractive) tartrates that have been precipitated by excessive cold. Sometimes small crystals are found stuck to the bottom of a cork, even in red wines. Again, these are tartrates, not, as some people imagine, sugar crystals.

The second aspect of color is the actual hue of the wine. The intensity of a wine's color can convey some idea of its character. A pale, watery white wine is likely to be lighter-bodied than a rich, gold one; a pale red wine will probably have less flavor than one that is dark, almost inky. This immediate judgment is really not much different from the one you automatically make about a cup of coffee—is it pale and therefore weak, or dark and strong?

As they age, red wines get lighter and white wines get darker. Young red wines have a purple-red color that soon turns to red, then to a bricklike orange-red before finally acquiring brown hues. This natural evolution reveals how far along the wine has come, irrespective of the vintage on the label. A six-month-old Beaujolais, for example, should still show hints of purple; if the wine in your glass displays faded red or red-orange hues, it's almost certainly too old. That same color would be acceptable, however, in a ten-year-old Bordeaux or California Cabernet Sauvignon.

A white wine, whether it's a pale straw-yellow or medium-gold color when young, will eventually darken with age. Just as a freshly cut apple begins to brown in a few minutes, so a white wine slowly browns over the years. Consequently, a young white wine that already shows signs of browning should be approached with some suspicion.

To judge the hue of a wine, don't look into the glass, as the depth of wine in the glass will affect its color. Tip the glass away from you and look at the outer edge of the wine against a white cloth or backdrop. (One indication of just how important color is in judging wines is evidenced by the design of the traditional Burgundian *tastevin*, once widely used to taste new wines still in barrels. It is a shallow silver cup—often used as a decorative ashtray here—with dimpled sides. Those dimples are there specifically to refract light through the wine, so that its color and appearance can be closely examined, even in a dimly lit cellar.)

The second step in judging wine is to smell it, and wineglasses are curved in at the top to focus and retain a wine's bouquet. You may ask, Why bother to smell a wine when I'm about to taste it? About 80 percent of what we imagine to be taste is actually based on our sense of smell. When we taste roast beef or a peach, it is in fact the olfactory nerves that are doing most of the work. You know that food loses much of its flavor when you have a head cold, and yet it's your nose, not your palate, that is affected by the cold. The reason that wine-glasses should be big (at least eight ounces) is that they are meant to be filled only halfway, so that a wine can easily be swirled in the glass. It is this gentle swirling that releases the wine's bouquet through evaporation.

A wine's bouquet gives you a strong first impression of the wine itself: if a wine has any serious faults, they can be discerned by smell, and you can avoid tasting bad wine. Occasionally, a wine may be corky, which is revealed by a moldy smell, rather than a clean, vinous one.

Not every wine has a distinctive bouquet. Some are fairly neutral and exude very little smell. This may be because they are simple wines that haven't much to offer, or because they are fine young wines that are still "closed in," requiring more bottle age to develop their bouquet. Some wines are immediately marked by off-odors. One of the most common is an excess of sulfur dioxide, the smell of a burning match. Sulfur dioxide is commonly used as a preservative, particularly for inexpensive whites, but an excessive amount is unpleasant when inhaled. (When you taste such a wine, the sulfur dioxide leaves an acrid bite in the back of your throat.) From time to time you may come across a white wine that has a suspiciously brown color and a bouquet reminiscent of Madeira or dry sherry without any of the fruit of a good wine. Such a wine is described as maderized (*maderisé*). Maderization is the result of excessive oxidation, and it may have been caused by overlong aging in wood or by a faulty cork that let air into the bottle, or it may be the natural evolution and decay of a white wine that is just too old. Another warning signal is a sour, vinegary smell, which indicates that the wine contains an excess of acetic acid, the vinegar acid. If you leave out a glass of wine overnight, what you smell and taste the next day is just such an excess of acetic acid.

Many off-odors are distinctive, but fortunately, they are not frequently encountered. More often you will be able to detect and recognize agreeable odors. Some of the easiest to identify are the aromas associated with specific grape varieties—the rose-petal or litchi smell of Gewürztraminer, the fragrance and floweriness of German Rieslings, the berrylike aromas of California Zinfandel. The bouquet of Cabernet Sauvignon, the classic grape of red Bordeaux, is often compared to green peppers, black currants, even cedarwood. The aroma of Sauvignon Blanc, the grape of Sancerre and Pouilly-Fumé, is often described as herbaceous, weedy, or grassy.

The bouquet of some wines is the result of the way they are made. Sauternes and sweet, late-harvest Rieslings from Germany and California have a honeyed, concentrated smell that comes from the overripe, slightly shriveled grapes from which they are made. Other smells may be the result of the way the wine was treated: wines aged in new oak barrels have nuances of wood and vanillin, a component of new oak. In general, young wines have more fruit in their aroma (more of the smell of the grape), whereas older wines exhibit a more refined and subtle character. The sense of smell is probably the most evocative of all the senses (as the perfume manufacturers discovered long ago), and many of us have a greater sense memory for smells than for tastes, so make the most of it.

Finally, you taste the wine. (Remember that judging a wine takes less time than reading about it. Your impressions of color and bouquet should have taken you only a few moments.) The tongue is covered with taste buds that can distinguish only salt, sour, bitter, and sweet, and they are located on different parts of the tongue. You must let the wine rest on your tongue for a few moments, so that you can separate the different taste sensations. At this point some professional tasters chew the wine to make sure that it comes into contact with all their taste buds. Others will "whistle in," drawing air into their mouths and through the wine, to help release its flavor. This slurping sound is an accepted part of serious tastings, but it can be dispensed with at dinner parties.

Although there are certain chemical salts in wine, picked up from the soil in which the vines are planted, they are rarely discernible to the taste. Sweetness will, of course, be more easily discernible, and is found in many white wines and rosés, and a few red wines as well. Most red wines are vinified so as to retain no sugar, and if a Beaujolais or dry red wine seems slightly sweet, it may simply denote the presence of glycerin or other elements that round out a wine and give it a certain richness. It's worth noting that not everyone's palate reacts the same way to sweetness: someone who drinks coffee with three spoonfuls of sugar may describe a dry red wine as "sour," and a medium-sweet white wine or rosé as "dry." Incidentally, cold diminishes the perception of sweetness, so if you've bought a wine that you find too sweet, serve it cooler than you would normally.

Acidity is essential to wine, especially to white wines. Just as a squeeze of lemon on fish, or lemon zest in a drink, perks up its taste, so a certain amount of acidity is always necessary to give a white wine liveliness. Acidity not only gives more character to dry white wines, but also balances sweetness in wines that are not dry, as lemon juice does in lemonade. Moselles, for example, may retain some sugar, but they have a lively, piquant taste, rather than a simple, one-dimensional sweet taste, because of the balancing acidity.

Acidity also enables white wines to age. White wines from some so-called great years are often short-lived because they are not acid enough; the heat and sun that produce extra sugar in the grapes (and therefore more alcohol in the wine) also burn away some of the acidity. This often results in big, powerful, but flabby white wines that are too low in acid and that therefore should not be put away for years of bottle aging. Too little sun produces grapes that are not fully ripe and contain too much acidity. The resulting wines are likely to be tart and unpleasant.

Bitterness usually indicates the presence of tannin in wine. Tannin—an important component of fine red wines—gives wine an astringent, puckerish taste that you will also find, for example, in very strong tea. Tannin acts as the spine or skeleton of a wine, and because tannin is an antioxidant that combines with the oxygen in wine, thereby slowing down the aging process, its presence enables a wine to evolve and mature in the bottle for many years. Tannin comes from grape skins and from the new oak barrels in which many red—and some white—wines are aged, and its presence is therefore the result of the vinification and aging methods used. In Beaujolais, where wines are to be drunk early while they retain their freshness, a short vatting (the time the skins are in contact with the juice) is the rule so that relatively little of the astringent tannin enters the wine. In Bordeaux, where red wines of good vintages are expected to last for ten years or more, vatting may take as long as three weeks, followed by up to two years of barrel aging, and the resulting wine is likely to be tannic and puckerish for several years. An important change in vinification around the world during the past twenty years is a trend toward shorter vatting, so that red wines can be consumed more quickly by a public that no longer cellars wine away for years of maturation.

The tannic edge in red wine is softened by foods that contain protein. For example, if you eat cheese while tasting red wines, the protein in the cheese combines with the tannin in the wine and reduces its bitter taste. It's the same effect that occurs when you add milk to strong tea: the protein in the milk combines with and diminishes the tannin in the tea. For this reason, young red wines are usually more appealing when drunk with food than when they are tasted on their own.

As a wine ages in bottle, the tannin combines chemically with the coloring matter to form a harmless deposit. That is why older red wines are both paler in color and less harsh to the palate. (When buying young red wines to mature in your cellar, it is important to distinguish between tannin and acid, because one diminishes with age, the other doesn't.) The amount of tannin you detect in a long-lived red wine tells you whether or not it is ready to drink, or rather, whether or not the wine has evolved sufficiently to make it attractive to you. Unfortunately, many consumers make the mistake of assuming that there is a particular point at which each bottle of fine wine is at its best. In fact, it is difficult to project the evolution of the wines of a region in any given vintage, even more so to determine when a specific wine from a particular vineyard or winery will be fully developed. Furthermore, different people enjoy wines at different stages of development. Some enjoy the vigor and intensity of young wines, others prefer a red wine that has lost virtually all its tannin and displays softness and harmony at the expense of a more positive character.

If you concentrate on a wine for the few moments that it's in your mouth, you should be able to isolate the elements that make up its taste, since it is not difficult to be aware of two or three taste sensations simultaneously. For example, lemonade is a simple combination of sweetness and acidity that most people have no trouble adjusting to suit their own preferences. Red vermouth is quite sweet, but it also contains bitter extracts, so that the initial impression of sweetness, which would be too cloying by itself, is balanced by a bitter aftertaste. Strong tea is a bitter solution dominated by tannin; if you put in a slice of lemon, you add acidity, and if you then add sugar to mask the first two elements, you have created a simple combination of bitter, sour, and sweet.

In addition to tastes, certain tactile sensations can be felt on the palate. Temperature is one; carbon dioxide gas, as in champagne, is another. An excess of alcohol is often perceived as a hot or burning sensation—although alcohol has little flavor, it can be felt, and it gives some wines an unwanted bite. One sensation that is especially important in evaluating a wine is its weight. Some wines are light and delicate, others are rather big and full, and this aspect of a wine's overall character is particularly relevant when you try to match a specific dish with an appropriate wine.

Finally, a wine should display harmony and balance, whatever its price. An inexpensive wine with no faults and a pleasant taste may be very good value. An expensive wine from a famous vineyard may be bigger and richer and, in many ways, more interesting, but may nevertheless lack the harmony that would make it a pleasure to drink.

Let me state again that the only way to learn about wines is to try different bottles and to be aware of what you are drinking. A good way to define your impressions more accurately is to compare two or three wines at a time: have two half-bottles for dinner, or invite like-minded friends over for an informal tasting. If you compare a Bordeaux to a Rioja or a Chianti, or a Sancerre to a California Sauvignon Blanc, or a Riesling from the Moselle to one from Alsace, or if you line up Chardonnays or Cabernet Sauvignons from California, Australia, and Chile—the possibilities are endless—you will soon acquire some useful impressions about the major wine regions and the principal grape varieties. More important still, you will discover new wines to enjoy, and good values from each region.

You will soon realize that one of the great pleasures of drinking wines is to talk about them and to compare impressions. Trying to describe the color, bouquet, and taste of a wine is much less difficult when you are talking to someone who is drinking the same wine. The vocabulary of wine tasting may seem vague or precious, at first, but you will discover that its terms are fairly specific and easily understood by anyone who has tasted a number of wines. Although professionals may use technical terms to pinpoint certain impressions, a tasting vocabulary need not be complex. A good wine may be described as delicate, fresh, lively, mature, spicy, deep, robust, complex, balanced, sturdy, clean, rounded, or crisp. An unattractive wine may be astringent, dull, heavy, harsh, thin, hard, bland, musty, cloying, or coarse. Some of these terms may be imprecise, but, if you focus your attention on each wine as you taste it, you should have little trouble distinguishing between a white wine that's rich and opulent and one that's lean and austere; or between a lively, aromatic white and one that's neutral and insipid; or between a sturdy, tannic red and one that's supple and round. It's fascinating to realize that although a wine chemist can easily spot a defective wine, he cannot distinguish by chemical analysis between, say, an inexpensive but soundly made red Bordeaux and a considerably more expensive wine from one of the great châteaux of the Médoc. He must eventually taste each wine to determine its character, intensity of flavor, complexity, subtlety, and true value.

One habit that will help to clarify your own taste, and will also help your wine buying considerably, is to keep some sort of record of the wines you drink both at your own table and away from home. Some hobbyists use a specially printed cellar book that has room for various entries. Many people simply use a pocket notebook, others prefer individual index cards. Whatever method you decide on, write down the name of the wine, who made it, and the vintage; when and where you bought it and the price; when you drank the bottle; and, of course, what you thought of it. If you look back at this record every few months you'll be amazed at the number of wines listed that you might otherwise have forgotten. You may also detect a change in your wine preferences and the evolution of a more precise tasting vocabulary.

Another way to keep track of what you drink is to soak off the label and record your comments on the back. The simplest method is to get an itemized bill from the store and to jot down your reactions to each wine as you drink it, if only to separate the wines you enjoyed most from those you found less to your taste.

As to smoking, a great many wine buyers and wine-makers are smokers, and experiments indicate that people who smoke can taste as well as those who don't. Anyone who doesn't smoke, however, is quickly thrown off by smoke in the air, and for that reason it is common courtesy not to smoke during a tasting or when fine wines are served.

THE WINES
OF FRANCE

France is traditionally considered the greatest wine-producing country in the world, and its annual output—the equivalent of 650 to 800 million cases—accounts for about one-fifth of the world's wines. Although France does not make the most wine (in most years Italy's total production is greater), it probably produces a greater variety of fine wines than any other country. The red wines of Bordeaux, the red and white wines of Burgundy, the sweet wines of Sauternes and Barsac, and the sparkling wines of Champagne attest to the quality and diversity of French wines, and the wines of the Charente region are distilled to make cognac, the most famous of all brandies.

The first French vineyards were planted about twenty-five hundred years ago near what is now Marseilles, and viticulture soon spread to the north and the west. There are nearly three million acres of vines in France, and of course, the great bulk of the wine produced is undistinguished. This is the *vin ordinaire* that the French drink every day, which is available in every grocery store, just as milk and soda are here. Only the top 35 percent or so of French wines are bound by the *Appellation Contrôlée* laws, but most of the wines shipped here come from this strictly defined category.

RHEIMS

PARIS • CHAMPAGNE

STRASBOURG

ALSACE

• Chablis

Vouvray
NANTES LOIRE Sancerre DIJON
Muscadet Anjou TOURS Pouilly-sur-Loire Beaune Nuits-Saint-Georges

BURGUNDY

Mâcon
COGNAC Beaujolais
LYONS

Côte Rotie
Hermitage

BORDEAUX
BORDEAUX CÔTES DU RHÔNE

Châteauneuf-du-Pape

ARMAGNAC MIDI Tavel AVIGNON
PROVENCE

MARSEILLES

FRANCE

The *Appellation Contrôlée* laws, established in the 1930s, are the key to understanding most French wine labels. The words mean controlled place-name, and they constitute a guarantee by the government that the place-name on the label is in fact just where the wine comes from. There are now about 250 individually defined *Appellation Contrôlée* wines, of which perhaps two hundred can be found here. When you have a bottle of French wine in front of you, look for the word directly above *Appellation Contrôlée* or between *Appellation* and *Contrôlée*. This will indicate the origin of the wine. It may be a region (Bordeaux, Côtes du Rhône), a district (Graves, Anjou), a village (Saint-Julien, Pommard), or even an individual vineyard, as in Burgundy (Chambertin, Montrachet). As the place-name becomes increasingly specific, the *Appellation Contrôlée* laws become increasingly strict, for they legislate not only the actual geographical limits of a particular place-name, but several other quality-control factors as well. Because certain soils are best suited to certain grape varieties, the law specifies which varieties are permitted. Minimum alcoholic content is another factor, not because the best wines have the most alcohol, but because too little alcohol in a wine will render it unstable. This prevents the use of an established place-name for certain wines produced there in a very poor year, when the worst of them will be too thin and washed-out to be typical. Perhaps the most important control of all, however, is that of quantity. It's been observed that most of the world's best wine regions do not, in fact, contain the best or most fertile soil: the vine seems to thrive in difficult terrain. In Bordeaux, for example, the richest soil, known as *palus*, lies along the riverbanks; wines produced there cannot be sold as Bordeaux, only as *vin ordinaire*. Furthermore, the best grape varieties rarely give a high yield, and should not be permitted to overproduce. An individual vine nourishes its fruit by sending roots down into the soil, as does any plant. If the vine is not pruned back in the winter to limit the number of bunches it can produce, the same root will have to nourish a lot more bunches, and the resulting wine will lack intensity of flavor and a clearly defined character.

Since the *Appellation Contrôlée* laws were first established, however, modern viticultural practices have enabled vineyard owners to produce somewhat more wine per acre while still maintaining the style and quality for which each appellation is noted. Although very abundant vintages generally produce lighter and less intense wines, there have also been some recent vintages in which excellent wines were produced in relatively large quantities. The *Appellation Contrôlée* laws are now flexible enough to permit some variation from year to year concerning maximum permissible yields. Nevertheless, in any given region the limits set for village appellations are always stricter than for a regional one, and those for individual vineyards strictest of all.

The *Appellation Contrôlée* laws were based on earlier attempts to control the authenticity and quality of French wines, which were in turn made necessary by the confusion resulting from the complete replanting of the

French vineyards after their destruction by phylloxera toward the end of the nineteenth century. Phylloxera, a plant louse that feeds on rootstocks, was unwittingly brought over from the United States on American rootstocks, and began to infest the European vineyards in the 1870s and 1880s. Various methods were proposed to combat the phylloxera epidemic, which was devastating the vineyards of one country after another, but the technique that finally worked was to graft European *Vitis vinifera* vines to native American rootstocks from the eastern United States that were resistant to this insect. Eventually just about every single vine in Europe (and many of those in California) was grafted onto an American rootstock.

There is another category of French wines, created in 1949, known as V.D.Q.S.—*Vins Delimités de Qualité Supérieure*, or Delimited Wines of Superior Quality. These wines rank below those of *Appellation Contrôlée* status because their quality is not quite as good or as consistent, and in a few instances, because the quantities produced are rather limited. There are about thirty V.D.Q.S. wines, and their total production is only 3 percent that of the *Appellation Contrôlée* category because, in the past two decades, so many of the V.D.Q.S. wines have been elevated to *Appellation Contrôlée* status. These include Cahors, Corbières, Coteaux d'Aix en Provence, Coteaux du Languedoc, Coteaux Varois, Côtes de Provence, Côtes du Luberon, Côtes du Ventoux, and Minervois. The labels of V.D.Q.S. wines, which include Saint-Pourçain, Sauvignon de Saint-Bris, and Gros Plant du Pays Nantais, are imprinted with an emblem that resembles a small postage stamp; it contains the appropriate words and an illustration of a hand holding a wineglass.

For many years a number of French wines were entitled to label themselves *Appellation d'Origine Simple*. The phrase misled some consumers into thinking that these wines, which rank somewhere between *vin ordinaire* and V.D.Q.S., were somehow associated with *Appellation Contrôlée* wines. In 1973, the name of this category of wines was changed to *Vins de Pays*, and there are now nearly a hundred defined areas whose wines are entitled to use this phrase on their labels. The category has become an important one, and accounts for as much as 20 percent of the total wine crop. More than three-quarters of the *Vins de Pays* come from the Midi region, which extends west from the Rhône to the Spanish border, and about 85 percent of these wines are reds and rosés. Among the names most often seen here are Vin de Pays de l'Aude, Vin de Pays d'Oc, Vin de Pays de l'Hérault, Vin de Pays des Coteaux de l'Ardèche, Vin de Pays de l'Ile de Beauté (which refers to Corsica), Vin de Pays des Côtes de Gascogne (from the Armagnac region), and Vin de Pays du Jardin de la France (which encompasses the Loire Valley). *Vins de Pays* are increasingly being produced from such grape varieties as Chardonnay, Sauvignon Blanc, Cabernet Sauvignon, Merlot, and Syrah, and so labeled. It is possible that as quality improves, some *Vins de Pays* will become V.D.Q.S., just as many V.D.Q.S. wines have been elevated to *Appellation Contrôlée* status. *Vin de Pays* now has a specific meaning, but the familiar phrase *vin du pays* is still used informally to refer to the wine of the region—that is, to whatever local wine is being discussed.

In addition to the various appellation wines described above, there are an increasing number of red, white, and rosé wines being shipped here that are simply blends of wines produced anywhere in France. Sold in magnums and labeled with proprietary names, they are meant to provide an inexpensive alternative to jug wines from California and Italy. Some may confuse consumers as to what they really are, because they are marketed by well-known firms in Bordeaux, Burgundy, the Rhône, and elsewhere whose names are traditionally associated with *Appellation Contrôlée* wines. Although these wines were created as a less expensive alternative to *Appellation Contrôlée* wines, consumers who recognize the shipper's name may imagine that they are buying wines of a higher class than is actually the case. In fact, these non-appellation wines, which fall into the European Community category *Vin de Table*, are usually no better than an anonymous *vin ordinaire*, despite the prices at which some of them are sold. The labels of such wines obviously do not show the words *Appellation Contrôlée*, and that is the simplest way to determine what they are, but at one time the shipper's name could be followed by the place in which the firm was located, such as Bordeaux,

Beaune, Nuits-Saint-Georges, and so on, and the wines could be vintage-dated. New regulations forbid the use, on a label of nonappellation wine, of a city or village whose name is associated with an *Appellation Contrôlée* wine, such as Bordeaux or Beaune, nor can such blends show a vintage date. The shipper's name can now be followed only by the French equivalent of a zip code, to avoid misleading the consumer as to the origin of the wine in the bottle. If a wine is produced or bottled in a town not associated with an *Appellation Contrôlée*, such as Blanquefort or Sète, its name may appear on the label of a *Vin de Table*, but these wines are nevertheless often referred to as "zip code wines." The *Vin de Table* category includes such brands as Partager, Moreau Blanc, Le Jardinet, René Junot, Valbon, Chantefleur, Boucheron, Sommelière, and Père Patriarche.

BORDEAUX

Bordeaux has long been considered one of the centers of the world's finest wines, and is unmatched within France for both quantity and variety. Red, white, and some rosé is produced, and the whites include both dry and sweet wines. Although the fifty to sixty million cases produced annually in Bordeaux amount to less than 10 percent of the wines of France, in many years they account for 20 to 25 percent of all wines entitled to *Appellation Contrôlée* status.

Bordeaux was shipping its wines to England as early as the twelfth century, when Henry II married Eleanor of Aquitaine and thus annexed the region of Bordeaux as part of his empire. At that time, thousands of barrels were shipped annually of a pale red wine called *clairet*. The word evolved into "claret," and properly refers only to red wine from Bordeaux, although it is often used to describe any dry red wine. It's only since the early nineteenth century, when the use of corks and cylindrical bottles became more common, making it possible for bottled wines to be stored on their sides for additional maturation, that claret as we know it today began to be produced: a deep-colored red wine that improves with

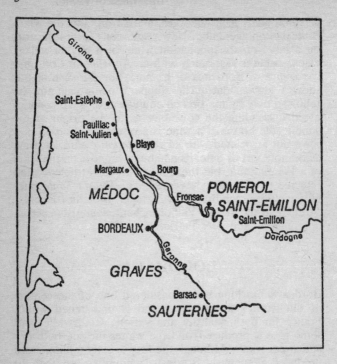

BORDEAUX

age and that, in fact, needs years in barrel and in bottle
to develop its best qualities.

The Bordeaux wine region lies within the *département*
of the Gironde, and its principal city is, of course, Bordeaux itself, with a population of about 210,000. Two
rivers, the Garonne and the Dordogne, meet just north
of Bordeaux and form the Gironde estuary, which flows
into the sea. It is in and around this triangle that the
vineyards of Bordeaux are situated.

There are more than forty wine districts in Bordeaux,
each one entitled to its own *Appellation Contrôlée*, but
there are only five that stand out as producing the very
greatest wines. They are the Médoc, Saint-Emilion, and
Pomerol, whose names are used only for red wines;

Graves, which produces both red and white wines; and Sauternes, containing the inner district of Barsac, whose sweet and luscious white wines are world-famous.

In addition to these five main districts, there are four communes, or parishes, in the Médoc district whose names are important: Margaux, Saint-Julien, Pauillac, and Saint-Estèphe. These are inner appellations of the Médoc, and a wine from one of these communes is generally of a higher class and has more individuality than one labeled simply Médoc. Although Bordeaux is a vast area, if you can remember these ten place-names (including Barsac), you will be well on your way to having a good idea of what you are drinking. For example, a red or white wine with the *Appellation Contrôlée* Bordeaux can come from anywhere within the entire region and will certainly not be from one of the better districts. A wine labeled Médoc, Saint-Emilion, Pomerol, or Graves will naturally come from vineyards within those respective districts, and you know you are getting a wine several steps up in quality from just a plain Bordeaux. If the label bears the name of one of the four communes in the Médoc, you are at a very high level within the hierarchy of Bordeaux appellations. This doesn't mean that a commune wine will always be better than a Médoc, but at least this provides a useful and fairly consistent ranking of relative quality.

Knowing these few names is also useful in reverse: that is, if a bottle of Bordeaux bears an unfamiliar *Appellation Contrôlée*, you know by the process of elimination that it must come from one of the many lesser districts. You may see names such as Entre-Deux-Mers, Côtes de Bourg, Premières Côtes de Blaye, Côtes de Castillon, and the like, and while such wines can be very agreeable indeed, they should cost less than wines from the major appellations.

When you are confronted with the label of an individual vineyard, traditionally called a château in Bordeaux, looking for its *Appellation Contrôlée* is the simplest way to place it geographically, which will help you recognize and remember the overall style of the wines from each major district. With the major appellations in mind, it becomes much easier to compare wines of different prices within an appellation, or to contrast wines of similar price from different appellations.

Although an individual vineyard in Bordeaux is called a château, there are very few homes that actually merit this description. Most properties consist of just a country house, some have more elaborate buildings dating from the late eighteenth or the early nineteenth century, and a few properties have no more than a large *chai*, or ground-level storage area, where the wines are made and stored. Nevertheless, labels for individual Bordeaux vineyards almost all contain the word *château* (a very few describe themselves as *domaine* or *clos*), and while there are properties elsewhere in France that also call themselves by a château name, when you see this word on a label, you can be pretty sure that the wine is from Bordeaux.

One way to approach the wines of Bordeaux is to divide them into two main categories; château wines, which are the product of an individual vineyard; and regional wines, which are marketed by their appellation of origin—Médoc, Saint-Emilion, Sauternes, and so on—rather than with the name of a specific property. The *négociants*, or shippers, of Bordeaux buy wines from a great many properties within a particular appellation of origin, as well as from the many cooperative cellars in the region, and blend them together to produce a wine of consistent quality and style. Most of the region's wines are shipped under two basic appellations, Bordeaux Rouge and Bordeaux Blanc, but the wines most frequently seen here are Médoc, Saint-Emilion, Graves, Sauternes, and Barsac. Margaux and Saint-Julien are occasionally available, but it is rare to find regional wines from Pauillac, Saint-Estèphe, or Pomerol, as almost all the wines from these appellations are bottled and sold by the vineyard proprietors as château wines. Since regional wines are blended, they do not express the characteristics of a particular vintage as clearly as do the wines of a single property. Nevertheless, there are vintage variations among regional wines, and it's always worth looking for the best recent vintages. Regional wines are meant to be consumed without much additional aging, and the best of them are consistent and dependable wines, although many lack the distinction and individuality of château wines selling for the same price. Some of the Bordeaux shippers whose names are featured on labels of regional wines are Baron Philippe, Barton & Guestier, Borie-Manoux, Calvet, Cordier, Dourthe, Dulong, Eschenauer, and Sichel.

In recent years, the traditional range of regional wines has been largely replaced, in this country, by proprietary wines, whose names are created and owned by individual shippers and promoted as brands. Mouton-Cadet, Maître d'Estournel, Michel Lynch, Lauretan, and La Cour Pavillon are some examples. These, too, are regional blends, almost always Bordeaux Rouge or Bordeaux Blanc, but their labels emphasize the brand name rather than the appellation of origin or the name of the shipper.

Although regional and branded wines make up the most important part of the Bordeaux market, it is the great château wines of Bordeaux that have established the reputation of this region among connoisseurs. Of the more than two thousand individually named properties in Bordeaux, there are approximately a hundred châteaux whose wines are considered the finest of all, and which most fully display the characteristics that have made the wines of Bordeaux famous. Most of these wines have been officially classified at one time or another—the vineyards of Pomerol are a notable exception—and are, therefore, referred to as *crus classés*, or classed growths (*cru* is synonymous with vineyard). Not all of these châteaux are readily available here, but there are probably fifty or sixty red wines and perhaps fifteen dry and sweet white wines whose names continually reappear in retail catalogs and on the wine lists of fine restaurants. Although the *crus classés* represent less than 5 percent of the wines of Bordeaux, this amounts to more than a million cases of very fine wine, and any discussion of Bordeaux wines will almost invariably turn to the classed growths. The classifications are explained and the wines listed district by district farther on.

The great châteaux of Bordeaux are comparatively easy to learn about because the properties are fairly large—150 acres is not uncommon—and they are traditionally under a single ownership. All of the wines from a specific vineyard that are to be sold under the château name are blended together before bottling; as a result, each property markets only one wine bearing the château label in any vintage. In contrast, most Burgundy vineyards are much smaller and almost all have several owners, each of whom makes a slightly different wine according to his skills and intentions. In Germany, also, the vineyards are small and under multiple ownership. In addition, each grower produces several different wines from the same vineyard in a good vintage, and these vary considerably in quality, taste, and price. By comparison with these other two great European wine regions, Bordeaux is relatively easy to understand, and the wines of the top châteaux are produced in sufficient quantities so that they are not difficult to acquire and compare. Many connoisseurs can discuss Bordeaux châteaux with great knowledge and enthusiasm, while remaining mystified about the wines of Burgundy or the Rhine.

It is possible to make comparisons among the wines of the many famous châteaux of Bordeaux because each of them has its own distinct characteristics. It may seem hard to believe, but each parcel of vines will produce a wine that is not only different from parcels nearby, but also consistently better or less good than those of its neighbors because of such factors as the soil and subsoil, drainage, exposure to the sun and other natural factors, proximity to a body of water, and so on. It is not unusual for a famous château to have, as its immediate neighbor, a vineyard that produces acceptable, but undistinguished, wine.

But there are other factors that enter into the quality and personality of the wine of a particular château, not least of them the proportion of different grape varieties planted. The varieties permitted for red Bordeaux are Cabernet Sauvignon, Cabernet Franc, Merlot, Petit Verdot, and Malbec, although the last two are present in rather limited quantities. Cabernet Sauvignon brings finesse, depth of flavor, tannic backbone, and longevity to a wine, the classic qualities of a claret; Cabernet Franc is similar, with perhaps more fruit and acidity and less depth; Merlot is prized for its suppleness and charm. Unlike California winemakers, who can buy the grapes they need and blend the resulting wine in whatever proportion they think most successful, a Bordeaux châteaux owner may only bottle the wine produced from his own vineyard. And the proportion of permitted varieties in a given property depends more on its soil than on the whim of the proprietor. The gravelly soil of the Médoc is particularly suitable for Cabernet Sauvignon, for example, but those sections of a vineyard that consist of clay and limestone are likely to be planted with Merlot, because Cabernet Sauvignon will not ripen as well there. Nor does it ripen well in the soils of Saint-Emilion and Pomerol—Merlot and Cabernet Franc are much more widely planted there. In any case, the proportion of different grape varieties in the wine of a particular château in a given year may not conform to that in the vineyard, because growing conditions may be more favorable for Merlot in one year, Cabernet Sauvignon the next.

Although Cabernet Sauvignon is considered the classic red-wine grape of Bordeaux, Merlot now accounts for about half the total acreage, Cabernet Sauvignon for only a quarter. Cabernet Sauvignon is the principal variety in the Médoc and Graves, however, as Merlot is in Saint-Emilion and Pomerol. Sémillon is the most widely planted white grape of Bordeaux; Sauvignon Blanc accounts for about 20 percent of the acreage and Muscadelle for about 8 percent. Colombard and Ugni Blanc are also planted in parts of Bordeaux, especially in the Bourg and Blaye regions. Overall, there are about 250,000 acres of vineyards entitled to the Bordeaux appellation, with red-wine grapes accounting for 80 percent of the total.

Among the factors that affect the style and quality of each wine (and which have been described in the chapter on winemaking) are the time of picking and vinification techniques. In recent years, the dry white wines of Bordeaux have been made from grapes that are picked earlier than in the past to retain their lively acidity, and fermentation takes place at comparatively low temperatures to preserve the wine's fruit and freshness. The grapes for red wines are picked later than they were twenty years ago, with the result that the grape tannins are more mature and the wines less harsh. Some proprietors prefer a shorter vatting—the time the grapeskins are in contact with the fermenting must—to produce a lighter and quicker-maturing wine. Other winemakers now employ a longer vatting, which extracts more color and flavor from the skins and, if properly controlled, results in wines that are rich, supple, and well structured.

One of a proprietor's most important decisions occurs within a few months of the harvest, when all the lots in the cellar are tasted to determine which ones will be set aside and which will be assembled to produce the wine eventually bottled with the château name. Since all the wine produced on the property can legally be sold with that name, this is the most expensive decision of all, but the one that is the most significant to the quality and reputation of the wine. The lots that are set aside usually consist of wines made from younger vines that are less than seven or eight years old or from parts of the vineyard that did not mature as well in that vintage. For this reason, the top châteaux generally pick and vinify young and old vines of each variety separately, and also try to vinify apart specific parcels of vines within the property, to permit a greater selection of lots for the final *assemblage*. The wines to be sold with the château name are traditionally referred to as the *grand vin*, and the rest of the crop as the *deuxième vin*, or second wine. In the past, most châteaux could not afford to set aside much of the crop as a second wine, which would have been sold to local wine merchants in bulk without the château name. In recent years, as Bordeaux proprietors have achieved bigger yields and higher prices, they have become more selective about the *grand vin*, and have also adopted the idea of bottling the second wine themselves and selling it under a different label at a lower price. The best known examples are Carruades de Lafite-Rothschild, Les Forts de Latour, and Pavillon Rouge du Château Margaux, but many other important châteaux have also adopted second labels.

After the *assemblage*, the new wine is put into the 225-liter, 60-gallon Bordeaux barrel known as a *barrique*. Many châteaux use a proportion of new oak barrels each year, which represents a considerable annual investment, but which adds complexity and nuances of taste to the wine. At the best properties, red wines were aged for eighteen to twenty-four months in the past, but a number of proprietors now prefer to use a higher proportion of new oak barrels and bottle their wines after only twelve to fifteen months to preserve more fruit and vigor.

Some years ago the best châteaux of Bordeaux began to bottle their wines themselves in their own cellars—rather than shipping them in barrels—as insurance that the wines bearing their labels are in no way tampered with; today, all *crus classés* must be château-bottled. A branded cork bearing the name of the château and the vintage is used as well. The labels of such wines bear the words *mis en bouteille au château*, that is, bottled at the château. Just about every important château wine imported into this country is now château-bottled. In recent years, as Americans have learned to look for *mis en bouteille au château* on a Bordeaux label, a number of smaller properties have taken to château-bottling their wines as well. Wines of these *petits châteaux*, as they are called, have become very popular here, and are now an important part of the Bordeaux trade; in fact, they have to a large extent replaced the regional wines of the leading shippers that dominated the Bordeaux market not so many years ago. Their quality will vary considerably, and it is well to remember that if a wine is château-bottled you are guaranteed of its authenticity, but not necessarily of its quality. It's perfectly possible to bottle a second-rate wine at the property, and this is being done to take advantage of the momentum for château-bottled wines. It is also permissible for a cooperative cellar to market certain of its wines with a château name, although in that case the phrase will read *mis en bouteille à la propriété*. There are, of course, a number of large, carefully tended properties in various districts that consistently produce good wines, and it's well worth experimenting with the selection of less expensive château-bottled wines available in local shops.

The word *supérieur*, as in Bordeaux Supérieur, only means that wines so labeled contain 1 percent more alcohol than those labeled simply Bordeaux. It is by no means an indication of superior quality, and in fact, many châteaux that could legally add *supérieur* to their appellations don't bother to do so. The word *monopole* on a shipper's label simply indicates that the firm has a monopoly, or exclusivity, on the particular brand name being used.

The Médoc

The Médoc district contains some of the most famous vineyards in the world, and most of its wines are on a very high level indeed. The wines of the Médoc have become well known only in the last two hundred years or so. The wines shipped to England in the Middle Ages, for example, were mostly from Graves. The Médoc, which begins a few miles from the city of Bordeaux and extends for sixty miles, remained a dangerous and unprotected place in which to travel, and it was not until the seventeenth century that important vineyards began to be established there.

The Médoc is actually divided into two parts, originally known as the Haut-Médoc and the Bas-Médoc. These references to high and low are based simply on the position of each district relative to the Gironde, but the proprietors in the Bas-Médoc, which is the part farthest from Bordeaux, objected to its possible connotations on a label, and their appellation is now simply Médoc. The famous communes of Saint-Estèphe, Pauillac, Saint-Julien, and Margaux are all situated in the Haut-Médoc. Although many châteaux entitled to the appellation Haut-Médoc will label their wines as such, the region is usually referred to informally as the Médoc.

Perhaps the best way to approach the wines of the Médoc is from the top, which is to say, with the Classification of 1855. In conjunction with the Paris Exhibition of that year, representatives of the Bordeaux wine trade were asked to draw up a list of the best vineyards of the Médoc and of Sauternes, which will be discussed separately. By this time the Médoc had become considerably more famous than Graves, and Saint-Emilion and Pomerol were not yet widely known. The resulting classification grouped the wines on five levels of excellence, from *Premiers crus* to *cinquièmes crus*. (Although Château Haut-Brion is located in the Graves district, it was already too important to leave out.) A fifth growth was by no means only one-fifth as good as a first growth—the ranking was gradual—and in any case all the classed growths represented the very best that Bordeaux had to offer.

THE CLASSIFICATION OF 1855 FOR THE MÉDOC

VINEYARD	COMMUNE

Premiers Crus—First Growths

Château Lafite-Rothschild	Pauillac
Château Margaux	Margaux
Château Latour	Pauillac
Château Haut-Brion	Pessac

Deuxièmes Crus—Second Growths

Château Mouton-Rothschild*	Pauillac
Château Rausan-Ségla	Margaux
Château Rauzan-Gassies	Margaux
Château Léoville-Las-Cases	Saint-Julien
Château Léoville-Poyferré	Saint-Julien
Château Léoville-Barton	Saint-Julien
Château Durfort-Vivens	Margaux
Château Lascombes	Margaux
Château Gruaud-Larose	Saint-Julien
Château Brane-Cantenac	Cantenac-Margaux
Château Pichon-Longueville	Pauillac
Château Pichon-Longueville-Comtesse de Lalande	Pauillac
Château Ducru-Beaucaillou	Saint-Julien
Château Cos d'Estournel	Saint-Estèphe
Château Montrose	Saint-Estèphe

*Reclassified as a *premier cru* in 1973.

Troisièmes Crus—Third Growths

Château Kirwan	Cantenac-Margaux
Château d'Issan	Cantenac-Margaux
Château Lagrange	Saint-Julien
Château Langoa-Barton	Saint-Julien
Château Giscours	Labarde-Margaux
Château Malescot-Saint- Exupéry	Margaux
Château Cantenac-Brown	Cantenac-Margaux
Château Palmer	Cantenac-Margaux
Château La Lagune	Ludon
Château Desmirail	Margaux
Château Calon-Ségur	Saint-Estèphe
Château Ferrière	Margaux
Château Marquis- d'Alesme-Becker	Margaux
Château Boyd-Cantenac	Cantenac-Margaux

Quatrièmes Crus—Fourth Growths

Château Saint-Pierre	Saint-Julien
Château Branaire-Ducru	Saint-Julien
Château Talbot	Saint-Julien
Château Duhart-Milon	Pauillac
Château Pouget	Cantenac-Margaux
Château La Tour-Carnet	Saint-Laurent
Château Lafon-Rochet	Saint-Estèphe
Château Beychevelle	Saint-Julien
Château Prieuré-Lichine	Cantenac-Margaux
Château Marquis-de-Terme	Margaux

Cinquièmes Crus—Fifth Growths

Château Pontet-Canet	Pauillac
Château Batailley	Pauillac
Château Haut-Batailley	Pauillac
Château Grand-Puy- Lacoste	Pauillac
Château Grand-Puy- Ducasse	Pauillac
Château Lynch-Bages	Pauillac
Château Lynch-Moussas	Pauillac
Château Dauzac	Labarde

Château d'Armailhac*	Pauillac
Château du Tertre	Arsac
Château Haut-Bages-Libéral	Pauillac
Château Pédesclaux	Pauillac
Château Belgrave	Saint-Laurent
Château Camensac	Saint-Laurent
Château Cos Labory	Saint-Estèphe
Château Clerc-Milon	Pauillac
Château Croizet-Bages	Pauillac
Château Cantemerle	Macau

Nearly 150 years have gone by, but this classification remains virtually unchanged to this day, and the names and ratings are more or less familiar to all lovers of claret. Most of the châteaux on the list continue to indicate on their labels that they are a *cru classé* or *grand cru classé*, and any discussion of the vineyards of the Médoc will always revolve around these wines. The classification remains valid in many ways, and many of these wines are still among the best produced in Bordeaux, but this listing must be approached with a certain perspective. Some châteaux have become rundown and produce only small quantities of undistinguished wine; others have been purchased by proprietors determined to increase the quality of a château's wines and to expand its production as well. Since the classification was drawn up, many of the *crus classés* no longer have the same boundaries as they did in 1855. A proprietor is legally permitted to buy vineyards anywhere within the appellation of his property—Margaux, Saint-Julien, Pauillac, or Saint-Estèphe—and sell that wine under the château label. Certain properties have, in fact, doubled or tripled their production in the past twenty years by acquiring land from their neighbors.

The classification gave such prominence to the châteaux of the Médoc that the excellent vineyards of Graves, Saint-Emilion, and Pomerol were neglected until fairly recently. It must be added, however, that the vineyards of the Médoc are much bigger, on the average,

*Formerly Château Mouton-Baronne-Philippe.

than those of the other districts. A château producing thirty or forty thousand cases is not unusual in the Médoc, whereas there are few châteaux producing even ten thousand cases in Saint-Emilion, Pomerol, and Graves.

Perhaps the most interesting development within the classification itself is that there has been so much attention focused on the four first growths, Lafite-Rothschild, Latour, Margaux, and Haut-Brion, that their prices are now two or three times that of almost all other classified wines. At the time of the classification, a second growth sold for only 10 or 15 percent less than a first, and a fifth growth cost about half as much as a first. To the four first growths of 1855 must be added Mouton-Rothschild, which never accepted its status as "first of the seconds." Its wines have almost always been as expensive as those of the first growths, and in 1973 it was officially reclassified as a first growth.

This leads to the important point that the classification was, in fact, based on the prices that each wine had sold for in a number of previous vintages. This pragmatic approach to the value of a property is the one still in use today among the brokers and shippers of Bordeaux. In the Bordeaux wine trade, the wines of the classification are referred to simply as the first growths and the classed growths, the latter category including all but the eight most expensive wines. (In practice, Châteaux Ausone and Cheval Blanc in Saint-Emilion and Pétrus in Pomerol are now included in the phrase "the first growths.") Among the classed growths are a number of wines officially rated as third, fourth, or fifth growths, such as Palmer, Talbot, Beychevelle, and Lynch-Bages, that consistently achieve the same prices as many of the classified seconds, and in some cases, a bit more. To use the classification effectively, look over the list from time to time, but do not pay undue attention to the exact rating of every wine, because a wine's relative price on an extensive retail listing of Bordeaux châteaux will give you a better indication of that wine's reputation today.

There were also a number of châteaux rated just below the *grands crus classés* as *crus exceptionnels* and *crus bourgeois*, and over the years these have been combined into the single category of *crus bourgeois*. There are now about 350 such properties altogether, and they account for nearly 45 percent of the total production of the Médoc district; 250 of these châteaux belong to an association called the Syndicat des Crus Bourgeois de Médoc, organized in 1962. Until 1989, any château could describe itself as a *cru bourgeois*, but that term has now been officially registered and its use is limited to members of the association. Some of the best-known *crus bourgeois* are listed below. (Note, however, that some well-known châteaux, including d'Avensan, Gloria, Lalande-Borie, Lanessan, Livran, and de Pez have chosen not to join the association.)

Château Beau-Site
Château Bel-Air-Marquis-d'Aligre
Château Bel-Orme
Château Capbern
Château Castera
Château Chasse-Spleen
Château Citran
Château Clarke
Château Coufran
Château d'Agassac
Château d'Angludet
Château du Glana
Château du Taillan
Château Dutruch-Grand-Poujeaux
Château Fonreaud
Château Fourcas-Dupré
Château Fourcas-Hosten
Château Gressier Grand Poujeaux
Château Greysac
Château Haut Marbuzet
Château La Bécade
Château Labégorce
Château La Cardonne
Château Lamarque
Château Larose Trintaudon
Château La Tour de By

Château La Tour de Mons
Château La Tour St. Bonnet
Château Les Ormes de Pez
Château Lestage
Château Lilian Ladouys
Château Liversan
Château Loudenne
Château Malleret
Château Marbuzet
Château Maucaillou
Château Meyney
Château Patache d'Aux
Château Paveil de Luze
Château Peyrabon
Château Phélan Ségur
Château Pibran
Château Plagnac
Château Potensac
Château Poujeaux
Château Ramage La Batisse
Château Siran
Château Sociando-Mallet
Château Tronquoy-Lalande
Château Verdignan
Château Vieux Robin

The wines of the Médoc are known especially for their breed and finesse, and are the most elegant of all Bordeaux. In good vintages, the best châteaux need several years of bottle age to reveal their distinctive qualities, and a wine that is still improving after twenty or thirty years in the bottle is not exceptional, although finding such a wine may be.

One way to tour the Médoc is to drive straight out to Saint-Estèphe, the village farthest from Bordeaux, and then to visit the principal properties in turn. Although Saint-Estèphe is the biggest wine-producing commune in the Médoc, it doesn't have as many famous châteaux as do Pauillac, Saint-Julien, and Margaux. The best-known properties are Cos d'Estournel, Montrose, Calon-Ségur, and Lafon-Rochet. Cos d'Estournel, in particular, under the direction of Bruno Prats, has produced excellent wines in recent vintages; its second label is Château de Marbuzet. Château Lafon-Rochet has been revitalized by the Tesseron family, who also own Château Pontet-Canet in Pauillac and Château Malescasse. The less familiar Château de Pez is another fine property, as is Château Les Ormes de Pez, owned by the Cazes family of Château Lynch-Bages. Château Phélan-Ségur has been revitalized by its new owner, Xavier Gardinier, and the newly created Château Lilian Ladouys has received attention for its first vintages. Saint-Estèphe wines are quite firm and tannic when young, and develop slowly: they are among the least supple of all clarets.

Pauillac probably has the highest average quality of wine of any village in France. Three *premier cru* châteaux are located there—Lafite-Rothschild, Latour, and Mouton-Rothschild—as well as a number of other vineyards whose wines are justifiably admired. Château Lafite-Rothschild is one of the few properties whose house actually resembles a château, and few sights are more impressive than the first view of its *chai* for the new wine—in a spacious and high-ceilinged ground-level warehouse, more than a thousand barrels of the most recent vintage are lined up in several long rows. Until 1967 a second wine was also made at the property, Carruades de Château Lafite-Rothschild, which came entirely from the Lafite vineyard, but was made up primarily of lighter and quicker-maturing wines from young vines. In 1974, Lafite began once again to market a second wine, first as Moulin des Carruades and then, since the late 1980s, as Carruades de Lafite-Rothschild. In 1962, the proprietors of Lafite purchased Château Duhart-Milon (which was, for some years, labeled Château Duhart-Milon-Rothschild); in 1984 they purchased a majority interest in Château Rieussec, in Sauternes, and later acquired Château l'Evangile, in Pomerol.

Château Mouton-Rothschild was in the hands of Baron Philippe de Rothschild from the 1920s until his death in 1988, and he gradually transformed the château into one of the showplaces of the Médoc. Apart from the dramatically lit cellars and the beautifully furnished main house, there is also a fascinating wine museum on the property that attracts a great many visitors every year. Nearly every year since 1945, the labels of Château Mouton-Rothschild have incorporated a design by a different artist. These have included Jean Cocteau (1947), Salvador Dali (1958), Henry Moore (1964), Joan Miró (1969), Marc Chagall (1970), Pablo Picasso (1973), Robert Motherwell (1974), Andy Warhol (1975), John Houston (1982), Saul Steinberg (1983), Keith Haring (1988), and Francis Bacon (1990). In 1933, Baron Philippe acquired Château Mouton d'Armailhacq, which he renamed Mouton Baron Philippe in 1956. Beginning with the 1975 vintage, the label was changed to Mouton Baronne Philippe, in honor of the Baron's late wife; with the 1989 vintage, Baroness Philippine de Rothschild, who succeeded her father as director of the family vineyards, changed the name of this property back to Château d'Armailhac (without the final *q*). A third vineyard in Pauillac, Château Clerc-Milon, was purchased by Baron Philippe in 1970. The firm that sells the wines of these three properties also markets a very successful red, white, and rosé regional Bordeaux called Mouton-Cadet, a name created by Baron Philippe in the 1930s.

At Château Latour, the seventeenth-century tower that gives the property its name, and appears on its label, still stands among the vines. In 1962, three-quarters of the shares of this famous vineyard passed from the de Beaumont family to British firms, and stainless-steel fermentation vats were installed in time for the 1964 vintage. Château Haut-Brion had already been using similar vats, and these innovations by two first growths encouraged many other châteaux to adopt more modern vinification methods. Since the 1966 vintage, Château Latour has been bottling a second wine, which comes entirely from the Latour vineyards, as Les Forts de Latour. In 1993, the property returned to French ownership when it was acquired by financier François Pinault. There are many Bordeaux vineyards that have incorporated the name Latour or La Tour on their labels, but the one great château of this name is this one, in Pauillac.

Château Pichon-Longueville, a second growth of Pauillac, was divided into two parts in 1850, one labeled Baron de Pichon-Longueville, the other Comtesse de Lalande; both have been considerably renovated and revitalized in recent years, and both have introduced second labels—Les Tourelles de Pichon for Pichon-Baron and Réserve de la Comtesse for Pichon-Lalande. Château Lynch-Bages, another deservedly popular Pauillac, is the property of the Cazes family; its second wine is labeled Château Haut-Bages Averous. Other well-known Pauillac châteaux include Pontet-Canet, Batailley, Haut-Batailley, Grand-Puy-Lacoste, and Grand-Puy-Ducasse.

Saint-Julien does not have any first growths, but it does have eleven classified châteaux within its borders. Just about all of them are available here, and they are excellent wines. Saint-Julien wines are somewhat softer and more supple than those of Saint-Estèphe and Pauillac, and may mature more quickly. In the early nineteenth century, the extensive Léoville estate was divided into three parts whose owners were the Marquis de Las Cases, the Baron de Poyferré, and Hugh Barton. Today, under the direction of the Delon family, Château Léoville Las Cases (whose second label is Clos du Marquis) produces rich, long-lived wines. Château Léoville-Poyferré has long been owned by the Cuvelier family, who recently expanded the vineyards and introduced a second label, Château Moulin Riche. Château Léoville-Barton, now owned by Anthony Barton, has always been vinified, aged, and bottled in the cellars of his other property, Château Langoa-Barton, yet the two are always different in style, a good example of the role that soil and microclimate play in the taste and quality of neighboring vineyards. Lady Langoa is the second label of these two properties. Château Beychevelle, whose seventeenth-century manor house and flowerbeds are among the most famous sights of the Médoc, is one of the best known Saint-Juliens, and Châteaux Talbot and Gruaud-Larose, both large estates, have long been popular with American consumers. Many connoisseurs agree that Château Ducru-Beaucaillou, the home of Jean-Eugène Borie, produces wines that are consistently among the finest of the Médoc. The Borie family also owns Châteaux Haut-Batailley and Grand-Puy-Lacoste, both in Pauillac; Château Lalande-Borie is a Saint-Julien property created by the Bories from vineyards purchased from Château Lagrange in 1970. Château Lagrange, acquired by Suntory of Japan in 1983, has been revitalized by its new owners, who expanded the vineyards and built a new winery; its second label is Les Fiefs de Lagrange. The popular Château Gloria was created by the late Henri Martin, the long-time mayor of Saint-Julien, who gradually expanded a few acres into an important property. Subsequently, he reunited the château and vineyards of Château Saint-Pierre, whose first vintage under his direction was in 1982.

Margaux produces wines noted for their elegance and rich texture: they are often described as suave. Château Margaux, a first growth, is its most famous vineyard, and the fact that it bears the same name as the commune itself has often led to confusion. A blend of wines from various properties within the village can be labeled Margaux. But there is only one Château Margaux, and there could be only a general family resemblance between a regional Margaux and the wine of this outstanding property. At the end of 1976, the Ginestet family sold Château Margaux to André Mentzelopoulos; after Mentzelopoulos' untimely death in 1980, his widow, Laura Mentzelopoulos, and their daughter, Corinne, took over the management of the property and completely renovated both the handsome nineteenth-century château and the cellars. Guided by Bordeaux enologist Emile Peynaud, the château, whose wines had been disappointing for some years, regained its former status with the 1978 and 1979 vintages. A second label, Pavillon Rouge du Château Margaux, is used for those lots that do not merit being bottled as Château Margaux.

The estate also produces a distinctive white wine, Pavillon Blanc du Château Margaux, from twenty-five acres of Sauvignon Blanc. As the Médoc appellation may be used only for red wines, any white wines produced in this region must be labeled as Bordeaux Blanc.

There are, in addition to Château Margaux, a number of excellent classed growths in Margaux and in the nearby communes of Cantenac, Labarde, Arsac, and Soussans, whose wines are entitled to be sold as Margaux. Château Palmer, classified as a third growth, now sells for more than any second growth; it is under the direction of Peter Alan Sichel, who lives nearby at Château d'Angludet. Château Prieuré-Lichine, another familiar property, was expanded, and its wines greatly improved, by its dynamic proprietor, Alexis Lichine, who died in 1989; he also directed and revitalized Château Lascombes before selling his interest in 1971. Château Giscours, purchased in 1952 by the Tari family, has considerably improved its reputation in recent years. Château Brane Cantenac is owned by Lucien Lurton and his family, who also own two other vineyards in Margaux, Château Durfort-Vivens and Château Desmirail; the Lurton family are also proprietors of Château Climens in Sauternes and Château Bouscaut in Graves. Other well-known properties in Margaux include Châteaux Rausan-Ségla, Rauzan-Gassies, Kirwan, Malescot-Saint-Exupéry, and Marquis-d'Alesme-Becker.

Two dependable classified growths that are not situated within the four main communes of the Médoc are Châteaux La Lagune and Cantemerle; each is entitled to the appellation Haut-Médoc. There are two additional Médoc communes, Listrac and Moulis, whose names are sometimes seen on château-bottled wines. It was in Listrac that Edmond de Rothschild, a shareholder of Lafite-Rothschild, decided to expand his vineyard holdings by buying an abandoned property, Château Clarke, in 1973; new vineyards were planted and the château produced its first wine in 1978. Châteaux Fourcas-Hosten and Fourcas-Dupré are also situated in Listrac, and some of the more familiar properties in Moulis include Châteaux Chasse-Spleen, Maucaillou, Poujeaux, and Malmaison, which adjoins Clarke and is owned by the same family.

Graves

The Graves district (whose name is derived from its gravelly soil) extends from just below the village of Langon all the way north beyond the city of Bordeaux to the stream of Blanquefort, which marks the southern end of the Médoc district. The extent to which the expansion of Bordeaux has encroached on the Graves vineyards can be gauged by the fact that the airport at Mérignac is actually within the boundaries of Graves, and a number of vineyards have, over the years, been transformed into urban housing.

Until the mid-1970s, most wine consumers associated the name Graves with an inexpensive, off-dry white wine that was bottled by many Bordeaux shippers as part of a line of regional Bordeaux, along with Sauternes and Saint-Emilion. Throughout the 1960s, white wines accounted for three-quarters of the crop of the Graves region; in the mid-1970s, red wines edged out the whites for the first time, and today reds represent nearly two-thirds of the crop. Graves is unusual among the major Bordeaux districts in that many of its top châteaux produce both red and white wines; in fact, both the reds and whites have been officially classified.

White Graves is usually a dry wine, but some regional bottlings are semidry or even noticeably sweet. Until recently, the relative sweetness of a Graves was rarely indicated on its label, but today dry wines are marketed as Graves, those with some sweetness as Graves Supérieures. In addition, producers throughout Bordeaux have been encouraged to use the traditional clear-glass bottle for slightly sweet white wines, and to use a dark green bottle for dry white Bordeaux. The slightly earthy quality of Graves—and of white Bordeaux in general—plus the mellowness that one frequently encounters have probably prevented the wine from being as popular as, say, Chablis or Pouilly-Fuissé. Furthermore, although it is accepted winemaking practice to stabilize white wines with a bit of sulfur dioxide, nowhere is this more evident than in the bouquet and taste of the cheapest Graves. Vinification techniques have improved considerably in recent years, and many dry white Graves are now well-made and distinctive, especially those from the top châteaux.

Most connoisseurs of Bordeaux would agree, however, that the best wines of Graves are red, and that those from the best-known châteaux are among the finest red wines of France. Château Haut-Brion, which is officially rated on a par with the first growths of the Médoc, was already famous in the seventeenth century, when it was owned by the Pontac family; in 1787, it merited a visit by Thomas Jefferson. The property, which also produces an exceptional white wine from Sémillon and Sauvignon Blanc, was acquired by an American, Clarence Dillon, in 1935. In 1983, the Dillon family purchased Château La Mission Haut-Brion, whose excellent wines are produced just across the road from Haut-Brion. Château La Tour Haut-Brion, whose name was for many years used as the second label of Château La Mission Haut-Brion, was re-established as a separate vineyard; Château Laville Haut-Brion, which is also part of this domain, continues to produce a fine white wine. Domaine de Chevalier, another top Graves estate, is known for its excellent red and white wines, made in limited quantities. Château La Louvière, an extensive estate that produces both red and white wines that are now the equal of the *crus classés*, was acquired by André Lurton in 1966; he also owns a part of Château Couhins that is planted entirely with Sauvignon Blanc and whose wines are labeled Château Couhins-Lurton.

The wines of Graves were classified in 1953 and again in 1959. Different levels of quality were not established, as in the Médoc and Saint-Emilion, and all of these wines are ranked equally as *crus classés*, although Château Haut-Brion is understood to be first among equals. Within the extensive Graves district, the vineyards in the northern part, in such villages as Pessac, Léognan, Martillac, and Talence, have traditionally produced the finest wines. In 1987, the new appellation Pessac-Léognan was created for this district, which encompasses more than fifty châteaux, including the thirteen *crus classés* of Graves. In recent vintages, this new appellation accounted for about one-quarter of the total Graves crop, 80 percent of it red. Although consumers may be slightly confused by an appellation that does not include the Graves name, all the châteaux of Pessac-Léognan also include the phrase Vin de Graves or, if appropriate, Cru Classé de Graves, on their labels.

GRAVES

Crus Classés—Classified Growths

Red Wines

Château Bouscaut
Château Carbonnieux
Domaine de Chevalier
Château de Fieuzal
Château Haut-Bailly
Château Haut-Brion
Château La Mission-
  Haut-Brion
Château La Tour-Haut-
  Brion

Château La Tour-
  Martillac
Château Malartic-
  Lagravière
Château Olivier
Château Pape Clément
Château Smith-Haut-
  Lafitte

White Wines

Château Bouscaut
Château Carbonnieux
Domaine de Chevalier
Château Couhins
Château Couhins-Lurton
Château La Tour-
  Martillac

Château Laville-Haut-
  Brion
Château Malartic-
  Lagravière
Château Olivier

Other good red and white wines from Graves include:

Château Ferrande
Château Larrivet Haut-
  Brion
Château La Garde

Château Magence
Château Pontac-
  Monplaisir
Château Rahoul

Saint-Emilion

The picturesque village of Saint-Emilion is about twenty miles northeast of Bordeaux, and to drive there one must cross both the Dordogne and the Garonne rivers. Saint-Emilion is a medieval village whose winding streets are paved with cobblestones, and one of its main tourist attractions is a monolithic church whose chapel was carved out of a granite hillside a thousand years ago, arches, pillars, and all. The local restaurants feature a dish that visitors are always encouraged to try without necessarily being told what it contains: it is *lamproie*, the local eel, cooked in red wine and one of the few fish dishes that is traditionally served with a red wine. The worldwide fame of Saint-Emilion, however, is its wine. Vineyards begin at the very edge of town and, unlike those of the Médoc and Graves, are to a large extent planted on slopes rather than flatlands. Saint-Emilion produces about two-thirds as much wine as the entire Médoc, but as its vineyards are not subdivided into inner appellations, the name Saint-Emilion is perhaps best-known of all the Bordeaux appellations.

The wines of Saint-Emilion are generally fuller and rounder than those of the Médoc—the result of somewhat richer soil and a greater proportion of Merlot grapes. Merlot produces a wine that is relatively charming and supple compared with those made from Cabernet Sauvignon, the principal grape of the Médoc. Cabernet Franc, also widely planted in Saint-Emilion (where it is known as Bouchet), gives structure to the Merlot. It's not that the growers of Saint-Emilion prefer Merlot or deliberately want to produce more supple wines; it's simply that Cabernet Sauvignon is unsuited to most of the soils there—it doesn't ripen well, and often produces wines that are comparatively hard and aggressive. Although Saint-Emilions tend to mature more quickly than the wines of the Médoc and Graves, they very much exhibit the classic qualities of Bordeaux.

The vineyards of Saint-Emilion were classified in 1954, and the rankings were formalized the following year, perhaps to coincide with the centenary of the famous 1855 classification of the Médoc. Twelve châteaux were ranked as *premiers grands crus classés*, with Châteaux

Ausone and Cheval Blanc in a category apart. The classification of Saint-Emilion wines differs from the one for the Médoc in that the former is incorporated into the *Appellation Contrôlée* laws, whereas the 1855 ranking exists apart from the Médoc appellations. The 1855 classification is unlikely ever to change, but the one for Saint-Emilion is supposed to be reviewed every ten years. In 1969, the Saint-Emilion classification was expanded to include another dozen *grands crus classés*, and then, in 1985, a new classification was published that reduced the total number of classed growths. Château Beau-Séjour-Bécot (formerly Beauséjour-Fagouet) was demoted from *premier grand cru classé* to *grand cru classé*, and several *grands crus classés* lost their ranking. In practice, only Châteaux Ausone and Cheval Blanc are ranked with the first growths of the Médoc; the nine other *permiers grands crus classés* of Saint-Emilion are considered on a par with the second and third growths of the Médoc. And, despite their classed status, few of the sixty-odd *grands crus classés* of Saint-Emilion are at the level of the classed growths of the Médoc and Graves, and fewer than twenty are easily found here.

There is, in addition, a third category of wines entitled to add *grand cru* to their labels. These châteaux are not permanently classified, but must submit their wines to a tasting panel on an annual basis to qualify for *grand cru* status. Nearly two hundred châteaux earn this distinction in a good vintage, and they account for about a third of the region's production. (There is an important cooperative cellar in Saint-Emilion that produces about 20 percent of the region's wines; some of the cooperative's wines may be labeled with a château name and the *grand cru* designation.)

The vineyards of Saint-Emilion are informally divided into two subdistricts, the *côtes* and the *graves*, neither of which has any official status. The clay-and-limestone *côtes*, or slopes, surrounds the town of Saint-Emilion and encompasses nine of the eleven *premiers grands cru classés*, including Château Ausone, whose production of twenty-five hundred cases makes it the smallest of the first growths. The two other top châteaux, Cheval Blanc and Figeac, are situated in the *graves*, a gravelly plateau that adjoins Pomerol; they are among the biggest of the classed growths of the region and, because of their grav-elly soil, are planted with a higher proportion of Ca-bernet Sauvignon vines than most Saint-Emilions.

Next to the extensive Saint-Emilion district are four communes whose wines may be marketed with the name Saint-Emilion added to their own. They are Montagne-Saint-Emilion (which includes the wines formerly sold as Parsac-Saint-Emilion), Saint-Georges-Saint-Emilion (whose wines may also be labeled as Montagne-Saint-Emilion), Lussac-Saint-Emilion, and Puisseguin-Saint-Emilion.

All of the *premiers grands crus classés* in the revised 1985 classification are listed here, as well as the better-known *grands cru classés*.

SAINT-EMILION

Premiers Grands Crus—First Great Growths

Château Ausone
Château Cheval Blanc
Château Beauséjour (Duf-
fau-Lagarrosse)
Château Belair
Château Canon

Clos Fourtet
Château Figeac
Château La Gaffelière
Château Magdelaine
Château Pavie
Château Trottevieille

Grands Crus Classés—Great Classified Growths

Château L'Angélus
Château Balestard-la-
Tonnelle
Château Beau-Séjour-
Bécot
Château Berliquet
Château Cadet-Piola
Château Canon-La-
Gaffelière
Château Cap de Mourlin
Château Corbin
Château Corbin-Michotte
Château Couvent des
Jacobins
Château Curé-Bon

Château Dassault
Château Fonplégade
Château Fonroque
Château Grand Barrail
Lamarzelle Figeac
Château Grand-Corbin
Château Grand Mayne
Château Grand-Pontet
Clos des Jacobins
Château La Clotte
Château La Dominique
Château La Marzelle
Château Larcis-Ducasse
Château Larmande
Château La Tour Figeac

Château Pavie-Decesse	Château Trimoulet
Château Pavie-Macquin	Château Troplong
Château Ripeau	Mondot
Château Soutard	Château Villemaurine
Château Tertre Daugey	Château Yon-Figeac

Other Saint-Emilion châteaux include the increasingly popular Château Monbousquet, now under the direction of Alain Querre; Château Simard, found on many restaurant wine lists; and:

Château Ferrande	Château Lapelletrie
Château Fombrauge	Château Puy-Blanquet
Château La Grace Dieu	

Pomerol

Pomerol is the smallest of the top wine districts of Bordeaux, and produces only 15 percent as much wine as Saint-Emilion. Pomerol adjoins the Saint-Emilion district, and for many years its wines were grouped with those of its better-known neighbor. About seventy years ago Pomerol was accorded a standing of its own, and its wines now have achieved the reputation they merit. As a matter of fact, a number of Pomerol vineyards consistently sell their wines for more than the second growths of the Médoc.

The vineyards of Pomerol are fairly small, as are those of Saint-Emilion, which partly accounts for their late-flowering reputations both in France and abroad. Vineyards were originally established in these two districts by members of the middle class. In contrast, the great vineyards of the Médoc were established in the early eighteenth century by an aristocratic class that was able to carve out much bigger estates in that undeveloped area. The greater production of the Médoc châteaux and the higher social standing of its owners gave this district a momentum from the very beginning. The Classification of 1855 did not even consider the vineyards of Saint-Emilion and Pomerol, and to this day, their limited production has prevented most of them from being as familiar to claret drinkers as the châteaux of the Médoc.

There is very little regional Pomerol available, as its

wines are mostly sold under the names of individual châteaux. Merlot is the principal variety planted in Pomerol, whose wines are rich and full-flavored, with a distinctive earthy or trufflelike quality. The ripe, generous taste of Pomerols often makes them more accessible when young than the firmer, more austere wines of the Médoc, but the finest examples are as long-lived as other top clarets.

The most famous Pomerol vineyard is Château Pétrus, which has become the most expensive red wine of Bordeaux. Its production is relatively small—about four thousand cases a year—and the vineyard is planted almost entirely in Merlot, with only 5 percent of Cabernet Franc. In 1969 the property was enlarged to its present size of twenty-eight acres by the acquisition of ten adjoining acres that belonged to Château Gazin. Jean-Pierre Moueix, the leading *négociant* of Saint-Emilion and Pomerol, has been a co-owner of Pétrus since 1964, and his son Christian has been in charge of making the wines since the early 1970s. Jean-Pierre Moueix also owns Châteaux Trotanoy, La Fleur Pétrus, and Lagrange in Pomerol, and Magdelaine and Fonroque in Saint-Emilion.

No classification has ever been established for Pomerol, but the following list indicates the best, and best-known, of its vineyards. Château Pétrus stands apart, on a level with the first growths of the Médoc. Other highly regarded Pomerol châteaux include Trotanoy, Vieux-Château-Certan, Latour à-Pomerol, La Fleur Pétrus, and La Conseillante.

POMEROL

Château Pétrus

Château Beauregard	Château Lafleur
Château Certan-de-May	Château La Fleur Pétrus
Château Certan-Giraud	Château Lagrange
Château Clinet	Château La Pointe
Château Gazin	Château Latour-Pomerol
Château La Conseillante	Clos L'Eglise
Château La Croix	Domaine de L'Eglise
Château Là Croix-de-Gay	Château L'Eglise-Clinet

Château L'Enclos
Château L'Evangile
Château Nénin
Château Petit-Village
Clos René

Château Rouget
Château de Sales
Château Taillefer
Château Trotanoy
Vieux-Château-Certan

Just above Pomerol is the relatively unfamiliar Lalande de Pomerol district, whose wines are often characterized as a lighter version of Pomerol. Fronsac and Canon-Fronsac are two appellations situated just west of Pomerol and the city of Libourne; these well-structured red wines, made primarily from Cabernet Franc, are becoming better known to consumers. Some miles away, facing the vineyards of the Médoc across the Gironde, are the extensive regions of Bourg and Blaye, whose official appellations are Côtes de Bourg and Premières Côtes de Blaye; both produce a great deal of agreeable red wine.

Sauternes

The luscious, sweet wines of Sauternes are among the most unusual in the world, and they are produced by a unique and expensive process that can take place only in certain years. The Sauternes district, which is about thirty miles from Bordeaux, is geographically contained within the southern part of Graves. Wines produced in the commune of Barsac are, technically speaking, Sauternes as well, but these wines are entitled to be marketed under their own *Appellation Contrôlée*. Some vineyards use the appellation Barsac, others use Sauternes, and a few use both names on their labels to make the most of the situation.

Although the name Sauternes is used (often without the final *s*) to label inexpensive white wines from other countries that range in taste from mellow to dry, they bear no resemblance to the sweet wines made in Sauternes itself, in a rather special way. When the owners of vineyards producing red wines or dry white wines are already picking their grapes, the critical time has just begun for those who make Sauternes and Barsac, as those proprietors wait for their grapes to be affected by a beneficial mold called *pourriture noble*, or noble rot.

(Sémillon is the principal grape variety planted in the Sauternes region; many châteaux also have 10 to 30 percent of Sauvignon Blanc, and a few have a little Muscadelle as well. Sauvignon Blanc, which contributes aroma and finesse, is usually harvested before it is affected by the noble rot.) The morning fog that rises from the Ciron River provides the moisture necessary for the noble rot to appear. As the grapes become covered with the unattractive white mold *Botrytis cinerea*, they gradually shrivel up. And as water evaporates from the grape pulp, there is an increased concentration of sugar and flavor elements in the remaining juice. When the grapes are pressed and the rich juice is fermented, not all of the sugar is transformed into alcohol. The resulting wine is rich and sweet.

Sauternes must contain a minimum of 13 percent alcohol, although 14 or 14.5 percent is not uncommon. The residual sugar often amounts to 7 or 8 percent in a good year, and may be as much as 10 percent in the finest years. But Sauternes is not simply a sweet wine: the noble rot not only increases the proportion of sugar in the grapes, it transforms the flavor of the juice as well. The resulting wine has a more intense aroma, a richer, more complex taste, and a more viscous texture than one that is merely sweet.

Although Sauternes can be made only when the right combination occurs—ripe grapes, alternating humidity and sunshine, and the absence of rain or frost in the fall—the finest Sauternes require even more care and risk. The vineyards must be harvested carefully so that only the fully botrytised, or "rotted," grapes are picked, and the rest are left to continue their transformation by the noble rot. This means not just one picking but several. It also means leaving part of the crop on the vines until late October or mid-November, in the hope that all the grapes will by then have been fully affected by the noble rot. Waiting those extra weeks involves risk, and sending harvesters through a vineyard six or eight times is expensive. In practice, much of the Sauternes region is harvested in only two or three pickings during late September or early October. As a result many wines produced in Sauternes are not much more than agreeable, sweet white wines that lack the intensity and concentration of the best Sauternes. Most important, they lack the distinctive botrytised taste, complex and honeyed, that distinguishes the finest wines, made from shriveled and rotted grapes, from those that are made primarily from ripe grapes only partly affected by *Botrytis cinerea*. Most of the wines from this region are blended and bottled by Bordeaux firms and sold as Sauternes or Barsac (or as Haut-Sauternes or Haut-Barsac, meaningless terms with no legal definition whatsoever). These regional bottlings almost invariably lack the character for which these wines are famous. Many are comparatively thin and weak sweet wines, and are likely to disappoint those who try them hoping to discover the qualities that make Sauternes unique. The finest Sauternes and Barsacs available here are château-bottled wines from about two dozen properties.

Sauternes is not as popular as it was in the last century, and in the recent past many of the château-bottled wines were undervalued; today, the best examples are at least as expensive as the second growths of the Médoc. At one time it was appropriate to serve a Sauternes or Barsac with a first course of foie gras, and this practice still exists today in Bordeaux to a limited extent. Although Sauternes is usually served with dessert, some connoisseurs feel that a sweet dessert tends to overwhelm the wine and diminish its natural sweetness. Many who enjoy the distinctive taste of Sauternes have discovered that Roquefort cheese is one of the best accompaniments to this wine, since it provides an excellent contrast to the richness of the wine and brings out its qualities, instead of smothering them. Sauternes is not to everyone's taste, but you must not deny yourself the experience of tasting a bottle of this unique wine.

There is one vineyard in Sauternes that is considerably more famous than all of the others, and that is Château d'Yquem. Its wines cost three or four times as much as those of the other châteaux, and its 250 acres constitute one of the most famous vineyards in the world. Yquem first produced a dry wine, labeled Y (and pronounced *ee-grec*), in 1959, and continues to do so in certain years.

Because producing Sauternes is a risky endeavor, a number of other properties now make a dry white wine as well. Château Guiraud produces a dry wine labeled

G, Château Rieussec makes R, Château de Malle makes Chevalier de Malle, and Château Coutet produces Vin Sec du Château Coutet, to cite a few examples. Some are made entirely, or primarily, from Sauvignon Blanc; others contain more Sémillon. (Château Doisy-Védrines produced a dry white from Sauvignon Blanc that became so popular that its name, Chevalier Védrines, is now a trademark for both red and white regional wines.) The dry wines are harvested first; thus, if a Sauternes vintage is spoiled, or considerably reduced, by rain in October or November, the proprietors still have the dry wine to sell. Because Sauternes must be sweet, the dry wines made in the region may be labeled only as Bordeaux Blanc.

The wines of Sauternes were classified in 1855 along with those of the Médoc, and many of these château-bottled wines are imported into this country. Note that Château Myrat no longer exists, and that Château de Fargues (under the same ownership as Château d'Yquem) and Château Raymond-Lafon are considered on a par with many of the first growths listed below.

THE CLASSIFICATION OF 1855
FOR SAUTERNES AND BARSAC

Grand Premier Cru—First Great Growth

Château d'Yquem

Premiers Crus—First Growths

Château La Tour-Blanche
Clos Haut-Peyraguey
Château Lafaurie-
  Peyraguey
Château de Rayne-
  Vigneau
Chateau de Suduiraut

Château Coutet
Château Climens
Château Guiraud
Château Rieussec
Château Rabaud-Promis
Château Sigalas-Rabaud

Deuxièmes Crus—Second Growths

Château Myrat	Château Nairac
Château Doisy-Daëne	Château Caillou
Château Doisy-Dubroca	Château Suau
Château Doisy-Védrines	Château de Malle
Château D'Arche	Château Romer
Château Filhot	Château Lamothe
Château Brouset	

Cérons, a small district next to Barsac, produces semi-sweet white wines. Across the Garonne River, within the larger appellation Premières Côtes de Bordeaux, the three districts of Cadillac, Loupiac, and Sainte-Croix-du-Mont also produce semisweet white wines. The extensive Entre-Deux-Mers region produces dry white wines whose quality has improved considerably in the past decade or so; its name, which means between two seas, is a rather grand reference to its location, between the Garonne and the Dordogne rivers.

BURGUNDY

Burgundy, perhaps the most evocative of all wine names, conveys different impressions to different people. The historian knows Burgundy as an independent duchy that was annexed to France in the late fifteenth century. The decorator associates the name with a deep red color, although Burgundy produces white wines that are among the finest in the world. Many consumers recognize Burgundy as a name used in several countries other than France to label inexpensive red wines, although the province of Burgundy, situated in east-central France, is strictly delimited. And to many wine drinkers Burgundy means wines that are rich and heavy, although many of the finest Burgundies are noted for their delicacy, finesse, and refinement.

All of Burgundy produces about half as much wine as Bordeaux, but most of this comes from Beaujolais and the Mâconnais. Perhaps a more relevant comparison might be between Bordeaux and the heart of Burgundy—the Côte d'Or—which contains such famous wine villages as Gevrey-Chambertin, Nuits-Saint-Georges, Pommard, Beaune, and Puligny-Montrachet. There are about twenty thousand acres of vines in the Côte d'Or, compared to 250,000 acres in Bordeaux, and the total amount of wine produced in the Côte d'Or is appreciably less than is made in the Saint-Emilion district of Bordeaux alone. This is another way of saying that the best wines of Burgundy will always be scarce and expensive. The vineyards of Burgundy are divided into several main districts: Chablis, to the north; the Côte d'Or, which consists of the Côte de Nuits and the Côte de Beaune; and to the south, the Chalonnais, the Mâconnais (including Pouilly-Fuissé), and the vast Beaujolais district.

White Burgundy from any district must be made entirely from the Chardonnay grape, although there is a small amount of Pinot Blanc still planted in a few scattered vineyards. (It is now believed that the famous white wine grape of Burgundy—traditionally called Pinot Chardonnay—is not actually a member of the Pinot family.) Red Burgundy from the Côte d'Or is made entirely from Pinot Noir; Gamay is used in Beaujolais and the Mâconnais. There is a substantial amount of white wine—occasionally seen in this country—made from the lesser Aligoté grape, and entitled only to the appellation Bourgogne Aligoté. Red wines that are made from a mixture of Pinot Noir and Gamay grapes are labeled Bourgogne-Passe-Tout-Grains.

Chablis

Chablis is probably the best-known white wine in the world, although mainly for the wrong reasons. As it happens, a number of wine-producing countries, including the United States, are permitted to label any white wine Chablis, and millions of cases of inexpensive wines are so marketed every year. True Chablis from France, however, is a specific and distinctive wine. It is produced in strictly delimited vineyards that encircle the village of Chablis, situated about 110 miles from Paris. Although considered a part of Burgundy, the vineyards of Chablis, surrounded by wheatfields, are somewhat isolated: Chablis is 80 miles northwest of Beaune and 130 miles from the vineyards of Pouilly-Fuissé, the wine with which

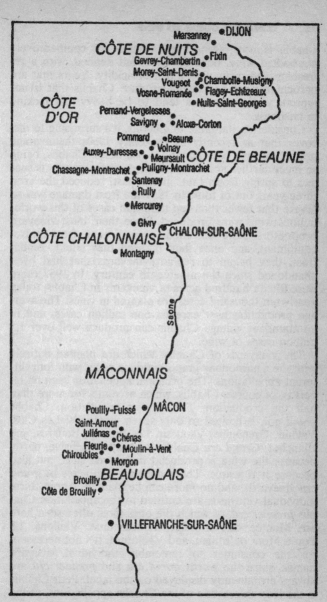

BURGUNDY

Chablis is most often linked. Chablis is a comparatively big-bodied wine, bone-dry and well defined, with a refreshing and distinctive touch of acidity. Years that are particularly hot and sunny produce Chablis that is not typical, and such wines tend to be heavy and lacking in crispness.

Considering the fame of Chablis, it's surprising to discover that as recently as the early 1960s the average production was only about 115,000 cases. Chablis, being so much farther north than the rest of Burgundy, is subject to spring frosts that, in the past, reduced the crop three years out of four. In 1957 the frost damage was so severe that fewer than ten thousand cases of this world-famous wine were produced. Since then, most vineyard proprietors have installed sophisticated frost-control equipment, and once they realized they could combat frost, they began to replant vineyards that had been abandoned since the nineteenth century. In 1957 there were fifteen hundred acres of vineyards in Chablis; today nearly ten thousand acres are planted in vines. The average production now exceeds one million cases, and in an abundant vintage Chablis can produce well over 1.5 million cases of wine.

The vineyards of Chablis, which are planted entirely with the Chardonnay grape, produce wines with four different appellations. The principal appellation seen on labels is, of course, Chablis, which accounts for more than half the production. The highest appellation, Chablis *grand cru*, is limited to only seven vineyards: Les Clos, Valmur, Grenouille, Vaudésir, Les Preuses, Bougros, and Blanchot. *Grand cru* Chablis is always expensive, partly because the wine is produced in favored sites, but also because it is scarce. There are only 250 acres of *grand cru* vineyards, and no more can be planted. About thirty individual vineyards are entitled to the appellation Chablis *premier cru*, of which the ones most often seen here are Montée de Tonnerre, Fourchaume, Vaillons, La Forêt, Mont de Milieu, and Vaulorent. It's not necessary for the consumer to remember individual vineyard names, since the words *grand cru* and *premier cru* are always prominently displayed on the label. Petit Chablis is the least interesting of the Chablis appellations, as the wines come from vineyards on the outskirts of the district. These lighter-bodied wines are attractive when young, but few examples retain their appeal much beyond a year. What's more, the price of Petit Chablis in recent years has been almost as high as that of Chablis, so it is not often imported into this country.

Côte d'Or

The Côte d'Or, or Golden Slope, gets its name from the appearance of these hillside vineyards when they have taken on their autumn foliage. The vineyards of the Côte d'Or begin just below Dijon and continue, with a break midway, for about thirty miles down to Chagny. This strip of soil, never more than half a mile wide, produces less than 15 percent of all the wines made in Burgundy, but it is here that are situated the famous villages and vineyards that most people associate with the name Burgundy. The northern half is the Côte de Nuits, and known primarily for its red wines. The Côte de Beaune, to the south, produces more red wine than white but is famous for its superb white wines.

Red Burgundies, which account for about 75 percent of the wines of the Côte d'Or, are considered easier to enjoy than Bordeaux, as they are softer, fuller, rounder wines. They have a more beguiling bouquet, generally described as more perfumed, and they seem to taste less austerely dry than claret. Unfortunately, many consumers think of red Burgundies as heavy, almost sweet wines, because of the many poor examples that are produced: such wines do not display the elegance and balance of the finest examples. The best white Burgundies have a richness and depth of flavor that justifies their reputation as one of the finest dry white wines in the world.

While good Burgundies may be very appealing to many wine drinkers, they are also considerably more difficult to understand than are the wines of Bordeaux. In the first place, there are more village names to remember in the Côte d'Or than in Bordeaux: about a dozen that are important, another dozen that are less frequently encountered and that therefore provide some good values. Apart from these village names and several regional appellations, there are thirty individual vineyards, officially rated as *grands crus*, which are legally entitled to their own *Appellation Contrôlée*. That is, the name of the vineyard—Chambertin, Montrachet, Musigny—may appear by itself on a label, without the name of the village in which it is situated. In Bordeaux, of course, even the best vineyards bear a commune or district appellation, which makes it considerably easier to place them geographically. Thus, Château Lafite-Rothschild has the *Appellation Contrôlée* Pauillac on its label, and Château Haut-Brion is identified as a Graves.

Not only is it necessary for the intelligent buyer of good Burgundy to know the wine villages and to have some familiarity with the *grands crus*, but one other important factor further complicates the choice of wine. Almost all of the vineyards in Burgundy, which are fairly small to begin with, are owned by several different growers. For example, Montrachet, only nineteen acres in size, has over a dozen owners. The twenty-three acres of Grands-Echézeaux are divided among ten owners; and Clos de Vougeot, whose 125 acres make it the biggest vineyard in Burgundy, has more than eighty owners today. This multiple ownership can be traced back to the French Revolution, when large domains owned by the Church and by members of the nobility were confiscated and sold in small parcels to the local farmers. The laws of inheritance in Burgundy have made these holdings even smaller, whereas in Bordeaux the large châteaux are maintained as corporate entities and have continued intact. Since each grower decides for himself when to replant old vines, how severely to limit his yield per acre, when to harvest, and exactly how to vinify his wines, the result is a number of different wines of different quality from the same vineyard. Two people can discuss the merits of Château Latour 1990, which they enjoyed separately, and be certain they are talking about the same wine. Two people comparing notes on previously consumed bottles of Chambertin 1988 or Volnay Caillerets 1990 must first establish who produced each wine.

There are three important levels of quality in the Côte d'Or: village wines, *premiers crus*, and *grands crus*. This rating system is incorporated into the official *Appellation Contrôlée* laws for Burgundy and was based on historical precedent and careful analysis of each vineyard. There has never been an official classification of the Côte d'Or vineyards similar in status to the 1855 classification for the Médoc, but an attempt was made in 1861. Each of the best vineyards was named a *Tête de Cuvée*, and this traditional distinction is still found on some labels, particularly for those vineyards that did not merit *grand cru* status under the *Appellation Contrôlée* laws. One indication of how difficult it must have been to rate each one of the small Burgundian vineyards is the fact that they are traditionally referred to as *climats*. In other words, it is understood that rain, for example, will affect each plot of land in a different way, depending on the ability of the subsoil to absorb water, that its exact position on a hillside will determine its exposure to the sun, and so forth. Perhaps a modern way of translating *climat* would be "microclimate."

The principal wine villages are shown on the map, and will be discussed in detail. One confusing aspect of some of these villages' names came about in the late nineteenth century when a number of villages appended to their names that of their most famous individual vineyard. Thus Gevrey became Gevrey-Chambertin, Chambolle became Chambolle-Musigny, Nuits changed to Nuits-Saint-Georges, and so on. As the great vineyard of Montrachet is partly situated in both Chassagne and Puligny, both of these villages added its name to their own. Consumers sometimes believe that they have drunk the wine of a specific great vineyard when in fact they have been served a village wine, which can come from vineyards anywhere in the named village. It must be remembered, however, that none of these villages produce a great deal of wine and their names on a label should by no means be thought of as a regional appellation. For example, Saint-Emilion produces twenty times as much wine as does Pommard, and there is a hundred times as much wine made in Beaujolais as in Nuits-Saint-Georges.

The *premier cru* vineyards of the Côte d'Or are not difficult to spot because their names always follow those of their respective villages. Thus, some *premier cru* wines from Volnay are Volnay Caillerets, Volnay Champans, Volnay Clos des Ducs, and so forth. Some *premier cru* wines from other villages include Gevrey-Chambertin, Clos Saint-Jacques; Pommard, Les Rugiens; Chassagne-Montrachet, Clos de la Boudriotte; and so on. Not infrequently you will see the words *premier cru* after a village name, without the name of a specific vineyard, such as Chassagne-Montrachet Premier Cru. This usually indicates that the wine was assembled from more than one *premier cru* vineyard or that the producer felt that the phrase by itself would make his wine more salable than the name of a specific, but unfamiliar, vineyard.

The highest rating in the Côte d'Or is that of *grand cru*, and the thirty vineyards so classed are listed further on, village by village, along with some of the better-known *premiers crus*. If you recognize the village names, certain *grand cru* vineyards are easy to locate: Chambertin, Musigny, Montrachet, Romanée-Saint-Vivant, for example. Other *grand cru* names, however, bear no relation to that of their village of origin, and only homework will lead to familiarity: for example, Clos de la Roche, Richebourg, Bonnes Mares. *Grand cru* wines account for perhaps 5 percent of all the wines of the Côte de Nuits and Côte de Beaune, and they are always expensive. They are also among the greatest red and white wines in the world, and their study will be repaid by their excellence.

A grower in Burgundy does not produce a single wine, as does a Bordeaux château. He deliberately has vines in several vineyards, and often in two or three adjoining villages, so that he is protected to some extent from the hailstorms and frosts that occasionally occur and that often affect only a very small area at a time. Of course, another factor leading to scattered holdings is that domains in Burgundy are built up slowly as money is accumulated and vines become available for sale.

A visitor to a Bordeaux château will be taken on a tour of the *chai*, see hundreds of barrels of new wine aging in spacious surroundings, and then be offered a glass of the one or perhaps two vintages currently maturing in wood. Visiting a cellar in Burgundy means crowding in among barrels, called *pièces*, piled two or three high, and tasting will include as many as a dozen different wines from different villages and vineyards. A famous Bordeaux château may produce fifteen thousand to forty thousand cases of a single wine in a year. A Burgundian grower whose domain is big enough to justify bottling his own wines at the property may produce only five hundred to one thousand cases each of several different wines. His share of a *grand cru* vineyard may only be big enough to produce four barrels, or one hundred cases, a year. A domain that produces four or five thousand cases is considered quite large in the Côte d'Or.

It is evident, then, that whereas in Bordeaux a knowledge of the main districts and of a few major châteaux will get you off to a good start, knowing Burgundy is a bit more time-consuming. You must know the villages and at least a few *grand cru* vineyards, and then pay strict attention to the name of the shipper or grower whose wine you are drinking.

The relative merits of wines blended and bottled by shippers and those estate-bottled by individual growers is a subject that often provokes discussion among Burgundy drinkers. Most growers in Burgundy sell their wines in barrel to the big shipping firms, who blend together wines from each appellation to make what they hope will be a consistently dependable Beaune, Pommard, Nuits-Saint-Georges, and so on. A number of growers have traditionally preferred to bottle their wines themselves, as do the châteaux of Bordeaux. Such wines bear the words *mis en bouteille au domaine, mis au domaine*, or *mis en bouteille à la propriété*, and these estate-bottled wines are the Burgundian equivalent of the château-bottled wines of Bordeaux. The phrase *mis en bouteille dans nos caves*, "bottled in our cellars," is often used by shippers and does not signify estate-bottling.

Those who prefer estate-bottled Burgundies suggest that the wines of each shipper tend to have a family resemblance that cuts across the individual appellations. Each shipper has certain ideas about what a good Burgundy should taste like and tries to maintain his standards and his style, sometimes at the expense of the particular characteristics of a village or vineyard. By comparison, the best of the growers produce wines that have more individuality and that define more clearly the style of each appellation. In reply, a shipper might point out that he is a specialist in the aging and bottling of fine wines, and that his judgment and experience in these matters are more reliable than that of many growers, especially those who have only recently decided to estate-bottle their wines. Furthermore, a shipper who buys from a great many growers is likely to have more perspective on the style of each appellation and greater flexibility in blending wines to a consistent style than a grower whose production and concerns are limited to wines from his own vineyards. Unfortunately, many estate-bottled wines today are of inferior quality, just as many shippers' wines are undistinguished and lack definition. Perhaps the most important element in this controversy is the reputation of the firm or person whose name is on the label. There are several dozen individual growers whose wines are recognized as outstanding examples of Burgundy, and a number of serious shippers who produce a wide range of excellent Burgundies. The controversy is somewhat complicated by the fact that a number of Burgundy shippers are themselves owners of substantial domains—sixty to two hundred acres—along the Côte d'Or, among them Bouchard Père & Fils, Chanson, Joseph Drouhin, Louis Jadot, and Louis Latour. What's more, many shippers today no longer simply buy wines from individual growers throughout the Côte d'Or; instead, they buy grapes (or, in some cases, the must—the unfermented juice—of white grapes) and vinify the wines themselves in their own modern cellars, thus retaining much greater control over the quality and style of the wines they market.

There is another controversial issue concerning the style and quality of fine Burgundy. Many people who enjoy red Burgundies feel that the overall style of these wines has been gradually transformed over the past twenty years or so by what is often referred to as the new vinification. According to this view, the longer vatting practiced years ago to produce deep-colored, tannic, and long-lived red Burgundies has given way to shorter vatting and lighter wines that are sooner ready to drink, but often lack intensity and flavor. It is undoubtedly true that some Burgundian winemakers have responded to the demand from many wine drinkers for red wines that can be consumed within a few years of the vintage, but it is also true that many shippers and growers continue to make long-lived wines in more traditional ways. As it happens, a number of Burgundian producers believe that the most significant factor affecting the quality of Burgundy has been that of overproduction, not vinification. As the demand for red and white Burgundies has intensified, many growers have increased their production per acre, which usually results in weak, light wines without much character or depth. Although *Appellation Contrôlée* laws for Burgundy limit the amount of wine that can be produced for each appellation, the maximum yields per acre have been increased over the years to reflect better viticultural practices. Growers therefore have a certain amount of leeway about yields, but the more conscientious ones—which includes a younger generation of serious, professionally trained Burgundian winemakers—are determined to reduce their crops to produce more complex and concentrated wines.

What follows is a closer look at the individual wine villages of the Côte d'Or, starting with the Côte de Nuits. With a few exceptions, all the wines of the Côte de Nuits are red; the limited amount of white wine produced in Chambolle-Musigny, Morey-Saint-Denis, Nuits-Saint-Georges, and Vougeot rarely exceeds five thousand cases altogether.

Just below Dijon is the little village of Marsannay, which produces red, white, and rosé wines that are sometimes seen here; the dry rosé, made from Pinot Noir, can be delightful. Fixin, pronounced by its inhabitants as *fee-san*, produces about a third as much wine as Nuits-Saint-Georges or Pommard, but good wines from its best vineyards can occasionally be found here.

The next village is world-famous: Gevrey-Chambertin. Its two principal vineyards, Chambertin and Chambertin-Clos de Bèze, sit side by side and extend for about seventy acres. Vines were planted in Gevrey by the abbey of Bèze as early as the seventh century, and its wines soon achieved a high reputation. In the thirteenth century, the story goes, a farmer named Bertin planted vines in the adjacent field, which was known as *champ de Bertin*, or Bertin's field. Although these two vineyards are now known for their outstanding red wines, it's interesting to note that at one time there was also a white

Chambertin, an early example of trial and error. Most of the proprietors of one vineyard own vines in the other, so it's hard to distinguish between the two plots. Moreover, whereas Chambertin can only be labeled as such, wines from Chambertin-Clos de Bèze can also be sold as Chambertin.

There are, in addition to these two vineyards, seven other vineyards of *grand cru* stature bearing the name Chambertin, including Chapelle-Chambertin, Charmes-Chambertin, Latricières-Chambertin, Ruchottes-Chambertin, Mazys-Chambertin, Mazoyères-Chambertin, and Griotte-Chambertin. Mazoyères-Chambertin is no longer seen on labels because its wines may be sold as Charmes-Chambertin. The two great vineyards produce about ten thousand cases a year, the other seven together about twenty thousand cases. Gevrey-Chambertin produces more wine than any other village in the Côte d'Or, and the best of them are the biggest-bodied of all Burgundies.

The village of Morey-Saint-Denis lies between the considerably more famous ones of Gevrey-Chambertin and Chambolle-Musigny. Its name is not often seen on wine labels here because its vineyards are not extensive, and also because a quarter of the wine produced in Morey comes from *grand cru* vineyards and is sold without reference to the village. These vineyards are Clos de la Roche, Clos des Lambrays, Clos Saint-Denis, Clos de Tart, and a small part of Bonnes Mares; Clos des Lambrays which has been entitled to *grand cru* status only since 1981, and Clos de Tart are among the few top vineyards in Burgundy under single ownership.

Chambolle-Musigny is known for its elegant and distinguished wines, and its two *grand cru* vineyards, Musigny and most of Bonnes Mares, are in the top rank of all Burgundies. A very small amount of white wine, Musigny Blanc, is also produced in that vineyard by the Comte de Vogüé.

The little hamlet of Vougeot produces some attractive red wines sold as such, but its fame is derived from its single great vineyard, Clos de Vougeot. First planted in vines by the Cistercian monks in the twelfth century, its 125 acres have been maintained as a single vineyard throughout the centuries. The vineyard is so extensive, however, that some parcels are much better situated than others. Moreover, there are so many proprietors who own vines in this vineyard—some of them producing only one or two barrels a year—that quality varies considerably from bottle to bottle. The Clos de Vougeot itself is now the headquarters of the Chevaliers du Tastevin, an organization founded in the 1930s to promote the wines of Burgundy, and the large hall is frequently the scene of convivial dinners. A white wine from Vougeot, Clos Blanc de Vougeot, is produced in limited quantities.

Flagey-Echézeaux does not have its own village appellation because its wines can be sold as Vosne-Romanée, but it does contain two *grand cru* vineyards. Grands-Echézeaux, which adjoins Clos de Vougeot, is divided among several proprietors. Wines from the eleven vineyards entitled to the Echézeaux appellation can also be sold as Vosne-Romanée Premier Cru. The production of Echézeaux is about four times that of Grands-Echézeaux.

Vosne-Romanée produces village wines of a very high level, and its best vineyards are among the most famous and most expensive in the world. The village includes the four-and-a-half-acre vineyard of Romanée-Conti, the most expensive of all Burgundies, whose total production never exceeds eight hundred cases. The property is owned by the Domaine de la Romanée-Conti, which also owns all fifteen acres of La Tâche, thirteen acres of Romanée-Saint-Vivant (acquired from the Marey-Monge estate in 1990), and parts of Richebourg, Grands-Echézeaux, and Echézeaux—about sixty-two acres within the Vosne-Romanée appellation; in addition, the Domaine also owns 1.7 acres of the famous Montrachet vineyard. La Romanée is a *grand cru* that is only two acres in size, which makes it the smallest vineyard in France to have its own *Appellation Contrôlée*; La Grande Rue, whose three acres are situated between Romanée-Conti and La Tâche, was recently granted *grand cru* status. The *grand cru* wines of Vosne-Romanée are all expensive, but a number of *premiers crus* produce excellent wines as well.

Nuits-Saints-Georges, with its five thousand inhabitants, is the biggest village in the Côte de Nuits, and its wines are among the best-known of all Burgundies. Nuits-

Saint-Georges and Gevrey-Chambertin produce between them about half the wines of the Côte de Nuits sold with village appellations, but this is not nearly enough to satisfy world demand. The wines of Prémeaux, which adjoins Nuits-Saint-Georges, can be marketed as Nuits-Saint-Georges. Its best-known vineyard is Clos de la Maréchale.

The appellation Côte de Nuits-Villages is a regional one for the whole district, and such wines come from the less important towns of the Côte de Nuits, such as Corgoloin, Comblanchien, and Brochon, not from Nuits-Saint-Georges itself. The lesser appellation Hautes Côtes de Nuits applies to wines produced in the hills behind the Côtes de Nuits.

At this point, the Golden Slope disappears for a few miles, and when it reappears it becomes the Côte de Beaune. The first important village is Aloxe-Corton, which produces some fine red wines. Behind the village is the impressive hill of Corton, whose extensive vineyards encompass two *grands crus*, the red Corton and the white Corton-Charlemagne. Within the large Corton appellation are a number of individual plots with their own names, such as Clos du Roi, Les Bressandes, Les Renardes, and Les Maréchaudes; wines from these vineyards may be labeled either as Corton or with the vineyard name, as Corton Clos du Rois, Corton Bressandes, and so on. Thus, a wine from the village of Aloxe-Corton is so labeled; one from a *premier cru*, such as Les Chaillots, would be labeled Aloxe-Corton, Les Chaillots. But a wine labeled Corton or Corton-something is a *grand cru*. Corton is, in fact, the only *grand cru* of the Côte de Beaune that produces red wine; all the other *grands crus* produce white wines, including Corton-Charlemagne, whose name bears witness to the influence of the Emperor Charlemagne, who owned vineyards in Burgundy in the eighth century. At its best, Corton-Charlemagne is a superlative wine of great power and breed. The best known of its several owners is the firm of Louis Latour, which markets the red wines from its *grand cru* vineyards on the hill of Corton under the proprietary name Château Corton Grancey.

The villages of Pernand-Vergelesses and Ladoix-Serrigny adjoin Aloxe-Corton; both produce attractive red and white wines. Savigny-les-Beaune is one of the biggest wine-producing villages of the entire slope, and almost all of its wines are red. Because they are less well known than those of its more illustrious neighbors, these excellent wines are usually less expensive as well.

Beaune is not only the center of the Côte de Beaune, but of Burgundy itself. It is the biggest town of all, and most of the shippers have their offices here. Beaune is also the scene of one of the world's most famous wine events. Every year, on the third Sunday in November, the wines of the Hospices de Beaune are auctioned off, and buyers from several countries arrive to participate in the auction and in the general festivity that prevails for three days.

The Hospices de Beaune is a charitable hospital built in the fifteenth century by Nicolas Rolin and his wife, Guigone de Salins. Over the years vineyard parcels have been bequeathed to the Hospices, and the money obtained from the sale by auction of their wine is used to support the institution. The wines are generally considered to be overpriced, but the sums they fetch often affect the general price levels of the year's crop throughout the Côte d'Or.

The Hospices de Beaune now owns about 135 acres in several villages, and produces about fifteen thousand cases a year. The wines are auctioned in lots identified for the most part by the name of a benefactor (who is not necessarily the donor of the particular parcel named in his honor) rather than that of an individual vineyard. One cannot simply refer to a bottle of Hospices de Beaune wine, but must properly identify it with the village and the specific parcel, or *cuvée* among the thirty-odd that make up the Hospices' holdings. What's more, the wines are aged and bottled by the buyer, not by the Hospices, so that if the many barrels that make up a particular *cuvée* are auctioned off to several buyers, as is usually the case, there will be variations among the different bottlings of that *cuvée*. Among the most famous red ones are Beaune, *Cuvée* Nicolas Rolin; Beaune, *Cuvée* Guigone de Salins; Corton, *Cuvée* Docteur Peste; and Pommard, *Cuvée* Dames de la Charité. The Hospices' white wines are almost all from Meursault and include Meursault-Charmes, *Cuvée* Albert Grivault, and Meursault Genevrières, *Cuvée* Baudot.

Beaune is one of the three or four largest wine-producing villages along the Côte d'Or, and virtually all of its wines are red. Perhaps the best-known of its white wines is Beaune Clos des Mouches of Joseph Drouhin. A wine labeled Côte de Beaune-Villages, often a good value, does not come from Beaune, but from any one of sixteen other villages, including such unfamiliar ones as Saint-Aubin, Saint-Romain, and Chorey-les-Beaune, whose agreeable red and white wines also go to market under their own names. Hautes Côtes de Beaune is an appellation used for wines produced in the hills behind the Côte de Beaune.

Pommard is probably the most famous name in Burgundy, and there can be no doubt, unfortunately, that some of the red wine sold as Pommard doesn't even bear a nodding acquaintance with the village itself. Good examples display a distinctive *terroir*, or undertaste, that characterizes the wines from this village. Although there are no *grands crus* in Pommard, most experts agree that the *têtes de cuvées* of the 1861 classification, Rugiens and Epenots, deserve the same status today.

Volnay, despite its simple name, has not achieved the same popularity in this country as Pommard and Nuits-Saints-Georges. Its elegant red wines, at best, display a delicacy and finesse that belie the popular misconception of Burgundy as a heavy wine.

Meursault is the first of the white-wine villages. Its vineyards, along with those of Chassagne-Montrachet and Puligny-Montrachet, produce almost all of the greatest white wines of Burgundy. Meursault actually produces as much white wine as the other two villages combined, and its wines are characterized by a certain texture and tangy dryness that set them apart. Although there are no *grand cru* vineyards in this village, Perrières, Charmes, and Genevrières are considered its best sites. Some red wine is produced in Meursault, notably Meursault-Blagny. Part of the Santenots vineyard is also planted in Pinot Noir: the whites are sold as Meursault-Santenots, the reds as Volnay-Santenots.

Set back from the main highway are the two villages of Monthélie and Auxey-Duresses. Monthélie produces red wines with the lightness of its neighbor, Volnay. Auxey-Duresses makes both red and white wines, and both are very agreeable. Wines from less-commercialized villages such as these are worth looking for.

Chassagne-Montrachet is famous for its white wines, but in fact more than half of its production is red. The white wines of Chassagne are, of course, outstanding, and within the village are parts of two great vineyards, Montrachet and Bâtard-Montrachet, as well as all four acres of Criots-Bâtard-Montrachet.

Puligny-Montrachet makes white wines only and of a very high quality. The rest of Montrachet and Bâtard-Montrachet are situated within its borders, as well as all of Chevalier-Montrachet and Bienvenue-Bâtard-Montrachet.

Montrachet, whose production usually varies between three and five thousand cases a year, is considered to be the best vineyard in the world for dry white wines, and it can indeed produce superlative wines. It's also true that not all of its several owners are equally conscientious, and the high price that Montrachet commands is often due as much to its fame and scarcity as to the quality of its wine. The adjoining *grand cru* vineyards should not be overlooked, nor should the many excellent village and *premier cru* wines of Chassagne-Montrachet and Puligny-Montrachet from good sources.

Santenay is the southernmost village of note in the Côte de Beaune, and its agreeable wines, almost all red, are well worth trying. Maranges is a new appellation that encompasses three small villages near Santenay whose wines usually go to market as Côte de Beaune-Villages.

CÔTE DE NUITS: *Red Wines*

Village	Grands Crus	Premiers Crus
Fixin		Clos de la Perrière
		Clos du Chapitre
		Les Hervelets
		Les Arvelets

Village	Grands Crus	Premiers Crus
Gevrey-Chambertin	Chambertin	Clos Saint-Jacques
	Chambertin-Clos de Bèze	Varoilles
	Latricières-Chambertin	Les Cazetiers
	Mazys-Chambertin	Combe-au-Moine
	Ruchottes-Chambertin	
	Chapelle-Chambertin	
	Charmes-Chambertin	
	Griotte-Chambertin	
Morey-Saint-Denis	Clos de Tart	Clos Bussière
	Clos Saint-Denis	
	Clos de la Roche	
	Clos des Lambrays	
	Bonnes Mares (part)	
Chambolle-Musigny	Musigny	Les Amoureuses
	Bonnes Mares (part)	Les Charmes
Vougeot	Clos de Vougeot	
Flagey-Echézeaux	Grands-Echézeaux	
	Echézeaux	
Vosne-Romanée	Romanée-Conti	Les Gaudichots
	La Romanée	Les Beaumonts
	La Tâche	Les Malconsorts
	Richebourg	Les Suchots
	Romanée-Saint-Vivant	Clos des Réas
	La Grande Rue	
Nuits-Saint-Georges (including Prémeaux)		Les Saint-Georges
		Les Vaucrains
		Les Cailles
		Les Pruliers
		Les Porrets
		Aux Boudots
		La Richemone
		Clos de la Maréchale
		Clos des Corvées
		Aux Perdrix

CÔTE DE BEAUNE: *Red Wines*

Village	Grands Crus	Premiers Crus
Aloxe-Corton	Le Corton (includes Clos du Roi, Bressandes, Renardes, etc.)	Les Chaillots Les Meix
Pernand-Vergelesses Savigny-les-Beaune		Ile des Vergelesses Les Vergelesses Les Marconnets La Dominode Les Jarrons Les Lavières
Beaune		Les Grèves Les Fèves Les Marconnets Les Bressandes Les Clos des Mouches Les Cent Vignes Clos du Roi Les Avaux
Pommard		Les Epenots Les Rugiens Le Clos Blanc La Platière Les Pézerolles Les Chaponnières
Volnay		Clos des Ducs Les Caillerets Les Champans Les Fremiets Santenots Le Clos des Chênes

Village	Grands Crus	Premiers Crus
Monthélie		Les Champs Fuillots
Auxey-Duresses		Les Duresses Clos du Val
Chassagne-Montrachet		Clos Saint-Jean Clos de la Boudriotte Morgeot La Maltroie Les Caillerets
Santenay		Gravières Clos Tavannes

CÔTE DE BEAUNE: *White Wines*

Village	Grands Crus	Premiers Crus
Aloxe-Corton	Corton-Charlemagne	
Beaune		Les Clos des Mouches
Meursault		Les Perrières Les Genevrières La Goutte d'Or Charmes Santenots Blagny Poruzot
Puligny-Montrachet	Montrachet (part) Bâtard-Montrachet (part) Chevalier-Montrachet Bienvenue-Bâtard-Montrachet	Les Combettes Le Champ Canet Les Caillerets Les Pucelles Les Chalumeaux Les Folatières Clavoillon Les Referts

Village	Grands Crus	Premiers Crus
Chassagne-Montrachet	Montrachet (part) Bâtard-Montrachet (part) Criots-Bâtard-Montrachet	Les Ruchottes Morgeot Les Caillerets Les Chenevottes

Southern Burgundy

Southern Burgundy is made up of three districts, the Chalonnais, the Mâconnais, and Beaujolais. Beaujolais is well known for its red wines, and the Mâconnais contains the inner appellation of Pouilly-Fuissé, but the Chalonnais wines are not established in world markets, despite their resemblance and proximity to the famous wines of Burgundy. The Côte Chalonnaise, which takes its name from the city of Chalon-sur-Saône, contains four villages entitled to their own appellations— Mercurey, Givry, Rully, and Montagny. Mercurey is the best known, and the area is sometimes referred to as the Région de Mercurey. As in the Côte d'Or, the whites are made from Chardonnay, the reds from Pinot Noir; not surprisingly, the wines are similar to those from the Côte de Beaune, and the best examples can be attractive and well-balanced. Givry and Mercurey are noted primarily for their red wines; Rully produces both red and white wines of good quality; and Montagny produces only white wines. The best-known firm of the region is Antonin Rodet, which owns the Château de Chamirey in Mercurey and the Château de Rully.

The Mâcon district produces red and white wine as well as some rosé, and the wines have long been available here. The red, made from the Gamay, lacks the style of the best wines of Beaujolais. The whites, from the Chardonnay, are generally better wines, and have become a popular alternative to the more expensive white Burgundies of the Côte de Beaune. In recent years some shippers have been marketing the white wines of Mâcon by its varietal name—Chardonnay—in imitation of the approach used by California wineries. Most of the wines of Mâcon are produced by cooperative cellars, the best-known of which are Lugny, Viré, and Prissé.

The most famous wine of the Mâconnais is Pouilly-Fuissé. The appellation is limited to wines coming from the five hamlets of Pouilly, Fuissé, Chaintré, Solutré, and Vergisson. Although this wine is extremely popular and often found on restaurant wine lists, there is actually not much of it made. An abundant year will produce perhaps 450,000 cases, and many vintages produce less. As a result of continually increasing demand, especially from consumers in the United States, this wine, which is often not much more than a good Mâcon Blanc, now costs twice as much as a Mâcon.

Close to the five communes of Pouilly-Fuissé are those of Loché and Vinzelles, which produce about one-tenth as much wine. They are marketed as Pouilly-Loché and Pouilly-Vinzelles, and are similar in style to those of Pouilly-Fuissé. Saint-Véran, a new appellation that went into effect with the 1971 vintage, comes from several communes that were formerly entitled to the appellation Beaujolais Blanc and Mâcon Blanc. Production is about two-thirds that of Pouilly-Fuissé.

BEAUJOLAIS

Beaujolais is one of the best-known of all red wines, and deservedly so, as the best of them are among the most enjoyable wines produced anywhere. Many people think that all Beaujolais is alike and are willing to settle for the cheapest example when they are looking for a pleasant red wine. Compared to the best wines of Bordeaux and the Côte d'Or, those of Beaujolais are not as exciting, as scarce, or as difficult to understand, but there is actually quite a variation in price, quality, and taste available from this extensive district in southern Burgundy. Poor examples lack the charm and distinctive flavor that makes Beaujolais almost unique among red wines, and bottles of this popular wine should be chosen with some attention.

The Beaujolais district begins near Mâcon (about sixty miles south of Beaune) and stretches down to the outskirts of Lyons, forty-five miles farther south. The vineyard district stretches about ten miles across, along the western bank of the Saône River. The region takes its name from the village of Beaujeu, originally a barony established more than a thousand years ago. Beaujeu is no longer an important town, and the center of the Beaujolais wine trade now is Villefranche, which lies about halfway between Mâcon and Lyons. The hills and valleys of Beaujolais make up one of the most picturesque and agreeable vineyard districts in France, and the landscape has charmed many tourists who have come to the area in search of Roman ruins or to visit the remains of the monastery of Cluny with its gigantic twelfth-century church.

In an abundant vintage, the Beaujolais district produces more than fourteen million cases of wine. (A certain amount of agreeable white and rosé wines are also produced, but 99 percent of Beaujolais is red.) Beaujolais is made from the Gamay grape. Although this variety is scorned in the vineyards of the Côte d'Or, the Gamay comes into its own in the granitic soil of southern Burgundy and produces wines much more charming and agreeable than would be produced from Pinot Noir. The wines of Beaujolais are at their best when consumed young, before they are two years old, and the wines are vinified with this in mind. Vatting is limited to three days or less so that a minimum of tannin is imparted to the wine. The wines are then bottled—and often consumed—within six months of the vintage, so that they retain the freshness and fruit that make Beaujolais so agreeable.

For many years bistros in Paris and Lyons have featured Beaujolais *nouveau* or *primeur* (the names are interchangeable), which are specially selected light and delicate wines that can be released for sale as early as mid-November, just weeks after the harvest. In the past twenty years or so, these fresh and charming wines have become popular in England and the United States as well, and it is no longer unusual to find new Beaujolais on sale here in late November. In fact, the popularity of this wine is such that in some years more than one-third of the entire Beaujolais crop is sold as *nouveau* or *primeur*. These wines are not meant to last, and are best consumed before Christmas. (*Beaujolais de l'année* is used informally to refer to wine from the most recent vintage.) New Beaujolais accounts for a limited proportion of the wines shipped here, which are rarely quite as delicate, since light-bodied wines don't keep very well. Wines chosen to be bottled for export are generally fuller-flavored and sturdier, although the best examples will naturally display the grace and charm typical of Beaujolais.

The Beaujolais district can be divided into three parts: Beaujolais, Beaujolais-Villages, and the ten *crus* of Beaujolais. The southern portion produces somewhat lighter wines entitled to call themselves simply Beaujolais. The appellation Beaujolais Supérieur differs from Beaujolais only in that this wine requires an extra degree of alcohol and production per acre is slightly less. Actually, most of the wine sold by its producers as Beaujolais could equally well be sold as Beaujolais Supérieur.

The next step up the ladder of *Appellation Contrôlée* laws for the Beaujolais district is Beaujolais-Villages. Wines so labeled come from about three dozen villages in the center of the region, whose vineyards consistently produce better wines than those farther south. Occasionally, the actual village name will appear on the label, but as these are not at all known here, the wines are usually labeled simply Beaujolais-Villages. About 25 percent of all Beaujolais is entitled to be called Beaujolais-Villages.

The finest of all Beaujolais comes from ten communes, or *crus*, in the northernmost part of the region: Moulin-à-Vent, Fleurie, Brouilly, Côte de Brouilly, Morgon, Saint-Amour, Chénas, Juliénas, Chiroubles, and Regnié. These communes produce the wines with the most distinction, they are longer-lived, and the price is somewhat higher than for a simple Beaujolais. As these wines are often labeled with only the name of the *cru*, without the word Beaujolais, it pays to remember their names if you are looking for something special from the district. Each wine has its special characteristics and its devotees, and these *crus* are among the most agreeable wines found anywhere. (Note that only the wines from Beaujolais and Beaujolais-Villages may be sold as Beaujolais *nouveau*; none of the *crus* may be sold as *nouveau*.)

The Beaujolais *crus* account for about one-quarter of all Beaujolais in an average year, and of the ten *crus*, Brouilly, Morgon, Moulin-à-Vent, and Fleurie alone produce about two-thirds of the total. Moulin-à-Vent is usually the most expensive, as its wines are considered the sturdiest and longest-lived. Although Moulin-à-Vent doesn't have the power or depth of a wine from the Côte de Nuits, it does have considerably more character than the typical Beaujolais and can be served with more robust foods.

Fleurie and Brouilly produce lighter and more elegant wines, with an enchanting perfumed bouquet. Although it might be imagined that Côte de Brouilly is a lesser appellation than Brouilly (as is the case with Beaune and Côte de Beaune), the opposite is in fact the case. Côte de Brouilly is an inner appellation reserved for vineyards on the slopes of Mont Brouilly. Morgon produces a very sturdy wine that needs some bottle age before it's ready to drink. Although the crop is comparatively large, the wine is not often seen in this country.

Juliénas and Chénas both have a rather distinctive *goût de terroir*, or taste of the soil, that sets them apart from their neighbors. Juliénas can be found here, but most of the production of Chénas is legally sold as Moulin-à-Vent. The wines of Saint-Amour, despite its romantic name, are not often exported to the United States, but those of Chiroubles, which was generally more attractive and distinctive, are becoming popular here. Regnié, which was elevated to *cru* status in 1989, is situated near Brouilly, and its wines are similar in style.

Beaujolais is made by thousands of small producers, most of whom sell their wine to local shippers. About one-third of all the Beaujolais produced, from the simplest wines to the best *crus*, comes from the eighteen cooperative cellars in the region. Although a number of individual estates—such as Château de Lacarelle in Beaujolais-Villages, Château de Juliénas, and Château de La Chaize and Château des Tours, both in Brouilly— have become known to consumers, most Beaujolais is marketed with the name of a shipper, many of whom offer a full range of *crus*. Georges Duboeuf is the leading shipper of the region; good examples are also produced by Paul Beaudet and Mommessin, and by such Burgundy shippers as Louis Jadot, Louis Latour, and Joseph Drouhin.

In sum, the wines of Beaujolais vary from rather light and fragile wines to the richer and fuller wines of some of the *crus*. There is naturally a tremendous choice, but it is a sad fact that there is much more Beaujolais drunk than is produced in the vineyards themselves. A cheap Beaujolais will rarely have the delightful characteristics of a true Beaujolais, and a Beaujolais or Beaujolais-Villages that is much more than a year old will almost always have lost most of its fruit and charm. As it happens, if you shop around you can often find a wine from one of the *crus* for only a little more money than one labeled simply Beaujolais or Beaujolais-Villages, and the differences in quality can be considerable. Beaujolais tastes best at cellar temperature (55° to 60° F), and you might try putting a bottle in the refrigerator for thirty or forty minutes to cool it down. The wine tastes all the fresher and seems even more delightful.

THE RHÔNE VALLEY

The Rhône River joins the Saône at Lyons and continues south, reaching the sea near Marseilles. The wines of the Côtes du Rhône come from vineyards planted on both banks of the Rhône, starting about twenty miles south of Lyons at Vienne and continuing 120 miles to Avignon. About 95 percent of Rhône wines are red, but the region includes a famous rosé—Tavel—and some unusual white wines.

The hot and sunny climate typical of the Rhône Valley produces red wines that are generally more robust and fuller-flavored than those of Burgundy. The growing conditions along this part of the Rhône are more dependable than in most parts of France, and consequently, the best vintages for Rhône wines do not always correspond, for example, to those for Bordeaux and Burgundy. The intense heat here produces wines that contain more alcohol—and hence more body—than in more northerly vineyards, and this is reflected in the minimums set by the *Appellation Contrôlée* laws. Whereas 9 percent is required for Beaujolais and only 10 percent for a Beaujolais *cru* such as Moulin-à-Vent, the minimum for Côtes du Rhône is 10.5 percent and for Châteauneuf-du-Pape 12.5 percent.

Although Rhône wines are usually all grouped together, there are actually two distinct districts within this region: the southern Rhône, near Avignon, whose best-known wines are Châteauneuf-du-Pape, Tavel, and the regional Côtes du Rhône; and the northern Rhône, between Vienne and Valence, which includes Côte Rotie, Hermitage, and Crozes-Hermitage.

Châteauneuf-du-Pape, a village located about ten miles from Avignon, produces about a million cases a year of what is surely the most famous of all Rhône wines. Although sixty thousand cases a year of white Châteauneuf-du-Pape are produced—the wine is distinctive and full-flavored—it is for its red wines that the village is world-famous. The name comes from a now-ruined castle, built in the fourteenth century as a summer house for Pope Clement V. During most of the fourteenth century the popes were French, and Avignon replaced Rome as the papal seat. The summer residence was called Châteauneuf, or new castle, to distinguish it from the existing papal fortress in Avignon. It was at this time that vines were first planted in the district. When the castle was destroyed two centuries later, the vineyards went untended until the nineteenth century. At that time the wines of Châteauneuf-du-Pape were reintroduced to Parisian society, and the wine has now established itself as one of the best-known red wines in the world.

Winemakers have discovered over the years that the intense heat of the Rhône Valley does not favor the growth of most of the finest grape varieties. Instead, a number of different varieties are used, each one contributing a particular characteristic to the finished wine. In Châteauneuf-du-Pape, thirteen grape varieties are permitted, but five are white-wine grapes used only in very small amounts in the production of red wines. And of the remaining varieties, only four are widely planted—Grenache, Syrah, Mourvèdre, and Cinsault. Grenache, which accounts for about three-quarters of the total acreage, contributes color and alcohol; Syrah and Mourvèdre are more tannic and enable a wine to age longer; and Cinsault adds fruit and aroma. Each grower plants his vineyards in somewhat different proportions, so that the wines of Châteauneuf-du-Pape vary from domain to domain. This variation in wine is further affected by the different vinification methods used in the district. Châteauneuf-du-Pape has long been known as a wine that needs several years of bottle age to reach maturity, and a number of growers continue to employ the long vatting and long maturation in barrel that produce long-lived wines. At the same time, the increasing demand for well-known wines throughout the world and the eagerness of the consumer to drink good vintages as soon as they are available have caused a number of domains to vinify their Châteauneuf-du-Pape to produce a full-bodied but relatively supple, fast-maturing wine that will be ready to drink sooner. You should, therefore, be prepared to experiment among the different shippers and domains to find the style you prefer. Although Châteauneuf-du-Pape is rarely an exceptional wine, it is usually dependable and widely available. Leading estates include Château de Beaucastel, Château Fortia, Château de la Gardine, Château Rayas, Château de Vaudieu, Château de Mont-Redon, Domaine du Nalys, Château La Nerthe, Domaine du Vieux Télégraphe, and Clos des Papes, as well as Les Cèdres of Paul Jaboulet Aîné and La Bernardine of Chapoutier.

About eight miles on the other side of Avignon is Tavel, which produces what many people consider the finest rosé of France. Made primarily from the Grenache grape, the wine is dry, has a most attractive and distinctive pink-orange hue, and, at best, combines character and balance. About 400,000 cases are made annually, and a great deal of that comes from the Cooperative of Tavel, although it goes to market under various names. There are, as well, a number of large domains producing estate-bottled Tavel.

Close to Tavel is the village of Lirac, which produces red and rosé wines and a small amount of white wine. The rosé is similar in style to that of Tavel, but less well known.

Most of the wines of the southern Rhône are sold simply as Côtes du Rhône. Production is abundant—about twenty million cases are produced, virtually all of it red. Côtes du Rhône is made from a number of different grape varieties, primarily Grenache and Carignan. Although many examples of Côtes du Rhône lack character or distinction, there are an increasing number of well-made, fuller-flavored wines to be found as well. More than a dozen villages within the region are entitled to label their wines Côtes du Rhône-Villages, and this appellation is generally of a higher quality. The village of Gigondas, which was granted its own *Appellation Contrôlée* in 1971, produces wines that are bigger and more distinguished than regional Côtes du Rhône, and more expensive. In 1990, the village of Vacqueyras was also granted its own appellation.

Côtes du Ventoux, situated just east of the Côtes du Rhône region, and Coteaux du Tricastin, which is just north of Côtes du Rhône, both achieved *Appellation Contrôlée* status in 1973. They produce large quantities of relatively inexpensive wines, primarily red, which are similar in taste to a lighter Côtes du Rhône; La Vieille Ferme is perhaps the best-known label from Côtes du Ventoux. Côtes du Luberon, situated just south of Côtes du Ventoux, was elevated to *Appellation Contrôlée* in 1988; Château Val-Joanis is one of its better-known properties. A small amount of sweet, intensely flavored Muscat wine is made in the Rhône village of Beaumes-de-Venise. The wine, whose fermentation is stopped by the addition of spirits, must contain a minimum of 11 percent sugar and 15 percent alcohol.

Although Châteauneuf-du-Pape, Tavel, and the regional appellation Côtes du Rhône account for almost all the shipments to this country of Rhône Valley wines, most connoisseurs agree that the finest wines of the Rhône come from the northern part of the region. Côte Rôtie and Hermitage are both powerful, deeply flavored red wines from a single grape variety—Syrah. (About 5 percent of the vineyards of Côte Rôtie are planted with the white Viognier grape, which is traditionally picked and vinified along with Syrah; Viognier contributes acidity and finesse to the final wine.) These two appellations produce about 100,000 cases of distinguished, long-lasting red wine. Hermitage is usually described as richer and more solid, Côte Rôtie as having perhaps more finesse. Crozes-Hermitage comes from vineyards that encircle those of Hermitage and that produce nearly ten times as much wine. The soil and exposure are different, the yield per acre is higher, and the wines are generally lighter-bodied as well as less expensive than those of

Hermitage. The villages of Cornas and Saint-Joseph, on opposite banks of the Rhône, produce good red wines from the Syrah grape; those of Cornas are generally longer-lived.

The northern Rhône also produces white wines, the best known of which are the dry, flavorful whites from the vineyards of Hermitage, Crozes-Hermitage, and Saint-Joseph, made from the Marsanne and Roussanne grapes. A soft and flowery white wine with a subtle bouquet is made at Condrieu from the Viognier grape. More famous is the little vineyard of Château Grillet, also planted with Viognier, which produces about a thousand cases a year of an expensive wine similar to Condrieu.

Well-known producers of northern Rhône wines include Paul Jaboulet Aîné, Chapoutier, Délas Freres, L. de Vallouit, and Guigal (which owns the Vidal-Fleury firm).

THE LOIRE VALLEY

The Loire is famous to tourists for its historic châteaux and for a variety of agreeable wines produced along its banks. But although the châteaux of the Loire are centered around Tours, the wines of the Loire Valley are produced along most of its 650-mile course. About two-thirds of the wines produced along the Loire are white, and a certain amount of agreeable and popular rosé is made. A limited amount of red wine is also produced, although the red wines are not so easily found in this country. If the Loire Valley produces no great wines (with the possible exception of some sweet wines that are rarely exported), it does produce quite a variety of delightful wines that can be—and should be—consumed young.

Starting at Nantes at the mouth of the Loire, the first wine district is Muscadet. This appellation is atypical of French wine names as it is not the name of a place, but the grape variety used to make the dry white wines of the region. The Muscadet grape, originally known as Melon de Bourgogne, was brought from Burgundy in the sixteenth century and ultimately gave its name to the vineyard region around Nantes. American wine drinkers may have been put off at first by its name, similar to that of the sweet Muscatel wines produced from the Muscat grape, to which Muscadet bears no relationship whatsoever. In the past a good deal of Muscadet was sold as Chablis, which gives some indication of its taste, although this refreshing wine is usually lighter-bodied and somewhat more acid. Nantes is the capital of Brittany, a region famous for its shellfish, and Muscadet is a perfect accompaniment to seafood, a first course, or lighter foods in general. It is the only *Appellation Contrôlée* wine of France with a maximum alcoholic content—12 percent.

The best examples of Muscadet come from the Sèvre-et-Maine district, and these words will be found on the label. Rather than being an inner appellation, however, Sèvre-et-Maine actually produces about 80 percent of all Muscadet, so most of the wines imported here come from this district. You will also find bottles labeled Muscadet *sur lie,* or on the lees. Theoretically, this indicates that the wine was bottled directly from the barrel or vat while still resting on its lees, or natural deposits, without first being transferred to another container. Current regulations, however, specify only that the wine must be bottled no later than June following the vintage, and many wines labeled *sur lie* lack the distinctive crispness and yeasty freshness that make these wines special. Well-known producers of Muscadet include Marquis de Goulaine, Barré Frères, Domaine de l'Hyvernière, Jean Sauvion & Fils (which owns Château de Cléray), Donatien-Bahuaud (which owns Château de la Cassemichère), Chéreau-Carré, and Louis Metaireau.

Another light, dry white wine produced in this region is Gros Plant du Pays Nantais. Gros Plant is the local name for Folle Blanche, and this V.D.Q.S. wine, occasionally shipped here, is at its best within a year or so of the harvest.

The next wine city up the Loire is Angers, which has given its name to the district of Anjou. The best-known of the Anjou wines is, of course, Rosé d'Anjou. This light, mellow, and agreeable wine is made primarily from the Groslot grape, plus Gamay and Cabernet Franc. The relative sweetness of the wine depends on the shipper's specifications, although none of the Anjou rosés on the market is dry. Another rosé, labeled Cabernet d'Anjou, is made from the Cabernet Franc grape of Bordeaux. This wine is generally less sweet and has somewhat more character than does Rosé d'Anjou.

The Anjou district also produces white wines ranging in character from fairly dry to quite sweet and rich. The wines are made from the Chenin Blanc grape, known locally along the Loire as Pineau de la Loire, although it is not related to the Pinot Blanc of Burgundy. The three main producing areas are the Côteaux de la Loire, the Côteaux de l'Aubance, and the Côteaux du Layon, the Aubance and the Layon being tributaries of the Loire. The Côteaux du Layon produces by far the most wine—mellow and rounded in character—but it is hard to find here. The wines produced in Quarts de Chaume and Bonnezeaux from grapes affected by *Botrytis cinerea,* as in Sauternes, can be especially rich and luscious. One of the most acclaimed dry white wines made from Chenin Blanc is produced in the small Savennières district, whose wines can be quite austere when young; its most famous vineyards are Coulée de Serrant and Roche aux Moines.

The village of Saumur produces white wines from Chenin Blanc and rosés and reds from Cabernet Franc. The reds are attractive, especially those from the village of Champigny, which are labeled Saumur-Champigny. Most of the white wines of Saumur are transformed into *mousseux,* or sparkling wines.

The city of Tours is the one most familiar to tourists, as it is here that most of the historic châteaux are found. Chambord, Azay-le-Rideau, Chenonceaux, and Amboise (where Leonardo da Vinci is buried) are among the most famous. Unfortunately, most of the Touraine wines are of minor interest and consumed locally. The most famous exception is the wine of Vouvray, a village ten miles from Tours. The town is noted for its chalk hills, and its inhabitants have dug caves into the slopes that are used both as wine cellars and as homes. A number of the houses built along the slopes are mere facades with the greater part of these homes situated within the hillsides themselves.

We know Vouvray in the United States as a pleasant and fairly dry white wine, but if you visit the local cellars, you'll discover that Vouvray can be very dry, mellow, or quite sweet, and that it can be still, *pétillant*—slightly sparkling—or fully sparkling like Champagne. The Chenin Blanc grape is used to make Vouvray and in sunny years it produces a most attractive mellow wine; when there is less sunshine, the wine will be drier in taste. In recent years, however, the trend here and elsewhere toward drier wines has encouraged the Vouvray winemakers to alter their vinification so that their wines are often fairly dry; in fact, much of it is made into *mousseux*. As for the rich dessert wines, they are carefully produced in exceptionally sunny vintages, and like Sauternes, are capable of aging for ten or twenty years. Vouvray producers include Gaston Huet, Monmousseau, Rémy-Pannier, Marc Bredif, Château Moncontour, and Prince Poniatowsky.

Across the river from Vouvray is Mountlouis, whose wines are similar to those of Vouvray, though perhaps not quite as good.

The Touraine also produces red wines in the villages of Chinon, Bourgueil, and Saint-Nicolas-de-Bourgueil. Rabelais was born in Chinon, and he often sang the praises of wine in general and of his local wine in particular. Made from the Cabernet Franc grape, these wines combine the tannic character of a light Bordeaux with an appealing fruitiness.

Up the Loire past Orléans and just before Nevers are two villages that produce the best dry white wines of the Loire Valley—Sancerre and Pouilly-sur-Loire. Although we know the hamlet of Sancerre for its wines, it is as famous to the French for its goat cheese. A few of the winegrowers also maintain a herd of goats, and they serve their homemade cheeses with as much pride as their wines. The wines of Sancerre have a distinctive character that has established their reputation in Paris and, now, in this country. The wine is made from the Sauvignon Blanc grape that is used to make the dry white wines of Bordeaux, but it takes on a completely different character in Sancerre— very dry, full-flavored, and with an attractive tang. For this reason Sancerre is a good wine to serve with full-flavored dishes that call for a white wine.

The growers of Sancerre have also planted part of their vineyards with the Pinot Noir grape, and they make very agreeable rosé and red wines as well. Some of the Sancerre labels found here are Clos La Perrière of Archambault, Domaine La Moussière of Alphonse Mellot, Clos de La Poussie of Cordier, Comte Lafond, and Michel Redde.

The village of Pouilly-sur-Loire produces two wines. The Chasselas grape (well known in Switzerland as the Fendant) produces a wine labeled, appropriately enough, Pouilly-sur-Loire. This is an agreeable country wine that is not often seen here and that is at its best within a year of the vintage. The village also produces in greater quantity a wine from the Sauvignon Blanc grape, locally known as the Blanc Fumé, or Smoky White (there are various explanations, none of them definitive). The correct name of this wine is Blanc Fumé de Pouilly-sur-Loire, to distinguish it from a Pouilly-sur-Loire. As it happens, a number of potential customers here and elsewhere, seeing the words Pouilly-sur-Loire on the label, incorrectly assumed that the lesser wine was being palmed off on them. The name was thus shortened to Pouilly-Fumé, an unusual appellation for France, as the village and grape name are combined. This, in turn, has led many people to confuse Pouilly-Fumé from the Loire with Pouilly-Fuissé from southern Burgundy, made from the Chardonnay grape. In any event, Pouilly-Fumé is readily found here, and its rich flavor makes it a good all-purpose accompaniment to food. The best-known label is de Ladoucette, produced at Château du Nozet.

The white wines of Quincy and Reuilly are also considered Loire wines, although these towns are actually situated along the Cher, a tributary of the Loire. The wines, made from Sauvignon Blanc, have a crisp, dry taste similar to those of Sancerre and Pouilly-Fumé, as do those of Ménétou-Salon, a village situated halfway between Sancerre and Quincy.

ALSACE, PROVENCE, AND OTHER REGIONS

Alsace

The hillside vineyards of Alsace are among the most beautiful in all of France, and the area is dotted with delightful little villages of the kind that are used as illustrations in children's storybooks. France is separated from Germany here by the Rhine, but the vineyards of Alsace are set back from the river's edge and extend for about seventy miles along the slopes of the Vosges Mountains. Alsace often produces ten or twelve million cases of white wine a year, which makes it the biggest producer of *Appellation Contrôlée* white wines after Champagne. Their flavorful and refreshing qualities complement perfectly the rich cuisine of the region, with its *foie gras,* sauerkraut dishes, and sausages.

Between 1870 and 1918 Alsace and the neighboring province of Lorraine were part of Germany. At the time, Germany did not want Alsatian wines to compete with her own Rhine and Moselle wines and encouraged the production of cheap, inferior wines, much of which was used for blending or in the manufacture of Sekt, German sparkling wine. After World War I, the growers of Alsace realized that their best chance for commercial success would be with finer wines, and they set about replanting their vineyards with better grape varieties. Today, about 80 percent of the vineyards of Alsace are planted in four varieties—Riesling, Gewürztraminer, Sylvaner, and Pinot Blanc (also known as Klevner). The rest is made up of Pinot Gris (marketed in the past as Tokay d'Alsace, although it bears no relation to the Tokay of Hungary), Muscat, Chasselas, and Pinot Noir. The last is used to make a small quantity of light red and rosé—95 percent of Alsatian wines are white.

The wines of Alsace were finally granted the *Appellation Contrôlée* Vin d'Alsace in 1962, but the wines themselves are traditionally labeled and marketed with the name of a specific grape variety. Riesling, Gewürztraminer, Pinot Blanc, and Pinot Gris are the best-known, and each is made entirely from the named grape. The *Appellation Contrôlée* laws also permit a blend of different grapes—in practice, usually Chasselas and Sylvaner—to be sold as *Edelzwicker,* or noble blend, but this name is rarely seen here. Crémant d'Alsace is a relatively new appellation that was created for sparkling wines.

The wines of Alsace are fermented until they are dry, and this is what distinguishes them from German wines, with which they are sometimes confused. Whereas German Rieslings, Sylvaners, and Gewürztraminers are fragrant and sweet, those made in Alsace are fuller-flavored, with more body and alcohol, and austerely dry. Sylvaner produces comparatively light, agreeable wines without much distinction. The Alsatians consider Riesling to be their finest wine, and many consumers agree that the dry Rieslings of Alsace are more appropriate with food than the sweeter wines produced in Germany. It is Gewürztraminer, however, that most people associate with Alsace. The wine has an intense bouquet reminiscent of rose petals or litchee and a pungent taste that makes it one of the most unusual and readily identifiable white wines in the world. The wine was originally made from the Traminer grape. *Gewürz* means spicy, and Alsatian shippers used to select the most intensely flavored lots of Traminer and market them as Gewürztraminer. Over the years, a natural clonal selection has occurred in the vineyards so that there is now a Gewürztraminer grape that has replaced the Traminer originally planted.

A number of specific vineyard sites have been classified as *grands crus,* and their names may appear on a label. Only wines made from Riesling, Gewürztraminer, Pinot Gris, and Muscat may be so designated, and the regulations concerning production per acre and minimum alcohol content are stricter than for the rest of the crop. The *grands crus* account for less than 5 percent of the wines produced in Alsace. Words such as *Réserve* or *Réserve Personnelle* are not legally defined and their significance depends on the standards of the individual shipper.

In especially sunny years, a number of producers make wines labeled *Vendange Tardive,* or late harvest, primarily from Gewürztraminer, Riesling, and Pinot Gris. To qualify for this designation, which was made official in 1984, the juice must contain a minimum sugar content about equal to that of a German Auslese; the wines, however, are usually dry, although some may be off-dry. Even rarer are wines labeled *Sélection de Grains Nobles,* the equivalent of a German Beerenauslese, made primarily from Gewürztraminer and Pinot Gris. Even in the most successful vintages, the production of *Vendange Tardive* wines might amount to about 250,000 cases and that of *Sélection de Grains Nobles* usually varies from forty thousand to sixty thousand cases, which together represents less than 3 percent of the crop.

Alsace shippers—Hugel, Trimbach, Willm, Josmeyer, Dopff, and Dopff & Irion are among the best-known here—market almost half the wines of the region; a third are produced by the many cooperative wine cellars; and the rest is estate-bottled by individual growers such as Domaine Weinbach and Zind-Humbrecht.

Provence

The region of Provence extends along the Mediterranean coast from Marseilles east to Nice. This 120-mile stretch is dotted with fishing villages and with such famous resorts as Saint-Tropez, Cannes, Antibes, and Juan-les-Pins. A holiday mood and a *salade niçoise* on a terrace overlooking the water can add a great deal of enchantment to the agreeable rosés of Provence, and it is disappointing to discover that these wines rarely taste quite the same when consumed at home. It's true that many of these delicate and charming wines served in carafes do not travel well, but then neither does the mood in which they were first enjoyed. Of the vast amount of wine produced in this part of France, mostly for local consumption, there is a certain amount that stands out from the rest. The best-known wines are labeled Côtes de Provence, and they were elevated from V.D.Q.S. status to *Appellation Contrôlée* with the 1977 vintage. About eight million cases are produced within the appellation, two-thirds of it rosé. An increasing amount of red wine is also made, as well as a certain amount of white wine. Château de Selle, owned by the Domaines Ott, is one of the region's most familiar wines.

Côteaux d'Aix en Provence, which was made an *Appellation Contrôlée* in 1984, includes reds, whites, and rosés produced near the town of Aix-en-Provence. Château Vignelaure, planted primarily with Cabernet Sauvignon, and Château de Fonscolombe are both situated in this region.

The seacoast villages of Bandol and Cassis each produce red, white, and rosé wines that are entitled to *Ap-*

pellation Contrôlée status. Bandol produces mostly reds and rosés—made primarily from the Mourvèdre grape, they are dry wines with a fairly well-defined character. Domaine Tempier is perhaps the best-known Bandol estate. Cassis is known primarily for its white wine, full-flavored and a favorite accompaniment to the local *bouillabaisse*. The wines of Cassis bear no relation to the *crème de cassis* made in Dijon. The latter is a black-currant syrup used on desserts and to flavor certain drinks, notably Kir, a popular aperitif that is a mixture of white wine and *crème de cassis*. The two small appellations Palette and Bellet produce red, white, and rosé wines that are rarely seen outside Provence; Palette is situated just east of Aix-en-Provence, Bellet is in the hills behind Nice.

Other Wines

Near the Swiss border, not far from Geneva, two white wines are produced that are occasionally seen in this country. Crépy, made a few miles from the lake of Geneva, is a light, dry wine made from the Chasselas grape. Being a wine made in the mountains near Switzerland and from a grape widely grown there, it's no surprise that Crépy resembles Swiss white wines. Seyssel is a dry white wine from the Haute-Savoie, and much of its production is transformed into a sparkling wine. Seyssel *mousseux* is well known to skiers at nearby Mégève and Chamonix, and is shipped to this country as well.

The vast area of the south of France, commonly known as the Midi, produces tremendous amounts of ordinary wine and is by far the largest viticultural area in the country, accounting for 40 percent of all its vineyards. The Languedoc-Roussillon, as this region is more properly called, extends west of the Rhône River along the Mediterranean to the Spanish border. Cooperative cellars produce about two-thirds of the region's wines, which are almost all red. Most of this wine is totally anonymous and is used to make the commercial blends sold within France and exported as *vin de table* under various brand names. There are, however, a number of *Appellation Contrôlée* wines produced here as well. The two basic appellations are Côteaux du Languedoc and

Côtes du Roussillon. Within the Languedoc are such districts as Corbières, Costières de Nimes, Faugères, Minervois, and Saint-Chinian; the Roussillon region includes Collioure and Fitou. These two regions are also the home of several unusual sweet, fortified dessert wines, such as Muscat de Frontignan, Muscat de Rivesaltes, Banyuls, and Maury.

The Languedoc-Roussillon region also produces most of France's *Vins de Pays:* Vin de Pays d'Oc encompasses the entire region; departmental names include Vin de Pays de l'Aude, Vin de Pays de l'Hérault, and Vin de Pays du Gard. In the 1970s, when the *Vin de Pays* category was being defined, a program of replanting was begun in the Languedoc-Roussillon, and to such traditional varieties as Carignan, Cinsault, and Grenache were added Syrah and Mourvèdre and, more recently, Cabernet Sauvignon, Merlot, Chardonnay, and Sauvignon Blanc. As a result, many *Vins de Pays* are now marketed as varietal wines under such labels as Fortant de France of Skalli and Réserve St.-Martin of the Val d'Orbieu cooperative. Perhaps the most famous vineyard within the *Vin de Pays* category is Mas de Daumas Gassac, a Vin de Pays de l'Hérault situated about twenty miles west of Montpellier; the fifty-acre estate produces a red wine made primarily from Cabernet Sauvignon, plus Syrah, Pinot Noir, and other varieties, and a white that includes Chardonnay and Viognier.

In the Dordogne region just east of Bordeaux, a number of relatively unfamiliar *Appellation Contrôlée* wines are produced from the same grape varieties as in Bordeaux. Among the wines that occasionally find their way here are the red and white wines of Bergerac, and the white wines of Montravel and Monbazillac.

The vineyards around Cahors, a city about 120 miles east of Bordeaux, produce deep-colored, full-bodied red wines made primarily from the Malbec grape (known locally as the Auxerrois). For many years this wine, greatly admired by those who were able to find it, was produced in limited quantities. In 1971, Cahors was elevated from V.D.Q.S. to *Appellation Contrôlée* rank; production has increased to more than two million cases, and most examples today are no longer as dark, tannic, and intense as in the past. About a third of the region's production comes from the Côtes d'Olt cooperative cellar at Parnac; in addition, a number of estates are also exporting their wines, including Château de Haut-Serre, Château Triguedina, Clos de Gamot, Château Pech de Jammes, and Château Lagrezette.

The Madiran district, situated just below the extensive Armagnac region, in southwest France, produces rather tannic and sturdy reds made primarily from the Tannat grape. The Buzet appellation (formerly Côtes de Buzet), north of Armagnac, is planted with the same varieties as Bordeaux and produces similar wines in a somewhat lighter version; almost all the wines of Buzet are made by a cooperative cellar.

The Armagnac region, also known as Gascony, produces white wines entitled to the name Vin de Pays des Côtes du Gascogne. The vineyards are planted primarily with Ugni Blanc and Colombard, and the wines have traditionally been distilled into Armagnac. In recent years, part of the crop has been vinified to produce crisp, lively white wines that are increasingly seen here; producers include Domaine de la Hitaire, Domaine de Pouy, Domaine de Puits, Domaine de Rieux, and Domaine Tariquet.

The Jura district, east of Burgundy, produces a limited amount of red, white, and rosé wines, of which Arbois rosé is the most often seen in Paris. There are also several thousand cases a year produced of a very special white wine, Château-Chalon, made in a rather unusual way. After fermentation, the wine is aged for at least six years in small barrels that are not completely filled, thus exposing the wine to air. The resulting oxidation causes a yeast film to form, similar to that produced in certain sherries by a similar process, and the finished wine is known as a *vin jaune,* or yellow wine. Château-Chalon (which is the name of a village, not a vineyard) is a most curious white wine; although not fortified, it is similar to a dry sherry, but perhaps less complex.

THE WINES
OF ITALY

Italy can claim to be the most completely vinous nation of all: vines are planted in every one of its twenty regions, from Piedmont to Sicily; in most years it produces more wine than any other country; and its wines offer a greater diversity of names and styles than are found anywhere else. Although Italy's annual production is the equivalent of 650 to 800 million cases—Italy and France together account for more than 40 percent of all the world's wines—the American consumer was for many years confined to a few well-known labels from a limited number of producers. Today, even a casual wine drinker can find a much more varied choice of attractive and moderately priced wines from Italy, as well as an extensive selection of that country's finest wines.

The range of white wines has expanded from the popular Soave, Frascati, Orvieto, and Verdicchio to include distinctive bottlings from such classic grape varieties as Chardonnay, Pinot Grigio, Pinot Bianco, Sauvignon, and Traminer, as well as from such local varieties as Tocai Friulano, Cortese, Albana, and Vernaccia. In addition to the familiar Chianti, Valpolicella, and Bardolino, the selection of red wines varies from the light, brisk Merlots and Cabernets produced in the northeast to such rich, complex, wood-aged wines as Barolo, Barbaresco, and

Brunello di Montalcino. Even as the best Italian wines have become more widely available here, however, many consumers have been slow to recognize their merits. One reason may be that the wines of each region are not structured into a clear upward progression from district to village to vineyard, as is the case in France and Germany. In fact, in Italy, as in California, there are relatively few single-vineyard wines; consequently there exists no ranking of classified vineyards, as in Bordeaux, or listing of *grands crus* and *premiers crus*, as in Burgundy, that make it easier for an informed consumer to identify the finest wines and determine their relative standing.

The consumer who wants to venture beyond the half-dozen best-known Italian wines faces a confusing array of names that do not seem to follow any specific pattern. Some wines are known by the grape variety from which each of them is made, some by their village or district of origin, others by a combination of both, and a few are still marketed with such colorful names as Lacryma Christi or Est! Est!! Est!!! Since the names of many Italian wine villages are not yet as familiar to consumers as are those of France and Germany, and since the grape varieties grown in Italy include many that are not readily found elsewhere, it's not always easy to recognize one or the other. Barolo and Barbaresco are villages, Barbera and Bonarda are grapes. Albana and Cortese are grapes, Lugana and Carema are villages. Verdicchio, Verduzzo, and Lambrusco are grapes. What's more, it's not unusual for the same name to be used for a wine that can be made either dry or sweet, still or sparkling.

Italy has been producing wine for more than three thousand years, and even twenty centuries ago wine was the daily drink of the people. Italians have always taken wine for granted, and this casual attitude is reflected in the easygoing way in which some of Italy's vineyards are cultivated to this day. Rows of vines are interspersed between plantings of wheat, corn, and olive trees, and this system of mixed cultivation, called *coltura promiscua*, goes back to a time when wine was only one of the products of a particular property. Forty years ago *coltura promiscua* accounted for 70 percent of Italy's vineyards. Nowadays, most of these vineyards have been uprooted, and extensive new plantings make better use of available land as well as permitting the use of tractors and other mechanical aids. *Coltura promiscua* now accounts for less than 25 percent of all vineyards, and in some areas— Soave, for example—less than 5 percent of the land is in mixed cultivation.

Another significant change that has affected most Italian wines is the adoption of modern winemaking techniques. Many of the dull, poorly vinified white wines of Italy, often aged in wood until they were oxidized, have been transformed into clean, crisp wines that are bottled early to retain their fruit and freshness. Regions whose wines had been accepted by local consumers but were previously unsuitable for the international export market have achieved great success in recent years as a result of new equipment and modern vinification methods. Many red wines, too, have been made more appealing by altering the winemaking and aging methods used previously.

Much of the improved quality of Italian wines, especially the less expensive whites, is due to the growth of cooperative cellars, which enable growers of limited means to have their grapes made into sound wines by the use of modern equipment and techniques that they would be unable to employ in their own small cellars. There are now nearly eight hundred cooperative cellars in Italy, and they account for nearly two-thirds of the country's wine production.

In the past, the Italians' informal approach to winemaking, combined with their traditionally individualistic attitude, made it difficult to establish quality controls similar to those enforced in many other countries. In a number of wine districts, growers and shippers banded together to form a *consorzio,* or association, to establish certain minimum standards. This self-discipline varied in intensity from one *consorzio* to another. The most famous *consorzio* was established by the producers in Chianti Classico. In 1963 the Italian government—spurred on by Italy's entry into the European Community—took an active role in establishing wine laws for the most important districts. These laws, which are in some ways more complete than the *Appellation Contrôlée* laws of France, are known as *Denominazione di Origine Con-*

trollata, or DOC. The first decrees were issued in 1966, and the DOC laws went into effect in 1967, when fourteen DOC wines accounted for about eleven million cases of wine. There are now about 240 DOC zones, all of whose wines display the words *Denominazione di Origine Controllata* on their labels, and they account for 85 to 100 million cases of wine a year, which usually amounts to 10 to 15 percent of Italy's total production. (By comparison, the production of French *Appellation Contrôlée* wines varies from 150 to 250 million cases a year.)

The DOC laws specify the geographical limits of each appellation, the grape varieties that may be used, the maximum amount of wine that can be produced per acre, and the minimum alcohol content of the wine, among other details. Reflecting the generally favorable climate that prevails throughout much of Italy, the DOC laws are more generous with regard to maximum production per acre than are the *Appellation Contrôlée* laws of France.

Although many Italian wines are labeled with the name of the grape variety from which each is made, every DOC wine must be produced within a specific region or district whose boundaries are strictly defined. Thus, the varietal name is combined with an appellation of origin—Barbera d'Asti, Nebbiolo d'Alba, Sangiovese di Romagna, Lambrusco di Sorbara, Cabernet del Trentino, or Pinot Grigio del Piave. Previously, non-DOC varietal wines could be labeled with only the name of the grape; now all varietal names must be accompanied by an appropriate geographical designation, as Barbera del Piemonte, Merlot delle Venezie, Pinot Grigio del Veneto, Sangiovese di Toscana, or Chardonnay dell'Umbria.

The DOC laws for many districts also specify that if a wine is made from grapes grown within an inner zone, it may be labeled *classico.* In some districts, such as Chianti and Soave, the *classico* zone may account for less than a third of the wines produced; in others, such as Valpolicella, as much as 60 percent of the wines can be marketed as *classico.* Most wines labeled *superiore* must have a slightly higher minimum alcohol content and must be aged somewhat longer before being sold, a few months for some white wines, perhaps a year for certain reds.

Some years ago a higher and even more select category of wines was created, *Denominazione di Origine Controllata e Garantita*, or DOCG. The principal differences between the DOC and DOCG laws are that the latter reduce the yield per acre and specify that every wine must be approved by a tasting commission before it can be sold with the DOCG seal. Four wines were originally granted DOCG status in the early 1980s—Brunello di Montalcino, Barolo, Barbaresco, and Vino Nobile di Montepulciano. In 1984, Chianti became the fifth DOCG wine, and more recently Albana di Romagna, Gattinara, Torgiano Rosso Riserva, Carmignano, Taurasi, Montefalco Sagrantino, Vernaccia di San Gimignano, Moscato d'Asti, and Asti Spumante have been elevated to the DOCG category.

Of the 250 or so DOC and DOCG wines, just five account for about a quarter of the total—Chianti, Soave, Valpolicella, Bardolino, and Moscato d'Asti (most of which is transformed into Asti Spumante). In fact, two-thirds of all the DOC and DOCG wines produced come from about twenty appellations, among them Caldaro, Montepulciano d'Abruzzo, Valdadige, Oltrepò Pavese, Piave, Grave del Friuli, Frascati, Orvieto, and Barbera d'Asti.

Although the DOC laws have now been in effect for many years, many of the *consorzi* are still functioning, and, in fact, a number of new ones were created after the advent of DOC. Their purpose is to provide an even stricter measure of self-regulation than the DOC laws, to encourage the production of wines of a higher quality within each district. Each *consorzio* has its own seal—the best-known is the black rooster used for Chianti Classico—and it appears on a strip attached to the neck of each bottle. A producer in any region who chooses not to join the local *consorzio* can nevertheless continue to sell his wine with the appropriate DOC name, of course, but without the *consorzio* seal.

Unlike the wine laws of France, the DOC and DOCG laws of Italy specify a minimum amount of wood-aging for many red wines, which may be as much as three or four years. The laws simply reflect the traditions of each region, but in recent years the long aging in large casks that has always been considered integral to the taste of such wines as Barolo, Barbaresco, and Brunello di Montalcino has led to controversy among winemakers and consumers, some of whom feel that the resulting wines are often faded and dried-out. No barrel-aging requirements exist for even the finest red wines of Bordeaux and Burgundy, for example, nor for those of California. By codifying existing attitudes toward aging in order to protect the quality of certain wines, the Italian laws impose a wood-aging minimum that a number of producers now feel diminishes their wines. Some winemakers now prefer to age at least some of their red wines for a limited amount of time in the small oak barrels used in France and California, rather than for several years in the large casks that are more traditional in Italian cellars.

The DOC laws also formalized the specific grape varieties that may be used for each appellation and, where more than one variety is used, the proportions of each. Since the DOC laws were established, however, a number of producers have planted such varieties as Chardonnay and Cabernet Sauvignon in areas where they were not previously cultivated; others have been experimenting with existing varieties, but in proportions different from those specified in the DOC regulations. What happened, in effect, was that wine laws were finally established—in the late 1960s and early 1970s—to protect and maintain traditional approaches to winemaking just as a number of Italian producers, influenced by France and California, began to alter their existing wines and to create new ones. As a result, an increasing number of excellent wines are being produced in Italy that are not entitled to DOC or DOCG status, but may be labeled only as *vino da tavola*, or table wine. Some examples include Sassicaia, Tignanello, Le Pergole Torte, Grifi, Ghiaie della Furba, Ornellaia, San Giorgio, Vintage Tunina, Luna dei Feldi, and Torcolato. This category also includes a number of excellent varietal wines made from Cabernet Sauvignon, Merlot, and Chardonnay, and labeled as such, but not entitled to DOC status because they are produced in regions, such as Piedmont and Tuscany, where these varieties are not yet officially recognized.

In 1992, a new law created a pyramid of quality for Italian wines, with *vino da tavola* as the base and individual vineyards, or *crus*, at the top. Thus, some of Italy's finest and most famous wines would be officially transferred from the bottom of the pyramid to the top. Also, a category known as *Indicazioni Geografiche Tipiche,* or IGT, would be created as an equivalent to France's *Vin de Pays* for wines that are more distinctive and of better quality than *vino da tavola* but not entitled to DOC status; such wines could be labeled with regional and varietal names.

Apart from a wine's appellation of origin and such supplementary indications as *classico* and *superiore,* there are a number of other words and phrases that are often encountered on Italian wine labels. These include *rosso* (red), *bianco* (white), *rosato* (rosé), *secco* (dry), *abboccato* or *amabile* (semisweet), *dolce* (sweet), *spumante* (sparkling), *frizzante* (lightly sparkling), *cantina* (cellar), *cantina sociale* (cooperative cellar), *azienda vinicola* (wine company), *casa vinicola* (winery), *tenuta* (estate), *fattoria, podere* (farm or estate), *azienda agricola* (estate winery), *vigna* or *vigneto* (vineyard) and *imbottigliato* (bottled).

The Italian Wine Regions

What follows is a description of Italian wines grouped into four sections and arranged in approximate geographical order: Piedmont and the Northwest includes Valle d'Aosta, Lombardy, and Liguria; Veneto and the Northeast includes Trentino-Alto Adige and Friuli-Venezia Giulia; Tuscany and Central Italy includes Umbria, the Marches, and Emilia-Romagna; and from Rome to the South includes the rest of Italy and Sicily.

PIEDMONT AND THE NORTHWEST

The Piedmont region, situated at the foot of the Alps that separate Italy from France and Switzerland, is known for the variety of fine red wines produced from its more than 230,000 acres of vineyards. Turin, the capital of the region, is the center of the vermouth trade; Asti, thirty miles southeast of Turin, is world-famous for its sweet, aromatic, sparkling wines. Asti Spumante and vermouth are discussed elsewhere, however. It is the table wines that concern us here, and Piedmont has a greater number of DOC and DOCG zones than any other region in Italy—more than three dozen, almost all of them red. The finest Piedmont reds are made from the Nebbiolo grape. *Nebbia* means mist, and the name of the grape apparently derives from the fog that often covers the hillside vineyards of Piedmont in the fall, when the Nebbiolo grapes are harvested.

The most famous Nebbiolo wine is Barolo, produced around the town of that name southwest of Alba. Like most Nebbiolo-based wines, Barolo is full-bodied, sturdy, and long-lived and needs several years to develop its qualities. According to the DOCG requirements for this wine, Barolo must have a minimum alcoholic strength of 13 percent when bottled (compared, for example, to a minimum requirement of 11.5 percent for the *grands crus* of Burgundy and 12.5 percent for Châteauneuf-du-Pape), and the wine must be aged for at least three years, two of them in cask. A Barolo labeled *Riserva* must be aged at least five years.

Barolo and several other big red wines of Piedmont are often compared to the Burgundies and Rhône wines of France, but the comparison can be misleading. Barolo is a rich, full-flavored wine, but it has its own distinctively earthy bouquet, often compared to tar, truffles, mushrooms, and faded roses, that sets it apart from French wines. Traditional Barolo is made with extended maceration—the time the wine spends in contact with the grapeskins—followed by aging in large casks that may go on for four or five years. Such a wine is likely to be harsh and tough when young and may then be relatively faded in color and flavor when it is eventually bottled, especially compared to the more vigorous fine reds of France and California. Today, a number of producers in Barolo—and elsewhere in Piedmont—have adopted a shorter, more gentle maceration followed by only two years or so of barrel age; and some use the small oak barrels that are traditional in Bordeaux. What this means to the consumer is that Barolo is now available in a number of styles, from the subdued and somewhat faded taste that was prevalent only a few years ago to wines with more color, fruit, and vigor.

Another significant change that has occurred in the Barolo district is the increasing use of specific vineyard names. A number of producers have begun to vinify and bottle wines from different sites separately, and such names as Brunate, Rocche, Rocchette, and Cannubi now appear on labels with growing frequency, sometimes preceded by *bricco* (hilltop) or *sorì* (denoting a site with a favorable southern exposure). The production of Barolo amounts to more than 500,000 cases a year, and there are more than two dozen firms whose labels can be found here, some in very limited quantities. Among the best-known Barolo producers (most of whom also make other Piedmont wines) are Elio Altare, Batasiolo, Borgogno, Ceretto, Pio Cesare, Michele Chiarlo, Clerico, Aldo Conterno, Giacomo Conterno, Contratto, Cordero di Montezemolo (Monfalletto), Fontanafredda, Angelo Gaja, Bruno Giacosa, Marchesi di Barolo, Giuseppe Mascarello, Prunotto, Renato Ratti, Vietti, and Roberto Voerzio.

The village of Barbaresco, a dozen miles northeast of Barolo, gives its name to another famous wine made entirely from Nebbiolo. Two years of age are required by law, of which one must be in wood. Barbaresco, too, has been granted DOCG status, and a Barbaresco *Riserva* must now be aged for at least four years. In general, the wine is somewhat lighter than Barolo, and it matures in less time, although fine examples may display more elegance and refinement. Most of the firms that make Barolo also produce Barbaresco, and it's not unusual to find a Barbaresco from one firm that is more tannic and richly textured than a Barolo from another. Producers that specialize in Barbaresco include Castello di Neive, Marchesi di Gresy, and Produttori del Barbaresco. Ceretto, which produces its finest Barolo at its Bricco Rocche estate, makes its best Barbaresco at its Bricco Asili estate, and the wines are so labeled. Perhaps the most famous winemaker in Barbaresco is Angelo Gaja, who has adopted the vinification and aging techniques of Bordeaux to produce long-lived wines that combine tannin,

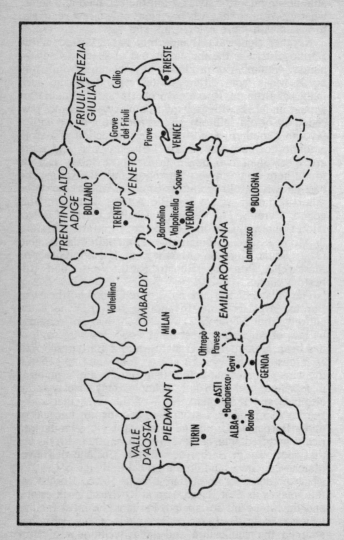

NORTHERN ITALY

fruit, and finesse. Gaja makes single-vineyard Barbarescos from his 140-acre estate—Sorì Tildin, Sorì San Lorenzo, and Costa Russi—as well as several other wines, including Vinòt, a *nouveau* wine made from Nebbiolo by carbonic maceration, and barrel-aged Cabernet Sauvignon and Chardonnay. Gaja also produces a Barolo, labeled Sperss, from a thirty-acre vineyard acquired in 1988.

The third famous Nebbiolo wine of Piedmont comes from vineyards around Gattinara, situated in the Novara-Vercelli hills, about seventy-five miles north of Barolo. Up to 10 percent Bonarda grapes is permitted in Gattinara, and the wine must age for at least four years, two of them in wood. Gattinara is the smallest of the three appellations, producing only fifty or sixty thousand cases of wine, compared to 250,000 or so for Barbaresco. Only wines from delimited hillside vineyards can be labeled Gattinara, and some producers market wines from adjoining vineyards as Spanna, which is the local name for Nebbiolo. Spanna is not a DOC wine, and the quality is variable, although some examples, such as those of Vallana, are on a par with the wines of Gattinara. Producers of Gattinara include Antoniolo, Dessilani, and Travaglini; Monsecco is the proprietary name for a Gattinara produced by Le Colline.

Six other villages around Gattinara produce DOC wines—Ghemme, Boca, Fara, Sizzano, Bramaterra, and Lessona. Although all these wines are made primarily from the Nebbiolo grape, each appellation has different minimum requirements, and as much as 50 or 60 percent of other varieties, primarily Vespolina and Bonarda, can be used as well. These wines must undergo two or three years of aging in cask, and their flavor is, unsurprisingly, similar to that of Gattinara. Ghemme is the best-known, but none of the wines is widely available here, as all six appellations together rarely produce more than forty thousand cases a year.

Two other Nebbiolo wines that get their names from the villages near which they are produced are Carema and Donnaz; both are made from grapes grown at fairly high altitudes, and these attractive reds, produced in limited quantities, tend to be lighter and fruitier than other Nebbiolo wines. Carema is on the border between Piedmont and Valle d'Aosta, Donnaz is in Valle d'Aosta, the smallest region in Italy, in the northwest corner of the country. Its vineyards are planted on steep hillsides overlooking the Dora Baltea River, and most of its red, white, and rosé wines are entitled to the regional DOC Valle d'Aosta or Vallée d'Aoste; inner zones, in addition to Donnaz, include Enfer d'Arvier and Blanc de Morgex and de La Salle.

A certain amount of Nebbiolo is also marketed as a varietal wine, either as Nebbiolo d'Alba, which is a DOC, or simply as Nebbiolo del Piemonte. In the 1980s, the DOC Roero was created for Nebbiolo wines produced in the Roeri hills, across the Tanaro River from Barolo and Barbaresco; because these wines are made with a small amount of the white Arneis grape, they are often lighter in style than Nebbiolo d'Alba. Although Nebbiolo produces the region's most famous wines, this grape is planted in less than 3 percent of the vineyards of Piedmont. The most widely cultivated grape is Barbera, which accounts for more than half the total acreage in Piedmont. There are five DOC wines in Piedmont produced from Barbera, the best-known of which are Barbera d'Asti and Barbera d'Alba; two others are Barbera del Monferrato and Barbera dei Colli Tortonesi— all four together account for only a small part of the total Barbera crop, most of which is marketed simply as Barbera or Barbera del Piemonte. The village of Gabiano has given its name to a fifth DOC for Barbera produced in the Monferrato hills. The late Giacomo Bologna created a complex, barrel-aged Barbera that he labeled Bricco dell'Uccellone. In addition, several Piedmont producers have created proprietary blends of Nebbiolo and Barbera that are matured in small oak barrels; among the best known of these well-structured wines are Bricco Manzoni of Valentino Migliorini and Barilot of Michele Chiarlo.

The other principal red-wine grape varieties of Piedmont are Dolcetto, Freisa, and Grignolino. All these names may appear on labels, but the varietal wines that are entitled to DOC status are also associated with a specific region of origin, for example Dolcetto d'Alba, Freisa di Chieri, and Grignolino d' Asti. What makes the different DOC names confusing at first is that different varieties may be planted in a given region—Barbera d'Asti, Dolcetto d'Asti, Freisa d'Asti, Grignolino d'Asti—and a given variety may be planted in more than one region, as in the case of the Barbera DOCs cited above. What's more, a number of these red wines may be dry or semisweet, still or sparkling. The examples shipped here are almost always dry, but, of course, their individual characteristics vary depending on the grape variety and the zone of origin. In general, Grignolino produces the lightest wines, and since both its quality and quantity are uneven, it is now less widely planted than in the past. Freisa is relatively light and fruity, and is the variety most likely to be made into an *amabile* or sparkling wine. Despite its name (*dolce* means sweet), Dolcetto is almost always dry and full-flavored; Dolcetto d'Alba, the most frequently encountered DOC, can be an excellent wine, combining youthful charm, ripe fruit, and tannic structure. Because it is an appealing red meant to be consumed young, Dolcetto is often compared to Beaujolais, but the Italian wine has more body and intensity of flavor; a better comparison might be to a California Zinfandel.

The best known white-wine grape of Piedmont is Moscato Canelli, used to make Asti Spumante. A number of producers also bottle Moscato d'Asti, which is made by stopping the fermentation when there is only 5 or 6 percent of alcohol; the resulting wine is sweet, aromatic, and may be *frizzante,* or lightly sparkling.

Although dry white wine accounts for a very small part of Piedmont's total production, that made from the Cortese grape at Gavi has achieved an excellent reputation in a relatively short time; the DOC Gavi or Cortese di Gavi was established only in 1974. Among the labels associated with this crisp, flavorful wine are La Scolca, La Battistina, La Giustiniana, and Principessa of Banfi. Arneis, a native grape, produces dry white wines that are now entitled to the DOC Arneis di Roero or Roero Arneis. Favorita is another local white grape, and dry wines so labeled are occasionally seen here. Also, several major Piedmont producers have planted Chardonnay in their vineyards, and are now making limited amounts of barrel-aged wines in the style of Burgundy and California.

Lombardy and Liguria

The Valtellina vineyards, situated northeast of Milan near the Swiss border, are in the Lombardy region, but as they are planted primarily with Nebbiolo, whose local name is Chiavennasca, the wines bear some similarities to those of Piedmont. The steeply terraced vineyards, situated on either side of the city of Sondrio, extend along the north bank of the Adda River, which flows from east to west at this point on its course to Lake Como. Although some white wines are made there, the DOC Valtellina applies only to red wines, and these must contain at last 70 percent Chiavennasca. Wines entitled to the higher appellation Valtellina Superiore, which account for about half of the region's production, must be made at least 95 percent from the Chiavennasca; their labels almost always feature the name of one of the district's inner zones—Valgella, Sassella, Grumello, and Inferno. In addition, an unusual dry red wine, similar to an Amarone from Valpolicella, is made from slightly dried grapes and labeled Sfursat or Sforzato; it has a minimum alcohol content of 14.5 percent and is likely to have more body than other Valtellina wines. Producers include Nino Negri, Rainoldi, and Enologica Valtellinese.

Another important DOC wine district in Lombardy is Oltrepò Pavese, situated about thirty miles south of Milan, beyond the city of Pavia and the Po River. Red wines labeled simply Oltrepò Pavese are made primarily from Barbera and Croatina grapes, but within the DOC Oltrepò Pavese are a number of wines labeled with such varietal names as Barbera, Bonarda, Riesling, and Pinot, as well as three unusual reds—Barbacarlo, Buttafuoco, and Sangue di Giuda. The Oltrepò Pavese contains Italy's most extensive plantings of Pinot Nero, most of which is used, as is the district's excellent Pinot Bianco and Pinot Grigio, for sparkling wines. Frecciarossa (red arrow) is the name of an estate in the Oltrepò Pavese that produces red, white, and rosé wines.

Franciacorta is a DOC district situated east of Milan, between Bergamo and Brescia. The reds marketed as Franciacorta are made from a blend that can include Cabernet Franc, Barbera, Nebbiolo, and Merlot; the

Franciacorta white is made primarily from Pinot Bianco; several producers have also planted Chardonnay and Cabernet Sauvignon. Much of the district's production is made into excellent *méthode champenoise* sparkling wine by such firms as Bellavista, Berlucchi (Brut, Cuvée Imperiale), and Ca' del Bosco (Brut, Crémant, Dosage Zero). Ca' del Bosco is also known for its table wines, which include barrel-aged Chardonnay, Pinot Noir, and a Cabernet-Merlot blend labeled with the name of the winery's owner, Maurizio Zanella.

The Liguria region, which adjoins Piedmont to the south, extends along the Ligurian Sea, with Genoa at its center. Liguria's two best-known DOC districts are Cinqueterre, near La Spezia, long famous for its white wines; and Dolceacqua, near San Remo, achieving a reputation for its reds, produced from the Rossese grape, and also labeled Rossese di Dolceacqua. Vermentino and Pigato are the principal white-wine grapes of Liguria.

VENETO AND THE NORTHEAST

The overall quality of the wines produced in the three northeastern provinces of Italy collectively referred to as the Tre Venezie—the Veneto, Friuli-Venezia Giulia, and Trentino-Alto Adige—is such that the area accounts for about a third of the country's total crop of DOC wines. The most famous wines of the Tre Venezie are Soave, Valpolicella, and Bardolino, but this part of Italy is becoming widely known for its extensive range of varietal wines. These include such well-known French and German varieties as Merlot, Cabernet Franc, Cabernet Sauvignon, Pinot Nero (Pinot Noir), Chardonnay, Pinot Bianco (Pinot Blanc), Pinot Grigio (Pinot Gris), Riesling Renano (Rhine Riesling), Sauvignon, Sylvaner, Traminer, and Müller-Thurgau. There are also a number of less familiar native varieties that include, among the reds, Lagrein, Marzemino, Raboso, Schiava, Teroldego, and Refosco, known in France as Mondeuse; the whites include Picolit, Prosecco, Verduzzo, and Tocai Friulano, not to be confused with the Tokay of Hungary, which is made primarily from the Furmint grape.

Merlot, Cabernet Franc, and Cabernet Sauvignon produce light, pleasing and distinctive red wines which are, for the most part, not barrel-aged, although a number of producers are now using small oak *barriques* to make more complex and long-lived reds. Cabernet Franc is more widely planted than Cabernet Sauvignon in northern Italy, and a wine labeled simply Cabernet is likely to be made primarily or entirely from the former. Excellent wines are also produced from Chardonnay, which is, in a way, a relatively new variety in Italy. In the late 1970s a number of northern Italian winemakers realized that much of what they had always assumed was Pinot Bianco, and sold as such, was actually Chardonnay. As Chardonnay was much better known as a varietal wine than Pinot Bianco, especially in the United States, many producers began to vinify and bottle Chardonnay separately, and to label it as such. Chardonnays produced in certain specific zones were first granted DOC status in 1984.

The Veneto

The Veneto region, whose capital is Venice, produces three of Italy's best-known wines—Soave, Valpolicella, and Bardolino, whose combined production is ten to twelve million cases a year.

The vineyards around the village of Soave produce a pale, dry white wine with a great deal of charm if it is cleanly made and bottled young. Not so long ago it was still common to bottle Soave two or three years after the vintage, which gave the best of them more character but less delicacy and fruit. Soave is made primarily from the Garganega grape, with some Trebbiano. The two red wines, Valpolicella and Bardolino, can be among the most enjoyable of Italy—fresh and light-bodied, with a characteristic dry aftertaste. Valpolicella is the sturdier of the two, Bardolino somewhat paler in color and lighter in body. The wines are made from Corvina Veronese, with varying proportions of Rondinella, Molinara, and other varieties. The picturesque town of Bardolino is situated on the eastern shore of Lake Garda, and many of its hillside vineyards are exposed to extra sunshine reflected off the surface of the lake. Valpolicella is a valley north of Verona whose hillsides are covered with vines. The inner zone of Valpantena, just above Verona, produces wines marketed as Valpolicella-Valpantena. The best-known shipper of Veronese wines is Bolla; other producers include Bertani, Folonari, Lamberti, and Tommasi. Two producers noted for Soave are Pieropan, one of the first to market single-vineyard wines, and the Cantina Sociale di Soave, one of Europe's biggest cooperative cellars.

An unusual red wine, Recioto della Valpolicella, is made in limited quantities from selected bunches of grapes that are spread out on trays or hung on hooks and left to dry in well-ventilated rooms, thus increasing the proportion of sugar in the juice. (*Recioto* is derived from *recie,* or ears, and refers to the top of the bunch, which has had the most exposure to sun and is likely to have the ripest grapes.) The wine made from these specially dried grapes—the technique is known as *passito*—has more alcohol and more flavor than a Valpolicella, and may be matured in large casks for several years. A wine labeled simply Recioto della Valpolicella is likely to be semisweet and often has a slight sparkle as well. If such a wine is left to ferment until it is dry, it has traditionally been labeled Recioto della Valpolicella Amarone. This red, which may now be labeled Amarone della Valpolicella, is a particularly sturdy, long-lived, and heady wine—14 or 15 percent alcohol is not uncommon—and very different in style from a straightforward Valpolicella. (Recioto di Soave, made in the same way from white grapes, is a semisweet white wine.) Well-known producers of Amarone include Allegrini, Anselmi, Masi, Quintarelli, Le Ragose, and Tedeschi. A few producers of Valpolicella and Amarone also make an unusual wine by the *ripasso* process. After Amarone is drawn from the fermentation vats, leaving the grapeskins behind, Valpolicella that has already finished its fermentation is transferred into those vats to extract additional color, body, and flavor from the mass of grapeskins. Examples of such wines include CampoFiorin of Masi, Capitel San Rocco of Tedeschi, and Catullo of Bertani.

Although Soave, Valpolicella, and Bardolino dominate the wine scene in the Veneto, a wide variety of other wines are produced throughout the region. Bianco di Custoza is a light, dry white wine made primarily from Trebbiano in vineyards situated in the southern part of the Bardolino district, southeast of Lake Garda. Several appealing wines produced on the Lombardy side of Lake Garda are usually associated with those of Verona: Lugana is another Trebbiano-based white wine; Groppello is a red-wine grape whose name is occasionally seen on labels. Wines produced on the western shore of Lake Garda, near Brescia, are entitled to the DOC Riviera del Garda Bresciano; the appellation includes red and white wines and Chiaretto, a dark rosé.

The Gambellara district, just east of Soave, produces a white wine made primarily from Garganega; Zonin is the leading producer. South of Vicenza are the extensive districts known as Colli Berici and Colli Euganei, whose hillside vineyards are planted with Cabernet, Merlot, Pinot Bianco, and several native varieties. North of Vicenza, the Breganze district produces a number of DOC wines, including a red based on Merlot and a white based on Tocai Friulano. The leading producer of the region is Fausto Maculan, whose range includes the red Brentino, the white Breganze de Breganze, single-vineyard Cabernets, and Torcolato, a barrel-aged sweet white wine made primarily from the Vespaiolo and Tocai grapes.

The vineyards of the Piave district, which extend on either side of the Piave River, are situated just north of Venice, in the province of Treviso. The principal varieties are Merlot, which accounts for more than half the total, Cabernet, Pinot Nero, Pinot Bianco, Pinot Grigio, Tocai Italico, and two local varieties, the white Verduzzo and the red Raboso. Each is entitled to DOC status in conjunction with the district name—Merlot del Piave, Piave Pinot Bianco, and so on.

East of Piave is the Lison-Pramaggiore district, which combines the three DOCs formerly known as Tocai de Lison, Cabernet di Pramaggiore and Merlot di Pramaggiore; the new DOC includes these three varieties plus several more including Chardonnay, Pinot Bianco, Refosco, and Verduzzo. The region's leading firm is Santa Margherita, best known for its popular Pinot Grigio, but also offering a range of red, white, and sparkling wines from the Veneto and Trentino-Alto Adige. North of

Piave, the Prosecco grape is widely planted in the district between the villages of Conegliano and Valdobiaddene; most of the crop goes to market as a dry, fruity sparkling wine made by the Charmat process and entitled to the DOC Prosecco di Conegliano-Valdobiaddene. Sparkling wines from a small district called Cartizze may be labeled as such. Also in the province of Treviso is the Venegazzù estate founded by Count Loredan-Gasparini, and under new ownership since the mid-1970s, which is known for a range of wines that includes a Bordeaux-style Cabernet-Merlot blend labeled Riserva della Casa and a *méthode champenoise* sparkling wine.

Friuli-Venezia Giulia

The Friuli-Venezia Giulia region is situated in the northeastern corner of Italy, on the border with Austria and Slovenia. Part of the region, whose capital is Trieste, once belonged to the former Yugoslavia, and that influence can be recognized in the local cuisine and the non-Italian names of some of its wine producers.

Among the varieties found in the vineyards of Friuli-Venezia Giulia are Merlot, Cabernet Franc, Cabernet Sauvignon, Pinot Nero, Chardonnay, Pinot Bianco, Pinot Grigio, Riesling Italico (Wälschriesling), Riesling Renano, Sauvignon, and Traminer, as well as such native varieties as Refosco, Tocai Friulano, Verduzzo, Ribolla, and Picolit. Although Merlot is the most widely planted grape in this region, it is the delicate and elegant white wines that have made the vinous reputation of this part of Italy. New equipment and modern technology, especially temperature-controlled fermentation, have enabled the producers here to achieve excellent results with many varieties.

The wide range of varieties cultivated in Friuli-Venezia Giulia are found in varying proportions in the DOC zones of the region—Grave del Friuli, Collio Goriziano, Colli Orientali del Friuli, Isonzo, Aquileia, Latisana, and Carso. As is the case in such viticultural areas of Alsace and California, where a number of different varieties are grown in the same sites, the name of the grape from which each wine is made is more significant than where it comes from. With few exceptions, all the DOC wines of Friuli-Venezia Giulia consist of a varietal name in conjunction with an appellation of origin.

The biggest DOC district is Grave del Friuli, an extensive plain named, as is the Graves district of Bordeaux, for its gravelly soil. More than half of Grave del Friuli's vineyards are planted with Merlot, which produces a relatively light but distinctive red. Most of the Cabernet wines are made from Cabernet Franc, as is the case throughout northern Italy, but Cabernet Sauvignon is also planted. Such wines may be labeled Cabernet, with no further qualification. A full selection of white varietal wines are produced in Grave del Friuli, of which Chardonnay and Pinot Grigio are the ones most likely to be found here. Producers include Collavini, Friulvini, and Plozner.

The Collio Goriziano district, whose name usually appears on labels simply as Collio, is the easternmost winegrowing area of northern Italy, and highly acclaimed for its crisp and stylish white wines; the producers in this region were among the first in Italy to employ temperature-controlled fermentation. Tocai Friulano, Pinot Bianco, Pinot Grigio, and Sauvignon are among the white varieties cultivated, and more recently Chardonnay and the native Ribolla Gialla have been granted DOC status. A white wine from this district labeled simply Collio—a blend of Ribolla Gialla, Malvasia, and Tocai—is an exception to the rule that the DOC wines of Friuli-Venezia Giulia be marketed as varietal wines. Another distinctive white wine from Collio is a flavorful style of Pinot Grigio, known as *ramato,* whose pale coppery color is the result of letting the juice stay in contact with the grapeskins for a time before fermentation. Merlot is the most widely planted red grape, and Cabernet Sauvignon and Cabernet Franc are now being made as well, either as varietal wines or blended together as in Bordeaux. Among the better-known producers, many of whom now age their wines in small oak barrels to create more complex whites and longer-lived reds, are Borgo Conventi, Livio Felluga, Marco Felluga (which also owns the Russiz Superiore estate), EnoFriulia, Conti Formentini, Gravner, Puiatti, Mario Schiopetto, and Jermann. The last produces a special wine labeled

Vintage Tunina, which is a blend of several varieties, including Pinot Bianco, Sauvignon, and Chardonnay.

Colli Orientali del Friuli (the Eastern Hills of Friuli) is a district situated to the north of Collio producing wines whose style and quality are similar to that of Collio. Here, too, Merlot and Tocai Friulano account for more than half the total, but a full range of varietal wines, including the unusual native varieties Verduzzo and Picolit. Verduzzo may be made dry or *amabile*, semisweet, and some examples of the latter are marketed as Ramandolo; Verduzzo *amabile* that actually comes from the village of Ramandolo many now be labeled Ramandolo Classico. Picolit, whose production rarely exceeds five thousand cases, in an unusual sweet white wine with a minimum alcohol content of 15 percent made from especially ripe grapes that are particularly difficult to cultivate. Leading producers in this district include Abbazia di Rosazzo, Giovanni Dri, La Viarte, Ronco del Gnemiz, Vigne del Leon, and Volpe Pasini.

Merlot is the most widely planted variety in three of the four smallest DOC districts of Friuli-Venezia Giulia: Isonzo, whose second most important variety is Tocai Friulano; Aquileia, where Refosco is second to Merlot; and Latisana, where Cabernet is also important. Carso, which stretches along the coast from Isonzo past Trieste, produces red wines from Refosco (known locally as Terrano) and whites from Malvasia.

Trentino–Alto Adige

The third of the regions grouped together as Tre Venezie is Trentino–Alto Adige, which contains the northernmost of Italy's vineyards. The region consists of two provinces—Trentino, whose principal city is Trento, situated about fifty miles north of Verona; and Alto Adige, whose capital is Bolzano, even farther north, and closer to the Alps that separate that part of Italy from Austria. The Adige River runs through both provinces.

The province of Trentino encompasses about twenty-five thousand acres of vineyards, and red wines account for more than 80 percent of its production. Schiava, a local variety, is the most widely planted red-wine grape; other native red varieties include Lagrein, Marzemino, and Teroldego, and the more familiar Merlot, Cabernet Franc, Cabernet Sauvignon, and Pinot Nero are also planted. White grapes cultivated in Trentino include Pinot Bianco, Chardonnay, Pinot Grigio, Riesling Italico, Riesling Renano, Müller-Thurgau, Sylvaner, Sauvignon, Traminer Aromatico, the local Nosiola, and two types of Muscat, Moscato Giallo and Moscato Rosa. The principal DOC of this district is Trentino in conjunction with a varietal name, as Merlot del Trentino, Pinot Bianco del Trentino, and so on.

A number of other DOCs have been established in Trentino as well. North of Trento is the village of Sorni, which gives its name to a red made primarily from Schiava and a white made primarily from Nosiola. Just above Sorni are vineyards planted with Teroldego on a wide plain known as Campo Rotaliano; the distinctive red wines are labeled Teroldego Rotaliano. Casteller is a light red wine produced from Schiava, Merlot, and Lambrusco in vineyards situated, for the most part, south of Trento. The Valdadige appellation, whose *rosso* and *bianco* are each made from a combination of several varieties, extends south from Trento and into the province of Verona. Wines from Trentino include those of Bollini, Cavit (an association of cooperative cellars), the Mezzacorona cooperative, Maso Poli, Pojer & Sandri, Zeni, and the enological institute of San Michele all'Adige. Also, such renowned sparkling-wine firms as Ferrari and Equipe 5 are located in Trentino.

The province of Alto Adige was once part of the Austro-Hungarian Empire, and even today many of its residents are more likely to speak German than Italian, and to refer to the area as Südtirol, or South Tyrol. The varieties cultivated in Alto Adige are virtually the same as in Trentino; Schiava is the dominant red and, now that it has been identified correctly, Chardonnay may be the most widely planted white. As in Trentino and Friuli, the Chardonnay produced in Alto Adige was granted DOC status in 1984. Incidentally, the Traminer grape, which achieved its principal success in Alsace, is thought to have its origins near the Alto Adige village of Termeno (Tramin in German).

Just as the most extensive DOC of Trentino is so named, so Alto Adige is the biggest appellation of the region around Bolzano. There are more than a dozen varieties whose names may be combined with Alto Adige, as Schiava dell'Alto Adige, Pinot Grigio dell'Alto Adige, and so on. Because many of these wines are exported to Germany and Austria, however, the appellation Alto Adige is likely to be replaced on a label with its German equivalent, Südtirol, as in Südtiroler Merlot or Südtiroler Cabernet. And because a number of grape varieties have different names in German than in Italian, a wine such as Schiava dell'Alto Adige becomes Südtiroler Vernatsch and Pinot Grigio dell'Alto Adige becomes Südtiroler Ruländer. Other varieties whose names may vary from one label to another are Pinot Nero and Blauburgunder, Pinot Bianco and Weissburgunder, Traminer Aromatico and Gewürztraminer, and Riesling Renano and Rheinriesling. A further complication occurs in the case of the wines made from the indigenous Lagrein grape—if vinified as a rosé, it is usually labeled Lagrein Kretzer, the red as Lagrein Dunkel; the Italian equivalents are Lagrein Rosato and Lagrein Scuro, respectively.

The DOC Terlano (Terlaner in German) is used for white wines made from half a dozen different varieties, and labeled accordingly, as Terlano Sylvaner, for example. A wine labeled simply Terlano (or Terlaner) is a blend of several varieties, with Pinot Bianco making up at least half the total. Valle Isarco is another white-wine district whose vineyards, northeast of Bolzano, extend along the Isarco River. Meranese di Collina is a light red wine made from Schiava near the town of Merano.

Perhaps the best-known DOC of Alto Adige is Lago di Caldaro or Caldaro (Kalterersee in German), whose light red wines are made primarily from Schiava. Although most of the vineyards that produce Caldaro are in Alto Adige, the zone extends into Trentino as well. The DOC Santa Maddalena (Sankt Magdalener in German) is situated just north of Bolzano; this light red wine, too, is made from Schiava. Firms that produce Alto Adige wines include Schloss Schwanburg, Hofstätter, Kettmeir, Alois Lageder, and in limited quantities, Tiefenbrunner and Giorgio Grai. Santa Margherita, whose headquarters are in the eastern Veneto, is best known for its Pinot Grigio and Chardonnay made from grapes grown in the Alto Adige and Trentino. The firm also produces many other wines from the Tre Venezie, including Cabernet, Merlot, and Tocai from Lison-Pramaggiore, a sparkling Prosecco, and such proprietary white wines as Cuvée Margherita and Luna dei Feldi, the latter a blend of Chardonnay, Müller-Thurgau, and Traminer.

TUSCANY AND CENTRAL ITALY

The region of Tuscany, with Florence as its capital, is the home of one of the most famous red wines in the world: Chianti. Forty-five to fifty million cases are produced annually in Tuscany, about a quarter of which are entitled to DOC and DOCG status; of that, Chianti, with an annual production of nine to ten million cases, accounts for more than three-quarters. Perhaps no wine was as closely associated with a particular bottle as Chianti was with the straw-covered *fiasco,* or flask. In recent years, the distinctive and picturesque *fiasco* has virtually disappeared from retail shelves here, and is now used primarily for wines sold to tourists in Italy. The expensive hand labor required to weave the straw meant that in many cases the consumer was paying more for the straw than for the wine in the bottle. And because *fiaschi* are difficult to store properly on their sides, they were unsuitable for the region's finest wines, which benefit from bottle age. But the principal reason that Chianti producers were delighted to discontinue the use of *fiaschi* is that they perpetuated the image of Chianti as a cheap and ordinary wine, obscuring the fact that the best examples can be taken seriously and are well worth the higher prices at which they must be sold.

The wines of Chianti are generally divided into two basic categories. One is the young, fresh, light-bodied, and occasionally *frizzante* wine served in the trattorias of Florence as early as March following the vintage; the other is a bigger, more tannic wine that needs time to mature in cask and bottle. Both styles are made from the same four or five grape varieties. According to the DOC law established in 1967, and in effect until 1984, Sangiovese accounted for 50 to 80 percent, blended with

10 to 30 percent of Canaiolo, and 10 to 30 percent of two white grapes, Trebbiano and Malvasia. Up to 5 percent of Colorino or certain other varieties could also be used. Sangiovese contributes body and character, Canaiolo delicacy and fruitiness, and the white grapes soften the wine. The original blending formula, established by Barone Bettino Ricasoli in the late nineteenth century, consisted of 85 percent Sangiovese, 10 to 15 percent Canaiolo, and 5 percent Malvasia, the latter to be included only for those wines meant to be consumed young. When the DOC laws were established, they reflected the relatively high proportion of white grapes planted in the Chianti region, and since the name Chianti Bianco was discontinued, producers were permitted to use white grapes in the production of the red wine.

Many producers believed that the use of white grapes in more than minimal amounts resulted in a Chianti that was relatively light-bodied, quick to age, and not typical of the appellation. When Chianti was granted a DOCG, in 1984, these considerations were taken into account. Sangiovese must make up to 75 to 90 percent of the total, and the proportions of white grapes now permitted for Chianti may vary from only 5 to 10 percent (and from 2 to 5 percent for Chianti Classico). Also, the proportion of nontraditional grapes that may be used for Chianti—Cabernet Sauvignon, for example—has been increased from 5 to 10 percent. Maximum production per acre has been reduced by about a third as well.

The traditional vinification of Chianti makes use of an unusual technique called *governo alla toscana*. Especially ripe grapes are placed on trays or hung on hooks for several weeks in well-ventilated rooms to dry out, which concentrates their sugar content. The grapes are then crushed, and when they begin to ferment, they are added to the wine already made in the normal way. The *governo* system adds body and alcohol to the new wine, and—because it induces malolactic fermentation—suppleness as well. This technique was traditionally associated with wines meant to be consumed young, but in practice it was also used by some producers for their better wines. Today, what is still referred to as the *governo* system rarely makes use of specially dried grapes, which is an expensive process, but rather of grape con-

CENTRAL AND SOUTHERN ITALY

centrate, which is juice whose natural sugar content has been concentrated by sophisticated means. Because chaptalization, the addition of sugar to fermenting must to increase a wine's alcohol content, is illegal in Italy, this adaptation of the *governo* process is now used for almost all Chianti, especially in poor years, when the grapes lack adequate sugar.

The quality of Chianti can vary greatly from one label to another, especially since some wines are bottled within a few months and fade quickly, while others are aged in wood for two or three years and improve in bottle for another five. Whereas each vintage of the famous red wines of Bordeaux and Burgundy, for example, is kept in barrel approximately the same length of time before being bottled, the wines of Chianti are aged depending on their character and quality. It is not unusual for a firm to be bottling the wines of a recent light vintage while the bigger wines of a previous vintage are still maturing in large casks. This leads to another distinction to be made among the wines of Chianti, based on the age of the wines. A Chianti that is at least three years old can be sold as a *Riserva*. The required aging need not take place entirely in wood, but may be a combination of cask and bottle, although the DOCG laws specify that a *Riserva* must be aged a minimum of one year in cask. Most producers bottle *Riservas* only in the best years, and use only the best part of the crop; wines so labeled generally represent the finest Chianti available.

Within the Chianti region is the inner Chianti Classico zone, which lies directly between Florence and Siena. Its boundaries were defined more than 250 years ago, and the producers within the zone claim that theirs is the only true Chianti. The best wines from the Chianti Classico zone are acknowledged to display more body, character, and longevity than most other Chianti, but since wine made in the surrounding area has been sold as Chianti for well over a hundred years, the vineyard proprietors in the original zone formed a Chianti Classico *consorzio* in 1924 to define the limits of the Classico area and to regulate the quality and authenticity of its wines. The seal of the Chianti Classico *consorzio,* which appears on the neck of the bottle, is the *gallo nero,* or black rooster, on a gold ground surrounded by a red circle, which has become one of the best-known quality symbols in the world of wine. When the DOC laws for Chianti went into effect in 1967, they confirmed the geographical limits of the Classico zone as originally defined by the *consorzio,* so a wine may be entitled to the DOC Chianti Classico even if its producer is not a member of the *consorzio.* Consequently, the *consorzio* no longer promotes the black rooster as a guarantee of a wine's appellation of origin, but of its superior quality and continues to act as a self-regulating body with somewhat stricter standards than those established by the DOC and DOCG laws. For example, a certain proportion of Chianti Classico wines are rejected each year by a *consorzio* tasting panel as not being up to the standards of the black rooster seal.

In the past fifteen years, the area planted in vines in the Classico zone has increased considerably, and production has more than doubled. About three million cases of Chianti Classico are produced today, which accounts for a third of all the wine made in the Chianti region. Most proprietors within the Classico zone belong to the *consorzio,* but some major shippers, including Brolio, Antinori, and Ruffino, prefer to trade on their own reputations without benefit of the black rooster. Melini and Cecchi are now among the biggest producers of Chianti Classico within the *consorzio,* whose name has been officially changed to Consorzio del Marchio Storico—Chianti Classico.

What this means to the consumer is that of the wines labeled with the DOCG Chianti Classico (which account for about two-thirds of the Chianti shipped to this country), some also carry the black-rooster neck strip, others do not. Among the dozens of Chianti Classico producers whose wines are found here are Antinori (which also produces the single-vineyard Peppoli and Badia Passignano), Badia a Coltibuono, Brolio, Castellare di Castellina, Castello d'Albola, Castello di Ama, Castello di Fonterutoli, Castello di Gabbiano, Castello di Querceto, Castello dei Rampolla, Castello di Uzzano, Castello di Verrazzano, Castello Vicchiomaggio, Castello di Volpaia, Felsina, Fontodi, Isole e Olena, Melini, Monsanto, Monte Vertine, Nozzole, Riecine, Rocco della Macie, San Felice, Terrabianca, and Ruffino (which is known for Riserva Ducale and also produces the single-vineyard Aziano and Santedame). A number of these firms also make non-DOC proprietary red wines that are described farther on.

There are six delimited areas within the Chianti region in addition to the Classico zone—Colli Aretini, Colli Fiorentini, Colli Senesi, Colline Pisane, Montalbano, and Rufina—but their names are not often seen on bottles shipped here. In 1927, producers in the Colli Fiorentini zone formed their own *consorzio,* whose emblem consists of a pink cherub, or *putto,* on a blue ground. In the past few years this *consorzio* has expanded to include producers in the other non-Classico zones, and they, too, may use the *putto* seal.

The best-known firm outside the Classico area is Frescobaldi, whose vineyards are situated east of Florence in the Rufina zone (not to be confused with Ruffino). Frescobaldi's best-known Chianti comes from their Castello di Nipozzano estate; Montesodi, produced only in the best vintages, and in limited quantities, comes from a specific vineyard within that estate. Pomino, a small district within the Chianti Rufina zone whose name has long been used by Frescobaldi for both red and white wines, was granted DOC status in 1983. The white, much better known, is made primarily from Pinot Bianco and Chardonnay; a barrel-aged version is labeled Il Benefizio. The red Pomino is a blend of Sangiovese and Cabernet, and may include Merlot and Pinot Noir.

Over the years, an increasing number of producers within the Chianti region have experimented with wines made only with red grapes, or with a proportion of Cabernet Sauvignon, and thus not entitled to the Chianti appellation. One of the best known is Tignanello, first made by the Antinori firm in 1971, again in 1975, and in most vintages since 1979. The wine consists of Sangiovese with about 20 percent of Cabernet Sauvignon and is aged in *barriques,* the small oak barrels traditionally used in Bordeaux. The concept of a rich, concentrated, *barrique*-aged red has appealed to many other producers. Monte Vertine created Le Pergole Torte, made entirely from Sangiovese, and red wines made entirely or primarily from Sangiovese include Ania of Gabbiano, Coltassala of Volpaia, Concerto of Fonterutoli, Flaccia-

nello della Pieve of Fontodi, Fontalloro of Felsina, San-
gioveto of Badia a Coltibuono, and I Sodi di San Niccolo
of Castellare. Antinori went on to produce Solaia, which
is made primarily from Cabernet Sauvignon with some
Sangiovese; other wines that emphasize Cabernet Sauvignon include Sammarco of Rampolla and Tinscvil of
Monsanto. Wines such as these fall outside the bounds
of existing DOC laws, and are thus entitled only to the
designation Vino da Tavola, or table wine; in practice,
many have become quite famous and are among the
most expensive wines of Italy. Producers elsewhere in
Tuscany have also created proprietary wines, and additional examples of these so-called "super Tuscans" are
mentioned farther on.

A few producers, led by Ruffino, have established a
category known as Predicato for special red and white
wines. The red-wine designations are Predicato di Bitur-
ica, for wines made primarily from Cabernet Sauvignon,
with up to 30 percent of Sangiovese; and Predicato di
Cardisco, for wines made with a minimum of 90 percent
of Sangiovese.

Although the DOC Chianti applies only to red wines,
most firms also produce a white wine. Some are labeled
simply as Bianco, others are marketed with proprietary
names. Several producers, including Antinori, Brolio,
Frescobaldi, and Ruffino, created the name Galestro for
a special Tuscan white wine. It must be fermented at a
low temperature, to retain its fruit and delicacy, and its
alcohol content may not exceed 10.5 percent. Galestro,
which is now produced by more than a dozen firms, is
made primarily from Trebbiano and Malvasia, along
with such varieties as Pinot Bianco, Pinot Grigio, and
Sauvignon.

Just as many producers have created non-DOC proprietary reds, so they have made nontraditional whites,
primarily barrel-aged Chardonnay, although Sauvignon
Blanc, Pinot Bianco, and Pinot Grigio have also been
planted in the region. Here, too, some firms have chosen
to use one of the two Predicato designations for white
wines—Predicato del Muschio for Chardonnay and Predicato del Selvante for Sauvignon Blanc.

Tuscan white wines for which DOCs have been established include Bianco di Pitigliano, Bianco Vergine Val-

dichiana, and Val d'Arbia. The well-known Vernaccia di San Gimignano, made from that grape variety on hillside vineyards near the picturesque medieval town of San Gimignano, about twenty-five miles southwest of Florence, has been elevated to DOCG. This attractive dry wine is one of only two officially defined whites in Tuscany not made primarily from Trebbiano and Malvasia (the other is Pomino); producers include Riccardo Falchini, Guicciardini Strozzi, and Teruzzi & Puthod, whose wine is labeled Ponte a Rondolino, and who also make a barrel-aged version labeled Terre di Tufo.

Vin Santo is an unusual white wine produced throughout Tuscany, usually from Trebbiano and Malvasia. The grapes are dried to concentrate their natural sugar, crushed and fermented in small barrels, where they are left for a minimum of three years. The resulting wine, which is likely to have 15 or 16 percent of alcohol, may be dry or sweet, and good examples are characterized by an intense, complex, and somewhat oxidized taste reminiscent of sherry.

Carmignano, a small district fifteen miles west of Florence, is actually contained within the Chianti Montalbano zone. Its wines traditionally contain a small proportion of Cabernet Sauvignon, and are usually firmer and longer-lived than the Chianti produced from adjoining vineyards. The best-known producer of this district, which was elevated to DOCG in 1990, is Contini Bonacossi, whose wines are labeled Villa di Capezzana and Villa di Trefiano. Barco Reale is a name used for a younger version of Carmignano, and Ghiaie della Furba is a proprietary name created by Contini Bonacossi for a barrel-aged Cabernet-Merlot blend. Other producers include Fattoria Ambra and Fattoria Il Poggiolo.

The Bolgheri district, near the Tuscan coast, southeast of Livorno, has been granted a DOC appellation for its white and rosé, but the region is far better known for its reds. Sassicaia, from the San Guido estate, is made from Cabernet Sauvignon, with a small proportion of Cabernet Franc; although the vineyard was planted in the 1940s, the wine was not put on the market until the 1970s, when it established a reputation as one of the finest reds of Italy. More recently, Lodovico Antinori created the Ornellaia estate, whose principal red wine, labeled Ornellaia, is a Cabernet-Merlot blend; Poggio alle Gazze is made from Sauvignon Blanc and Sémillon, and Masseto is made entirely from Merlot. Grattamacco, also produced in this district, is a blend of Sangiovese and Cabernet.

The village of Montalcino, about twenty miles southeast of Siena, gives its name to one of Italy's most famous red wines—Brunello di Montalcino. Brunello is the local name for a variant of Sangiovese known as Sangiovese Grosso. The wine in its present form—rich, wood-aged, long-lived, and from the Brunello grape alone—was first made in the late nineteenth century by Ferruccio Biondi-Santi, whose estate, Il Greppo, continues to produce the best-known and most expensive examples. The increasing fame of this wine has resulted in extensive new plantings which have increased from two hundred acres in the 1960s to more than twenty-five hundred acres producing the equivalent of 300,000 to 400,000 cases a year, although not all of this wine as bottled as Brunello di Montalcino. The wine marketed as Brunello di Montalcino, which has been elevated to DOCG status, may not be sold until the fifth year after the harvest and must age for a minimum of three and a half years in cask, four and a half for a *Riserva*. The best of them are among the finest and longest-lived of all Italian red wines, but there are those who feel that the mandatory three and a half years in cask can result in wines that are too tannic, woody, and somewhat dried-out, especially in lesser vintages. As a result, many firms also produced a second wine from Brunello grapes that was not aged as long in wood and was more accessible when young. In 1984, the DOC Rosso di Montalcino was established for such wines, which may be sold a year after the vintage and need not be aged in wood; in practice, more than half the crop from this district is sold as Rosso di Montalcino rather than as Brunello di Montalcino. Besides Biondi-Santi, the leading producers include Altesino, Argiano, Case Basse, Castelgiocondo, Tenuta Caparzo, Tenuta Col d'Orcia, Emilio Costanti, Fattoria dei Barbi, Lisini, Mastrojanni, Il Poggione, Val di Suga, and Castello Banfi. Many producers also make a proprietary wine, such as Ca' del Pazzo of Caparzo, Palazzo Altesi of Altesino, and Brusco dei Barbi of Fattoria dei Barbi.

In the early 1980s, the owners of Banfi Vintners, the American firm that imports Riunite Lambrusco, created extensive new vineyards and a large modern winery in the Montalcino area. Under the direction of enologist Ezio Rivella, more than two thousand acres were planted on a seven-thousand-acre property called Castello Banfi. Part of the vineyards produce Moscadello di Montalcino, a sweet, low-alcohol, lightly sparkling white wine; the remaining acreage is planted with Brunello, for Brunello di Montalcino and for a Rosso di Montalcino labeled Centine; Cabernet Sauvignon, marketed with the name Tavernelle; Chardonnay, labeled Fontanelle; and several other varieties, including Pinot Grigio, Sauvignon Blanc, Pinot Noir, Merlot, and Syrah.

From Montepulciano, situated fifteen miles east of Montalcino, comes a red wine called Vino Nobile di Montepulciano. The *nobile* does not derive from the character of the wine, but from the fact that it was first produced by the local nobility in the fourteenth century. Vino Nobile di Montepulciano is made primarily from the Sangiovese grape (known locally as Prugnolo) in a district that overlaps part of the Chianti region—both Montepulciano and Montalcino are in the Colli Senesi zone—and many of the producers make both a Chianti and a Vino Nobile from their vineyards. Although Vino Nobile, unlike Chianti, must be aged a minimum of two years in wood, the quality of these wines is uneven— some are distinctive, complex, and long-lived, others are similar to Chianti. The DOC Rosso di Montepulciano was established for a younger, less complex version of Vino Nobile di Montepulciano. Producers include Avignonesi (who also make a proprietary wine labeled Grifi from Sangiovese and Cabernet), Fassati, Fattoria del Cerro, Fattoria di Fognano, Poderi Boscarelli, Poliziano, and Tenuta Trerose.

Umbria

Adjoining Tuscany to the southeast is the region of Umbria, whose capital is Perugia, and whose best-known wine is Orvieto. The hilltop village of Orvieto, situated about halfway between Florence and Rome, is dominated by its famous cathedral, begun in the late thirteenth century. The white wine of Orvieto has a long history, but its popularity was gradually eclipsed by such wines as Soave and Verdicchio. In the past few years, however, a number of Tuscan firms have taken a greater interest in this wine; well over a million cases a year are produced, and it is now much more widely available here. Orvieto, made primarily from Trebbiano (known locally as Procanico), with lesser amounts of Malvasia, Grechetto, and Verdello, is marketed either as *secco*, dry, or *abboccato*, semisweet. It is the *abboccato* version of this wine that established its fame, but today, in response to consumer demand for dry white wines, it is Orvieto *secco* that is most often seen. Castello della Sala of Antinori, the best-known estate of Orvieto, also produces several proprietary wines, including Cervaro della Sala, a barrel-aged blend of Chardonnay and Grechetto, and Borro della Sala, a blend of Sauvignon Blanc and Procanico; other producers include Barberani, Bigi, Decugnano dei Barbi, Ruffino, Le Velette, and Conte Vaselli.

The red and white wines of Torgiano, produced a few miles south of Perugia, have achieved recognition in recent years due to the efforts of its leading producer, Giorgio Lungarotti. The red wine, which the Lungarotti firm markets under the proprietary name Rubesco, is made primarily from Sangiovese, plus some Canaiolo; special lots are given longer wood-aging and bottled as Rubesco Riserva, whose official appellation, Torgiano Rosso Riserva, has been elevated to DOCG. The white wine, made from Trebbiano and Grechetto, is labeled Torre di Giano. Lungarotti's extensive vineyards include plantings of Chardonnay and Cabernet Sauvignon, bottled and labeled as such; a proprietary red wine, San Giorgio, is a blend of Sangiovese, Canaiolo, and Cabernet Sauvignon.

The town of Montefalco, some miles southeast of Torgiano, gives its name to a red wine made primarily from Sangiovese. The district also produces a rich, full-flavored red from the Sagrantino grape called Montefalco Sagrantino; this wine, sometimes compared to Amarone, has been granted DOCG status.

The Marches

Verdicchio, one of Italy's most popular white wines, is produced in the region of the Marches, situated east of Umbria, along the Adriatic Sea. Just as Chianti was long associated with the straw-covered *fiasco*, so Verdicchio, named after the grape variety from which it is primarily made, owes some of its success to the distinctive amphora-shaped bottle in which it is sold. The complete name of the DOC is Verdicchio dei Castelli di Jesi—Jesi is a village northwest of the city of Ancona—and most bottles are so labeled. Southwest of Jesi is another, smaller district whose wines are entitled to the DOC Verdicchio di Matelica, but this name is rarely seen here. Fazi-Battaglia is the best-known producer; others include Garafoli and Umani Ronchi.

The most extensive DOC district in the Marches produces light red wine entitled to the appellation Rosso Piceno; the wine is made from Sangiovese and Montepulciano. Rosso Cònero, another red wine from this region, is made primarily from Montepulciano.

Emilia-Romagna

Emilia-Romagna, the region that adjoins Tuscany to the north, is famous for its hearty cuisine, and its capital, Bologna, is as esteemed by Italian gastronomes as Lyons is by the French. Emilia-Romagna's best-known wine is Lambrusco, which has become the best-selling Italian wine in America. Lambrusco, made by the Charmat process used for many of the world's sparkling wines, is a slightly sweet red wine, relatively low in alcohol, with just enough sparkle so that it sometimes foams up when poured and leaves a prickly sensation on the tongue when drunk. The wine is moderately priced and, served chilled, has become quite popular with people who find most red wines too dry.

Lambrusco is made from the grape of that name near Modena, northwest of Bologna. There are four DOC Lambrusco wines, the best-known of which is Lambrusco di Sorbara. Lambrusco entitled to a DOC accounts for only a small part of the total production, however, and virtually all the wines shipped to this country are non-

DOC; furthermore, the wines produced for export are grapier and sweeter than the fresh, light dry wines that are enjoyed in the restaurants of Bologna. The popularity of Lambrusco is such that in the mid-1980s it accounted for as much as two-thirds of all the Italian wines sold here. Current figures, however, also include the white and rosé wines shipped by Lambrusco producers under the same brand name. Riunite is the leading brand; others are Cella and Zonin.

A great deal of pleasant red and white wine is made in an extensive area that stretches from Bologna southeast to the Adriatic. The DOC for the white wine is Trebbiano di Romagna, for the red wine, Sangiovese di Romagna. In addition, the appellation Albana di Romagna was elevated from DOC to DOCG, the first white wine so honored. This change has been controversial because many observers believe that the dry white wines made from the Albana grape are, for the most part, undistinguished. There has been an improvement in quality since the DOCG was established, however, and several firms now specialize in semisweet versions, labeled *abboccato* or *amabile;* leading producers include Fattoria Paradiso and Fattoria Zerbina.

FROM ROME TO THE SOUTH

Visitors to the restaurants and cafés of Rome will find themselves drinking the attractive white wines of the Castelli Romani, a group of once-fortified hill towns a few miles southeast of the city. Although this district produces red wines as well, the whites are much better known and are entitled to DOC status. The wines are made primarily from Malvasia and Trebbiano grapes, and although they can all be vinified either dry or semisweet, the ones shipped here are almost always dry. Among the various DOCs, the wines of Marino, Colli Albani, and Colli Lanuvini can be found here, but it is the light-bodied dry white wine from the village of Frascati that is the best-known of all; Fontana Candida is the most familiar brand. Gotto d'Oro is produced by the cooperative cellar of that name. Fiorano is a proprietary wine made in limited quantities by Boncompagni Ludovisi at an estate on the outskirts of Rome; the more famous red is based on Merlot and Cabernet, the white is made from Sémillon.

Beyond the Castelli Romani is the Aprilia district, whose white wine is labeled Trebbiano di Aprilia, and whose two red wines are Merlot di Aprilia and Sangiovese di Aprilia.

A white wine with the colorful name Est! Est!! Est!!! di Montefiascone comes from vineyards situated about fifty miles north of Rome. The name derives from a story—whose details vary from one version to another—about a German bishop who was journeying to Rome and instructed his servant to travel ahead and chalk *Est!* (it is) on the side of those inns whose wines were worth a stop. The servant was so taken with the wines of Montefiascone that he wrote *Est! Est!! Est!!!* on the wall of a local inn. The bishop stopped and apparently concurred, as the legend states that he settled in Montefiascone and spent the rest of his days enjoying its wine. The story is better than the wine, which is not often seen here.

Two wines from the Abruzzi region that are produced in relatively large quantities are the red Montepulciano d'Abruzzo and the white Trebbiano d'Abruzzo. The red, made primarily from Montepulciano grapes to which a small proportion of Sangiovese may be added, should not be confused with Vino Nobile di Montepulciano, a Tuscan wine made from the Sangiovese grape in the village of Montepulciano. Casal Thaulero is the best-known brand of Montepulciano d'Abruzzo.

The region of Campania, whose capital is Naples, includes such tourist attractions as Amalfi, Pompeii, Mount Vesuvius, and the islands of Capri and Ischia. Perhaps the best-known wine name of this region is Lacryma Christi (Tears of Christ), which was finally incorporated into the DOC Vesuvio in 1983. The appellation includes red, white, and rosé wines produced in vineyards just south of Naples; the better wines are entitled to the name Lacryma Christi del Vesuvio. Red and white wines are made on Capri and Ischia and near the town of Ravello, which is also known for its rosé.

The finest wines of the region, however, are made in the province of Avellino, about thirty miles east of Naples, by Mastroberardino, one of Italy's most distinguished producers. The firm makes two distinctive, dry white wines from vineyards in the Irpinia hills, Fiano di Avellino and Greco di Tufo—Fiano and Greco are local grape varieties—and a red wine that takes its name from the village of Taurasi. Made from the Aglianico grape, Taurasi, which was elevated to DOCG, must be aged a minimum of three years. Mastroberardino's Taurasi and Taurasi Riserva, the latter made only in the best vintages, are considered among the finest and longest lived of Italy's red wines.

Apulia, the region that forms the heel of Italy, has gained some unexpected attention because it is the home of Primitivo, a red-wine grape that some ampelographers believe to be identical to the Zinfandel of California. The best-known DOC of Apulia is probably Castel del Monte, whose vineyards are on the hills northwest of the city of Bari. The popular rosé, whose production is greater than that of the red and white together, is made primarily from the local Bombino Nero variety; Rivera, the leading producer, is also known for a barrel-aged red labeled Il Falcone. Salice Salentino is a sturdy red made from the Negroamaro grape; leading producers are Cosimo Taurino and Leone De Castris. The Torre Quarto estate is best known for its red wine made primarily from the Malbec grape. Favonio is the brand name used by Attilio Simonini to market his distinctive varietal wines made from Pinot Bianco, Chardonnay, Cabernet Franc, and Pinot Nero. Aglianico del Vulture, from the adjoining region of Basilicata, is a red wine made from the Aglianico grape grown near Mount Vulture. Cirò, whose red, white, and rosé wines come from hillside vineyards, is the best-known DOC of Calabria.

The island of Sicily produces more than 10 percent of Italy's wines, but much of it is used for the production of vermouth, or to add body and alcohol to wines made elsewhere. Sicily is the home of Marsala, a fortified wine described elsewhere, and of a number of appealing red and white wines whose quality has improved dramatically since the 1960s. The principal grape varieties cultivated in Sicily are likely to be unfamiliar even to those who enjoy the island's wines: Catarratto, Inzolia, and

Caricante for the whites; Nerello Mascalese, Perricone, Calabrese, and Nero d'Avola for the reds.

The island's best-known red and white wines are probably those sold with the proprietary name Corvo, which are produced by the Duca di Salaparuta firm in Casteldaccia, near Palermo; special lots of the white wine are labeled Colomba Platino and a barrel-aged red is labeled Duca Enrico. Regaleali, an estate in the mountains southeast of Palermo, with more than four hundred acres of vineyards, has been revitalized by its owner, Count Tasca d'Almerita, who now produces Chardonnay and Cabernet Sauvignon in addition to traditional wines; a special red is labeled Rosso del Conte, and Nozze d'Oro is a white that includes Sauvignon Blanc. Wines from the slopes of Mount Etna, on the eastern end of Sicily, are entitled to the DOC Etna. Faro is a red wine made on the northeastern tip of the island; Alcamo is a white produced near the town of that name. Settesoli is a cooperative at Menfi; Segesta is a brand name.

Some unusual sweet wines are produced on islands off the coast of Sicily. Malvasia delle Lipari is an appellation for semisweet and sweet wines from the Lipari islands; Carlo Hauner is the best-known producer. Pantelleria, an island southwest of Sicily, is known for its Moscato di Pantelleria; De Bartoli, the leading producer, makes a particularly rich and sweet version, labeled Bukkuram, from sun-dried grapes.

The red and white wines of Sardinia, made from a wide variety of grapes that includes Nuragus, Vermentino, and Cannonau, are occasionally seen here. Sella & Mosca, the island's best-known firm, produces two dry whites, Torbato di Alghero and Vermentino di Sardegna; a dry red from Cannonau; and a sweet, barrel-aged dessert wine labeled Anghelu Ruju.

THE WINES
OF GERMANY

Germany produces only 3 or 4 percent of the world's wines, and its vineyards—situated within a relatively small area in the southwestern part of the country—amount to about a tenth those of France or Italy. Nor is wine the national beverage, as it is in those two countries; beer is the German's daily drink. Nevertheless, Germany makes what are acknowledged to be among the very greatest white wines in the world. The classic Riesling grape, when planted in the best sites along the Rhine and Moselle, produces a truly superb wine with an incomparable bouquet and with extraordinary elegance and breed.

Until the eighteenth century most German wines were red, but today about 85 percent of Germany's vineyards produce white wine. Red wines are still made—primarily from the Blauer Spätburgunder (Pinot Noir), Portugieser, and Trollinger grapes—in Baden and Württemberg, in the Rheinpfalz, along the Ahr, and in the villages of Assmannshausen in the Rheingau and Ingelheim in the Rheinhessen, but with a few notable exceptions, they are generally too light to compare favorably with red wines available from other countries. All of Germany's white wines, with the possible exception of those from Franconia, bear a family resemblance: a distinctive, flowery

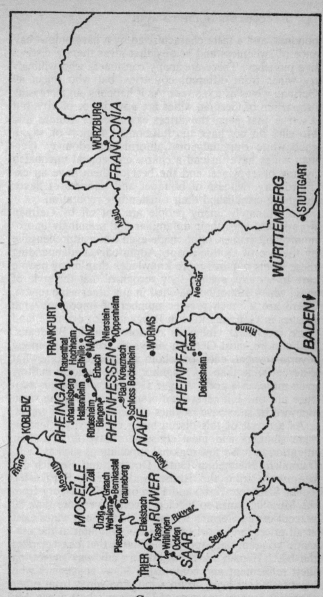

GERMANY

bouquet, and a taste characterized by a harmonious balance of sweetness and acidity that gives them a distinctive piquancy. There are many consumers who willingly try wines from different countries, but who reject all German wines as too sweet. As it happens, an increasing proportion of German wines are now dry or off-dry, but it's true that even the driest examples of Rhines and Moselles do not have the full-bodied dryness of, say, a good white Burgundy or California Chardonnay. German wines have instead a charm and appeal unequaled by any other wines, and the best of them have an extraordinary richness of bouquet and ripeness of flavor that have established their outstanding reputation.

Unfortunately, many people are put off by German wine labels, with their unfamiliar and seemingly unpronounceable names, often made even less comprehensible by the use of Gothic script. Admittedly, understanding these labels requires more knowledge than many people care to acquire, even if they recognize that the style of these wines cannot be matched in any other wine region. There are a much greater number of important wine villages in Germany than in Burgundy, for example, and more individual vineyards of note than in Bordeaux. Futhermore, most German vineyards are split up among several owners, each of whom will make a somewhat different wine than his neighbor. To complicate matters even more, in a good vintage German winemakers produce not one but several different wines from the same vineyard by successive pickings of increasingly ripe grapes.

As a result of this discouraging complexity, German wine shippers and most consumers have limited their attention to just a few regional appellations such as Liebfraumilch, Niersteiner Gutes Domtal, and Bereich Johannisberg from the Rhine, and Bereich Bernkastel, Zeller Schwarze Katz, and Piesporter Michelsberg from the Moselle; wines so labeled account for more than 80 percent of the German wines sold here. Such wines exist at all prices, and most of them can only hint at the aromatic bouquet and opulence of taste that characterizes the best German wines, without in any way suggesting their refinement and complexity. Many consumers who have tasted, at least on occasion, fine wines from other countries remain unaware of Germany's best wines. My own experience suggests that anyone who is offered a good German wine for the first time will almost invariably express amazement and delight that wines of this style and caliber exist.

The German vineyards extend up to, and even slightly beyond, what is known as the northern limit of the vine. Farther north, excessively cold winters will kill the vines, and summers lacking in adequate sunshine would prevent grapes from properly ripening. The best wines are made on slopes and steep hillsides facing south, where their height and direction enable the grapes to catch the maximum amount of sunshine. The poor soil that characterizes these vineyards is unsuitable for any other crop, and the steep incline of many vineyards makes it impossible to use modern machinery. It is by the hand labor of thousands of growers that these vines are tended, and it's only because the wines produced can be so remarkable—and expensive—that it is still commercially worthwhile for these vineyards to be cultivated. There are about fifty thousand growers tending their own vines in Germany, and 75 percent of them own less than five acres. Fewer than a thousand estates consist of more than twenty-five acres, but it is among these larger domains that most of the famous wine-producing names are found.

The Rhine is the informing river of German viticulture, and all German wines are produced either along the Rhine or along the banks of its many tributaries. (The two small regions of Sachsen and Saale-Unstrut, in the former East Germany, are situated south of Berlin along the Elbe River and its tributaries; these vineyards account for less than 1 percent of the German crop.) The principal wine regions along the Rhine itself are the Rheinpfalz, or Palatinate, known for its soft, full, rounded wines; the Rheinhessen, which produces a tremendous quantity of agreeable wines; and the Rheingau, a comparatively small district that produces the very finest of the Rhine wines—elegant, rich, and well balanced. The Nahe joins the Rhine at Bingen, and despite its geographical position halfway between the Rhine and Moselle, its wines have the richness and style of Rhine wines. The Moselle (spelled Mosel in German) joins the Rhine at Koblenz. Its wines, and those of its two tributaries, the Saar and the Ruwer, are light-bodied and fragrant and possess a refreshing crispness derived from their acidity.

The vineyards of Franken, or Franconia, along the Main, produce wines quite different from those of the Rhine and Moselle, and less often seen here. These drier wines have less bouquet and more body, and a distinctive earthy taste. Franconia wines, once referred to generically as Steinweins after its most famous single vineyard, are easy to spot because they are always shipped in the distinctive *Bocksbeutel,* a squat, flat-sided, gourdlike bottle.

The two regions of Baden and Württemberg produce about 25 percent of Germany's wines, and a third of that is red. Stuttgart is the principal city of Württemberg, whose wine villages are spread out on both sides of the Neckar River. Baden is the southernmost of the German wine regions, and part of its vineyards extend between the Black Forest and the Rhine, opposite the Alsace region of France.

Except for the wines of Franconia, just about all German wines are sold in slender tapering bottles—Rhine wines in brown bottles, Moselles in pale green. This distinction can be of help in remembering their general characteristics: the rich, full, deep flavor of the Rhines, and the pale, fresh, delicate, and graceful wines of the Moselle.

Virtually all of Germany's fine wines are made from the Riesling grape, and it is along the Rhine and Moselle that this grape has most successfully demonstrated why it is considered one of the world's half-dozen classic varieties. Riesling needs a long growing season, however, and does not ripen fully every year, so that despite the quality of its wines, it accounts for only 20 percent of the acreage in Germany. It is the principal variety in the Mosel-Saar-Ruwer and the Rheingau, but is planted in less than 20 percent of the Rheinpfalz vineyards, and only 5 percent of those in the Rheinhessen. Until quite recently it could be assumed that the finest wines of the Rheingau and the Mosel-Saar-Ruwer—those from individual vineyards and top estates—were made from Riesling, whether or not the variety was named on the label. Because of increased plantings of other varieties in recent years that assumption can no longer be made, and with few exceptions producers whose wines are made from Riesling now indicate that on their labels.

Riesling is widely planted throughout the world, and although it sometimes retains its name, as in France's Alsace region, the true Riesling of Germany is often identified by a somewhat different name in other countries—Johannisberg Riesling or White Riesling in California, Rheinriesling in Austria, Riesling Renano in Italy, Rjanski Rizling in Yugoslavia, Rhine Riesling in Australia, and so on. More often than not, wines from other European countries that are simply labeled Riesling are made from a variety known as the Welsch Riesling or Italian Riesling, and are rather neutral in taste. A California wine labeled Riesling may actually be made from Sylvaner. It would therefore be a mistake to expect any of the so-called Rieslings produced around the world to have any similarity whatsoever to those of Germany. With few exceptions, even wines made from the true Riesling in other countries lack the elegance, distinctive aroma, and particular combination of fruit and acidity of German Rieslings.

Sylvaner (spelled *Silvaner* in German) was once the most widely cultivated variety, and accounted for almost a third of all plantings as recently as 1960. Today, it covers less than 10 percent of the vineyards, but is still widely found in the Rheinhessen, Rheinpfalz, and Franconia, where it is sometimes called Franken Riesling. Sylvaner produces wines without much finesse or distinction, neutral and low in acid, which makes them useful for blending. Nevertheless, the best examples from good vintages, especially from vineyards in the Rheinhessen, can be very good.

Müller-Thurgau, now the most extensively planted variety in Germany, was developed about a hundred years ago by Professor Müller, who came from Thurgau in Switzerland. It was long assumed to have been a cross of Riesling and Sylvaner, but some ampelographers now believe that it was produced from two clones of Riesling. It has the advantage of being adaptable to a wide variety of soils and ripening early, making it a good all-purpose variety. It produces wines that have an aromatic bouquet when young, and that are mild and low in acid, which makes them useful in blending, although when bottled on their own they age rather quickly.

Traminer, famous in Alsace for its spicy, aromatic wines, is not widely planted in Germany. Ruländer, known as the Pinot Gris in France, Gutedel, known as the Chasselas in Switzerland, and Weissburgunder, or Pinot Blanc, are cultivated to some extent, primarily in Baden. The most significant recent development has been the increased plantings of new varieties. Some, such as Morio-Muskat and Scheurebe, have been known for some time. Others, including Kerner, Bacchus, Faberrebe, Huxelrebe, Ortega, Optima, and Ehrenfelser, have been registered only in the past twenty or thirty years, and these new varieties are now found in some of the best-known estates along the Rhine and, to a lesser extent, the Moselle. Each has particular attributes that make it worth cultivating—resistance to frost, early ripening, higher sugar contents, low acidity—and they are useful for blending with Riesling in lesser years. Some of them are also bottled individually, and marketed with their own names, especially Kerner and Scheurebe.

In most of the world's vineyard districts, a good vintage is one in which the grapes ripen fully and the resulting wine is dry, balanced, and complete, with a proper degree of alcohol. In Germany, the best vintages are those in which the grapes are not only ripe, but overripe, so that the grape sugar and natural flavor extracts present in the grapes will produce wines that are sweet, intense, and complex. These considerations are the basis of the new German wine regulations that went into effect in 1971. The new laws established three basic categories for German wines based not simply on geographical origin, but also on the ripeness of the grapes at the time of picking as expressed by their natural sugar content.

The lowest category of wine is *Deutscher Tafelwein*, German table wine. These wines, which rarely account for more than 5 percent of Germany's total production, can be labeled with only the broadest regional appellations of origin—Rhein-Mosel (which includes the subregions Rhein, Mosel, and Saar), Bayern, Neckar, and Oberrhein—and only if at least 85 percent of the wine was produced in the named region. A wine labeled simply *Tafelwein* can be blended from wines produced out-side Germany. Relatively little *Deutscher Tafelwein* is shipped to this country, even though the category includes the once popular regional wine Moselblümchen. (In 1982 the subcategory *Landwein* was established as the equivalent of the French *vin de pays* for better wines within the *Deutscher Tafelwein* category. A *Landwein* must come from one of fifteen specified regions; its minimum natural alcohol content is slightly higher than for a *Tafelwein;* and it may contain no more than 1.8 percent sugar.)

The most important category of German wines, in terms of volume, is *Qualitätswein bestimmter Anbaugebiete,* quality wines from specified regions, also known as *Q.b.A.* or simply as *Qualitätswein.* There are thirteen delimited regions within the *Qualitätswein* category— Mosel-Saar-Ruwer, Rheingau, Rheinhessen, Rheinpfalz, Nahe, Franken, Württemberg, Baden, Ahr, Hessische Bergstrasse, Mittelrhein, and, since 1990, Sachsen and Saale-Unstrut. Wines from the last five regions listed, which produce about 2 percent of Germany's wines, are almost never seen here. The name of one or another of these regions must appear on the label of every *Qualitätswein,* which gives the consumer at least a general idea of where the wine comes from, no matter how puzzling or unfamiliar the rest of the label may be.

The third and highest category of German wines is *Qualitätswein mit Prädikat,* or quality wine with a special attribute. The special attribute—designated on the label by the word *Kabinett, Spätlese, Auslese, Beerenauslese, Trockenbeerenauslese,* or *Eiswein*—does not reflect the origin of the wine but the ripeness of the grapes when they were picked. Chaptalization, adding sugar to the must, is permitted, for *Tafelwein* and *Qualitätswein,* but is prohibited for *Prädikat* wines. Before 1971, the word *Kabinett*—or *Cabinet,* as it could then be spelled—was used at a grower's discretion to indicate a wine of special quality. Kabinett is now clearly defined as the first level among *Prädikat* wines. *Spätlese* means late-picked, and now refers to wines made from fully ripe grapes that have been left on the vines at least a week after the harvest has begun so that they will ripen even further. Such wines are somewhat sweeter and richer than a Kabinett wine from the same vineyard. A wine labeled *Auslese*, selected picking, is made from especially ripe bunches of grapes that are fermented separately. Auslese wines are even sweeter and richer in taste than those labeled Spätlese, and have a more concentrated flavor. *Beerenauslese*, selected berry picking, is several steps higher in quality and scarcity: grapes that are unusually ripe are picked individually and set aside to make a particularly sweet and intense wine. The very scarcest and most highly prized wines of all are called *Trockenbeerenauslese*, which means selected picking of naturally dried berries. They are made from overripe grapes that have been attacked by *Botrytis cinerea*, the noble rot called *pourriture noble* in Sauternes and *Edelfäule* in Germany. The juice that remains in these shriveled grapes has a very high proportion of natural sugar, and its flavor is intensified to a remarkable degree. The resulting wine, which ferments very slowly and with great difficulty, is the rarest and most extraordinary wine that a German vineyard can produce. It is very sweet, of course, but has a balancing acidity that makes it harmonious rather than cloying.

Beerenauslese and Trockenbeerenauslese wines are made only in exceptionally fine years, and then only in minute quantities. A large estate that produces, say, 500,000 bottles of wine altogether might harvest a thousand bottles of Trockenbeerenauslese and perhaps three times that amount of Beerenauslese; the prices for these rare wines are correspondingly high.

There is one other designation that occasionally appears on a label of *Prädikat* wine—*Eiswein*, or ice wine. An Eiswein is made late in the year from fully ripe grapes that have frozen on the vine when the temperature has dropped to 20°F or less. The frozen grapes are gathered in the early-morning hours, before the sun appears, and are carefully crushed to obtain only the rich unfrozen juice. Because the juice from which this rare wine is made concentrates not only the sugar in the grapes but also the acid, Eiswein is characterized by a relatively high acidity that gives it a distinctive elegance and finesse, as well as exceptional longevity. Until 1982 the Eiswein designation appeared on a label only in conjunction with one of the special attributes, such as Auslese or Beerenauslese. Today, Eiswein has been established as a *Prädikat* on its own, and the minimum sugar requirements are the same as for a Beerenauslese.

Before the new wine laws went into effect, each producer was allowed a certain amount of leeway in determining which of the special designations to put on his labels. Now the minimum requirements for a *Prädikat* wine, and for each additional level of ripeness up to Trockenbeerenauslese, are determined by the wine's Oechsle degree. The Oechsle scale, named after the scientist who invented it in the early nineteenth century, measures the sugar content of unfermented juice. For example, to qualify for the category *Qualitätswein mit Prädikat,* a Rhine wine made from the Riesling must have a minimum natural sugar content of 73° Oechsle; a Moselle, 67° (which is equivalent to about 16 or 17 percent sugar, and to a potential alcohol content of about 9 percent). Such wine could be labeled Kabinett, the lightest and least-expensive level of *Prädikat* wines. The Oechsle degree required for each of the special attributes varies from region to region and from one grape variety to another; the minimums established for a Riesling from the Rheingau are 85° for a Spätlese, 95° for an Auslese, 125° for a Beerenauslese, and 150° for a Trockenbeerenauslese (which is equivalent to about 33 percent sugar; the bottled wine is likely to contain only 6 or 7 percent alcohol).

Since the quality of German wines is to a large extent determined by the ripeness of the grapes as defined by the Oechsle scale, it is possible to make some interesting comparisons among German vintages. In 1984, for example, only 7 percent of the crop was entitled to the *Prädikat* designation, and *Prädikat* wines accounted for only 20 percent or so of the 1986 and 1987 vintages, and most of that was Kabinett. In such excellent vintages as 1988, 1989, 1990, 1992, and 1993, however, 45 to 60 percent of the crop consisted of *Prädikat* wines, and most of that was of Spätlese and Auslese quality. The variations within a specific district can be even more dramatic—barely 2 percent of Kabinett wines one year, then 60 or 70 percent of Spätlese and Auslese wines the next.

Ripeness plays a role not simply in the quality, but also in the variety of German wines. In most wine regions around the world, a producer makes wine from the same vineyard or group of vineyards every year—the number of wines does not change, only their quality. In Germany, a large estate on the Rheingau may own vines in, say, thirty vineyards in half a dozen villages. In a fine year, when each vineyard yields a wide range of *Prädikat* wines, the estate may bottle more than a hundred different wines. In a lesser year, when few wines exceed the *Qualitätswein* category, the estate may produce only a third as many wines.

Grape juice that contains a high proportion of natural sugar will not be able to complete its fermentation, and it is the residual sugar remaining in the wine that has traditionally given German wines whatever degree of sweetness they possessed. About forty years ago some German winemakers began to use *Süssreserve*, or sweet reserve, and this technique has now been adopted by most producers. *Süssreserve* is unfermented grape juice, rich in sugar, that is kept aside and then added to a wine just before bottling to increase its sugar content. This permits the winemaker to ferment his wines out until they are dry, since he will have the opportunity of adding sweetness back later on. The winemaker no longer has to arrest the fermentation of a Kabinett, Spätlese, or even Auslese when just the right amount of residual sugar remains in the wine, and he can control the exact degree of sweetness of the bottled wine. About 15 percent of a good crop is set aside as *Süssreserve*, which may be used to sweeten the wines of a poor year as well. Not all producers are *Süssreserve*, and in exceptionally ripe years, when very high Oechsle degrees are achieved, some producers prefer to arrest the fermentation in an Auslese wine while residual sugar remains, although they will probably permit Kabinett and Spätlese wines to ferment until they are dry.

By way of suggesting the relative sweetness of the different *Prädikat* wines, there might be 25 to 30 grams per liter—2.5 to 3 percent—of sugar in a Kabinett wine (compared to 25 grams or so in a typical Liebfraumilch); 35 to 50 grams in a Spätlese, 60 to 80 grams in an Auslese, 100 to 125 grams in a Beerenauslese, and 150 to 200 grams—15 to 20 percent—in a Trockenbeerenauslese. These are only general figures, however, because

there are bound to be variations in the sugar content—
and intensity of flavor—of wines labeled Spätlese or
Auslese from different regions, different vintages, and
different producers. Note that minimum sugar requirements—expressed in Oechsle degrees—apply to the unfermented juice when the grapes are picked, not to the
wine when it is bottled.

Although the sweetness of one of these wines is the
most obvious aspect of its taste, the winemakers consider
that the amount of acidity present is just as important
because it determines whether the wine is harmonious
and well-balanced or simply sweet and clumsy. In addition, the presence of botrytised grapes, those affected
by the noble rot, adds a distinctive, honeyed flavor and
complexity of taste that sweetness alone cannot provide.
Although the particular taste that comes from botrytised
grapes is almost always found in Trockenbeerenauslese
and Beerenauslese wines, there are years—such as 1976,
1989 and 1992—in which the noble rot is so prevalent
in the vineyards that even Auslese and Spätlese wines
display the characteristically honeyed taste. Sometimes
Botrytis cinerea does not occur even in a good vintage.
In 1959, 1983, and 1988 for example, grapes dried up on
the vines without being affected by the noble rot. Even
though Trockenbeerenauslese wines were produced,
they lacked a botrytised character.

The presence of the noble rot also affects the sequence in which grapes are harvested in Germany. In a
typical good vintage, each level of *Prädikat* wines is harvested in order of increasing ripeness. When there is a
great deal of noble rot, however, growers may begin the
harvest by picking the grapes for Auslese and Beerenauslese wines, and there are even instances when the
first wines to be made were Trockenbeerenauslese. The
usual description of the German winemaker consciously
deciding whether or not to risk leaving his grapes on the
vine for an additional two or three weeks of ripening is
not always an accurate one. What the winemaker must
decide in an outstanding year is just how much Trockenbeerenauslese and Beerenauslese wines to make, since
the grapes he sets aside for these superb wines will, to
some extent, diminish the richness and concentration of
the rest of the crop. The one wine that is always pro-

duced by a conscious decision is Eiswein. Since a grower may have to wait until December or even January for the grapes to freeze on the vines, he can produce an Eiswein only by deliberately leaving a part of the crop unpicked and hoping that the necessary frost occurs before the fully ripe grapes simply spoil.

None of the wines described so far is dry, but there are two relatively new styles of wines that are now being made in Germany—Trocken, dry, and Halbtrocken, half-dry. Since the late 1970s, a number of producers have been marketing these wines in an effort to provide the German consumer with a wine he or she can drink with meals, and in some recent vintages Trocken and Halbtrocken wines accounted for as much as a third of all *Qualitätswein*. The proportion is even higher in such regions as Baden and Franconia, and some of the most important estates along the Rhine and Moselle now vinify about half their wines as dry. The maximum permissible sweetness of these wines is determined by a formula based on both sugar and acid. Basically, a Trocken wine cannot exceed 9 grams of sugar, and most have only 4 or 5 grams; a Halbtrocken cannot contain more than 18 grams of sugar, and most have about 14 grams. In a good vintage, a grower may decide to make Trocken and Halbtrocken wines of Spätlese and even Auslese quality by fermenting them out until they are dry, and such wines, made from extra-ripe grapes, have noticeably more body and flavor. Because these wines are so different from traditional German wines, and because most countries have adequate sources of dry white wines, Trocken and Halbtrocken wines are not widely exported. Nevertheless, many estates and shippers market such wines, and they can be found here; consumers often prefer the off-dry, rounder Halbtrocken to the more austere, lighter-bodied Trocken.

Although the success of a vintage and of individual wines in Germany is to a large extent measured in Oechsle degrees, the origin of each wine is still of prime importance, as it is throughout the world, in determining its particular style and personality. The new wine laws have established three increasingly specific appellations of origin within the thirteen *Qualitätswein* regions: *Bereich,* or district; *Grosslage,* or collective vineyard site;

and *Einzellage,* or individual vineyard site. There are thirty-four *Bereiche,* most of whose names are those of well-known wine villages. Since the average size of a *bereich* is about 7,500 acres, these district appellations should not be confused with wines from the village whose name is used. For example, Bereich Johannisberg includes virtually all of the wine-producing villages along the Rheingau. There are only five *Bereiche* for the Mosel-Saar-Ruwer, and the best-known, Bereich Bernkastel, encompasses sixteen thousand acres of vineyards and sixty villages. Bereich Nierstein in the Rheinhessen and Bereich Schloss Böckelheim in the Nahe are other examples of these rather extended regional appellations. It is under such names as these, plus Liebfraumilch, that most branded German wines are sold.

The most specific appellations of origin, as in most wine-producing countries, are those of individual vineyards, now called *Einzellagen.* German labels for individual vineyards almost always indicate the village of origin followed by the vineyard. Thus, a wine labeled Bernkasteler Graben comes from the Graben vineyard in the village of Bernkastel (which takes the possessive *er,* as a person from New York is called a New Yorker). Piesporter Treppchen, Rauenthaler Baiken, and Forster Jesuitengarten are wines that come from individual vineyards, or *Einzellagen,* in the village of Piesport, Rauenthal, and Forst respectively. Exceptions to this rule, vineyards so famous that their names may appear on a label without that of the village in which each is located, include Schloss Johannisberg, Schloss Vollrads, Steinberg, Scharzhofberg, and Maximin Grünhaus.

The new laws reduced the number of individual vineyards in Germany from more than thirty thousand to 2,600, and the minimum size of an *Einzellage* was set at five hectares, or a little more than twelve acres. Many small vineyards were combined, and even sizable vineyards were considerably expanded. Bernkasteler Bratenhöfchen was expanded from six acres to forty-five, Piesporter Goldtröpfchen from eighty-six acres to nearly 260. The average size of the *Einzellagen* created by the new laws is over ninety acres.

Despite the dramatic reduction in the number of individual vineyard names, there are still quite a few for the consumer to keep in mind—118 in the Rheingau, for instance, and over five hundred in the Mosel-Saar-Ruwer. The new laws established an intermediate appellation called a *Grosslage,* which is made up of a number of neighboring *Einzellagen.* A *Grosslage* appellation consists of a village name followed by what seems to be an individual vineyard—Bernkasteler Kurfürstlay, Piesporter Michelsberg, Rauenthaler Steinmächer, Forster Mariengarten. In fact, Bernkasteler Kurfürstlay is a name that can be used for wines made in any one of eleven villages along the Moselle, and six villages along the Rheingau can market their wines as Rauenthaler Steinmächer. There are 152 *Grosslagen* in Germany, including twenty in the Mosel-Saar-Ruwer and ten in the Rheingau. The average size of a *Grosslagen* is fifteen hundred acres. A consumer who does not recognize the names of the principal *Grosslagen* is likely to confuse wines so labeled with those from individual vineyards, especially since many names now used for *Grosslagen,* such as Bernkasteler Badstube and Johannisberger Erntebringer, were actually those of individual vineyards before 1971. The names of the most important *Bereiche, Grosslagen,* and *Einzellagen* for the major wine regions are listed further on.

With few exceptions, each *Einzellage,* or vineyard site, is divided among several owners. Consequently, the names of individual proprietors and domains, whose holdings may be scattered among a number of vineyards in several villages, must also be taken into consideration when choosing German wines. The label of an estate-bottled wine bears the word *Erzeugerabfüllung,* bottled by the producer, followed by the name of the producer. (Before 1971, *Originalabfüllung* was used to indicate an estate-wine.) As in Burgundy, the consumer must have some familiarity with the names of the best producers as well as those of the best vineyards. Unlike Burgundy, however, where most growers bottle only a few thousand cases, there are quite a few large domains in Germany that produce twenty-five thousand to fifty thousand cases of wine a year, and their names consistently appear on any list of German wines. The owners of these large domains—which will be listed region by region farther on—include noble families, orders, and the German state.

Many German winemakers traditionally bottle the contents of each large cask or tank separately, rather than blending them together. Before 1971, the number of the actual cask from which a wine came was sometimes indicated on a label, preceded by *Fass* for Rhine wines, *Fuder* for Moselles. Also, *feine* or *feinste* (as in *feine* Auslese) was an indication by the producer that the wine was especially fine. These designations are no longer permitted, as they are considered too arbitrary. Nevertheless, some estates still bottle the contents of each day's picking separately, and may, therefore, market several different wines labeled Spätlese, Auslese, and so on from a given vintage. Today, the relative qualities of similarly labeled wines might be indicated by the use of different lot numbers on a producer's list, or by the use of different colored capsules on the bottles. The consumer who has already made an effort to remember the names of the best vineyards and best estates may be discouraged to learn that two bottles of Auslese from a particular domain may not, in fact, be identical, but the winemaker's insistence on preserving the quality and individuality of each barrel of his wine must at least be recognized.

In addition to the vineyard proprietors who bottle their own wines and those who sell their wines in bulk to the many German wine shippers, nearly two-thirds of all growers are members of cooperative wine cellars. More than three hundred cooperative cellars exist in Germany today, and they account for about a third of all the wines made. Cooperatives produce a relatively small proportion of wines in the Rheingau, but more than a quarter of the wines of the Mosel-Saar-Ruwer come from cooperatives, half the wines of Franconia, and more than three-quarters of those from Baden and Württemberg. *Winzergenossenschaft* or *Winzerverein*, wine grower's cooperative, are the words you are most likely to see on the label of one of these wines.

Other German words that are useful to know are *Kellerei*, cellar; *Weingut*, wine domain; *Erben*, heirs; *Freiherr*, baron; *Graf*, count; and *Fürst*, prince. Weissherbst, not often seen here, is a rosé produced for the most part in Baden and Württemberg from Blauer Spätburgunder grapes. Schillerwein is a rosé made in Württemberg, from red and white grapes pressed and fermented together.

One other indication that must appear on the labels of all *Qualitätswein* and *Prädikat* wines is the *Amtliche Prüfungsnummer,* or certification number. This is usually shortened to *A.P. Nr.* followed by a numbered code. To obtain a certification number, each lot of wine must undergo laboratory analysis and must be approved at a quality-control tasting.

Despite the exceptional quality of the best German wines, the branded regional wines marketed by a number of German shippers dominate the market here. Most consumers are put off by the diversity of German wine names, and in any case weather conditions do not permit individual producers to make fine wines every year. The simplified labeling and consistent quality of the leading brands, as well as their appealing taste, account for their popularity.

The single best-known wine of Germany is Liebfraumilch, which accounts for half of all the wines exported. The name may have originally referred to the wines produced in the small vineyard belonging to the Liebfrauenkirche in Worms (situated on the border between the Rheinhessen and Rheinpfalz), but the name has long been used for wines produced throughout the Rheinhessen, Rheinpfalz, Rheingau, and Nahe. The laws concerning Liebfraumilch were amended in 1982 and again with the 1990 vintage: the wine must be made primarily from Müller-Thurgau, Sylvaner, Kerner, and Riesling; it must come exclusively from the Rheinhessen, Rheinpfalz, Rheingau, or Nahe (that is, wines from different regions may no longer be blended together); and the name of the region of origin must now appear on the label. In practice, most Liebfraumilch—which must contain a minimum of 1.8 percent sugar—comes from the Rheinhessen and Rheinpfalz and it is unlikely that much Riesling finds its way into the blend. Among the best-known brands are Sichel Blue Nun, Kendermann Black Tower, Deinhard Hanns Christof, Valckenberg Madonna, Goldener Oktober, and Madrigal.

Apart from Liebfraumilch, the most frequently seen

regional appellations are Bereich Bernkastel, Bereich Johannisberg, and Bereich Nierstein. Two brands based on Bereich Bernkastel are Deinhard Green Label and Rudolf Müller Bishop of Riesling. A number of *Grosslagen* wines are also readily available from several shippers, including Bernkasteler Kurfürstlay, Piesporter Michelsberg, Zeller Schwarze Katz, Johannisberger Erntebringer, and Niersteiner Gutes Domtal. At least 85 percent of a wine must come from the *Bereich, Grosslage* or *Einzellage* on the label, and at least 85 percent of a vintage-dated wine must come from that vintage. If a label also indicates the name of a specific grape variety, as in Bereich Bernkastel Riesling or Piesporter Michelsberg Riesling, 85 percent of the wine must be made from the named grape. These requirements apply not only to regional wines, but to estate-bottled wines from individual vineyards as well. In the case of *Prädikat* wines from the top estates, however, it is likely that the wine comes entirely from the vineyard, vintage, and variety shown on the label.

One problem that everyone who admires German wines must face is how to match them with food. *Qualitätswein,* which includes branded regional wines and Liebfraumilch, can certainly be drunk with a meal, especially in warm weather, as can many Kabinett wines. The finer *Prädikat* wines, Spätlese and up, are too sweet to accompany most foods, and not sweet enough to stand up to rich desserts, which tend to overwhelm them. The Germans themselves drink these wines on their own, in the afternoon or late in the evening. The delicate flavor and refreshing acidity of many German wines, especially Moselles, make them a delightful wine to serve as an aperitif before dinner. Since German wines are comparatively low in alcohol—few contain more than 10 percent—they can be drunk more casually and copiously than many of the headier white wines produced elsewhere.

Although white wines are usually consumed young, the finest German whites—Auslese, Beerenauslese, Eiswein, and Trockenbeerenauslese—will improve with a few years of bottle age. The initial sweetness and opulence will give way to a more harmonious and complex taste. Even Spätlese wines, especially those from the Rhine, will acquire added interest with bottle age.

German wine labels are considered the most specific in the world, especially for the finest wines, but a knowledge of German wines is not so easily acquired. There are nearly fourteen hundred wine villages and twenty-six hundred vineyards whose names may appear on a label. Add to that the various levels of ripeness among *Prädikat* wines and the result is a truly awesome number of possibilities. Nevertheless, a rule of thumb can be formulated when selecting German wines: once you decide whether you want a Rhine or Moselle, if you choose a *Prädikat* wine of Spätlese or Auslese quality made from the Riesling in a good vintage, you will be well on your way toward a good bottle. If you then select a wine from one of the top estates, you will often be getting a single vineyard wine as well. In time you can make your own evaluations of wines from different vineyards and from different estates, but by focusing on the vintage, special attribute, and the reputation of a major estate, you can drink fine wines without having to learn the names of villages and vineyards. Anyone who has enjoyed a few bottles of fine German wine, however, will want to know more about just where each wine comes from, and the following pages contain some basic information about the major regions.

THE GERMAN WINE REGIONS

Rheinpfalz

The Rheinpfalz usually produces more wine than any other region in Germany, and enjoys the warmest weather as well. Its wines are generally fuller, softer, and less acid than those of more northerly regions, and Auslese and Beerenauslese wines are not uncommon. The Pfalz vineyards are not actually situated along the Rhine, but extend for about fifty miles along the slopes of the Haardt Mountains, ten or fifteen miles west of the river. The Deutsche Weinstrasse, or German wine road, runs through the entire region almost to the northern end of Alsace. Nearly half the Pfalz wines are made from Müller-

Thurgau, Sylvaner, and Kerner, and this region supplies much of Germany's carafe wines. Riesling predominates in the Middle Haardt, however, the central section that contains the best wine-producing villages: Forst, Deidesheim, Ruppertsberg, Wachenheim, and Bad Dürkheim (whose wines are labeled simply Dürkheimer). When choosing wines from this district, it is helpful to remember that three producers in particular are famous for the high quality of their wines: Bassermann-Jordan, Bürklin-Wolf, and von Buhl. In addition, Müller-Catoir and Lingenfelder (known especially for barrel-aged Spätburgunder) are well respected.

The two *Bereiche* names of the Pfalz are rarely seen, and of its twenty-six *Grosslagen*, the best-known are Forster Mariengarten and Deidesheimer Hofstück.

VILLAGE	IMPORTANT VINEYARDS
Forst	Kirchenstück, Jesuitengarten, Ungeheuer, Pechstein
Deidesheim	Leinhöhle, Hohenmorgen, Herrgottsacker, Grainhübel, Nonnenstück
Ruppertsberg	Hoheburg, Nussbien, Reiterpfad
Wachenheim	Goldbächel, Rechbächel, Gerümpel
Dürkheim	Speilberg, Herrenmorgen, Steinberg

Rheinhessen

The Rheinhessen begins where the Rheinpfalz ends, at Worms, and these two regions account for almost half the vineyard acreage in Germany. The Rheinhessen is not an elongated region, but triangular, with Worms, Mainz, and Bingen as its three points. Müller-Thurgau and Sylvaner account for a third of the acreage, and a certain amount of full, ripe Spätlese and Auslese wines are made from these grapes. The Rheinhessen is also the area with the most extensive plantings of new varieties, and nearly a third of the vineyards consist of Scheurebe, Bacchus, Kerner, and Faberrebe. The bulk of Rheinhessen wines are used to make up shippers' regional blends, however, notably Liebfraumilch.

The best wines of the region come from a number of villages situated along the Rhine as it flows north toward Mainz. Riesling is extensively planted in this section, whose best-known villages are Nierstein, Nackenheim, and Oppenheim. To this group must be added the village of Bingen, situated some miles away opposite the Rheingau village of Rüdesheim; Scharlachberg is Bingen's best-known vineyard. The estates of Heyl zu Herrnsheim and Anton Balbach, both located in Nierstein, produce some of the region's best wines.

Bereich Nierstein is the best-known of the region's three *Bereiche*. Of the twenty-four *Grosslagen*, the ones most frequently seen are Niersteiner Spiegelberg, Niersteiner Gutes Domtal, and Oppenheimer Krötenbrunnen.

VILLAGE	IMPORTANT VINEYARDS
Nierstein	Hipping, Orbel, Pettenthal, Hölle, Olberg
Oppenheim	Sackträger, Herrenberg, Daubhaus

Rheingau

The Rheingau accounts for only 3 percent of Germany's vineyards, but it has a higher proportion of Riesling—about 80 percent—than any other region. Its best wines are, with the very best of the Moselle, the finest wines of Germany. Rheingau wines have more body and depth, and perhaps more character, than those of the Moselle, which impress more with their grace and delicacy. Spätlese and Auslese wines from the Rheingau are richer and more opulent than those of the Moselle, and generally longer-lived as well.

The Rheingau extends along the Rhine for about

twenty-five miles as it flows from east to west. The vineyards face south, which enables them to obtain the maximum amount of sunshine, and they are protected from cold winds by the Taunus Mountains to the north. There are two villages that are situated along this stretch of the Rhine, but that are considered as part of the Rheingau: Hochheim, which is actually on the Main River just before it joins the Rhine; and Assmannshausen, known primarily for its red wines. The English traditionally refer to all Rhine wines as Hocks, derived from the village of Hochheim, from which the wines of this region were originally shipped to England. To this day, many English wine lists divide German wines into Hocks and Moselles.

There are many outstanding vineyards in the Rheingau, but three of them are so famous that each of their names may appear alone on a label without being preceded by that of a village: Schloss Johannisberg, Schloss Vollrads, and Steinberg. These vineyards are unusual because they are quite large, eighty acres or more, and because each has a single owner. Steinberg is owned by the Hessian state, and at one time its wines were made at Kloster Eberbach, a twelfth-century monastery located in Hattenheim. The Hessian state is actually the largest single owner of vineyards along the Rheingau with nearly four hundred acres in several villages, including the former Schloss Eltz estate. Its simple label, with a stylized black-and-gold eagle and the identification *Staatsweingüter*, is a familiar one.

Schloss Vollrads belongs to the Matuschka-Greiffenclau family, who built the imposing castle in the fourteenth century. A distinctive feature in the presentation of the wines of Schloss Vollrads is that a different-colored capsule is used for each category—green for *Qualitätswein,* blue for Kabinett wines, pink for Spätlese, white for Auslese, and gold for Beerenauslese and Trockenbeerenauslese. In addition, specially selected lots within each of the first four categories are indicated by adding gold bands to the capsules. The present Graf Matuschka-Grieffenclau has taken a particular interest in Trocken and Halbtrocken wines, and such wines are identified by silver bands on the capsules.

Schloss Johannisberg is probably the single most famous vineyard in Germany, and its renown is such that the Riesling grape is known as Johannisberger in Switzerland, and as Johannisberg Riesling in California. The vineyard was given to the von Metternich family by the emperor of Austria in 1816, but it was famous long before that; some of the buildings date back to the seventeenth century and Riesling was first planted at this estate in the early eighteenth century. For many years, the wines of Schloss Johannisberg were marketed with two labels—one showed the family crest, the other a drawing of the castle; since the mid-1980s, all the wines are marketed with the same label.

The interested consumer will enjoy comparing wines from each of the Rheingau villages and from the different estates, many of which are quite extensive. Langwerth von Simmern, Schloss Reinhartshausen, Schloss Groenesteyn, and Schloss Schönborn are some of the most respected names. The largest privately owned domain is that of Graf von Schönborn, whose 150 acres include holdings in forty-five individual vineyard sites located in thirteen different villages. The wines are labeled Schloss Schönborn, with the village and vineyard designation appearing in smaller type. In fact, a number of estates have adopted this Schloss method of labeling, in which the estate name is more prominently displayed than that of each vineyard. The names Schloss Vollrads and Schloss Johannisberg, however, actually refer to a single vineyard, as does Schloss Reichartshausen, a small vineyard belonging to the Balthasar Ress family. Another large estate is that of Wegeler-Deinhard, whose 140 acres, almost all Riesling, are situated in seven villages. The estate is owned by the Deinhard firm, which also owns vineyards along the Moselle and in the Rheinpfalz.

In 1984, a number of Rheingau estates formed the Charta association, whose aim is to produce Riesling wines that are rich but dry, rather than light, soft, and sweet. Wines eligible to bear the Charta symbol must be estate-bottled, made entirely from Riesling, and may have no more than 18 grams of residual sugar.

Only one *Bereich* has been established for the Rheingau—Bereich Johannisberg. There are ten *Grosslagen,* the most familiar of which are Hochheimer Daubhaus, Rauenthaler Steinmächer, Eltviller Steinmächer, Hatten-

heimer Deutelsberg, Johannisberger Erntebringer, and
Rüdesheimer Burgweg.

VILLAGE	IMPORTANT VINEYARDS
Hochheim	Domdechaney, Kirchen-stück, Königin Victoria Berg
Rauenthal	Baiken, Gehrn, Wülfen
Eltville	Taubenberg, Sonnen-berg, Sandgrub
Kiedrich	Wasseros, Sandgrub
Erbach	Marcobrunn, Steinmorgen
Hattenheim	Steinberg, Nussbrunnen, Wisselbrunnen, Mannberg
Hallgarten	Schönhell, Hendelberg
Oestrich	Lenchen, Doosberg
Winkel	Schloss Vollrads, Hasensprung
Johannisberg	Schloss Johannisberg, Klaus, Hölle
Geisenheim	Rothenberg, Kläuserweg
Rüdesheim	Bischofsberg, Berg Rott-land, Berg Schlossberg

Nahe

The wines of the Nahe are not very well known in
this country, and even German consumers are relatively
unfamiliar with its best sites. The best of the Nahe wines
are very good indeed, and although they are said to combine the best characteristics of the two districts that adjoin it—the Rheingau and the Moselle—they are much
closer in style to the better Rheingaus. The best wine-
producing villages are Bad Kreuznach (which shortens
its name on a label to Kreuznacher), Niederhausen, and
Schlossböckelheim. Although *Schloss,* or castle, is associated with two famous Rheingau vineyards—Schloss Johannisberg and Schloss Vollrads—Schlossböckelheim is
the name of the village, not a specific vineyard. Leading

producers include Paul Anheuser, August Anheuser, Crusius, Diel, Salm-Dalberg, and the State Domaine at Niederhausen.

There are two *Bereiche,* Bereich Kreuznach and Bereich Schloss Böckelheim, and seven *Grosslagen,* including Schlossböckelheimer Burgweg and Rüdesheimer Rosengarten (not to be confused with Rüdesheimer Rosengarten in the Rheingau).

VILLAGE	IMPORTANT VINEYARDS
Schlossböckelheim	Kupfergrube, Felsenberg, Königsfels
Niederhausen	Hermannshöhle, Hermannsberg
Kreuznach	Hinkelstein, Krotenpfuhl, Narrenkappe

Moselle

Compared to the majestic flow of the Rhine, the erratic path of the Moselle seems frivolous and nowhere more so than in the section known as the Middle Moselle. Yet it is along these steep banks that are found the world-famous wine villages of Piesport, Bernkastel, Wehlen, Zeltingen, Urzig, Graach, and a few others whose names, coupled with that of their best vineyards, identify some of the finest wines to be found anywhere. The Moselle zigzags here to such an extent that the greatest vineyards, always planted so as to face toward the south, are located first on one bank, then on the other. In some cases, the village itself is on the opposite bank, so that these choice slopes can be used entirely for the production of wine. During the vintage, the growers must keep crossing the river to bring the grapes back to their press houses.

Twenty years ago, the Riesling grape accounted for 80 percent of the acreage along the Moselle; today, that figure has dropped to less than 60 percent. Furthermore, because Riesling yields less wine per acre than do other varieties, it now accounts for less than half the wine produced along the Moselle. The finest wines still come from Riesling, but the consumer can no longer assume that a Moselle has been made from that grape unless its name appears on the label. The wines of the Moselle are noted for their flowery and fragrant bouquet, for their delicacy and elegance, and for a fruity acidity that gives them a lively and refreshing taste. They are light-bodied wines that are comparatively low in alcohol—8 or 9 percent is not uncommon—which makes them very appealing with many foods and also by themselves as an aperitif.

The most famous vineyard along the Moselle is Bernkasteler Doctor, which was expanded in 1971 from three to twelve acres by incorporating parts of the Badstube and Graben vineyards. In 1984 the size of the vineyard was reduced to eight acres, whch includes the original site and the best parts of the adjoining Graben vineyard. The principal owners are Thanisch-Knabben, Thanisch-Müller-Burggraeff, Wegeler-Deinhard, and Lauerberg. The Sonnenuhr, or sundial, vineyard of Wehlen, about one hundred acres in size, is also famous. The Joh. Jos. Prüm estate has the biggest share of this vineyard; other owners include Selbach-Oster, Dr. Loosen, Pauly-Bergweiler, and S. A. Prum. These producers, and those associated with the Doctor vineyard, are among the best known in the region, as is the Reichsgraf von Kesselstatt estate, owned by the Reh family, whose 160 acres of vines include the fifteen-acre Josephshof vineyard.

There are also several hospitals, schools, and religious orders with extensive holdings along the Moselle (and the Saar and Ruwer as well): Vereinigte Hospitien, St. Nikolaus Hospital, Friedrich-Wilhelm-Gymnasium, Bischöfliches Konvikt, and Bischöfliches Priesterseminar. The last two estates were combined with that of the Hohe Domkirche in 1966 to form the Bischöfliche Weingüter, but the wines are still labeled with the name of each estate.

The villages of Zell and Kröv have given their names to two popular wines, Zeller Schwarze Katz, or Black Cat, and Kröver Nacktarsch, or Bare Bottom, whose labels usually illustrate their names. Both these names are now *Grosslagen,* but the new boundaries for Kröver Nacktarsch are so limited that this wine is not often seen anymore.

Along the Moselle, Bereich Bernkastel is by far the best known, as it encompasses virtually the entire Middle Moselle. Bernkasteler Kurfürstlay and Piesporter Michelsberg are the most popular *Grosslagen,* and widely used by shippers as regional wine appellations. Ürziger Schwarzlay, Graacher Münzlay, and Bernkasteler Badstube are other *Grosslagen,* as are Zeller Schwarze Katz and Kröver Nacktarsch, already referred to.

VILLAGE	IMPORTANT VINEYARDS
Trittenheim	Apotheke, Altärchen
Piesport	Goldtröpfchen, Günterslay, Falkenberg
Brauneberg	Juffer
Bernkastel	Doctor, Lay, Graben
Graach	Josephshöfer, Himmelreich, Domprobst
Wehlen	Sonnenuhr
Zeltingen	Sonnenuhr, Himmelreich
Ürzig	Würzgarten, Goldwingert
Erden	Treppchen

Saar

The Saar joins the Moselle just below Trier, the Ruwer just above that historic city. Wines from these two districts are labeled, as are those of the Moselle, with the overall regional appellation Mosel-Saar-Ruwer. In fine years, Saar and Ruwer wines are even more delicate and elegant than those of the Moselle, and some connoisseurs prefer the particular finesse of these wines to the softer and rounder flavor of Moselles. In lesser years, however, Saar and Ruwer wines are disappointingly thin and acid.

The most famous vineyard of the Saar is Scharzhofberg, whose name may appear by itself on a label, without that of Wiltingen, the village in which it is located.

In 1971, the vineyard was expanded from forty-five acres to sixty-seven acres, and is now split up among ten owners, the most respected of which is Egon Müller. Scharzberg, which was the name of an individual vineyard prior to the new laws, has now been transformed into the *Grosslage* name Wiltinger Scharzberg, which can be used to label wines produced anywhere in the entire Saar region. Bereich Saar-Ruwer encompasses both regions. Dr. Fischer and the State Domain are vineyard proprietors along the Saar.

VILLAGE	IMPORTANT VINEYARDS
Serrig	Kupp, Würzberg
Ayl	Herrenberg, Kupp
Ockfen	Bockstein, Geisberg, Herrenberg
Wiltingen	Scharzhofberg, Kupp
Oberemmel	Altenberg, Rosenberg
Kanzem	Altenberg, Sonnenberg

Ruwer

There are two particularly famous vineyards along the Ruwer, each with a single proprietor. Maximin Grünhaus, owned by von Schubert, is in Mertesdorf, but since 1971 its name has been treated as if it were that of a village, and may appear by itself on a label. The vineyard name is followed by that of a specific section of the property: Abtsberg is considered the best, followed by Herrenberg and Bruderberg. In Eitelsbach, the Karthäuserhofberg vineyard is divided into five sections, the biggest of which are Kronenberg, Sang, and Burgberg. Perhaps with a sense of irony, the proprietors have devised one of the smallest of all German wine labels to bear so many long names. The *Grosslage* Kaseler Römerlay is used for the entire Ruwer.

VILLAGE	IMPORTANT VINEYARDS
Avelsbach	Herrenberg, Altenberg
Waldrach	Laurentiusberg, Krone
Kasel	Nieschen, Kehrnagel, Hitzlay
Maximin Grünhaus	Abtsberg, Herrenberg, Bruderberg
Eitelsbach	Karthäuserhofberg

Franconia

The wines of Franconia, shipped in the distinctive *Bocksbeutel,* are comparatively dry, less typically German in flavor, and characterized by a *Bodengeschmak,* or taste of the earth, that sets them apart from the more fragrant wines of the Rhine and Moselle. In the past, Sylvaner was the variety most typically associated with the wines of this region, but Müller-Thurgau now accounts for half the plantings. Although Franconia is not a major wine district in terms of volume, its vineyards are rather extensively spread out along the Main River and its tributaries. Frankenwein and Steinwein have often been used as regional names for these wines, but the latter may be used only for the wines from the Stein vineyard in Würzburg. The Staatliche Hofkellerei, Juliusspital, and Bürgerspital have extensive holdings in this region.

Franconia is divided into Bereich Mainviereck, Bereich Maindreieck, and Bereich Steigerwald, and two of its *Grosslagen* are Würzburger Himmelspforte and Randersacker Ewig Leben.

VILLAGE	IMPORTANT VINEYARDS
Würzburg	Stein, Innere Leiste, Schlossberg
Escherndorf	Lump, Berg
Randersacker	Teufelskeller, Sonnenstuhl
Iphofen	Julius-Echter-Berg, Kronsberg

OTHER EUROPEAN WINES

SPAIN

With nearly four million acres of vineyards, Spain has
more land devoted to wines than any other European
country, although lower yields per acre place Spain third
in wine production, after Italy and France. For many
years, most of the wine shipped here from Spain consisted of sweet, fruit-flavored *sangría* and sherry, especially cream sherries; sherry may be Spain's most famous
wine, but it accounts for only 3 or 4 percent of all the
wine made in that country. More recently, the increasingly popular *cava*—the *méthode champenoise* sparkling
wines produced, for the most part, in the Penedés district, near Barcelona—have been the best-selling Spanish
wines among American consumers. But as any visitor to
Spain soon learns, a varied range of red, white, and rosé
table wines are made throughout the country, and many
of these are becoming more widely available here.

The appellation of origin laws of Spain, known as *Denominación de Origen,* or DO, now include more than
three dozen names. (Sherry, Montilla, Málaga, and the
cava wines are described elsewhere.) As is the case with

SAN SEBASTIAN

Ebro

Logroño

RIOJA

BARCELONA

VINHO VERDE

Douro

Vilafranca del Penedés

OPORTO ●PORT

DÃO

Tarragona

MADRID ●

LA MANCHA

●LISBON

● Valdepeñas

Montilla ●

SHERRY

Jerez de la Frontera

Málaga

SPAIN AND PORTUGAL

the *Appellation Contrôlée* laws of France, the DO regulations determine the boundaries of each appellation, the grapes that may be grown there, maximum yields per acre, minimum alcohol content, and other factors that affect quality. Some of the newly elevated DO districts are still unknown and others have yet to achieve their potential quality, but such appellations as Rioja, Rueda, Ribera del Duero, and the wines of Penedés are already familiar to many consumers. The category *Denominación de Origen Calificada,* or DOC, has been established for the top wines, and was awarded to Rioja in 1991. The less familiar category *Vino de la Tierra* has been created for regional wines and is similar to the *Vin de Pays* of France. The *Denominación de Origen* wines account for about 100 million cases a year, which represents one-quarter to one-third of the total crop; within the DO category, five appellations make up about half the total—*cava*, sherry, Rioja, La Mancha, and Valdepeñas.

Although such well-known grape varieties as Chardonnay, Sauvignon Blanc, Cabernet Sauvignon, and Merlot have been planted in a few wine districts, especially Catalonia, almost all Spanish wines are made from traditional varieties that include such reds as Tempranillo (known as Cencibel in Valdepeñas, Ull de Llebre in Catalonia, and Tinto Fino or Tinta del País in Ribera del Duero), Garnacha (the Grenache of France), Cariñena (the Carignane of France, known as Mazuelo in Rioja), and Monastrell. The best-known white varieties include Airén, Albariño, Macabeo (known as Viura in Rioja and Rueda), Palomino, Parellada, Verdejo, and Xarello. As in other wine-producing countries, Spanish winemakers have adopted such practices as earlier picking to produce wines with less alcohol and more lively acidity; temperature-controlled fermentation to retain more fruit, delicacy, and elegance; and less aging in wood—or none at all—for both red and white wines.

Some of the best wines of Spain, and the ones most often seen here, come from the Rioja district in northeastern Spain, not far from the French border. The vineyards extend for about seventy miles along the Ebro River, from Haro to Logroño and on to Alfaro. The district gets its name from a little river, the Rio Oja, that flows toward the Ebro near Haro. Wine has been made in this region for several centuries, and in fact the first attempt to guarantee its authenticity dates back to 1560. Rioja has long been one of the most carefully controlled wine districts in Spain, and since 1926 labels of authentic Rioja are imprinted with a seal that resembles a small postage stamp.

Rioja is a comparatively large viticultural area, producing between twelve and sixteen million cases of wine a year. About three-quarters of the region's 120,000 acres are planted with red grapes, primarily Tempranillo and Garnacha, plus limited amounts of Graciano and Mazuelo. The white wines are made almost entirely from Viura, plus Malvasía and Garnacha Blanca. Because white-wine varieties are traditionally planted among the red varieties, and the grapes harvested and vinified together (the white grapes contribute lightness and acidity to the red wines), white wines make up only 10 percent of the Rioja crop.

The Rioja region is divided into three districts—La Rioja Alta is cooler and produces wines with more finesse and acidity; the wines from La Rioja Alavesa are somewhat fuller; and the hotter, drier climate of Rioja Baja results in sturdier wines that are generally less distinguished. In practice, however, most producers blend together wines from at least two of the districts. Some Rioja firms own no vineyards, others own three hundred to a thousand acres or more, but with very few exceptions they buy grapes from farmers and wine from the cooperative cellars that now account for about half the production of the region; these purchases are eventually blended to produce a consistent house style.

Although the wines of Rioja have a long history, the character of the wines produced was altered about a hundred years ago, when phylloxera struck the vineyards of Bordeaux. A number of French winemaking families moved across the Pyrenées to the nearby Rioja district and Bordeaux merchants appeared looking for wines to ship back to France; these people introduced their vinification techniques, which are still used in some Rioja cellars. The fermenting must is kept in contact with the grapeskins for an extended period, so that the red wines are particularly rich in color and tannin, and the better wines are then aged in 225-liter oak barrels for a comparatively long time—four or five years is not uncommon. The white wines, too, may be aged in wood for one or two years. These practices often resulted in wines that seemed faded, dried out, and too woody to consumers used to the livelier and more youthful tastes of French and California wines. In the early 1970s, a number of important new firms were established in Rioja and equipped with the latest cellar equipment, including temperature-controlled fermentation tanks. These firms began to produce fresh, lively whites that were bottled within months of the harvest and appealing reds that were matured in oak barrels for only a year or two; some reds were not aged in wood at all. Although some long-established Rioja firms continue to produce rich, woody, old-fashioned red and white wines, most have adopted modern vinification and aging techniques.

Rioja is a blended wine and most shippers traditionally market their wines with several different brand names, each representing a different style of wine. Thus, a firm's dry white wine will have one name, its mellow white another; a young red wine and an older, barrel-aged red will each be labeled with a different name. Viña Real, Viña Pomal, Viña Monty, Añares, Banda Azul, and Monte Real are some proprietary names used by Rioja producers. (Note that *viña* means vineyard, but not when it is used as part of a proprietary name in Rioja.) Although these names have been created by each firm, there are other words found on Rioja labels that have specific meanings. *Bodega* means cellar or winery. *Cosecha* and *vendimia* refer to the vintage year. A Rioja labeled *sin crianza* is one that has not been aged in wood; *crianza* means that the wine has been aged a minimum of one year in wood. A wine labeled *reserva* must be aged for a minimum of three years before being released for sale, including at least one year in oak barrels; a *gran reserva* must be aged for at least five years, including at least two years in oak barrels. It is understood that a producer's *reservas* and *gran reservas* are specially selected lots that merit additional aging, and that such wines are likely to be produced only in the best vintages. Also, many firms are likely to age their *reservas* for at least two years in wood and their *gran reservas* for three years or more in wood. Rioja is one of the few wine regions where the finest red wines are aged by the producers and released when they are mature; such wines are more likely to be polished and graceful than tannic and harsh. The importance of the 225-liter oak barrel of Bordeaux, known in Rioja as a *barrica,* is such that many of the leading firms have ten thousand to thirty thousand of these barrels in their cellars. The traditional *barrica* of Rioja is made of American oak, which imparts a distinctive spicy or vanilla note, but a number of wineries are now using French oak barrels as well.

Some well-known Rioja firms (and their popular proprietary brands) are AGE Bodegas Unidas (Siglo), Bodegas Berberana (Carta de Plata), Bodegas Beronia, Bodegas Bilbaínas (Viña Pomal, Viña Zaco), Bodegas Campo Viejo (Marqués de Villamagna), Compañía Vinícola del Norte de España, or CUNE (Viña Real, Imperial, and the single-vineyard Contino), Bodegas Domecq (Marqués de Arienzo), Faustino Martínez (Faustino V),

Bodegas Franco-Españolas (Diamante), Bodegas Gurpegui (Viña Berceo), Bodegas Lan, López de Heredia (Viña Tondonia, Viña Bosconia), Marqués de Cáceres, Marqués de Murrieta (Castillo Ygay), Marqués de Riscal (Barón de Chirel), Martínez Bujanda (Conde de Valdemar), Bodegas Montecillo (Viña Cumbrero, Viña Monty), Bodegas Muerza (Rioja Vega), Bodegas Muga, Bodegas Olarra (Añares, Reciente), Bodegas Palacio (Cosme Palacio y Hermanos, Glorioso), Federico Paternina (Banda Azul, Viña Vial), Remelluri, La Rioja Alta (Viña Ardanza, Reserva 904), Bodegas Rioja Santiago (Gran Condal), and Bodegas Riojanas (Monte Real).

The Ribera del Duero district, which has been widely acclaimed for its fine red wines, was established as a *Denominación de Origen* in 1982; since then, the vineyards have expanded to more than twenty-five thousand acres and the wines marketed with the DO (many of which were previously sold off in bulk rather than bottled by the producers) have increased from forty thousand cases to more than one million a year. The district, situated about eighty miles north of Madrid, extends for nearly seventy miles east of Valladolid along the Duero River, which continues into Portugal, where it is known as the Douro. The wines are made primarily from Tinto Fino or Tinta del País, the local names for Tempranillo; Garnacha is also planted and a few estates are experimenting with Cabernet Sauvignon and Merlot. The most famous estate in the district, and one of the legendary vineyards of Spain, is Vega Sicilia, established in the mid-nineteenth century. Its first owner planted Cabernet Sauvignon, Merlot, and Malbec along with Tempranillo, and to this day the Bordeaux varieties account for about 40 percent of the three hundred acres planted, and of the wine made from that vineyard. The special wine made at Vega Sicilia, labeled Unico, is unusual in that most vintages are aged for seven to ten years in a combination of large vats, casks, and barrels; some vintages are not bottled until they have matured in wood for fifteen years or more. A second wine, labeled Valbuena, is bottled after eighteen months or three years in wood, depending on the vintage. Total production of the estate is about twenty-five thousand cases, of which Unico accounts for less than a third.

The best known of the new wineries in Ribera del Duero is that of Alejandro Fernández, whose wine is labeled Pesquera. First produced in the mid-1970s, this rich, supple wine is made almost entirely from Tempranillo and aged in a combination of American and French oak barrels. Other labels include Victor Balbás, Viña Pedrosa of Pérez Pascuas, Peñafiel and Protos of the Ribera Duero cooperative, Señorio de Nava, and Ismael Arroyo; Mauro is a wine, similar in style, produced just outside the boundaries of Ribera del Duero.

The Rueda district, southwest of Valladolid, has become known for its crisp, dry white wines. For most of this century, the wines typical of Rueda were similar to sherry, whether made from the Palomino grape of Jerez, or from Verdejo or Viura. In the early 1970s, the Marqués de Riscal firm of Rioja introduced modern equipment and techniques to produce dry white wines from the Verdejo grape. Their success has been such that other producers have followed, and today a wine labeled Rueda must contain at least 25 percent of Verdejo, 60 percent if it is labeled Rueda Superior. Viura has also been planted, and some wineries have experimented with Sauvignon Blanc and Chardonnay as well. In addition to Marqués de Riscal, other labels include Martínsancho (made entirely from Verdejo) and Marqués de Griñón. (Carlos Falcó, the Marqués de Griñón, is also known for a barrel-aged red made primarily from Cabernet Sauvignon at his family estate west of Toledo, along the Tajo River.)

Catalonia, with Barcelona as its capital, is an autonomous region within Spain, and even has its own language, Catalán. The area encompasses several wine districts, the most interesting of which is Penedés. Most of the firms producing *cava—méthode champenoise* sparkling wines—are situated in Penedés, which accounts for the extensive plantings of the three white varieties used for these wines, Xarello, Macabeo, and Parellada. The principal red grapes are Tempranillo (known locally as Ull de Llebre), Garnacha, and Monastrell. In the 1960s, Jean León, a Catalan and the owner of the restaurant La Scala in Los Angeles, planted Chardonnay and Cabernet

Sauvignon on what is now a four-hundred-acre vineyard. Soon after, Miguel Torres, Jr., planted those varieties as well as Sauvignon Blanc, Riesling, Gewürztraminer, Pinot Noir, and Merlot in the family vineyards, which have expanded to more than two thousand acres. The combination of these varieties and modern vinification techniques enabled the Torres firm, founded in 1870, to lead the way for other Penedés producers. The range of wines offered by Torres suggests how the firm uses both native and French varieties. Among the white wines, Viña Sol is made from Parellada, Gran Viña Sol from Chardonnay and some Parellada, and Fransola is primarily Sauvignon Blanc plus some Parellada; of the red wines, Sangre de Toro is made from Garnacha and Cariñena, Coronas is made primarily from Tempranillo, Gran Coronas contains mostly Cabernet Sauvignon plus some Tempranillo, and Gran Coronas Black Label Mas La Plana is made entirely from Cabernet Sauvignon. Torres also makes Merlot and Pinot Noir, as well as a barrel-aged Chardonnay from grapes grown in Conca de Barberá, just west of Penedés. In addition to Torres and Jean León, the René Barbier firm, owned by Freixenet, produces agreeable red, white, and rosé wines.

About 120 miles west of Barcelona, in the province of Lérida, the Raimat estate, created by the Raventós family of Codorníu, dominates the DO Costers del Segre. Raimat encompasses three thousand acres of vineyards, with Cabernet Sauvignon and Chardonnay making up nearly two-thirds of the total; the rest consists of a number of native varieties as well as Merlot and Pinot Noir. The estate produces a range of wines, including Chardonnay, Cabernet Sauvignon, Merlot, and Abadía, a blend of Cabernet Sauvignon and Tempranillo, as well as several *méthode champenoise* sparkling wines. The Codorníu firm also owns the Masía Bach estate and winery in Penedés, known for Extrísimo, a sweet dessert wine, and a dry white wine labeled Extrísimo Seco; a red labeled Viña Extrísima Reserva is made from Tempranillo, Garnacha, and some Cabernet Sauvignon.

Alella is a small district northeast of Barcelona known for pleasant white wines made primarily from Pansa Blanca, the local name for Xarello; Chardonnay and

Chenin Blanc have also been planted. Marqués de Alella and Marfil are the best-known labels.

Tarragona, a city along the Mediterranean coast, southwest of Barcelona, gives its name to an extensive region once famous for its rich, fortified red wines, similar in style to port. Now the region produces mostly white wines, much of it destined for the sparkling wine trade. Priorato, a small district within Tarragona, produces rich, powerful red wines.

Galicia, in northwestern Spain, has achieved a reputation for crisp, dry white wines in recent years. Its most famous appellation is Rías Baixas, created in 1988, which includes three districts, one along the Atlantic coast, the two others along the Miño River, which forms the border with Portugal. The wines of Rías Baixas must contain a minimum of 70 percent Albariño, but many producers use that grape exclusively for their best wines. Labels include Martín Códax, Morgadío, Castel de Fornos, and Condes de Albarei. Many growers in the Ribeiro district, also in Galicia, have been replacing the Palomino grape, which makes dull whites, with new plantings of Treixadura and Torrontes, capable of producing fresh, lively white wines.

The extensive La Mancha area, in the center of Spain, is the biggest vineyard region in that country and accounts for more than a third of all Spanish wines, about two-thirds of them produced by cooperative cellars. Only a part of the traditional La Mancha area is entitled to the DO, but its half a million acres make it, perhaps, the largest region in the world with a single appellation. The white Airén grape represents about 80 percent of the acreage, with most of the rest devoted to Cencíbel, the local name for Tempranillo. Until recently, the white wines of La Mancha were undistinguished, and much of the crop was distilled into brandy. Today, many cooperatives and private firms have introduced new equipment and are producing lighter, fresher whites and more appealing reds.

Valdepeñas, a district within La Mancha, has long been known for its light red wines. In fact, most of its vineyards are planted with Arién, the rest with Cencibel and some Garnacha. Cencibel contributes so much color, however, that the traditional light red Valdepeñas was made from Airén with about 20 percent Cencibel.

Today, many producers are making red Valdepeñas with less Airén or none at all, and barrel-aging their best wines. Wineries include Los Llanos, Félix Solís, Luis Megía, and Casa de la Viña.

Other *Denominación de Origen* wines include Toro, a full-bodied red made primarily from Tinta de Toro in a district that adjoins Rueda. Cariñena is another full-bodied red produced around the city of that name (which gave its name to the variety better known as Carignan); the wine is made primarily from Garnacha and Tempranillo, plus some Mazuelo, the local name for Carignane. The Navarra district, south of Pamplona, once best known for its dry rosés, has now established a reputation for red wines made from Garnacha and, increasingly, from Tempranillo blended with Cabernet Sauvignon and Merlot.

PORTUGAL

Perhaps the most famous wines of Portugal are port and Madeira, which account for less than 10 percent of the country's wine production. And for many years, the most popular table wines of Portugal shipped here have been the agreeable, off-dry rosés, many of them marketed in distinctive bottles and crocks, which have undoubtedly converted many people to the pleasures of wine drinking; the best-known brands are Lancers and Mateus. But Portugal also produces a great deal of moderately priced red and white wine from a number of regions throughout the country, and these wines are becoming more widely known here.

Until recently, most Portuguese reds were sturdy, rustic, even harsh, and many whites were dull and oxidized. There were few appellations of origin, and they included several that were mostly of historical interest. As a result, the leading producers created proprietary names to market their wines, and these blends often made no reference to specific districts of origin. Terms such as *garrafeira* and *reserva* were used to indicate specifically selected and aged wines. Today, the latest cellar equipment and contemporary vinification and aging techniques are used by many of the shippers and leading estates to produce more supple reds and fresher, livelier whites. In addition, the government has defined more regions and districts, and there is an increasing emphasis on appellations of origin.

There are now about a dozen districts entitled to a Região Demarcada (RD), similar to the *Appellation Contrôlée* of France; the term *Denominacão de Origem Controlada* (DOC) has been introduced and is gradually supplanting Região Demarcada on labels. Another three dozen districts are entitled to *Indicação de Proveniência Regulamentada* (IPR), similar to France's VDQS category; as in France, some of the IPR districts may eventually be elevated to RD or DOC status. More recently, a number of regions have been defined for a new category called *Vinho Regional,* which is equivalent to the *Vin de Pays* of France. The *Vinhos Regionais* include Terras do Sado, Alentejo, Rios do Minho, Trás-os-Montes, Beiras, Algarve, Ribatejo, and Estremadura. What follows is an overview of the principal wine districts of Portugal, from north to south.

Vinho Verde, very popular in Portugal, is now becoming better known in this country. Its name literally means "green wine," but only in the sense of new wine, in contrast to aged wines, which are referred to as *vinhos maduros,* or mature wines. Vinho Verde, which can be red or white, is produced in the northwest of Portugal, in the Minho province, north of the Douro River. These light-bodied wines are comparatively low in alcohol and, when consumed locally, are noted for their refreshing acidity. Red Vinho Verde, normally served chilled, has a rather harsh taste and is rarely exported; the whites can be crisp and fresh, and may have a light natural sprightliness that adds to their charm. Many white Vinhos Verdes are made from the Loureiro grape; some of the best examples are made from the Alvarinho grape in the Monção district, and are so labeled. Of the white Vinhos Verdes shipped here, some have the lively acidity that makes these wines so distinct, others have a softer, off-dry taste that is less typical. Aveleda and Casal Garcia are the best-known brands, and there are now a number of estate-bottled wines available as well, such as Quinta de Azevedo.

The extensive Douro region is best known for port,

but only about half the crop is used to produce this fortified wine; the rest is vinified in the traditional manner to produce red (and some white) wines. The same grapes are used for these reds as for port, but they are likely to be picked earlier, so that the wines are not overly alcoholic, and many producers have learned to blend the fuller-bodied wines from lower altitudes with those from cooler areas, which contribute elegance and balancing acidity. Fine Douro reds come from a number of estates, including Quinta do Cotto, Quinta de la Rosa, and Quinta da Pacheca, but the best-known wine of the region is Barca Velha, a long-lived, barrel-aged wine made by the Ferreira port firm; only the best vintages are sold as Barca Velha, lesser vintages go to market as Reserva Especial. Ferreira, which also makes the Douro wines Esteva and Vinha Grande, is now owned by Sogrape, creators of the Mateus brand, and producers of Douro wines labeled Vila Regia and Mateus Signature.

The Dão region, in central Portugal, gets its name from the river that winds through it toward the Atlantic Ocean; although best known for its reds, white wines account for about a third of the crop. Until recently, shippers were not allowed to buy grapes directly from the growers, so all the Dão wines were made by cooperative cellars, many of them lacking modern equipment. Today, the shippers can vinify their own wines, vineyards have been replanted, and new wineries constructed in the region; as a result the proportion of soundly made Dão wines—both red and white—has increased considerably. Grão Vasco is a well-known label; others include Terras Altas, Duque de Viseu, Quinta das Carvalhais, Casa da Insua, and Conde de Santar.

The Bairrada district, situated south of the Douro, between Dão and the ocean, produces deep-colored, tannic reds from the Baga grape and dry whites from several varieties, including Maria Gomes. Familiar names include Caves Aliança, Caves São João, and Terra Franca and such estates as Quinta do Ribeirinho of Luis Pato and Quinta de Pedralvites. The Estremadura region extends along the coast from Leiria down to Lisbon; long a source of inexpensive bulk wines, it is now becoming known for the wines from such estates as Quinta de Pancas and Quinta de Abrigada. The large Ribatejo region is situated northeast of Lisbon, on either side of the Tagus River. Although the vineyards are planted primarily with white grapes, the red wines of Ribatejo are considered superior; these include such wines as Serradayres, the *garrafeira* bottlings of several large firms, including Caves Dom Teodósio, and such estate wines as Falcoaria and Quinta Lagoalva de Cima.

About twenty miles from Lisbon, along the Atlantic coast, are the vineyards of Colares, which produce a long-lived red wine (and a small amount of undistinguished white wine). Although Colares is rarely seen here, the vineyards themselves are quite unusual and deserve mention. For one thing, the vines grow in sand dunes near the ocean, and planting new vines requires digging special reinforced trenches ten or twenty feet deep in the sand. For another, the Ramisco vines of Colares have never been attacked by phylloxera, so this wine is one of the very few in Europe still being made from vines that have not been grafted onto American rootstocks.

Bucelas, now produced in limited quantities, is a dry white wine from a village of that name about fifteen miles north of Lisbon. Carcavelos, on the coast near Colares, was once an important wine district, but this sweet, fortified wine is now difficult to find even in Lisbon.

The Setúbal peninsula, just south of Lisbon across the Tagus River, is best known for its Moscatel de Setúbal, a sweet, fortified white wine made from the Muscat of Alexandria grape. Today, there is little Muscat left, and the district is becoming better known for an interesting range of red and white wines produced primarily by two firms who are experimenting with traditional Portuguese varieties as well as with Chardonnay, Sémillon, Cabernet Sauvignon, and Merlot. José Maria da Fonseca Successores, which makes Pasmados and the popular Periquita, a sturdy red, own the Quinta de Camarate, planted with Cabernet Sauvignon and native varieties; J. P. Vinhos produces a dry Muscat labeled João Pires and makes the wines at Quinta da Bacalhôa, a vineyard planted with Cabernet Sauvignon and Merlot. The wines of the Setúbal district are entitled to the regional appellation Terras do Sado, and are often so labeled.

The vast Alentejo region, which encompasses most of

southern Portugal, has been subdivided into several districts whose vineyards and wineries are being revitalized; some wines from this region, which is better known for its reds, include Tinto da Anfora, JS Rosado Fernandes, Paço dos Infantes, Morgado do Reguengo, and Quinta do Carmo. The Algarve, which is the southernmost region of Portugal, is more famous for its tourist attractions than for its light red and rosé wines.

SWITZERLAND

The per capita consumption of wine in Switzerland is more than seven times that of the United States, and the thirsty Swiss import about three times as much wine as they make themselves. The Swiss vineyards produce twelve to fourteen million cases a year, about as much wine as is made in the Beaujolais region of France; dry, crisp, refreshing whites account for a little more than half the total, light reds and dry rosés make up the rest.

Some wine is made in the Italian-speaking part of the country, notably the attractive red Merlot del Ticino, but almost all of Switzerland's wines come from the French-speaking region known as La Suisse Romande. The cantons, or districts, that are best known for their wines are those of Neuchâtel, Vaud, and the Valais. The most widely planted white-wine grape is Chasselas, known in the Valais as Fendant and in Vaud as Dorin; Gamay and Pinot Noir are the leading red-wine grapes.

Neuchâtel, one of the most familiar of Swiss wines, comes from vineyards along the northern shore of the Lake of Neuchâtel. The pleasant, sprightly white is made from Chasselas, the red and rosé from Pinot Noir. Some of the best reds come from the village of Cortaillod, and the appealing dry rosé may be labeled Oeil de Perdrix.

The canton of Vaud, along the shore of Lake Geneva, is divided into two main wine districts: La Côte extends west of the city of Lausanne, Lavaux extends to the east of the city. Within Lavaux are the wine villages of Dézaley and Saint-Saphorin, whose names may appear on wine labels. Beyond Lavaux is the Chablais district, which encompasses five villages, including Aigle and Yvorne, whose names may also be seen on labels. Individual village names may be used alone or with that of the appropriate district, as Dézaley de Lavaux and Aigle de Chablais. Two recently defined appellations in Vaud are the white Bonvillars, made from Chasselas, and the red Salvagnin, made from Pinot Noir and Gamay. Wines are also produced closer to the city of Geneva, from vineyards along the Rhône River and the shores of Lake Geneva—the red Gamay de Genève and the white Perlan, made from Chasselas.

The vineyards of the Valais lie along the Rhône River, on either side of the city of Sion. The wines of this district are labeled with the name of the grape from which they are made—Fendant, Johannisberg (actually Sylvaner), and Pinot Noir. Dôle is a red wine made from Pinot Noir and Gamay, with the former accounting for at least half the blend. Other white varieties grown in the Valais in limited quantities are Arvine and Amigne, native to the region, and Ermitage, which is the local name for the Marsanne of France.

AUSTRIA

Vienna may be famous for its coffee and pastry, but wine is very much a part of the Austrian way of life: the per capita consumption of wine in that country is about forty-five bottles a year. Nearly 150,000 acres produce about thirty million cases, with white wines accounting for 80 percent of the total. The Austrian's casual approach to wine is nowhere more evident than in the *Heurigen,* or wine taverns, that are found throughout each wine region. Everyone who has *Heurige,* or new wine, to sell hangs a bough or wreath outside his establishment to alert passersby, and these refreshing wines are consumed on the premises—by the glass or from open carafes—in a tradition that dates back more than two hundred years. Some *Heurigen* are open all year round, others sell wines for only a few weeks in the spring and summer. The new wine may actually be more than a year old, since a wine can be sold as *Heurige* until November of the year following the vintage.

The most widely planted grape in Austria is Grüner Veltliner, whose mild, agreeable wines account for about a third of the total production. Other white-wine grapes include Müller-Thurgau (usually called Riesling-Sylvaner in Austria), Welschriesling, Rheinriesling (which is the true Riesling of Germany), Traminer, Neuberger, and Weissburgunder (Pinot Blanc) as well as lesser plantings of Zierfandler (also known as Spätrot) and Rotgipfler; Chardonnay and Sauvignon Blanc, produced in limited quantities, have become increasingly sought after. Austria's pleasant, light-bodied red wines are made from such varieties as Portugieser, Blaufränkisch, Blauburgunder (Pinot Noir), Saint Laurent, and Zweigelt (a cross of Blaufränkisch and Saint Laurent); Cabernet Sauvignon, first planted in the 1860s, is also cultivated.

As in Germany, the better wines bear such designations as *Qualitätswein* and Kabinett, and the *Prädikatswein* category includes—in order of increasing ripeness—Spätlese, Auslese, Eiswein, Beerenauslese, Ausbruch, and Trockenbeerenauslese. These words have been clearly defined and have virtually the same meaning as in Germany. The sugar content of the grapes is expressed in degrees KMW (Klosterneuberger Mostwaage), just as the Oechsle scale is used in Germany, and minimum requirements have been established for each category. In 1985, a number of Austrian producers were found guilty of adding diethylene glycol to certain wines; this potentially harmful chemical contributed a rich, viscous texture to wines that were also sweetened and then passed off as expensive, late-harvest wines. A number of strict new laws were subsequently established, including some that reduced the maximum permitted yields per acre.

A Viennese who wants to drink local wines does not have far to travel because many of the country's most agreeable wines are produced just west of Vienna, near the celebrated Vienna Woods, in such villages as Grinzing and Nussberg. Gumpoldskirchen, a village some fifteen miles south of Vienna, enjoys an even higher rating; Gumpoldskirchner (the suffix *er* is added to a village or district name when it appears on a label) is made primarily from Zierfandler and Rotgipfler. Farther south is the village of Vöslau, best known for its reds; and a few miles northwest of Vienna is the town of Klosterneuberg, whose famous monastery is one of the country's most important vineyard owners. About forty miles west of Vienna, along the north bank of the Danube River, is the Wachau district, whose most famous villages are Dürnstein and Loiben, best known for the appealing wines made from Grüner Veltliner and Riesling. Just east of the Wachau are the equally famous wine villages of Krems and Langenlois; Falkenstein and Poysdorf are the best-known villages in the extensive district north of Vienna known as the Weinviertel. The small Styria region is situated in the southeast corner of the country.

The Burgenland district, southeast of Vienna, is unusual among Austria's wine regions in that it is best known for its sweet wines. The mist that rises off the Neusiedlersee, a long narrow lake, permits the development of *Botrytis cinerea*, also known as noble rot, in most years, and results in Auslese, Beerenauslese, and Trockenbeerenauslese wines, most of them made from Weissburgunder, Müller-Thurgau, and Neuberger rather than the more traditional Riesling. Rust and Apetlon are the most famous wine villages of Burgenland, and the best-known of the region's sweet wines is probably Ruster Ausbruch, the latter term used for wines that are even sweeter than a Beerenauslese. Mörbisch, Oggau, and Donnerskirchen are other wine villages in Burgenland.

Austrian wines may be labeled with the name of a grape variety, with that of the district or village of origin, or with a combination of both, such as Kremser Grüner Veltliner, Durnsteiner Rheinriesling, Apetloner Weissburgunder, and Oggauer Blaufrankisch. In addition, a number of popular Austrian wines are labeled with proprietary brand names.

HUNGARY

Although Hungary is not one of Europe's biggest wine-producing countries, it has always maintained a special position among connoisseurs as the home of the famous sweet wines of Tokay. At one time these luscious dessert wines were considered an essential part of any complete cellar, and the finest examples, labeled Eszencia, were served at royal banquets and state occasions. Bottles of nineteenth-century Tokay still show up at wine auctions, and invariably fetch high prices, but the wine is no longer as popular as it was in the past, and most consumers today are more familiar with the range of red and white Hungarian wines that are increasingly available here. Nevertheless, Tokay is an interesting and unusual wine, enhanced by the legends that surround it.

The village of Tokay (spelled *Tokaj* locally) is situated in the northeast corner of the country, at the foothills of the Carpathian Mountains. A number of neighboring villages, also situated along the Bodrog River, are permitted to market their wines as Tokay, and these hillside vineyards are planted almost entirely with Furmint and Hárslevelü grapes. The volcanic soil of the district imparts a distinctive tang or undertaste that distinguishes Tokay from the sweet dessert wines of Sauternes and the Auslese and Beerenauslese wines of Germany.

Tokay is made in a very special way. After the normal harvest, grapes are left on the vines to develop the same noble rot that affects the grapes in Sauternes and along the Rhine and Moselle. These shriveled grapes, with their much higher concentration of sugar, are known as *aszu.* The *aszu* grapes are carefully harvested and put into containers, or butts, known as *puttonyos,* each of which holds about twenty liters; the *aszu* grapes will eventually be crushed into a rich paste. After the regular harvest has been vinified into a dry white wine, a certain number of *puttonyos,* usually three to five, are added to each vat of wine, which holds about 135 liters; the more *puttonyos* are added, the sweeter the resulting wine will be. The addition of the *aszu* paste induces a slight second fermentation of the enriched wine, which nevertheless retains a certain amount of residual sugar. The sweet wine then undergoes extensive barrel aging in damp, cold cellars, which adds richness and an element of oxidation. When the wine is bottled, it is labeled Tokaji Aszu and the number of *puttonyos* that were added is also indicated; a three-*puttonyos* wine is likely to contain sixty grams, or 6 percent, of residual sugar, a five-*puttonyos* wine may contain ninety grams, or 9 percent, of residual sugar. A wine labeled Tokaji Aszu Eszencia contains six *puttonyos;* one labeled Tokaji Eszencia, exceptionally sweet and rarely encountered, is made entirely from the free-run juice that drips from the containers of *aszu* grapes before they are crushed. The sweet wines of Tokay are traditionally sold in 500-milliliter bottles, which hold two-thirds of a regular bottle.

Apart from Tokaji Aszu, other wines are also made in the Tokay vineyards. Tokaji Furmint is the normal wine of the district, and its label may carry the word *edes*, meaning sweet. Tokaji Szamorodni is made from grapes harvested without special attention to the proportion of *aszu* berries that may be present (*szamorodni* means "as it is grown"). The wine may consequently be dry or sweet, and this will be indicated on its label.

Famous as it is, Tokay accounts for less than 5 percent of Hungary's wines, which are produced in a number of districts throughout the country from a combination of state-run vineyards and wineries, cooperative cellars, and privately owned vineyards, with the last accounting for more than half the total acreage. The principal grape varieties cultivated for white wine include Ezerjó, Furmint, Hárslevelü (which means linden leaf), Kéknyelü, Szürkebarát (which means gray friar, and is actually Pinot Gris), Olaszriesling (which is the Welschriesling, not the Riesling of Germany), and Leányka (which means young girl, and is identical to the Fetească of Romania). Kadarka and Kékfrankos (known in Austria as Blaufränkisch) are the principal red-wine grapes. For the most part, Hungarian wines are labeled with a combination of the village of origin (which takes the possessive *i*) and the grape variety—Debröi Hárslevelü, Móri Ezerjó, Soproni Kékfrankos. A notable exception is the most famous red wine of Hungary, Egri Bikavér. The wine comes from vineyards around the village of Eger, but Bikaver means bull's blood, and the wine is made from Kadarka and Kékfrankos. There are other exceptions as well: Vörös means red wine, as in Szekszárdi Voros, and another red wine is labeled Villányi Burgundi.

A number of wines are produced along the shore of Lake Balaton, which is the largest lake in central Europe, and are so labeled—Balatoni Olaszriesling, Balatoni Furmint, and so on. Two well-known white wines from the slopes of Mount Badacsony, on the north shore of the lake, are Badacsonyi Kéknyelü and Badacsonyi Szürkebarát. In addition to the native varieties, some producers have also planted Cabernet Sauvignon, Merlot, Chardonnay, and Sauvignon Blanc, and Hungarian wines labeled with these varietal names can be found here as well.

GREECE

The vine may have appeared in Greece as early as 1500 B.C., and wine was certainly a common beverage in Homer's time, twenty-seven hundred years ago. Ancient Greek literature abounds in references to wine, and it's quite possible that these early Greek wines were of exceptional quality. For most of the past century, Greek wines were undistinguished, and production was dominated by Retsina, a generic name applied to any wine that has been flavored, during fermentation, with a small but unmistakable amount of pine resin. Retsina has an unusual and pungent flavor that is described by those who do not like it as the taste of turpentine. Those who enjoy Retsina find it to be an excellent complement to the oil-based dishes that abound in Greek cuisine. Retsina is usually a white wine, but it is also made as a red wine and a rosé, and may then be labeled Kokinelli. Nonresinated red and white wines were marketed, for the most part, with proprietary brand names created by the leading firms, such as Castel Danielis and Demestica of Achaia Clauss and Hymettus and Pendeli of Cambas.

In the early 1970s, Greek firms began to introduce modern equipment and winemaking techniques, and more than two dozen appellations of origin were created in anticipation of Greece's entry into the European Community. Several of these appellations refer to sweet dessert wines, such as the white Muscat of Rhodes, Muscat of Patras, and Muscat of Cephallonia and the unusual red Mavrodaphne of Patras and Mavrodaphne of Cephallonia. Appellations were also established for a variety of red, white, and rosé wines from wine districts throughout the country and on adjoining islands. White wines (and the grape varieties from which they are made) include Patras (Roditis), Côtes de Meliton (Roditis), Santorini (Asyritko), and Rhodes (Athiri). Some red appellations are Nemea (Agioritiko), Naoussa (Xynomavro), Paros (Monemvasia, Mandilaria),

Côtes de Meliton (Limnio), Rhodes (Mandilaria), and Kantza (Savatiano). A few producers are experimenting with Cabernet Sauvignon, Cabernet Franc, and Chardonnay, but consumers looking for contemporary Greek wines will have to familiarize themselves with a new set of place-names. The whites of Patras and Santorini and the reds from Nemea and Naoussa have already achieved some success. Producers include Achaia Clauss, Boutari, Domaine Carras, Hatzi Michalis, and Kourtakis, who also use the name Kouros.

BULGARIA

Once a part of ancient Thrace, whose wines were celebrated nearly three thousand years ago, Bulgaria has about 400,000 acres of vineyards, which produce thirty to forty-five million cases a year. Until the 1950s, Bulgaria's vineyards were planted almost exclusively with such native grapes as the red Gamza, Mavrud, and Pamid, and the white Dimiat, Misket, and Rkatsiteli. Today, classic varieties account for more than half the acreage: Cabernet Sauvignon is the most widely planted red grape, with Merlot second; white-wine grapes include Chardonnay, Italian Riesling, Rhine Riesling, Sauvignon Blanc, Pinot Gris, and Aligoté. The principal wine-producing regions of Bulgaria include Shumen, best known for its white wines; Suhindol, known for Cabernet Sauvignon and Gamza; and Haskovo, the Sungulare Valley, and the district around the village of Melnik. In practice, virtually all of the Bulgarian wines shipped here are sold under the Trakia label (Bulgarian for Thrace); the range includes a Cabernet Sauvignon and Merlot from the Slivin region, and a Chardonnay, Sauvignon Blanc, and Johannisberg Riesling from Shumen.

ROMANIA

With an annual production that usually varies from 80 to 100 million cases, Romania is one of Europe's major wine producers. Its extensive vineyards are planted with such native grapes as Grasa, Babeasca, Tamaioasa, and the red and white Feteasca, as well as with such familiar varieties as Cabernet Sauvignon, Merlot, Pinot Noir, Chardonnay, Traminer, Sauvignon Blanc, Pinot Gris, and Welschriesling (the lesser Italian Riesling). At one time, Romania's most famous wine was Cotnari, a sweet white wine similar to Tokay or Sauternes, produced in Moldavia. Today, the country's principal regions are Tarnave, known for its white wines; Dealul Mare, north of Bucharest, known for its reds; and Murfatlar, near the Black Sea. Almost all of the Romanian wines shipped here are marketed with the Premiat label; the selection includes a Cabernet Sauvignon and Merlot from Dealul Mare; a Sauvignon Blanc and Riesling from Tarnave; and a Chardonnay from Murfatlar.

The most famous wine regions of the former Yugoslavia are Slovenia, whose best-known wine is an off-dry Riesling from Lutomer and Maribor; and the Dalmatian coast of Croatia, which produces red wines from such native grapes as Plavac, Prokupac, and Vranac. The wines shipped to this country, however, consist primarily of such varietal wines as Cabernet Sauvignon, Merlot, Chardonnay, Sauvignon Blanc, and Riesling marketed under the brand name Avia.

Not long ago, the former Soviet Union vied with Spain for third place, after Italy and France, among the world's biggest wine producers; its 3.5 million acres of vineyards produced 400 million cases or more in some vintages. Most of the vineyards in the country once known as Russia were planted since the 1950s in a governmental attempt to promote wine as an alternative to vodka; production consisted primarily of sweet, fortified wines in the style of port and sherry, and much of the rest was made up of semisweet table wines and sparkling wines. Current production seems to be considerably less than in the recent past, and even the best-known wines, from the Crimea and Georgia, are rarely encountered here.

THE WINES OF
CALIFORNIA

For the American consumer, California continues to be
the most interesting and exciting of the world's new wine
regions. For several decades, California has supplied
about three-quarters of the wine consumed in this country. (The rest is made up of wines produced in other
states and imported wines.) For much of that time, the
bulk of these shipments consisted of moderately priced
jug wines whose quality and value had long been acknowledged. It is only in the past twenty years or so
that the excellence and diversity of the best California
wines have attracted the attention and admiration of
wine drinkers here and abroad, and that California has
been widely recognized as one of the world's fine wine
areas. Considering that many of the great European
wine regions were already well-established two or three
centuries ago, it's all the more remarkable how far California winemakers have come in such a comparatively
short time.

One indication of the pace at which changes have occurred is that as recently as the 1950s, three-quarters
of the state's wine production consisted of inexpensive
fortified and flavored wines; it was not until 1968 that

table wines—red, white, and pink, from the least expensive jugs to the finest bottles—accounted for even half of California's total production. Today, table wines and sparkling wines represent about 80 percent of the wines made in California.

The increased production of table wines, and especially fine varietal wines from such grapes as Cabernet Sauvignon, Chardonnay, Merlot, Pinot Noir, and Sauvignon Blanc, is a reflection of growing consumer interest. Just as the great wine châteaux of Bordeaux prospered only when, in the nineteenth century, an affluent French middle class was prepared to pay a higher price for wines of better quality, so the increased plantings of the best grape varieties in California became possible when enough American consumers began to discriminate among wines and were willing to pay a premium for the best of them. In 1959, there were only eighty thousand acres of wine grapes in California, and half of that consisted of Carignane, Grenache, and Zinfandel. Extensive plantings of new vineyards occurred in the late 1960s and early 1970s, and by 1974 there were more than 300,000 acres of wine grapes; some of this acreage was later uprooted or abandoned, much of it was converted from one grape variety to another, and new plantings have also taken place, raising the total to nearly 350,000 acres. But it was not simply the expansion of vineyards that affected quality, it was the kinds of grapes that were planted. The acreage of such classic varieties as Cabernet Sauvignon, Chardonnay, Sauvignon Blanc, Pinot Noir, Merlot, and Johannisberg Riesling increased from fewer than ten thousand acres to more than 130,000 acres. There is now twice as much Cabernet Sauvignon in California as in the Médoc district of Bordeaux, twice as much Chardonnay as in all of Burgundy, including Chablis, the Côte d'Or, and the Mâcon region.

The quality of California wines has developed so quickly that many of the wines that are considered among the finest produced in the state, and on a par with the best in the world, come from wineries that did not introduce their first wines until the late 1970s or early 1980s. Whereas almost all of Europe's great vineyards are already well-known, California's best sites are still being discovered. And because much of California's acreage is planted with vines that are not yet mature, and many of the wines made by young winemakers who are still experimenting with different styles, it is certain that as good as California wines are today, the state has yet to produce its finest bottles.

It was only two hundred years ago that the first vines were planted in southern California by Spanish missionaries. These Franciscans established additional missions throughout the state, and they planted vineyards as far up the coast as Sonoma, north of San Francisco. By the 1830s, when these clerical holdings were secularized, European immigrants and farmers from the East had begun to set up commercial vineyards in California.

In the 1850s a Hungarian, Agoston Haraszthy, made a significant contribution to the wine industry by publishing the results of his experiments in grape growing and winemaking. He later brought over about 100,000 vine cuttings from Europe, which greatly increased the number of *vinifera* grape varieties available to California winemakers.

The gradual development of the California wine industry owes a great debt to the many Europeans who established wineries in the second half of the nineteenth century and the early years of this one. They include Italians (Giuseppe and Pietro Simi, John Foppiano, and Samuele Sebastiani), Frenchmen (Paul Masson, Pierre Mirassou, Georges de Latour at Beaulieu Vineyard, and Etienne Thée and Charles Lefranc at Almadén), Germans (Carl Wente and the Beringer brothers), Czechs (the Korbel brothers), a Finn (Gustave Niebaum at Inglenook), an Irishman (James Concannon), a Prussian (Charles Krug), and a Hungarian (Agoston Haraszthy at Buena Vista). Then, less than a hundred years after it began, this industry was crippled by Prohibition. Many wineries went out of business and only a few were able to survive by producing sacramental wines or by growing grapes for home winemaking, which was still legal. The better wine varieties were uprooted and replaced by high-yield, thick-skinned grapes that could be shipped east without damage. As recently as 1971 two-thirds of the California crush—as the wine harvest is usually referred to—was made up of table and raisin grapes, primarily Thompson Seedless. Wine grapes accounted for more than half the total crush for the first time in 1974.

After the repeal of Prohibition, commercial winemaking started again almost from scratch, as there was a shortage of vinification equipment, of tanks and barrels to store the wine, of land planted in anything but high-yield varieties, of skilled personnel, and of a public accustomed to drinking table wines. It's not unfair to say that winemaking in California is not much more than sixty years old.

Actually, most of California's current success has been achieved in the relatively short period that began in the late 1960s. Part of that success was the result of adopting new winemaking technology, such as the use of temperature-controlled stainless-steel tanks to ferment white wines slowly at low temperatures, thus retaining the wine's fruit and delicacy while diminishing the possibility of browning and oxidation: controlled fermentors also permit winemakers to use higher temperatures to bring out the flavor of certain red wines. Just as important as technology has been the willingness of Californians to experiment with every aspect of winemaking, and to explore more fully the options that are available to winemakers everywhere. These include such techniques as skin contact—leaving the juice of white grapes in contact with their skins for a few hours before fermentation begins, to extract more flavor and aroma; and barrel fermentation—fermenting selected lots of white wine in small oak barrels rather than large tanks, to add to their richness and complexity.

Perhaps the most significant aspect of California winemaking, and the one that most clearly sets it apart from the traditional European approach, is its flexibility. A European winemaker is to a large extent bound within established norms: the boundaries of a given vineyard or appellation have already been defined; the grape varieties he may use are limited by law; and the winemaking techniques are traditional. In contrast, a California winemaker can choose the site on which to establish his vineyard and plant whichever varieties he cares to. Or he can buy grapes with which to make wines from any region, and is free to add a new variety or discontinue an old one from one vintage to the next. A winemaker from

Bordeaux cannot suddenly produce Burgundy or Rhine wine, but a California winemaker who specializes in Cabernet Sauvignon, the classic grape of Bordeaux, can begin to make Chardonnay or Johannisberg Riesling, varieties associated with Burgundy and the Rhine, respectively, just by finding a source for those grapes.

Not only can a winemaker change direction, but a grape-grower, too, can change over his vineyards, either by uprooting his vines and planting new ones, or by cutting an existing vine off above the ground and grafting on a different variety, a technique known as T-budding or budding over. Thus growers can convert from red varieties to more profitable white varieties, or replace varieties unsuitable for a particular region with more appropriate ones.

This flexibility was especially useful to growers who discovered that many of the vineyards created in the late 1960s and early 1970s were planted with the wrong varieties or in districts not suitable for grape-growing. Although the total vineyard acreage of several classic varieties has increased dramatically since 1969, the growth was not always a steady one, and has been subject to trial and error. New plantings of Pinot Noir, for example, expanded from fifteen hundred acres to ten thousand in five years, then dropped to half that before increasing again, in more appropriate sites, to more than nine thousand acres. Johannisberg Riesling acreage, which increased from twelve hundred in 1969 to ten thousand in the mid-1980s, has since diminished to a third of that. Merlot, too, went from two hundred acres to four thousand in five years, then dropped to half that before new plantings in different districts increased the total to more than ten thousand acres. These dramatic swings were not limited to the most famous varieties— the acreage of Petite Sirah, Ruby Cabernet, and Rubired increased from six thousand to nearly forty-five thousand acres in just a few years before gradually dropping back to less than a third of that.

As California winemakers were mastering different aspects of vinification and aging, the focus shifted from the cellar to the vineyard, where new viticultural techniques began to affect the quality and style of different varieties. These include clonal selection, choosing the most appropriate example of a specific grape variety, such as Pinot Noir or Chardonnay, for a particular site and its microclimate; trellising, training the branches of each vine to assure the best growing conditions; and canopy management, shaping the canopy of leaves on each vine to obtain optimum exposure to sunlight and air. Many growers are also experimenting with vine density, the number of vines planted per acre: the vineyards of Bordeaux, for example, are traditionally planted with four thousand vines to the acre, California vineyards with about 425, yet the yield per acre is similar; greater density is thought to produce smaller and riper grapes, which results in wines with more concentration of flavor. Also, a number of producers, including such large firms as Gallo, Fetzer, Buena Vista, and Sutter Home are experimenting with organic farming, which avoids the use of herbicides, pesticides, fungicides, and chemical fertilizers in the vineyards, and employs natural insect and pest controls and cover crops to nourish the soil. Note that grapes from organically farmed vineyards do not necessarily become organic wines, which are vinified without the use of sulfites and other preservatives.

Winemakers in Europe and California are likely to have different goals, which affects the styles of their wines. The European, producing wines from specific grape varieties in a delimited region, will strive for appellation character, that is, for wines that reflect their place of origin. In California, where appellations of origin are only beginning to be established, and where many different varieties are grown in the same region, the winemaker strives for varietal character, that is, for wines that express the potential of the grape from which each is made. As a result, many of the California wines made in the 1970s from such varieties as Chardonnay and Cabernet Sauvignon emphasized power and intensity of flavor at the expense of subtlety and refinement. By the 1980s, producers and consumers alike had realized that although ripe, full-bodied, heady wines often stand out in a comparative tasting, they may not be enjoyable at the dinner table, and the style of California wines began to evolve accordingly, and continues to evolve in the 1990s.

Many elements contribute to a wine's style, but two

that seem to have considerable impact are the degree of ripeness of the grapes at harvest (which affects the wine's alcohol content), and the extent to which the wine is aged in oak barrels. California has more sun during the growing season than do the top wine regions of Europe, so the grapes contain more sugar when they are picked, and do not need to have sugar added, as is usually the case in France and Germany. But the comparatively warm temperatures in many of California's grape-growing regions often result in wines with a relatively high alcohol content—13.5 to 14.5 percent is not uncommon. In the recent past, many winemakers believed that maximum ripeness meant more varietal character; some still do, but others feel they can get the flavor, structure, and weight they want in a wine with less alcohol. They are trying to counteract California's abundant sunshine by picking their grapes earlier, when they contain less sugar and more natural acidity, which results in wines with less power and better balance.

Perhaps the most widely discussed aspect of making California wines is the use of small, sixty-gallon French oak barrels from the forests of Nevers, Limousin, Allier, and Tronçais, as well as the use of fifty- and sixty-gallon American oak barrels. Although many delicate, fruity, charming red and white wines are bottled without being aged in wood, most winemakers agree that oak provides additional depth and complexity to such wines as Cabernet Sauvignon and Chardonnay, as well as a tannic structure that enables fine red or white wines to mature more gracefully. Too much oak obscures a wine's taste, instead of enhancing it, however, and as the preference for rich, oaky wines has evolved into a greater appreciation for balanced, elegant ones, winemakers are using oak more judiciously. But just as some producers were striving for restraint and complexity from the start, so others still prefer the big, impressive, powerful style, and make their wines accordingly.

The choices available to California winemakers represent a challenge and an opportunity, but they also pose a problem for the consumer. As winemakers are finding their way with specific varieties and with the overall style of the wines they produce, the wines themselves do not always maintain a continuity of style. Among the established European wines, the primary difference between one year and the next is based on the character of the vintage; in California, the style of a particular wine may change arbitrarily. This provides the interested consumer with an ongoing sense of discovery, but it sometimes makes it difficult to define the style of a winery and of its individual wines, or to choose wines on the basis of past experience.

Reading a California Label

California table wines are often divided into two broad categories based on the way they are marketed: *generic wines,* labeled for the most part with the names of famous European wine regions; and *varietal wines,* labeled with the name of the specific grape variety from which each wine is primarily made. The most familiar generic names for red wines are Burgundy and Chianti, and for white wines, Chablis, Sauterne (usually spelled without the final *s* in California), and Rhine Wine. These names are among the best known to wine drinkers and have, therefore, been used almost from the beginning of California winemaking to suggest, in a general way, the kind of wine contained in the bottle. Actually, generic wines have more in common with each other than with the European wines whose names are being used. Many California wineries sell generic wines, and although they are still very popular and widely available, they no longer dominate the table wine market as they did for so many years since the repeal of Prohibition. Also, while generic names are here to stay, there is also a trend away from the use of European place-names, and some wineries now label their less expensive wines simply as Red Table Wine, Mountain White Wine, Premium Red, Classic Red, Vintage White, and so on.

This category includes the least-expensive table wines available in this country, and many of them provide excellent value. Most of them are sold in jugs, and now that metric sizes have been adopted, the familiar half-gallons and gallons have been replaced by the 50.7-ounce magnum and the 101.4-ounce jeroboam. If there is a problem with generic wines, however, it is not that they don't taste like the European originals, but that there are no standards to help the consumer find his or her way among different brands. Perhaps the most important variable among generic wines is that some are dry and many are not. While a certain amount of sweetness in both white and red wines appeals to a large segment of the public, those who prefer completely dry table wines cannot simply assume that a Chablis will be drier than a Sauterne or a Rhine wine. For one thing, some wineries market identical wines under different generic labels. For another, many wineries maintain a minimum amount of sweetness in all their wines, others in none of them. The sweetness, which usually comes from grape concentrate added just before bottling, is often 1 percent and not infrequently 2 percent, which is far from dry.

Although many well-made generic wines at moderate prices continue to offer good values, it is among varietal wines that almost all the finest California wines are to be found. Consumers have not always been as familiar with the names of individual grapes as they are today—in the 1950s many wineries found it easier to sell a wine made primarily from Cabernet Sauvignon as Claret than as Cabernet Sauvignon. Today the situation is reversed. As consumers have discovered that varietal wines are likely to be more distinctive than generic wines, and that the best varietal wines represent the best that California has to offer, varietal labeling has caught on to such an extent that these wines, which once accounted for less than 10 percent of table wine sales, now amount to more than half the market. White Zinfandel, Chardonnay, and Cabernet Sauvignon are the most popular varietal wines, and others include Sauvignon Blanc, Pinot Noir, Merlot, Zinfandel, and Johannisberg Riesling. There are more than two dozen varietal names in general use, and they are described further on.

Since 1983, a varietal wine must be made at least 75 percent from the grape named on its label. In practice, the finest wines are made entirely, or almost entirely, from the named grape, and few winemakers would claim that such varieties as Pinot Noir and Chardonnay are improved by blending in another variety. Inexpensive varietal wines, however, are often stretched by blending in neutral wines. Since it is the character of a specific grape variety that distinguishes varietal wines and gives them their personality, the extent to which they are diluted can have an important effect on their taste. On the other hand, many winemakers believe that certain varieties can be improved by judicious blending with a complementary one. Cabernet Sauvignon, for example, may be blended with Merlot or Cabernet Franc, as in Bordeaux; and the intensity of Sauvignon Blanc, another Bordeaux variety, may be softened by adding Sémillon. If more than 25 percent of a complementary variety is added, that fact may be shown on the label, but the wine cannot be labeled with a single varietal name.

Because more winemakers want greater flexibility in assembling blends based on Cabernet Sauvignon and Sauvignon Blanc, a number of producers formed an association and chose the name Meritage (rhymes with *heritage*) to label such wines. If that name appears on the label, only Bordeaux varieties may be used—Cabernet Sauvignon, Merlot, Cabernet Franc, Malbec, and Petit Verdot for the reds; Sauvignon Blanc, Sémillon, and Muscadelle for the whites. Many members of the association, which also includes wineries outside California, use the name Meritage, others prefer to label their blends with proprietary names.

In addition to generic names and varietal names, a third way to label wines is with a *proprietary name*, which a winery creates to market a specific wine: Emerald Dry, Bravissimo, Paisano, and Soléo are such examples. Although proprietary names were most often used for moderately priced wines, as an alternative to generic names, they are now increasingly used for a winery's most expensive wines, as an alternative to varietal names. Insignia, Opus One, Dominus, Rubicon, Réserve Alexandre, and Trilogy are some names used for red wines based on Cabernet Sauvignon or blended from the Bordeaux varieties. Le Cigare Volant, Le Mistral, and Oakley Cuvée are proprietary names used for red wines made from the varieties usually associated with France's Rhône Valley.

An increasingly important category of California wine that is not legally defined is that of reserve wines—that is, wines labeled Reserve, Private Reserve, Special Selection, Proprietor's Selection, Vintage Selection, and so on. A winery's reserve bottling of a given varietal wine—usually Cabernet Sauvignon, Chardonnay, Pinot Noir, or Sauvignon Blanc—is always more expensive than its regular bottling, yet the basis of selection varies considerably from one producer to another. A reserve wine may come from one or two specific vineyards whose grapes are vinified and aged apart, it may be selected from the winery's entire inventory of a given variety some months after vinification and then aged separately, or it may simply be the regular wine aged a few months longer in wood. Whatever criteria are used, the reserve bottling is likely to be more concentrated in flavor, is expected to be longer lived, and is one that the winemaker finds in some way more impressive; whether or not it is worth a higher price depends on the taste and preferences of each consumer. Note that although most wineries use the reserve designation for their finest wines, a few wineries use terms such as Proprietor's Reserve for their least expensive bottlings.

Appellations of Origin

If one factor that affects a wine's quality and taste is the grape variety from which it is made, another that is becoming increasingly important is where the grapes are grown. Although some consumers may still think of California as a single area, the state includes regions as cool as Bordeaux, Burgundy, Champagne, and the Rhine and as warm as the Rhône Valley, central Italy, southern Spain, and North Africa. Certain parts of the state are best suited to high-yield grape varieties that can be distilled into brandy or blended to produce fortified dessert wines, others to ordinary table wine, and certain limited areas to the production of red and white wines with the finesse and individuality of the best European wines.

One basic distinction to be made among California wines—both generic and varietal—is that between the wines produced in the cooler coastal counties that extend north and south of San Francisco and those produced in the San Joaquin Valley. Also known as the Central Valley, the San Joaquin Valley stretches for more than two hundred miles from Lodi (pronounced *low*-die) down to Bakersfield, and it is in this warm interior valley that most of California's wine grapes are grown, as well as almost all of its table and raisin grapes. Despite the tremendous increase in coastal vineyards, about three-quarters of all California wine comes from the San Joaquin Valley.

The interior valley has always been a source of generic wines, but as more consumers have associated varietal wines with quality there has been a tendency to label comparatively undistinguished wines with varietal names. Every wine, after all, is made from one or more grape varieties, but in the past, producers of inexpensive generic wines saw no advantage in labeling such wines with the name of the grape from which each was primarily made. The extensive new acreage in the San Joaquin Valley made it possible for varietally labeled wines to be produced in large quantities from such grapes as Barbera, Ruby Cabernet, Zinfandel, Chenin Blanc, and French Colombard, as well as Cabernet Sauvignon and Chardonnay. Generally speaking, wines made from grapes grown in the warm interior valley tend to have less varietal character, individuality, and liveliness than those from cooler regions. Consequently, while some varietal wines from the San Joaquin Valley are well made and moderately priced, a number of others are no more distinctive than the generic Burgundy and Chablis they are meant to replace.

Just as European winemakers have established, through trial and error, that specific varieties produce the finest wines only in certain regions, so California growers are gradually determining the best sites for each of the major wine grapes. The traditional technique used in California is that of heat summation, based on the average daily temperature during the six-month growing season from April to October. The coolest areas are designated as Region I, the warmest as Region V, whatever their actual location, and these five designations have been widely used to determine which grape varieties will flourish best in a particular district. In recent years, more exacting and sophisticated techniques are being used to match grape varieties with specific microclimates throughout the state.

The traditional fine-wine area in California has been the North Coast counties that fan out from San Francisco—Napa, Sonoma, Mendocino, Alameda (which contains the Livermore Valley), and Santa Clara. In the last twenty-five years, winemakers have discovered that fine wines can also be made in such counties as Monterey, San Luis Obispo, Santa Barbara, and Amador, among others. As new vineyards and new wineries have been created, there has been an increasing use of appellations of origin in California labels. In the past, the names most frequently seen were those of counties—Sonoma, Mendocino, Monterey, Santa Barbara—and if such a name appears on a label, at least 75 percent of the wine must come from that county. New appellations of origin, known as viticultural areas, were first established in 1983. A viticultural area (officially known as an American Viticultural Area, or AVA) is a delimited grape-growing region whose geographical features and boundaries have been recognized and defined; it is the growers in a given area who must define its boundaries and then petition the government for the right to use the name of the area on their labels. If a viticultural area appears on a label, at least 85 percent of the wine must come from that area. There are now about seventy viticultural areas in California (and another fifty or so in other states), and they vary greatly in size. The North Coast appellation has now been defined to include the counties north of San Francisco—Napa, Sonoma, Mendocino, Lake, Solano, and Marin. The Central Coast appellation includes an extensive area south of San Francisco—Alameda, Santa Clara, Santa Cruz, Monterey, San Benito, San Luis Obispo, and Santa Barbara. The Napa Valley appellation includes virtually all of Napa County's thirty-five thousand acres; Mendocino's Anderson Valley and San Luis Obispo's Edna Valley are much more narrowly defined. Sonoma County includes about a dozen appellations, many of which overlap. Some areas are known as one-owner appellations—there is only one producer in Guenoc Valley, Chalone, Mount Harlan, and York Mountain. Other appellations extend across political borders to include two or more counties—Carneros, Sierra Foothills, Santa Cruz Mountains.

The idea of appellations of origin is still a relatively new one in California, and the stylistic differences between wines coming from different areas are as likely to reflect the philosophy of a given winemaker as the area in which the grapes were grown. Just because an area can be defined geographically doesn't mean that the wines produced from its vineyards are necessarily special, or even distinctive (it's the area that's defined, not the quality of the fruit grown there nor the specific grape varieties permitted), but the increased emphasis on appellations will encourage wineries and the growers from whom they buy their grapes to focus more intently on the particular varieties best suited to a specific combination of soil and microclimate. Even now, many consumers are already aware of such felicitous pairings as Carneros Pinot Noir, Dry Creek Valley Zinfandel, Santa Maria Valley Chardonnay, Livermore Valley Sauvignon Blanc, and Stags Leap District Cabernet Sauvignon.

Wines with the most specific place of origin are those that come from individual vineyards. No less than 95 percent of a vineyard-designated wine must come from the named vineyard. As in Europe, the wine from a particular vineyard may display a distinctive personality, and an increasing number of California wineries are producing single-vineyard wines. Of course, vinifying, aging, and bottling wine from a specific plot of land separately and putting its name on the label may retain the wine's individuality, but is no guarantee of better quality.

Phrases such as *made and bottled, produced and bottled, estate-bottled,* and *proprietor-grown* all have specific meanings, but they are less significant than the reputation of the winery. In California many of the finest wines are made from purchased grapes rather than from grapes grown by a producer in his own vineyards, so the concept of estate bottling is less important than in Bordeaux, for example, where the best wines come from specific, named vineyards and are bottled at the property.

Vintages

A vintage-dated wine must contain no less than 95 percent of grapes harvested in the vintage indicated. It has often been claimed that there are no bad vintages in California, along with the corollary statement that there are no variations from one California vintage to another. The first claim has some validity. In most of Europe's fine-wine districts grapes don't ripen fully every year, whereas in California it is unusual for grapes to be unripe at the time of the harvest. Nevertheless, there are years when a very cool growing season in parts of California has resulted in grapes that never fully ripened; there have been years when rains during the vintage caused a certain amount of rot to form on the grapes; and years when extensive drought conditions affected the quality of the wines. In some years a heat spell in the fall may cause certain grapes to become overripe, which results in raisiny, unbalanced wines high in alcohol; in other years, several different varieties, which normally ripen one after the other over six to eight weeks, may be ready for picking within two weeks of each other, making timely harvesting and vinification difficult.

As the range of vintage-dated varietal wines has increased, consumers have become much more aware of vintage variations in California, as well as of varietal and regional differences. After all, when grapes as different as Cabernet Sauvignon, Chardonnay, Pinot Noir, and Johannisberg Riesling grow side by side, it's inevitable that a particular growing season will favor one variety over another. And just as there are differences to be found in a given vintage between wines produced in the Médoc and in Saint-Emilion, or between Rieslings from the Moselle and the Rheingau, so there are bound to be differences between Cabernet Sauvignon from Napa and Mendocino, or between Chardonnays produced in Sonoma and Monterey, which are nearly two hundred miles apart. Ironically, just as Bordeaux vintages represent, for many consumers, all of France, so the relative success of Napa Valley Cabernet Sauvignon is often, and erroneously, used as a vintage guide to all California wines.

In addition to the basic information contained on a California wine label, which can be more or less explicit depending on the wine, many wineries volunteer additional details about how each of their wines is made. Special back labels indicate, for example, the sugar content of the grapes when they were picked (expressed in degrees Brix), and the date of picking; the temperature at which the wine was fermented, and for how long; the kind of wood in which the wine was aged; when it was bottled; the amount of alcohol and acid in the finished wine; and the wine's exact varietal content. While this is more information than most consumers need to know when they pull the cork, it does indicate the extent to which California winemakers are prepared to experiment with, and discuss, every aspect of winemaking.

Late-Harvest Wines

One of the most dramatic developments in recent years has been the recognition of *Botrytis cinerea* in California vineyards. This beneficial mold, called *pourriture noble* in Sauternes and *Edelfäule* in Germany (both mean noble rot), shrivels ripe grapes, intensifies their flavor, and increases the sugar content of the juice. It was long believed that climatic conditions in California would not permit *Botrytis cinerea* to develop, but in 1969 Wente Bros. harvested naturally botrytised Johannisberg Riesling grapes in its Arroyo Seco vineyards in Monterey County. In 1973 Wente Bros. made an even sweeter wine, and Freemark Abbey, in the Napa Valley, produced a botrytised Johannisberg Riesling, which it called Edelwein, with 10 percent residual sugar. By the mid-1970s Joseph Phelps Vineyards, Chateau St. Jean, and other wineries were producing remarkable late-harvest Johannisberg Rieslings with an intensity and richness equal to Beerenauslese and Trockenbeerenauslese wines from the Rhine.

The earliest examples of such wines were labeled Spätlese and Auslese to suggest their similarity to German wines, but the use of German words was soon prohibited. Such wines are now labeled Late Harvest, Select Late Harvest, and Special Select Late Harvest; minimum sugar levels have been established for each of these categories, which correspond to the German categories Auslese, Beerenauslese, and Trockenbeerenauslese. In any case, the label must also indicate the sugar content of the grapes at the time of picking and the wine's residual sugar after fermentation, so that the consumer can determine just how sweet each late harvest wine is. The first late-harvest wines were made primarily from Johannisberg Riesling and Gewürztraminer, as in Germany, but a number of wineries now produce such wines from Sémillon and Sauvignon Blanc, as in the Sauternes region of France. Also, some producers label their late-harvest wines with proprietary names, such as Edelwein Gold, Eldorado Gold, Délice du Sémillon, and Dolce.

Light Wines

Light wines, which are lower in alcohol than most table wines and contain fewer calories as well, were introduced in 1981. They were aimed at the same calorie-conscious consumers who buy light beer, diet soft drinks, and bottled water. Light wines are lower in calories because they have less alcohol—most contain only 7 to 9 percent—but it was only recently that they could be produced by California wineries. Previously, California law required a minimum alcohol content of 10 percent for white wines and 10.5 percent for reds, even though the federal requirements were only 7 percent. Consequently, wines with 8 or 9 percent alcohol—such as German Moselles and Italian Lambruscos—could be imported, but California winemakers could not produce similar wines.

At the end of 1979 the California law was changed to conform to federal regulations in order to accommodate wineries that wanted to produce "soft" wines, sweet, low-alcohol wines made by stopping fermentation while a substantial amount of residual sugar remained in the wine. As it happens, the change in the California law also permitted producers of late-harvest wines to retain even more residual sugar in their luscious dessert wines; previously, such wines had to be fermented until they contained at least 10 percent of alcohol. The new regulations also enabled California wineries to introduce moderately priced bottles and magnums of low-alcohol "light" wines with one-quarter to one-third fewer calories than their regular wines. A number of firms market such wines, the best known of which are Masson Light of Paul Masson and Light Chablis of Los Hermanos.

Special Natural Wines and Wine Coolers

In addition to table wines, dessert wines, sparkling wines, and vermouth, there is a category known as special natural wines, which are flavored, usually sweet, and sometimes lightly carbonated, and which include wines made from apples or pears as well as from grapes. Some contain 20 percent alcohol; others, which are also known as pop or refreshment wines, contain about 10 percent alcohol. Thunderbird and Boone's are among the best-known labels. In the early 1970s, special natural wines accounted for as much as one out of every six bottles of wine consumed in this country, but the audience for these fruit-flavored wines has diminished.

Wine coolers are a sprightly, wine-based beverage with 4 to 6 percent alcohol; most are a blend of neutral wine, carbonated water, sugar, and various flavors, usually fruit. First created in 1981, wine coolers increased their sales from four thousand cases the first year to more than fifty million cases five years later, and accounted for about 20 percent of total American wine sales, led by such brands as California Cooler, Seagram's Coolers, and, from Gallo, Bartles & James. Coolers are no longer as popular as they once were and, as it happens, many brands are now made with malt rather than wine.

THE PRINCIPAL GRAPE VARIETIES

Most European wines are labeled with the name of the district, village, or vineyard from which each comes, as defined by its appellation of origin. In California, a wine's origin plays a less important role than the grape variety from which it is primarily or entirely made. Although a wine's place of origin has become increasingly significant to the quality and style of California wines, most consumers still focus on varietal names when choosing wines, and anyone with an interest in California wines soon learns to distinguish among the different varietal names with which these wines are labeled.

Important plantings of the classic European grape varieties took place in the early 1970s, and in subsequent years many new plantings have occurred, a number of existing vineyards have been replanted with different varieties, and the acreage of several traditional California varieties has decreased substantially. A few overall figures suggest the extent to which the acreage of certain popular varieties has increased in California in the past twenty-five years or so. The acreage of Chardonnay, for example, has expanded dramatically from eighteen hundred in 1969 to more than sixty thousand; Cabernet Sauvignon has increased from four thousand to thirty-five thousand; Sauvignon Blanc from six hundred to thirteen thousand; Merlot from one hundred to ten thousand; and Pinot Noir from two thousand to nine thousand. During the same period, Carignane has diminished from thirty thousand acres to nine thousand, Barbera from twenty thousand to ten thousand, Grenache from twenty thousand to thirteen thousand, and there are also fewer acres of such varieties as Alicante Bouschet, Grey Riesling, and Sylvaner.

Red Wines

Cabernet Sauvignon, the classic red grape of Bordeaux, produces many of the finest red wines of California, noted for their concentration of flavor and firm structure, and for their tannic, puckerish qualities when young, which enables them to age in the bottle for many years; ripe examples may display nuances of blackcurrant, lighter examples may suggest bell pepper. In the Médoc region of Bordeaux, a certain amount of *Merlot*, which produces relatively supple wines, is used to soften the austerity of Cabernet Sauvignon, and this practice has been adopted in California as well. As more Merlot was planted in California, an increasing number of wineries began to bottle this variety on its own, often blending in a proportion of Cabernet Sauvignon to add backbone. *Cabernet Franc*, which produces aromatic wines with lively acidity, has also been planted in California, as have the lesser-known Bordeaux varieties *Malbec* and *Petit Verdot*, and many wineries use one or another of these varieties to complement Cabernet Sauvignon.

Pinot Noir, from France's Burgundy region, was for many years the least successful of the classic varieties in

California; some examples were light and indistinct, others were full-bodied but lacked the complexity and finesse of fine red Burgundies. In recent years, selected clones, or variants, of Pinot Noir have been planted in cooler districts, such as Carneros, the Russian River Valley, and parts of Monterey and Santa Barbara counties, and the combination of more suitable microclimates, lower yields, and different vinification techniques for this fragile variety has resulted in an expanding range of excellent wines. Note, too, that a significant portion of the Pinot Noir crop is used to make *méthode champenoise* sparkling wines.

Gamay Beaujolais is now officially classified as a clone of Pinot Noir, and wines made from this variety may legally be sold under either name. Since the name Gamay Beaujolais has become familiar to consumers, many wineries continue to sell lighter-bodied examples with that name and market fuller ones as Pinot Noir. The variety called *Gamay* or *Napa Gamay* was thought to be similar to the one cultivated in the Beaujolais region, but some ampelographers now believe that Napa Gamay is really the lesser variety Valdiguié, from southern France. Both Napa Gamay and Gamay Beaujolais are usually bottled early and meant to be drunk young. Several wineries even produce a Gamay Beaujolais Nouveau, in the style of France's Beaujolais Nouveau, which is bottled and sold within weeks of the harvest.

Although the *Zinfandel* grape is of European origin, its wines are often referred to as typically American because they are unlike those produced anywhere else. The origin of Zinfandel, long considered a Hungarian variety, remains something of a mystery. It has now been identified as similar if not identical to the Primitivo of southern Italy, but it seems likely that the Primitivo is not native to Italy, but was brought there from another country. Plantings of Zinfandel increased considerably in the 1970s, and it displaced Carignane as the most widely cultivated red-wine grape in California. When grown in the Central Valley, it usually produces undistinguished wine suitable for blending in generic reds. In cooler areas, it makes a very individual and appealing wine with a distinctive spicy or berrylike aroma and taste. Winemakers can vinify this grape to produce a range of styles, from a light, fruity wine to be consumed young, like Beaujolais, to one that is rich, tannic, intensely flavored, and long-lived. In the early 1980s, Zinfandel had lost some of its popularity, partly because the diversity of styles confused many consumers, and acreage of this variety decreased. By the mid-1980s, however, White Zinfandel—a simple, slightly sweet pink wine (described further on)—had become very popular, and acreage of Zinfandel increased, as did the number of producers making medium-bodied, well-balanced red Zinfandel.

Petite Sirah produces intensely colored, full-flavored, and tannic wines that have long been used in generic blends; in addition, a number of wineries in the coastal counties market Petite Sirah as a varietal wine. Plantings increased considerably in the 1970s, to thirteen thousand acres, but have since been reduced to fewer than three thousand. It is now generally agreed that California Petite Sirah is not the Syrah of the northern Rhône, but more likely a variety called Durif, from southern France. The true *Syrah* of the Rhône is now cultivated in California, and accounts for more than six hundred acres; despite its limited acreage, Syrah produces some of California's most interesting red wines.

Carignane, widely planted in southern France, is a high-yield variety used almost entirely as a blending wine, although a few wineries market it as a varietal wine. *Grenache,* another variety from southern France extensively planted in the Central Valley, is best known as a varietal rosé labeled Grenache Rosé or, more recently, White Grenache. In the past decade, a number of California winemakers have become interested in Rhône varieties, such as Syrah, Mourvèdre (long known in California as Mataro), Carignane, and Grenache, and are producing varietal wines or proprietary blends from these grapes, especially those grown in old vineyards whose crop produces more concentrated wines.

Barbera is widely grown in northern Italy and in California's Central Valley, where it produces agreeable wines that contribute lively acidity to generic blends. A limited amount of Barbera is also made in the coastal counties, some of which is marketed as a varietal wine. *Charbono,* another north Italian variety, is similar to Barbera, although fuller-bodied; fewer than one hundred acres now exist, and the wine is only occasionally encountered as a varietal wine. A few winemakers are experimenting with such classic Italian varieties as *Sangiovese* and *Nebbiolo,* and these may be now found as varietal wines.

Ruby Cabernet, a cross of Cabernet Sauvignon with Carignane, has been widely planted in the Central Valley, where it gives an abundant yield of agreeable wines. *Rubired,* another cross, is noted for the deep red color of its juice, which makes it especially useful for blending. Although Carignane, Grenache, Barbera, Ruby Cabernet, and Rubired are not acclaimed varieties, and even though the acreage of each variety has decreased in recent years, these five grapes still account for more than 40 percent of California's red-grape crop.

Carnelian, a cross of Cabernet Sauvignon, Carignane, and Grenache, was developed as a high-yield variety for use in the Central Valley; *Carmine* and *Centurion* are other Cabernet-based crosses.

White Wines

Chardonnay, the classic grape of Burgundy, is considered the most successful white-wine variety in California. The wines, which do not have a strong varietal personality, may suggest melon and fig or, in some cases, tropical fruit. Fine Chardonnays are often barrel-fermented and most are aged in small oak barrels to add complexity and nuances of toast and vanilla. At their best, Chardonnays are rich, full-flavored, complex, and elegant, and are among the longest lived of dry white wines. It should be added that, as a result of extensive new plantings, this variety now represents more than 20 percent of the white-grape crop, and many examples are relatively simple and undistinguished.

Sauvignon Blanc is the grape used, in combination with Sémillon, to make white Bordeaux and Graves and is also used on its own along the Loire to make such assertive dry wines as Sancerre and Pouilly-Fumé. California Sauvignon Blanc had never been a popular varietal wine until Robert Mondavi introduced a dry, flavorful Sauvignon Blanc labeled Fumé Blanc in the late 1960s. Sauvignon Blanc and Fumé Blanc (the names are interchangeable) is now marketed by a great many wineries as a dry wine whose grassy, herbaceous character makes it one of California's most distinctive white wines. Just as Merlot is blended with Cabernet Sauvignon, *Sémillon,* which makes a somewhat softer, fuller-bodied wine, is often blended with Sauvignon Blanc to produce a less assertive and more complex white wine; some of these Sauvignon Blanc-Sémillon blends are labeled as Meritage or with a proprietary name. A few wineries also bottle Sémillon as a dry varietal wine, and some winemakers make a sweet, *botrytis*-infected Sémillon in the style of Sauternes.

The Riesling grape that is cultivated along Germany's Rhine and Moselle rivers is called *Johannisberg Riesling* or *White Riesling* in California. It produces fragrant and charming wines that usually have more body and alcohol than Rieslings from Germany; a few wineries make a dry Johannisberg Riesling, as in Alsace, but most retain a certain amount of sugar to produce a semidry wine. In addition to the wide range of medium-dry Johannisberg Rieslings produced in California, winemakers there have also been remarkably successful in making sweet, honeyed, late-harvest wines similar to the Auslese, Beerenauslese, and even Trockenbeerenauslese wines of Germany.

In California, *Sylvaner* may be labeled Riesling, and most of them are, although the names Franken Riesling or Riesling-Sylvaner may occasionally be seen. The wine, which is usually semidry, does not have the fragrance or elegance of a true Riesling. *Grey Riesling,* which is not a Riesling at all, is capable of producing wines that are dry and crisp, but most examples are semisweet and undistinguished. *Emerald Riesling,* a cross of Riesling with Muscadelle, produces pale-colored, light-bodied, rather neutral wines. The acreage of Sylvaner, Grey Riesling, and Emerald Riesling has decreased considerably in recent years.

Chenin Blanc, used to make such Loire Valley wines as Vouvray and Anjou Blanc, produces fruity, appealing wines in California, where it has long played an important role in generic white wines. Many wineries market Chenin Blanc as a varietal wine; a few are completely dry, but most range from semidry to semisweet. Some years ago, Chenin Blanc was occasionally labeled, misleadingly, as Pinot Blanc, perhaps because the grape is also known as Pineau de la Loire. As it turns out, the grape long known in California as *Pinot Blanc* is probably Melon de Bourgogne, which produces the light, dry wines of Muscadet. More recently, some California sparkling wine firms have planted true Pinot Blanc to use in their blends.

French Colombard, an anonymous component of many generic blends, was for many years the most widely planted white-wine grape in California. (It is now second to Chardonnay.) Often bottled as an inexpensive varietal wine, it can be made into a pleasant off-dry wine with a touch of acidity, especially in the cooler coastal regions. French Colombard and Chenin Blanc, most of it cultivated in the Central Valley, and capable of much higher yields than Chardonnay, account for nearly two-thirds of California's white-wine crop.

Wines labeled *Gewürztraminer* have a pungent aroma and pronounced taste that place them among the most distinctive white wines. *Gewürz* means spicy, and even muted versions of this wine retain its characteristic rose-petal bouquet and intense flavor. In France's Alsace region, Gewürztraminer is almost always dry; in California, most examples range from semidry to semisweet.

Viognier, an unusual and fragile variety from the northern Rhône, has been planted in California, where it makes a delicate dry wine with a subtle, floral aroma. Two other Rhône varieties, *Marsanne* and *Roussanne,* are also being cultivated by a few growers.

Muscat Blanc, also known as Muscat Canelli, is used to make sweet, aromatic table wines, fortified wines, and sparkling wines. Some producers also blend Muscat into neutral white wines to add aroma and flavor.

Green Hungarian, once a popular wine—as much for its name as for its taste—is not often seen anymore. *Folle Blanche,* known along the Loire as Gros Plant, makes a light-bodied, dry wine.

Flora, a cross of Sémillon and Gewürztraminer, has not been widely planted and is rarely seen as a varietal wine. *Symphony,* a new cross of Muscat of Alexandria and Grenache Gris, was introduced in the 1980s; it can produce wines that range from dry to sweet.

Rosés and Blanc de Noirs

Most California rosés are blended from different varieties and sold as Vin Rosé, Pink Chablis, Chablis Blush, or with a proprietary name. Of the varietal rosés, Grenache Rosé, first popularized by Almadén, was for many years the best known. Rosés are also made from Zinfandel, Gamay, Pinot Noir, and Cabernet Sauvignon. The best of them, which retain the varietal characteristics of the grape, are among the most distinctive and attractive rosés available.

Some years ago, in response to the increased demand for white wines, a number of wineries began to market white wines made from black grapes, which are often referred to as *blanc de noirs*. The color in red wine is extracted from the skins during fermentation, so if black grapes are pressed immediately after picking and the juice fermented away from the skins (as is done in the Champagne district of France), the result is a white wine. In practice, California versions are usually light pink in color, so the word White or Blanc that almost always appears on the label is not really accurate, although it permits wineries to avoid the less desirable word Rosé. The wines are marketed as if they were white, however, and are meant to be served chilled.

At first, Pinot Noir was the variety most often used to make a *blanc de noirs*. Then, in the mid-1980s, White Zinfandel, popularized by Sutter Home Winery, began to dominate the market for these wines, and soon became the best-selling varietal wine of California. Most examples range in color from pale salmon to pink and in taste from semidry to semisweet. The grapes used for White Zinfandel are usually harvested earlier than those made into red wines so that they have less color, less sugar (which results in wines with less alcohol), and more crisp acidity. Such grapes also produce wines with relatively little flavor, so many producers blend in a proportion of wines made from such aromatic varieties as Gewürztraminer and Muscat. The success of White Zinfandel resulted in similar wines made from other varieties, such as White Grenache and Cabernet Blanc.

The California Wine Regions

The changes that are continually taking place in California mean that any description of its wine regions and wineries must necessarily be tentative. New wine-producing districts are still being created where vines were not previously cultivated, microclimates particularly suited to one or another variety are being discovered within established vineyard regions, and new viticultural areas continue to be officially defined and recognized. Many wineries, too, are in a state of flux. The size and ambitions of a winery may change because of new ownership, the style of its wines may be affected by a new winemaker, a winery that produces a particular range of varietal wines may drop some and add others, the Reserve designation may be changed to another term or to a proprietary name, single-vineyard bottlings may be introduced. The following discussion of the principal wine regions and viticultural areas, and brief descriptions of some of the better-known wineries, is meant to be no more than an introduction to the diversity that characterizes the California wine scene.

NAPA

Of all the California wine regions, Napa is probably the most famous to consumers and the one with the finest reputation. The reasons for this are not hard to discover: not only does the Napa Valley contain some of California's best-known wineries, but the number of fine wines produced there since Repeal is greater than anywhere else. There are vintage-dated varietal wines, especially Cabernet Sauvignon, from such wineries as Beaulieu Vineyard, Inglenook, Charles Krug, and Louis M. Martini going back to the 1930s and 1940s, while Sonoma and Monterey, for example, began to produce such wines only in the 1960s. Today, outstanding wines are made in other regions as well, and many winemakers would agree that certain varieties grow even more successfully in other counties than in Napa. Nevertheless, Napa retains its reputation, which has been further enhanced by a number of excellent new wineries created in the 1970s and 1980s.

The Napa Valley wineries are particularly accessible to visitors. The city of Napa is fifty miles north of San Francisco, and the distance from Napa to Calistoga, at the northern end of the valley, by way of Yountville, Oakville, Rutherford, and St. Helena is about twenty-five miles. The Silverado Trail, at the base of the Vaca Range east of the valley floor, parallels the main highway that runs through the Napa Valley; to the west the Mayacamas Mountains separate Napa and Sonoma counties.

There are about thirty-five thousand acres of vineyards in Napa, of which Cabernet Sauvignon and Chardonnay each account for more than ten thousand acres. These two varieties, plus Sauvignon Blanc, Pinot Noir, and Merlot, make up more than three-quarters of Napa's total acreage. In the late 1980s, a strain of phylloxera—the plant louse that feeds on rootstocks and that devastated the vineyards of Europe in the late nineteenth century—began to infest Napa Valley vineyards, and an extensive program of replanting on phylloxera-resistant rootstocks is under way. In a few years, more than half the total acreage will have been replanted, and it is likely that Cabernet Sauvignon and Chardonnay will account for an even bigger share of Napa's vineyards.

The Napa Valley appellation encompasses virtually all of the vineyards in the county, including those in the Chiles, Pope, and Wooden valleys. Growers and winemakers recognize that a region as extensive as the Napa Valley includes many different microclimates. The area around Calistoga to the north, for example, is actually warmer than the southern part of the valley; another distinction is made between grapes grown on the valley floor and those from hillside vineyards to the east and west. Established viticultural areas within the Napa Valley include part of the Carneros region, the Stags Leap District, Howell Mountain, Mount Veeder, Atlas Peak, Spring Mountain, Oakville, and Rutherford.

Carneros (also referred to as Los Carneros) has become one of the best-known districts in California, noted especially for Pinot Noir, Chardonnay, and *méthode champenoise* sparkling wines made from those grapes.

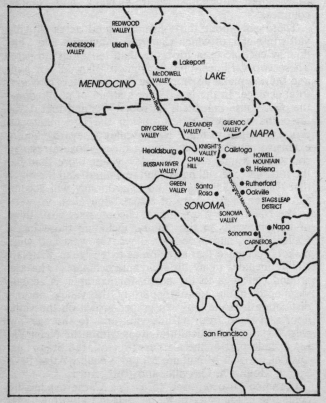

NORTHERN CALIFORNIA

The district lies at the southern end of Napa and Sonoma counties; it extends from the southern foothills of the Mayacamas Mountains, below the towns of Napa and Sonoma, almost to San Pablo Bay (as the northern part of San Francisco Bay is called), and from the Napa River on the east to the Sonoma Mountains on the west. Carneros, which is about thirty miles northeast of San Francisco, was defined by factors that affect grape-growing, rather than by such political boundaries as county lines, and the principal factor is the proximity of the bay, which has a moderating influence on the region's temperature and permits a long, cool growing season.

There are about seven thousand acres planted in Carneros (which means sheep, in tribute to its earlier fame as a sheepherding region); about two-thirds of this is planted in Napa and is also entitled to the Napa Valley appellation, the rest is in Sonoma and is also entitled to the Sonoma Valley and Sonoma County appellations. About 80 percent of the acreage is Chardonnay and Pinot Noir, but Cabernet Sauvignon, Merlot, Sauvignon Blanc, and Johannisberg Riesling are also planted. Such Napa Valley wineries as Beaulieu Vineyard, Charles Krug, and Louis Martini established vineyards here some time ago, as have Cuvaison, Domaine Chandon, Clos Du Val, Clos Pegase, and Robert Mondavi more recently. The Sangiacomo family, whose name is often seen on labels, has nine hundred acres of vineyards in Carneros; in 1986, Winery Lake Vineyard, established by Rene di Rosa in the 1960s, was acquired by Seagram's and its grapes now go to Sterling Vineyards and Mumm Napa Valley. The first winery in Carneros was Carneros Creek Winery, established in 1972. Others now include Acacia Winery, Saintsbury Cellars, Bouchaine Vineyards, Mont St. John Cellars, Kent Rasmussen, Truchard Vineyards, and the sparkling wine firms Domaine Carneros and Codorníu Napa, all on the Napa side; Buena Vista Winery, Gloria Ferrer, Roche Winery, Viansa Winery, Sonoma Creek Winery, Cline Cellars, and Schug Carneros Estate are on the Sonoma side.

The Stags Leap district, which is east of Yountville, extends for about two miles on either side of the Silverado Trail at the base of the Vaca Range, which faces the Mayacamas Mountains across the Napa Valley. The area, which began to be developed in the 1960s, is particularly known for its rich, supple Cabernet Sauvignons, many of which are blended with Merlot and Cabernet Franc. Among the wineries in this district is Warren Winiarski's Stag's Leap Wine Cellars, whose Cabernet Sauvignons include one labeled SLV from the vineyard that adjoins the winery and a reserve bottling labeled Cask 23; Chardonnay, Sauvignon Blanc, and other wines are also made, and less expensive varietal wines are sold under the Hawk Crest label. Carl Doumani's Stags' Leap Winery, originally known for its Petite Syrah, now also makes Cabernet Sauvignon and Merlot. Clos Du Val, under the direction of Bernard Portet, began by producing Cabernet Sauvignon and Zinfandel, and now makes a range of varietal wines, including Chardonnay and Pinot Noir from Carneros. Other wineries in the Stags Leap district known for their Cabernet Sauvignon (and other varietal wines) include Shafer Vineyards, Pine Ridge Winery, Steltzner Vineyards, Silverado Vineyards, and Chimney Rock Winery; Robert Sinskey Vineyards produces Pinot Noir, Chardonnay, and Merlot from its acreage in Carneros, S. Anderson Vineyard focuses on sparkling wines and Chardonnay.

Howell Mountain is situated northeast of St. Helena; the appellation applies only to vineyards at least fourteen hundred feet above sea level, and encompasses just a few hundred acres. The volcanic soil produces especially rich wines, which include the Cabernet Sauvignons of Dunn Vineyards, Forman Winery (also known for its Chardonnay), and La Jota Vineyard (also known for its Viognier), the Zinfandel of Lamborn Family Vineyards, and the vineyard-designated Chardonnays of Chateau Woltner.

Mount Veeder is part of the Mayacamas Mountains, and the appellation includes about one thousand acres of hillside vineyards located west of Yountville and planted, for the most part, with Cabernet Sauvignon and Chardonnay. Mayacamas Vineyards (established in 1941 and purchased by Robert and Elinor Travers in 1968), Mount Veeder Winery, The Hess Collection (which produces less expensive varietal wines under the Hess Select label), and Chateau Potelle are all on Mount Veeder.

The Atlas Peak viticultural area is part of the Vaca Range, above the Stags Leap district, on the east side of the Napa Valley. The appellation includes one winery, Atlas Peak Vineyards, whose nearly five hundred acres are planted primarily with Chardonnay, Cabernet Sauvignon, and Sangiovese; the first wines it released were a Sangiovese and a Cabernet Sauvignon-Sangiovese blend labeled Consenso. About a dozen wineries are situated within the Spring Mountain viticultural area, also part of the Mayacamas Mountains, just northeast of St. Helena. Perhaps the best-known winery is Spring Mountain Vineyards, which provided the setting for the Falcon Crest television show; new owners have assembled more than four hundred acres of vineyards (including the Chateau Chevalier and Streblow properties) and are producing a red wine based on Cabernet and Merlot and a white from Sauvignon Blanc and Sémillon. Other wineries in the Spring Mountain district include Smith-Madrone Vineyards; Newton Vineyard; Robert Keenan Winery; Philip Togni Vineyard; Domaine Karakash, which also produces a pot-still brandy; Stony Hill Vineyards, which has been known for its Chardonnay since the 1950s; and Cain Cellars, best known for a proprietary wine labeled Cain Five. Diamond Mountain, at the northern end of the Mayacamas Mountains, is the home of Diamond Creek Vineyards, known for three vineyard-designated Cabernet Sauvignons labeled Volcanic Hill, Red Rock Terrace, and Gravelly Meadow. Sterling Vineyards produces a Diamond Mountain Ranch Cabernet Sauvignon and Chardonnay, and Von Strasser made its first Diamond Mountain Cabernet Sauvignon in 1990.

A number of large, well-established wineries are situated along a stretch of Highway 29 from Oakville to just past St. Helena. One of the most famous is Beaulieu Vineyard, founded by Georges de Latour in 1900, and known particularly for its Cabernet Sauvignon. The winery, often referred to as BV, produces three Cabernets—one is labeled Rutherford; another, Beautour, is lighter in style; the third, produced in limited quantities, is the famous Georges de Latour Private Reserve, first made in 1936. BV makes several other varietal wines, including Chardonnay and Pinot Noir from grapes grown in the Carneros district. André Tchelistcheff, a Russian-born enologist, joined BV in 1938 and was responsible for the style and quality of its wines for thirty-five years. He pioneered the use of small American oak barrels as an adjunct to large redwood tanks to age wines, and was one of the first to recognize the potential of the Carneros district for Pinot Noir and Chardonnay.

Inglenook, founded by Gustave Niebaum in 1879, is less than a mile from BV, and now under the same ownership. The estate-bottled Napa Valley wines include Cabernet Sauvignon, Chardonnay, Merlot, Sauvignon Blanc, and Charbono, an unusual red; the best lots of Cabernet Sauvignon continue to be bottled with the well-known Reserve Cask designation. The firm also produces a range of single-vineyard varietal wines labeled Gustave Niebaum Collection. The Inglenook Vineyards label (formerly Inglenook Navalle) is used for a line of inexpensive jug wines that are bottled in Madera, in the San Joaquin Valley. The Christian Brothers, a teaching order founded in France in the seventeenth century, first planted vineyards in California in 1882 and moved to the Napa Valley in 1930; in addition to its varietal wines, the Christian Brothers line also includes the Muscat-based Chateau La Salle, several dessert wines, and a brandy. In 1989, the Christian Brothers label, winery, and vineyards were acquired by Heublein, the firm that owns BV and Inglenook; the wines are now bottled at the Madera facility.

Louis M. Martini wines were first made in Napa in 1934. The firm, which owns about five hundred acres of vineyards, including the 240-acre Monte Rosso vineyard in Sonoma, produces a full range of varietal wines and has achieved a particular reputation for its Cabernet Sauvignon, Zinfandel, Barbera, and Petite Sirah; limited amounts of Reserve and single-vineyard wines are also made. Charles Krug Winery, founded in 1861, was purchased by Cesare Mondavi in 1943, and was later under the direction of his two sons, Peter and Robert (who eventually left to found his own winery). The firm, which produces a full range of wines, was the first to successfully market Chenin Blanc as a varietal wine and continues to bottle its Vintage Selection Cabernet Sauvignon;

Krug also markets a separate line of jug wines under the name CK Mondavi.

North of St. Helena is the picturesque nineteenth-century Rhine House, which serves as a tasting room for Beringer Vineyards. Beringer was revitalized in 1971, when it was purchased by Wine World, a division of Nestlé of Switzerland, which also owns Chateau Souverain in Sonoma and Meridian Vineyards in San Luis Obispo; a new winery was built and its vineyards were subsequently expanded to about three thousand acres in Napa and Sonoma. Beringer offers a full range of varietal wines, including Private Reserve bottlings of Cabernet Sauvignon and Chardonnay; a Cabernet Sauvignon and a Sauvignon Blanc-Sémillon blend from its acreage in Knights Valley; and Nightingale, a sweet, botrytis-affected Sémillon named after Beringer's former winemaker. A selection of less expensive varietal wines, bottled in Sonoma, are marketed under the Napa Ridge label, and Los Hermanos is the name used for a line of jug wines.

The Robert Mondavi Winery, which was built near Oakville in 1966, was the first large new winery established in the Napa Valley since Prohibition. When Mondavi left Charles Krug, he decided to produce only vintage-dated varietal wines, which was a considerably more unusual concept at the time than it seems today. The winery, which owns fifteen hundred acres in Napa and more than six hundred acres in the Santa Maria Valley, is best known for its Cabernet Sauvignon, Chardonnay, Pinot Noir, and Fumé Blanc, which is the name Mondavi originated for a dry Sauvignon Blanc, and each of these wines is also produced in a Reserve bottling. Robert Mondavi and the late Baron Philippe de Rothschild of Château Mouton-Rothschild in Bordeaux created a joint venture to produce a Napa Valley Cabernet Sauvignon which was given the proprietary name Opus One; the first vintages of Opus One, 1979 and 1980, were released in 1984, and the Opus One winery was completed in 1991. Mondavi also owns the Woodbridge winery, near Lodi, where less expensive varietal wines are produced. In 1985, the Mondavi family bought Vichon Winery in Napa Valley, known for its Stags Leap district Cabernet Sauvignon and for Chevrignon, a proprietary blend of Sauvignon Blanc and Sémillon; Byron Vineyard, in Santa Barbara County, was acquired in 1990.

Farther up the Napa Valley, near Calistoga, is Sterling Vineyards, whose winery is one of the most distinctive in California; an aerial tramway transports visitors from the base of the hill to the winery, modeled on the spare white churches found on some Greek islands. The first wines marketed by Sterling were from the 1969 vintage, and included California's first vintage-dated Merlot. Current production, from more than one thousand acres of vineyards, includes Cabernet Sauvignon, Chardonnay, Sauvignon Blanc, and Merlot; a Cabernet-based Reserve bottling, and such single-vineyard wines as Chardonnay and Cabernet Sauvignon from Diamond Mountain Ranch, Chardonnay and Pinot Noir from Winery Lake, in Carneros, and Merlot from the Three Palms vineyard.

Joseph Phelps Vineyards, in the hills east of St. Helena, produced its first wines in 1973 and has achieved success with a number of different wines, including Cabernet Sauvignon, Chardonnay, Sauvignon Blanc, and Gewürztraminer; the winery is also known for its Johannisberg Rieslings, which range from a light, crisp, dry version to very sweet, botrytised late-harvest bottlings that rival the best of Germany. Insignia, first produced in 1974, is a proprietary wine made from Cabernet Sauvignon, Merlot, and Cabernet Franc in proportions that vary from year to year; and wines made from varieties associated with the Rhône Valley, marketed under the Vin du Mistral label, include Viognier, Syrah, Grenache Rosé, and Le Mistral, a proprietary blend. Innisfree Cabernet Sauvignon and Chardonnay are produced in association with Joseph Phelps.

Heitz Cellars was established in 1961 by Joe Heitz, one of California's most respected winemakers, who is probably best known for the Cabernet Sauvignon that comes from Martha's Vineyard, owned by Tom and Martha May. When the wine was first made, in 1966, there were only twelve acres planted with Cabernet Sauvignon; today, all of the vineyard's forty acres are planted with that variety. Since 1976, Heitz has also produced a Cabernet Sauvignon from the eighteen-acre Bella Oaks vineyard.

Dominus, first produced in 1983, is a proprietary wine made under the supervision of Christian Moueix, director of Château Petrus in Bordeaux; the wine is made primarily from Cabernet Sauvignon, plus 25 percent or so of Cabernet Franc and Merlot. The grapes come from the 124-acre Napanook vineyard, situated along the foothills of the Mayacamas Mountains, and now the property of Moueix's partners, Robin Lail and Marcia Smith, the daughters of the late John Daniel, who owned Inglenook Vineyards.

Rubicon, another proprietary wine, is produced by the Niebaum-Coppola Estate, owned by filmmaker Francis Ford Coppola; first made in 1978, the wine is a blend of Cabernet Sauvignon, Merlot, and Cabernet Franc from the estate's 120-acre vineyard, which is part of Coppola's sixteen-hundred-acre property, once owned by Gustave Niebaum of Inglenook.

When Robert Mondavi set out on his own, in 1966, there were fewer than twenty wineries in the Napa Valley; today, there are nearly two hundred. Most of them now focus their attention on Chardonnay and Cabernet Sauvignon and many produce lesser amounts of Sauvignon Blanc and/or Merlot. Many Napa Valley wineries have already been cited within their geographical designations. In addition, some of the producers that are perhaps best known for Cabernet Sauvignon include Buehler Vineyards (also known for its Zinfandel), Cafaro Cellars (also known for its Merlot), Caymus Vineyards (which produces a proprietary white wine called Conundrum and other wines under the Liberty School label), Chappellet Vineyard, Chateau Montelena (also known for its Napa and Alexander Valley Chardonnays), Conn Creek Winery, Corison Wines, Dalla Valle Vineyards, Etude (created by Tony Soter, who also produces Pinot Noir), Groth Vineyards, Livingston Vineyards, Pahlmeyer Winery, Silver Oak Cellars (whose principal Cabernet is made from Alexander Valley grapes), Spottswoode (also known for its Sauvignon Blanc), Tudal Winery, Turnbull Cellars (formerly Johnson Turnbull), and Viader (which produces a proprietary blend of Cabernet Sauvignon and Cabernet Franc).

Among the wineries known for Chardonnay are Crichton Hall Vineyard, Cuvaison Winery (which has extensive acreage in Carneros and is also known for its Cabernet Sauvignon and Merlot), Folie à Deux, Girard Winery, Goosecross Cellars, Long Vineyards (also known for Johannisberg Riesling), Raymond Vineyard, Revere Winery, St. Andrews Vineyards, and ZD Wines.

Wineries associated with Merlot include Duckhorn Vineyards and Jaeger Inglewood Vineyard. Zinfandel is a specialty of Storybook Mountain Vineyard, Green & Red Vineyard, and Sky Vineyards. Sauvignon Blanc is a specialty of Honig Cellars and Robert Pepi Winery (which also produces a Cabernet Sauvignon from Vine Hill Ranch).

Other Napa Valley wineries, most of which emphasize Chardonnay and Cabernet Sauvignon, include Beaucannon Winery, Bergfeld Winery, Burgess Cellars, Cakebread Cellars, Clos Pegase, Cosentino Winery, De Moor Winery, Far Niente Winery (which also produces a late-harvest wine called Dolce), Flora Springs Winery (which produces a proprietary red called Trilogy and less expensive varietal wines labeled Floréal), Franciscan Oakville Estate, Freemark Abbey Winery (known for Cabernet Sauvignon from the Bosché vineyard and a late-harvest Johannisberg Riesling labeled Edelwein Gold), Frog's Leap Winery, Grgich Hills Cellar, Hagafen Cellars, William Hill Winery, Lakespring Winery, Markham Vineyards, Merryvale Vineyards (which produces a Meritage white and a proprietary red called Profile), Monticello Cellars, Neyers Winery, Robert Pecota (also known for Sauvignon Blanc and a sweet Muscat), Peju Province, Philippe Lorraine (a label created by winemaker Phil Baxter), Plam Vineyards, Quail Ridge Cellars, Raymond Vineyard, Rombauer Vineyards, Round Hills Vineyards (whose wines include the Rutherford Ranch label), Rutherford Hill Winery (known for its Merlot), St. Clement Vineyards, St. Supéry Vineyards (whose owner, Robert Skalli, also produces the Fortant de France wines from France's Pays d'Oc region), Sequoia Grove Vineyards, Signorello Vineyards, Sunny St. Helena Winery, Sutter Home Winery (the biggest winery in Napa, best known for its White Zinfandel), Swanson Winery, Trefethen Vineyards (which produces a less expensive Chardonnay and Cabernet-Merlot blend under the Eshcol label), Villa Mt. Eden, and Whitehall Lane.

East of Napa County, in the Solano-Green Valley viticultural area, Chateau de Leu produces wines from vineyards first planted in the 1950s.

SONOMA

Sonoma does not project as clear an image to consumers as does Napa. One reason is that the county encompasses several distinct districts, each with its own microclimate and its own appellation of origin. Another is that Sonoma has a particularly varied mix of producers that includes traditional wineries that have been changing their marketing policies and winemaking techniques; large new wineries that have experienced growing pains; and dozens of small new wineries whose first wines were released as recently as the 1980s. Whereas Napa's fame is attributable to a number of long-established wineries whose reputations added prestige to that of the county, there are relatively few existing wineries in Sonoma whose identities go back more than thirty years: most of them did not sell much wine under their own labels until the 1960s, and much of what they did sell was in jugs with generic names. For example, as recently as 1970, Sebastiani still sold more wine in bulk to other wineries than it did under its own name; and Foppiano, founded in 1896, marketed its first Cabernet Sauvignon in 1972, its first Chardonnay in 1979.

The shift toward the production of fine wines can be seen in Sonoma, as in other California counties, by new plantings of better grape varieties. In 1965, there were about ten thousand acres under cultivation in Sonoma, two-thirds of them planted with Zinfandel, Carignane, Petite Sirah, and French Colombard. Such classic varieties as Cabernet Sauvignon, Merlot, Pinot Noir, Chardonnay, Sauvignon Blanc, and Johannisberg Riesling accounted for less than a thousand acres. Today there are more than thirty-five thousand acres of vineyards in Sonoma, and more than two-thirds consist of Cabernet Sauvignon, Chardonnay, Pinot Noir, and Merlot. Sonoma had long been a proven, if neglected, area for fine wines, but it wasn't until the early 1970s, when vineyard land in Napa became very expensive, that a number of new winemakers turned to Sonoma. There are now about 180 wineries in Sonoma.

The extensive new vineyards created throughout Sonoma County present a special problem for the casual wine drinker because the geographical origin of Sonoma's wines cannot be grasped as easily as those of Napa. The well-known wineries that created the Napa Valley's reputation, and many of the newer ones as well, are concentrated along a fifteen-mile stretch from Oakville to Calistoga, and easily grouped on a map. In Sonoma County, however, there are two main wine regions, one in and around Sonoma itself, and the other near Healdsburg and Geyserville, almost fifty miles away. What's more, many Sonoma wineries do not feature the county appellation on their labels. Some large wineries that buy grapes or wine from other counties must use California or North Coast, but even those wineries that are entitled to use the Sonoma County appellation often choose a more specific inner appellation such as Alexander Valley, Dry Creek Valley, Russian River Valley, or Sonoma Valley.

Sonoma County contains a number of defined viticultural areas: Alexander Valley, Dry Creek Valley, Russian River Valley, Sonoma-Green Valley, Chalk Hill, Knights Valley, Sonoma Valley, Sonoma Mountain, and part of Carneros. The extensive Sonoma Coast area includes the cooler districts of the county along the coast from the Mendocino border down to Carneros; the large Northern Sonoma appellation includes Alexander Valley, Dry Creek Valley, Knights Valley, and most of the Russian River Valley. What follows is a description of these areas and some of their wineries.

The Alexander Valley, which extends for about twenty miles along the Russian River from the Mendocino border to just east of Healdsburg, was settled by a fur trader named Cyrus Alexander in the 1840s. The Alexander Valley name began to appear with some regularity on wine labels in the late 1970s and 1980s, and the region has achieved a particular reputation for stylish, elegant Cabernet Sauvignon, ripe, opulent Chardonnays, and distinct Sauvignon Blanc. Cabernet Sauvignon and Chardonnay account for most of the valley's seven thousand acres of vineyards; Cabernet Sauvignon (and, increasingly, Merlot and Cabernet Franc) are planted in well-drained, gravelly soils; Chardonnay (and Sauvignon Blanc) are usually planted in the deeper, richer soils nearer the river. The Alexander Valley contains several well-known vineyards, such as the Belle Terre and Robert Young Vineyards, whose names appear on Chardonnays made by Chateau St. Jean; and Alexander's Crown, a sixty-one-acre Cabernet Sauvignon vineyard owned by Rodney Strong Vineyards.

Among the wineries located in the Alexander Valley is Alexander Valley Vineyards, which produced its first wines in 1975 from vineyards planted by the Wetzel family in the 1960s; the winery focuses on Chardonnay and Cabernet Sauvignon, as does Chateau Souverain, acquired in 1986 by Wine World, which also owns Beringer in the Napa Valley. Estancia Estates, under the same ownership as Franciscan in Napa, markets Cabernet Sauvignon and a Meritage red from its 240 acres in the Alexander Valley; its Chardonnay, Sauvignon Blanc, and a Meritage white are made from Monterey grapes. Tim Murphy and Dale Goode established Murphy-Goode Estate Winery and produced their first wines in 1985 from vineyards originally planted in the 1970s; the winery focuses on Chardonnay and Fumé Blanc, plus Cabernet Sauvignon and Merlot. Simi Winery, which dates back to 1876, was revitalized in the 1970s and acquired by Moët-Hennessy in 1981; it has since established extensive Cabernet Sauvignon vineyards in the Alexander Valley and Chardonnay vineyards in the Russian River Valley. In addition to Chardonnay and Cabernet Sauvignon, the winery also produces Sauvignon Blanc, Chenin Blanc, and a Rosé of Cabernet Sauvignon; more recently, Simi introduced Sendal, a Sauvignon Blanc-Sémillon blend, and Altaire, an unusual blend of Pinot Noir, Cabernet Franc, and Pinot Meunier. Jordan Winery, established in 1972, made its first Cabernet Sauvignon in 1976, its first Chardonnay in 1979, both from its 275-acre vineyard; a *méthode champenoise* sparkling wine labeled J is produced nearby.

Clos du Bois produced its first wines in 1974 from vineyards planted a decade earlier in the Alexander Valley and Dry Creek Valley; best known for its Merlot and barrel-fermented Chardonnay, Clos du Bois produces a full range of wines as well as a vineyard-designated Chardonnay from the Calcaire vineyard, a Cabernet Sauvignon from the Briarcrest vineyard, and a blend of the five Bordeaux varieties from the Marlstone vineyard. Geyser Peak Winery, one of the biggest wineries in Sonoma, was founded in 1880 and eventually acquired in 1982 by the Trione family, who own more than twelve hundred acres of vineyards in Sonoma, Lake, and Mendocino counties; the winery produces a range of varietal wines and inexpensive magnums, as well as a proprietary red labeled Réserve Alexandre and a blend of Sémillon and Chardonnay called Semchard. Field Stone Winery, Johnson's of Alexander Valley, and Trentadue Winery are also in the Alexander Valley, as are Sausal Winery, which is noted for its intense Zinfandels, and deLorimier Winery, which produces a proprietary red called Mosaic and a white labeled Spectrum. Black Mountain Vineyard produces several varietal wines; other table wines and ports are marketed with the J. W. Morris label. Marietta Cellars is known for Zinfandel, Cabernet Sauvignon, and a proprietary wine labeled Old Vine Red. J. Stonestreet Vineyards is under the same ownership as Kendall-Jackson Vineyards. The Lyeth winery produced a proprietary red based on Cabernet Sauvignon and a proprietary white made from Sauvignon Blanc and Sémillon, both labeled simply as Lyeth (pronounced *leeth*). The name is now owned by French wine merchant Jean-Claude Boisset, who has added a Lyeth Chardonnay; his firm also acquired the William Wheeler Winery in Dry Creek Valley and produces the wines marketed as Christophe Vineyards and Joliesse.

The Dry Creek Valley runs parallel to the Alexander Valley; sixteen miles long and two miles wide, it contains about six thousand acres of vineyards. The district, particularly known for its Zinfandel and Sauvignon Blanc, is also planted with Chardonnay and Cabernet Sauvignon as well as a number of other varieties. David Stare established Dry Creek Vineyards in 1972; in addition to Chardonnay and Cabernet Sauvignon, the winery is known for its Fumé Blanc and Dry Chenin Blanc. Preston Vineyards produces Zinfandel, a Sauvignon Blanc-based wine labeled Cuvée de Fumé, and several wines made from Rhône varieties, including Syrah, Viognier, Marsanne, and a proprietary red wine labeled Faux. Ferrari-Carano Vineyards, with extensive vineyards in Dry Creek Valley, Alexander Valley, Knights Valley, and Carneros, offers a range of varietal wines, a Cabernet-Sangiovese blend labeled Siena, and a late-harvest wine called Eldorado Gold. A. Rafanelli Winery is known for its Cabernet Sauvignon and Zinfandel; Nalle Winery specializes in Zinfandel, as does Quivira Vineyards, which also makes Sauvignon Blanc and a Cabernet Sauvignon-based wine labeled Cabernet Cuvée; J. Fritz Cellars is best known for Chardonnay; Michel-Schlumberger (formerly Domaine Michel) produces selected lots of Cabernet Sauvignon, Merlot, and Chardonnay; and J. Pedroncelli, founded in 1904, offers a full range of varietal wines. Bellerose Vineyard produces a proprietary blend based on the Bordeaux varieties labeled Cuvée Bellerose; Mill Creek Vineyards was the first California winery to use the term "blush" for a pink wine when, in the late 1970s, it labeled a wine Cabernet Blush. Other Dry Creek wineries include Alderbrook Vineyards, Frick Winery, Mazzocco Vineyards, and Meeker Vineyard. E. & J. Gallo, which owns nearly two thousand acres of vineyards in the Alexander Valley, Russian River Valley, and Dry Creek Valley, also has a winery in Dry Creek Valley.

The Lytton Springs district, within the Dry Creek Valley, became known for its Zinfandel as a result of wines made by Ridge Vineyards; Lytton Springs Winery, established in 1975, was acquired by Ridge in 1991.

The Knights Valley appellation abuts the Alexander Valley and Chalk Hill districts and extends back to the Mayacamas Mountains. Beringer produces a Knights Valley Cabernet Sauvignon and a Sauvignon Blanc-Sémillon blend from its vineyards in this area; Peter Michael Winery, established in 1989, is known for its Chardonnay and for a Cabernet Sauvignon labeled Les Pavots.

Wineries situated in or near Healdsburg include Seghesio Winery, which traces its origins back to 1894, and which began to produce wines under its own name in 1983, from its four hundred acres of vineyards; White

Oaks Vineyards; and Weinstock Cellars, which makes kosher varietal wines from its vineyards in Dry Creek Valley.

The Russian River Valley viticultural area includes only that part of the river's course as it flows west from Healdsburg to Sebastopol and then to Guerneville, less than ten miles from the Pacific Ocean. About nine thousand acres are planted in this cool region (which also encompasses the smaller appellations Sonoma-Green Valley and Chalk Hill); the vineyards include a full range of varieties, including Gewürztraminer and Johannisberg Riesling, but the area is best known for its Pinot Noir and Chardonnay, and for selected lots of Zinfandel. The Russian River Valley is also an important source of Pinot Noir and Chardonnay for *méthode champenoise* sparkling wines. Korbel Champagne Cellars, established in 1862, is located near Guerneville; Piper-Sonoma is near Healdsburg.

The extensive Russian River Valley region is home to many of Sonoma's wineries, among them De Loach Vineyards, known especially for its Chardonnay, Zinfandel, and Gewürztraminer; Sonoma-Cutrer, which focuses on its three Chardonnays—Russian River Ranches and the single-vineyard Les Pierres and Cutrer Vineyard; Dehlinger Winery, which has established a reputation for its Chardonnay and Pinot Noir; and J. Rochioli Vineyards, best known for Pinot Noir, as is Williams Selyem Winery, established by Burt Williams and Ed Selyem. Rodney Strong Vineyards produces a full range of varietal wines and such single-vineyard bottlings as a Cabernet Sauvignon from Alexander's Crown, Chardonnays from the Chalk Hill and River West vineyards, and Charlotte's Home Sauvignon Blanc. Foppiano Vineyards, established in 1896 and still owned by the founding family, is known for its Petite Sirah and Zinfandel; its reserve bottlings are labeled Fox Mountain and its less expensive wines are marketed under the Riverside Farm label. Domaine St. George produces moderately priced varietal wines; Christopher Creek winery focuses on Syrah and Petite Sirah; Merry Vintners, created by winemaker Merry Edwards, concentrates on Chardonnay; Z Moore Wines is best known for its bottlings of oak-aged Gewürztraminer and also produces a proprietary red, primarily

Zinfandel and Petite Sirah, labeled Danato; Gary Farrell makes a number of single-vineyard bottlings from Chardonnay, Pinot Noir, Zinfandel, and Cabernet Sauvignon; Joseph Swan Vineyards first achieved a reputation for its Zinfandel, then for its Pinot Noir, both produced in limited quantities; Sonoma-Loeb, created by former ambassador John Loeb, Jr., is best known for Chardonnay, produced from Loeb's vineyards in the Alexander Valley and Russian River Valley; and Chateau de Baun has made a specialty of Symphony, a cross of Grenache Gris and Muscat. Other wineries include Armida Winery, Belvedere Winery, Davis Bynum, Hanna Winery, Hop Kiln Winery, Mark West Vineyards, Rabbit Ridge Vineyards, and Taft Street Winery.

Green Valley, a cool district in the southwestern part of the Russian River Valley region, is known particularly for its Pinot Noir and Chardonnay, and for sparkling wines based on those two varieties. The best-known winery in Sonoma-Green Valley (as the appellation is officially listed, to distinguish it from another Green Valley in Solano County) is Iron Horse Vineyards, which makes Chardonnay, Pinot Noir, and a range of crisp *méthode champenoise* sparkling wines from its acreage in Green Valley; vineyards in the Alexander Valley produce a Fumé Blanc blended with a small proportion of Viognier and a proprietary blend of Cabernet Sauvignon and Cabernet Franc labeled Cabernets. Marimar Torres, whose brother, Miguel, directs the family winery in the Penedés region of Spain, makes Chardonnay and Pinot Noir from a 55-acre vineyard in Green Valley. Gan Eden, which produces a range of kosher varietal wines, is best known for its Cabernet Sauvignon and Chardonnay.

Chalk Hill, a small district contained in the northeast part of the Russian River Valley, is best known for Chardonnay; the leading producer is Chalk Hill Winery.

The Sonoma Valley appellation extends for about twenty-five miles from just below Santa Rosa almost to San Pablo Bay, and encompasses the Sonoma portion of the Carneros appellation and the small district called Sonoma Mountain, as well as the towns of Sonoma, Glen Ellen, and Kenwood. The valley proper, which is also known as the Valley of the Moon, lies between the Mayacamas Mountains and the Sonoma Mountains, and this area has a long history of grape-growing and winemaking. The Sonoma Mission was established here, and vines planted, in the 1820s; in 1857, Agoston Haraszthy founded Buena Vista, and the Rhinefarm vineyard of Gundlach-Bundschu was first planted in 1858. The Sonoma Valley includes a number of different microclimates, and plantings—about six thousand acres in all—vary from Pinot Noir and Chardonnay in the cool Carneros district to Cabernet Sauvignon and Zinfandel in the warmer region to the north, with Sauvignon Blanc and other varieties also represented.

The biggest winery in the area, and one of the oldest, is Sebastiani Vineyards, founded in 1904; originally a supplier of bulk wines to other wineries, it has achieved success under its own name with a full range of varietal wines, reserve Chardonnays and Cabernet Sauvignons, less expensive varietal wines labeled Vendange, and a line of jug wines under the August Sebastiani name. Buena Vista Winery has been revitalized since its purchase, in 1979, by Racke, a German wine and spirits firm; more than nine hundred acres have been planted in the Carneros region and the winery produces regular and Carneros Grand Reserve bottlings of Chardonnay, Cabernet Sauvignon, and Pinot Noir and also a Sauvignon Blanc from Lake County. The owners of Buena Vista also acquired two well-known labels: Robert Stemmler Winery, known for its Pinot Noir; and Haywood Winery, known for Chardonnay, Cabernet Sauvignon, and Zinfandel from the Los Chamizal vineyard.

Among the wineries in the Carneros district of the Sonoma Valley are the Schug Carneros Estate, which specializes in Pinot Noir and Chardonnay; Viansa Winery, established by Sam and Vicki Sebastiani; Roche Winery, which focuses on Chardonnay and Pinot Noir; MacRostie, which concentrates on Chardonnay, as does Sonoma Creek Vineyards; and Gloria Ferrer, owned by the Freixenet firm of Spain, which produces *méthode champenoise* sparkling wines. Cline Cellars, which was originally situated in the town of Oakley, specializes in Rhône varieties; its wines include such proprietary blends as Côtes d'Oakley, Oakley Cuvée, and Angel Rosé as well as Mourvèdre and Sémillon.

Wineries situated in or near the town of Sonoma—in

addition to Sebastiani, Haywood, and the Buena Vista reception center—include Gundlach-Bundschu Winery, whose Rhinefarm vineyard dates back to 1858 and whose winery, re-established in 1973, draws on the Bundschu family's four hundred acres of vineyard; and Ravenswood, which has established a special reputation for its different bottlings of Zinfandel and for the red wine made from the Pickberry vineyard, planted with Bordeaux varieties.

Hanzell Vineyards, in the Mayacamas Mountains north of Sonoma, was created in the 1950s by James Zellerbach, who was determined to make Pinot Noir and Chardonnay equal to the best of Burgundy. He is generally credited with having introduced small French oak barrels to California, a practice that has been widely adopted throughout the state to give many red and white wines additional complexity; the winery continues to produce these two wines and limited amounts of Cabernet Sauvignon. Carmenet was created by the owners of Chalone, in Monterey County, and its seventy acres of hillside vineyards are planted with Cabernet Sauvignon, Cabernet Franc, and Merlot; in addition to the estate red, labeled Moon Mountain Estate Vineyard, the winery also produces a more accessible red labeled Dynamite Cabernet, a Sauvignon Blanc-Sémillon blend from Edna Valley grapes, and a Carneros Chardonnay.

The best-known winery associated with the town of Glen Ellen is the Glen Ellen winery, established by the Benziger family, which has been very successful with a line of inexpensive varietal and generic wines labeled Proprietor's Reserve; similar wines are marketed with the M. G. Vallejo label. In 1993, the Glen Ellen and M. G. Vallejo brands were acquired by Heublein. The Benziger family continues to use its own name for a range of varietal wines, including estate-bottled wines from its Sonoma Mountain vineyards, and for red and white proprietary wines labeled A Tribute. B. R. Cohn is best known for Cabernet Sauvignon from its Olive Hill vineyard.

The Sonoma Mountain viticultural area, which encompasses vineyards up in the mountains west of Glen Ellen, is especially noted for Cabernet Sauvignon, although other varieties also do well. Pickberry Vineyard, Jack

London Ranch, and the estate vineyard of Benziger are located in the Sonoma Mountain district, as is Patrick Campbell's Laurel Glen Vineyard, known for its Cabernet Sauvignon; the winery also markets a less expensive Cabernet under the Terra Rosa label.

Kenwood is home to a number of wineries, including Chateau St. Jean, established in the early 1970s, and focused primarily on white wines; these include such vineyard-designated wines as Chardonnays from the Robert Young and Belle Terre vineyards in the Alexander Valley; Fumé Blanc from La Petite Etoile in the Russian River Valley; and Chardonnay and Fumé Blanc from the winery's own St. Jean vineyard in the Sonoma Valley, as well as a succession of late-harvest Johannisberg Rieslings and Gewürztraminers that are among the best produced in California. Chateau St. Jean's original winemaker, Richard Arrowood, established his own winery near Glen Ellen to concentrate on Chardonnay and Cabernet Sauvignon. Kenwood Vineyards, established in 1970, produces a full range of varietal wines and is perhaps best known for its Sauvignon Blanc and Chardonnay, and for such single-vineyard wines as Chardonnay from Beltane Ranch and Cabernet Sauvignon and Zinfandel from Jack London Ranch; special selections of Cabernet Sauvignon are labeled Artist Series.

Kistler Vineyards, whose first wines were made in 1979, has made a reputation with its single-vineyard Chardonnays, which come from several appellations; St. Francis Vineyards is best known for its Merlot and Chardonnay; Landmark Vineyards specializes in Chardonnay, including Damaris Reserve from the Alexander Valley; Adler Fels is known for its distinctive Fumé Blanc; and Kunde Estate Winery, whose vineyards were originally planted in 1879, produced its first wines in 1990. Matanzas Creek Winery, situated in the Bennett Valley, between Kenwood and Santa Rosa, has established a reputation for its Chardonnay, Sauvignon Blanc, and Merlot. Fisher Vineyards, situated in the Mayacamas Mountains, but well north of Sonoma Valley, is known for its vineyard-designated Chardonnay, Cabernet Sauvignon, and Merlot.

MENDOCINO AND LAKE COUNTY

Mendocino

Mendocino County is situated just above Sonoma County, and its principal city, Ukiah, is about 120 miles north of San Francisco. Vineyard acreage increased substantially in the early 1970s and now exceeds twelve thousand acres. In the late 1960s, Mendocino was planted with such traditional varieties as Carignane and French Colombard, and Chardonnay accounted for fewer than one hundred acres; today, there are about four thousand acres of Chardonnay, plus Cabernet Sauvignon, Sauvignon Blanc, Zinfandel, and lesser amounts of Pinot Noir and Merlot. A number of viticultural areas have been defined in Mendocino, among them such less-familiar ones as Cole Ranch, which consists of about sixty acres planted primarily with Cabernet Sauvignon; Potter Valley, the northernmost appellation in the county, whose thousand acres are planted with such cool-climate varieties as Chardonnay, Sauvignon Blanc, and Pinot Noir; and the Sanel Valley, between Talmage and Hopland, known primarily for Sauvignon Blanc. Better-known appellations include Anderson Valley, McDowell Valley, and Redwood Valley.

The Redwood Valley, which extends north from Ukiah for about fifteen miles along the Russian River, is the area where Mendocino vineyards and wineries were first established. For many years the only winery associated with Mendocino was Parducci Wine Cellars, established in 1932, and among the first to bottle French Colombard, Chenin Blanc, and Petite Sirah as a varietal wine. Today, the winery, which owns four hundred acres of vineyards, offers a full range of wines. Fetzer Vineyards, founded by the late Bernard Fetzer, produced its first wines in 1968 from vineyards planted a decade earlier. Now one of California's biggest wineries, Fetzer (acquired in 1992 by Brown-Forman Distillers) offers such popular bottlings as Sundial Chardonnay, Valley Oaks Cabernet Sauvignon, Fumé Blanc, and a semisweet Gewürztraminer, as well as selected varietal wines labeled Barrel Select and Reserve; a range of less expensive wines are marketed under the Bel Arbors name.

Other wineries in the Redwood Valley area include Weibel Vineyards, known for its popular sparkling wines and a full range of varietal wines, including Green Hungarian; and Dunnewood (formerly Cresta Blanc). Frey Vineyard and Konrad Estate specialize in organic varietal wines made from their own organically farmed grapes. Wineries in the Sanel Valley include Jepson Vineyards, which produces Chardonnay and Sauvignon Blanc as well as sparkling wines and a pot-still brandy; Tijsseling Vineyards, which makes both table wines and sparkling wines; and Milano Winery. Other wineries in this part of Mendocino are Whaler Vineyard, which specializes in Zinfandel; Hidden Cellars; and Lolonis Winery.

The McDowell Valley appellation was established by McDowell Valley Vineyards, known for Chardonnay and for several wines based on Rhône varieties; these include Syrah, Grenache Rosé, and a Grenache-Syrah blend called Le Trésor.

The Anderson Valley, some miles west of Ukiah, extends along the Navarro River from Booneville past Philo to the town of Navarro. Cooled by Pacific breezes, the valley is particularly suitable for such white varieties as Gewürztraminer, Johannisberg Riesling, Chardonnay, and Sauvignon Blanc, and also for Pinot Noir and Chardonnay used for sparkling wines; in recent years, Cabernet Sauvignon and Merlot have also achieved success. The region's best-known wineries are the two that produce *méthode champenoise* sparkling wines: Scharffenberger, established in the early 1980s by John Scharffenberger and subsequently acquired by the French champagne firm Pommery; and Roederer Estate, which has planted about four hundred acres of vineyards and released its first wine in 1988. Among the Anderson Valley wineries noted for their Gewürztraminer and other white wines are Husch Vineyards, established in 1968; Navarro Vineyards, established in 1974, and also known for its late-harvest wines; and Lazy Creek Vineyards. Handley Cellars, with vineyards in the Anderson Valley and the Dry Creek Valley, has a reputation for its Chardonnay, Sauvignon Blanc, and *méthode champenoise* wines; other wineries include Greenwood Ridge,

Obester Winery, Pepperwood Springs, and Christine Woods Vineyards.

Lake County

Lake County, just north of Napa and east of Mendocino, had a flourishing wine business in the 1880s, with five thousand acres of vineyards and three dozen wineries. When Prohibition ended, there were no wineries left and almost no vineyards. New plantings occurred in the early 1970s, and the Lake County name began appearing on labels of wines produced from these vineyards by wineries in neighboring counties. There are now about thirty-five hundred acres of grapes in the county, much of it planted at higher elevations to benefit from cooler growing conditions, with Cabernet Sauvignon, Chardonnay, and Sauvignon Blanc accounting for two-thirds of the total.

There are two viticultural areas in Lake County—Clear Lake, which surrounds that lake and accounts for almost all the acreage except that in the second appellation, Guenoc Valley, which has only one winery. The Magoon family began planting vineyards in the Guenoc Valley, which is just above the Napa border, in the early 1970s on a twenty-three-thousand-acre tract they had acquired some years before, and founded Guenoc Winery in 1981. The winery produces a full range of varietal wines as well as a proprietary red and white Meritage blend labeled Langtry, in honor of the actress Lillie Langtry, who owned part of the estate at the turn of the century.

The biggest producer in Lake County is Kendall-Jackson Winery, which began modestly but soon achieved tremendous success with its Vintner's Reserve Chardonnay, produced from grapes grown in several coastal districts. The Vintner's Reserve line was expanded to include Cabernet Sauvignon, Sauvignon Blanc, Zinfandel, Merlot, Syrah, Pinot Noir, and other varieties; selected lots of varietal wines are labeled Grand Reserve; and the winery also makes a number of vineyard-designated wines. Other wines include a proprietary Cabernet-Merlot blend labeled Cardinale, a Sémillon-Sauvignon Blanc wine labeled Royale, and Grand Finale, a late-harvest Sémillon. The proprietors of Kendall-Jackson also own vineyards and the Edmeades winery in Mendocino's Anderson Valley; a thousand acres of vineyards in Santa Barbara County, where they established Cambria Winery to produce Chardonnay and Pinot Noir; and additional vineyards and the J. Stonestreet winery in Sonoma's Alexander Valley. Jed Steele, for many years the winemaker at Kendall-Jackson, established his own winery, Steele Wines, to focus on Chardonnay and Pinot Noir, including vineyard-designated bottlings. Mount Konocti Winery (pronounced con-*oc*-tie) was established at the foot of that mountain in 1979 by an association of Lake County grapegrowers, who have since been joined by John Parducci of Mendocino and other partners; the winery produces a range of varietal wines.

ALAMEDA, SANTA CLARA, AND THE SANTA CRUZ MOUNTAINS

Almost all of the vineyard acreage in Alameda County, southeast of San Francisco, is in the fifteen-mile-long Livermore Valley, whose best-known wineries are Wente Bros. and Concannon Vineyard. As a result of urbanization, the vineyards in this county were considerably reduced in the mid-1970s, to fewer than two thousand acres; new legislation permitted new plantings, but in recent years the overall acreage has diminished to about sixteen hundred acres, primarily Chardonnay, Sauvignon Blanc, and Sémillon.

Wente Bros. is a family-owned winery that dates back to 1883. The Wentes now own more than two thousand acres of vineyards, two-thirds of them in the Livermore Valley, the rest in the Arroyo Seco region of Monterey County. About 90 percent of the winery's production is of white wines, including Chardonnay, Sauvignon Blanc, Sémillon, and Le Blanc de Blancs, made primarily from Chenin Blanc; Cabernet Sauvignon and Merlot are also made. The winery first marketed Sauvignon Blanc and Chardonnay as varietal wines in the 1930s, and in 1969 Wente produced the first Spätlese type of wine made in California from botrytised Johannisberg Riesling grapes grown in its Arroyo Seco vineyard. At a separate facility, Wente also makes *méthode champenoise* sparkling wines from Pinot Noir, Chardonnay, and Pinot Blanc. Concannon Vineyard, just down the road from Wente Bros., was also established in the 1880s; after several changes of ownership, it was acquired by the Wente family in 1992. Concannon was among the first to market Petite Sirah as a varietal wine, and is still known for that wine and for Sauvignon Blanc. The winery's 180 acres of vineyards, used for its estate-bottled wines, are now planted almost entirely with Sauvignon Blanc, Sémillon, Cabernet Sauvignon, and Petite Sirah; Chardonnay is made primarily from Santa Clara grapes.

Sergio Traverso, formerly co-owner and winemaker at Concannon, has established Murrieta's Well to produce proprietary wines labeled Vendimia; the red is based on Cabernet Sauvignon, Cabernet Franc, and Merlot; the white is primarily Sauvignon Blanc and Sémillon. The Iván Tamás varietal wines, which include a Trebbiano, are associated with the Livermore Valley; other producers include Fenestra Winery and Stony Ridge Winery.

A number of small wineries are situated in the northern part of Alameda, near Berkeley and Emeryville. These include Edmunds St. John, which specializes in such Rhône varieties as Grenache, Syrah, and Mourvèdre and produces limited amounts of varietal wines and such proprietary reds as Les Côtes Sauvages and New World Red. Rosenblum Cellars is best known for small lots of intense, vineyard-designated Zinfandels; Audubon Cellars and Bay Cellars are also located in this area. Kalin Cellars, established by Terry Leighton, is located across the San Francisco Bay in Marin County; the winery produces single-vineyard wines, each labeled with a different *cuvée* designation, from Chardonnay, Sémillon, Pinot Noir, and other varieties, as well as limited amounts of sparkling wines. Sean Thackrey produces wines from Rhône varieties, including a Syrah labeled Orion and a Mourvèdre labeled Taurus.

Vineyard acreage in Santa Clara diminished from more than eight thousand acres in the 1940s to fewer than three thousand in the mid-1970s, and now stands at about a thousand acres. Although the Santa Clara appellation is not often seen on labels, the region has

CENTRAL CALIFORNIA

long been familiar to wine-minded tourists because for many years Almadén's home winery was located near San José and Paul Masson's reception center was in Saratoga; even today there are dozens of small family wineries in Santa Clara that sell much of their production to visitors. These days, the biggest wineries in the San José area are Mirassou Vineyards and J. Lohr. (Weibel, long associated with Santa Clara, has established vineyards and a winery in Mendocino.) The history of Mirassou goes back to 1854, but it was only in the 1960s that the family began to actively promote its own name rather than selling its wine in bulk to other wineries. Mirassou was one of the first to plant vineyards in Monterey, and now has extensive acreage there. Mirassou offers a full range of varietal wines, including special lots labeled Family Selection and Harvest Reserve, and also makes several styles of *méthode champenoise* sparkling wines.

J. Lohr Winery owns more than one thousand acres of vineyards in several regions, including the Arroyo Seco district of Monterey, Clarksburg, Paso Robles, and the Napa Valley; it produces a full range of varietal wines, including the popular Wild Flower Gamay, Bay Mist Johannisberg Riesling, Riverstone Chardonnay, Seven Oaks Cabernet Sauvignon, and a line of less expensive varietal wines labeled Cypress. J. Lohr also helped create the Ariel brand of de-alcoholized wines, now produced in the Napa Valley.

A number of wineries, both old and new, are situated near the highway between Morgan Hill and Gilroy, and in the Hecker Pass district west of Gilroy. Sarah's Vineyard, a small winery established in 1978, specializes in Chardonnay. Other wineries in the area include Kirigin Cellars, Thomas Kruse, Fortino Winery, Hecker Pass Winery, Sycamore Creek, Rapazzini, Emilio Guglielmo, and Pedrizzetti.

The Santa Cruz Mountains viticultural area encompasses parts of Santa Cruz, San Mateo, and Santa Clara counties. Santa Cruz has only a hundred acres of vineyards, and San Mateo even less, so almost all the wineries within this appellation buy grapes from other regions. One of the best-known wineries of the Santa Cruz Mountains is Ridge Vineyards, founded in 1962; winemaker Paul Draper joined Ridge in 1969 and helped change the image of Zinfandel from a simple picnic wine to that of a complex, long-lived red. Ridge has specialized in making individual lots of wine, primarily Zinfandel and Cabernet Sauvignon, from grapes purchased in different regions, and identifying the source of the grapes on the label. Examples include Zinfandels from Lytton Springs in Sonoma and from Paso Robles; Cabernet Sauvignon and Petite Sirah from York Creek, on Napa's Spring Mountain; Merlot from Bradford Mountain, in the Russian River Valley; and Cabernet Sauvignon and Chardonnay from the Santa Cruz Mountains. Ridge also makes two proprietary reds: Geyserville, from northern Sonoma, is made primarily from Zinfandel; Monte Bello comes from the winery's home vineyard, planted with Cabernet Sauvignon, Merlot, and Petit Verdot.

Randall Grahm of Bonny Doon Vineyard, who began by focusing on Chardonnay and Pinot Noir, was one of the first to recognize the possibilities of the Rhône varieties in California, and now cultivates such grapes as Syrah, Mourvèdre, Grenache, Marsanne, Roussanne, and Viognier, from which he makes a number of varietal wines, as well as such proprietary reds as Le Cigare Volant, the Mourvèdre-based Old Telegram, the Grenache-based Clos de Gilroy, and a pale pink wine labeled Vin Gris de Cigare. Grahm has also become interested in Italian varieties, some of which are marketed under the Ca' del Solo label, and he also produces a selection of grappas and several ice wines, labeled Vin de Glacière, made from grapes that are put into a freezer before they are crushed.

Martin Ray, who owned the Paul Masson winery for a few years, established his own vineyards on Mount Eden in the 1940s. Ray died in 1976, and his winery and part of the vineyards are now known as Mount Eden Vineyards; the winery produces Chardonnay, Pinot Noir, and Cabernet Sauvignon from the estate vineyards and another Chardonnay from Edna Valley grapes. David Bruce began making wines from Santa Cruz vineyards in the 1960s, including a number of powerful Chardonnays, Pinot Noirs, and Zinfandels; he now focuses on Chardonnay and Pinot Noir from his own vineyards and also produces Chardonnay, Pinot Noir, and Cabernet Sauvignon labeled Vintner's Select. Santa Cruz Mountain Vineyard, which was established by Ken Burnap in 1974 to concentrate on Pinot Noir, also produces Cabernet Sauvignon and Chardonnay. Hallcrest Vineyards, active in the 1950s and 1960s, was closed in 1969, then revived as Felton-Empire; more recently, new owners restored the Hallcrest name for several varietal wines, including some that are alcohol-free, and the winery also markets varietal wines from organically farmed grapes under the Organic Wine Works label.

Other wineries associated with the Santa Cruz Mountains include Cronin Vineyards, which makes small lots of Chardonnay from different appellations; Kathryn Kennedy Winery, which makes a limited amount of Cabernet Sauvignon; Cinnabar Vineyards, which makes Cabernet Sauvignon and Chardonnay; Fellom Ranch Vineyards, which cultivates Cabernet Sauvignon on a vineyard contiguous to Ridge's Monte Bello; and also Ahlgren Vineyard, Thomas Fogarty Winery, Roudon-Smith Vineyards, and Storrs Winery.

MONTEREY, SAN LUIS OBISPO, AND SANTA BARBARA

Monterey

Much of the expansion that has occurred in the acreage of fine wine grapes has taken place south of San Francisco, and the most dramatic example is that of Monterey. In 1970, there were fewer than two thousand acres of vines in that county; by 1974, thirty-two thousand acres had been planted. There are now about thirty thousand acres of vineyards, but the vineyard sites and the proportion of different varieties cultivated today has changed considerably from the original plantings of the early 1970s. Wente Bros., Mirassou, and Paul Masson were the first major companies to create vineyards in Monterey, starting in the early 1960s. Almadén and a few small wineries followed; and a number of ranching companies, which sold their grapes to established wineries in other countries, planted large vineyards as well. Almost all of the vineyards in Monterey County are situated in the Salinas Valley between the Santa Lucia Mountains on the west and the Gavilan Mountains on the east. The vineyards are cooled by ocean breezes, and water for irrigation is supplied by wells drilled into an underground river. The rows of vines were deliberately set out far enough apart to allow mechanical harvesting, whereby the grape bunches are shaken loose from the vines by machine rather than being cut and picked by hand. Since the vineyards were created in land that was never before planted with vines (the Salinas Valley is famous for lettuce, broccoli, and artichokes), it was assumed that the phylloxera louse would not be present in the soil. Most of the vines in Monterey were, therefore, planted on their own roots. Phylloxera did eventually appear in Monterey and all new plantings are now grafted onto phylloxera-resistant American rootstocks.

All of the principal varieties were planted in Monterey, which was originally thought of as a single microclimate; but growers soon realized that not all of the varieties planted were equally successful in every vineyard site. Monterey winemakers discovered that the region produces white wines with a particularly intense and cleanly defined varietal character, but an odd vegetal flavor marred some of the first Monterey red wines. The exceptionally cool growing season in the upper part of the region made it difficult for most red-wine varieties to mature properly, and experience suggested that the cooler upper Salinas Valley, nearest the ocean, would be more appropriate for white varieties, while Cabernet Sauvignon, Merlot, Petite Sirah, and Zinfandel would be more successfully cultivated in the warmer, inland part of the valley—which extends northwest to southeast— and on hillside vineyards. More than two-thirds of the vineyards created in the early 1970s were made up of red varieties; today, white varieties account for two-thirds of the acreage, with Chardonnay representing about a third of the total Monterey plantings, followed by Chenin Blanc, Sauvignon Blanc, Johannisberg Riesling, and lesser amounts of Pinot Blanc and Gewürztraminer. Cabernet Sauvignon is the leading red-wine grape, followed by Zinfandel, Pinot Noir, and lesser amounts of Merlot and Petite Sirah; not only has the acreage of red grapes diminished considerably, but these varieties are, to a large extent, planted in different parts of the valley than in the 1970s.

Monterey includes several viticultural areas, notably Arroyo Seco, which extends west of Greenfield to the foothills of the Santa Lucia Mountains; the Santa Lucia Highlands, which extends to the west of Soledad and Gonzales and is just northwest of the Arroyo Seco district; Carmel Valley, which begins southwest of the town of Carmel and runs parallel to the Salinas Valley; and Chalone, which includes the winery of that name, and is situated on the eastern slopes of the valley, about fifteen hundred feet above the valley floor.

Many firms that own vineyards in Monterey are located elsewhere. One of the best-known wineries in Monterey is the Monterey Vineyard, established in the early 1970s; after several changes of ownership, it is now part of the Seagram's group and produces a range of varietal wines under the Classic label and selected lots that are labeled Limited Reserve. Adjoining facilities are used to produce the wines marketed as Paul Masson and Taylor California Cellars. Jekel Vineyard was first planted in 1972 in the Arroyo Seco district and a winery built in 1978; it is best known for Chardonnay, Johannisberg Riesling, and Cabernet Sauvignon. Ventana Vineyards was established as a winery in 1978 by Doug Meador, whose three-hundred-acre vineyard continues to provide grapes to other wineries, many of whom designate the vineyard on their labels. Smith & Hook, whose hillside vineyards in the Santa Lucia Highlands district are planted primarily with Cabernet Sauvignon and Merlot, is known for those two wines; the Hahn Estates label is used for Cabernet Sauvignon, Merlot, and Chardonnay. San Saba Vineyard, planted in the 1970s, uses that name for its Cabernet Sauvignon; a second label, Bocage, is used for Cabernet Sauvignon and Merlot. Winemaker Dan Lee established Morgan Winery to make Chardonnay, Pinot Noir, Cabernet Sauvignon, and Sauvignon Blanc. Robert Talbott Vineyards produces Chardonnay from both the Monterey and Carmel Valley appellations, the latter labeled Diamond-T Estate; Logan is the winery's second label. La Reina Winery also concentrates on Chardonnay, as does Richard Boyer. The five-hundred-acre Pinnacles vineyard, originally planted by Paul Masson in the 1960s, was acquired by the owners of Franciscan, who now bottle Chardonnay and Pinot Noir under the Pinnacles name; the vineyard also supplies Chardonnay and Sauvignon Blanc for the Estancia Estates label, under the same ownership. Lockwood Vineyard produces a range of varietal wines from sixteen hundred acres planted in the San Lucas district. Paraiso Springs Vineyards produces a limited amount of wine from its acreage in the Santa Lucia Highlands.

The pioneer winery in the Carmel Valley was Durney Vineyard, whose wines—primarily Cabernet Sauvignon—come from vineyards first planted in the 1960s. Chateau Julien, also in the Carmel Valley, produced its first wines in 1983; its emphasis is on regular and reserve bottlings of Chardonnay and Cabernet Sauvignon. Joullian Vineyards, whose forty-acre vineyard was planted in 1984, produces Chardonnay, Sauvignon Blanc, and Cabernet Sauvignon. Bernardus Vineyards, established by Bernardus Pon in the Carmel Valley, is planted primarily with the traditional Bordeaux varieties. Domaine de Clarck concentrates on Chardonnay and Pinot Noir.

Chalone Vineyard, the oldest winery in Monterey, and the most remote, is situated on a benchland of the Gavilan Mountains. In 1969, the winery was revitalized by Richard Graff, who expanded the acreage, now more than two hundred acres, planted with Chardonnay, Pinot Noir, and Pinot Blanc. The winery, which has established the viticultural area Chalone for its vineyards, is best known for its rich Chardonnay and Pinot Noir; Gavilan is a second label used for wines from the estate. The Chalone group also owns Carmenet Vineyard in Sonoma, Acacia Winery in the Carneros district of Napa, and is co-owner of the Edna Valley Vineyard winery in San Luis Obispo.

The vineyards in San Benito County, which adjoins Monterey on the other side of the San Benito Range, were first developed by Almadén, which also established the Paicines and Cienega Valley viticultural areas; nearly five thousand acres were planted by the mid-1970s, but after a change of ownership the Almadén vineyards were abandoned, and current plantings in San Benito amount to about fifteen hundred acres. The county's best-known producer is Calera Wine Company, established by Josh Jensen to concentrate on Pinot Noir; he planted twenty-four acres of that variety in the mid-1970s on a limestone site in the mountains and then planted more Pinot Noir, plus Chardonnay, and Viognier, in the 1980s. Pinot Noir from the four vineyard sites are bottled separately as Reed, Selleck, Jensen, and Mills and the estate Chardonnay bears the Mount Harlan viticultural designation; Jensen produces additional Pinot Noir and Chardonnay from Central Coast grapes. Cygnet Cellars is also located in San Benito.

San Luis Obispo

The vineyard acreage in San Luis Obispo has developed more slowly than in Monterey, from just a few hundred acres in the late 1960s to about three thousand in the mid-1970s, and now amounts to about nine thousand acres. Chardonnay and Cabernet Sauvignon account for nearly two-thirds of the total, and most of the rest consists of Zinfandel, Sauvignon Blanc, and Merlot. The county's viticultural areas include the large Paso Robles district, which extends from just south of the Monterey border down past the towns of Paso Robles and Templeton almost to San Luis Obispo; Edna Valley, a small district southeast of the town of San Luis Obispo; and Arroyo Seco, another small district just south of Edna Valley and about a dozen miles southeast of San Luis Obispo. The York Mountain district is contained along the western edge of the Paso Robles appellation, at a fifteen-hundred-foot elevation in the Santa Lucia Mountains; its one producer, York Mountain Winery, established in 1882 and revitalized in the 1970s, is best known for its red wines.

The Paso Robles area, separated from the ocean by the Santa Lucia Mountains, is a relatively warm area whose growers have had particular success with Zinfandel and Cabernet Sauvignon, although Chardonnay and many other varieties, including Nebbiolo and Syrah, are also cultivated there. In fact, the Perrin family, owners of Château Beaucastel in France's Châteauneuf-du-Pape district, in partnership with wine merchant Robert Haas, have established a vineyard near Paso Robles which is

planted with a number of red and white Rhône varieties.
(The town of Paso Robles, incidentally, is due east of
William Randolph Hearst's San Simeon estate, a well-
known tourist attraction situated along the coast.) Per-
haps the best-known winery in Paso Robles is Meridian
Cellars, under the same ownership as Beringer Vine-
yards and Chateau Souverain. The winery is the former
Estrella River Winery, which was purchased by Wine
World along with nearly six hundred acres of vineyards;
the Meridian name was acquired from winemaker Chuck
Ortman, who was then put in charge of the new firm.
(The Estrella River Winery name and additional acreage
was retained by the winery's former owner.) Meridian,
which draws on its acreage in San Luis Obispo and
an additional three thousand acres in Santa Barbara
County owned by Wine World, is best known for its
Chardonnays from Santa Barbara County and the
Edna Valley; Syrah, Cabernet Sauvignon, and Pinot
Noir are also produced.

Wild Horse Vineyards, established by Ken Volk,
achieved a reputation for Pinot Noir and also produces
Chardonnay, Cabernet Sauvignon, and Merlot. Eberle
Winery focuses on Cabernet Sauvignon and Chardonnay, as does Adelaida Cellars. Martin Brothers Winery
produces several wines, including Nebbiolo; Caparone
Vineyards, too, produces wine from Italian varieties in
addition to its Cabernet Sauvignon and Merlot. Creston
Manor offers a full range of wines from its hillside vineyards; Mastantuono specializes in Zinfandel; and Arciero
Winery offers a wide range of wines from more than
five hundred acres of vineyards near Paso Robles. Justin
Vineyards produces Chardonnay, Cabernet Sauvignon,
and a proprietary red labeled Isosceles Reserve. Other
wineries include Castoro Cellars.

The cool growing conditions of the Edna Valley,
which is open to ocean breezes, favor Chardonnay,
which is by far the most widely planted variety in this
district. Edna Valley Vineyards, whose first wines were
produced in 1980, concentrates on Chardonnay; it is co-
owned by Chalone and the owners of Paragon Vineyard,
whose six hundred acres, also planted with other varieties, supplies grapes to other wineries. Corbett Canyon
Vineyards, the biggest winery in Edna Valley, produces

moderately priced varietal wines with the Coastal Classic designation. Chamisal Vineyards, which established the first winery in the Edna Valley, focuses on estate-bottled Chardonnay.

The cool Arroyo Grande district became known when the Deutz champagne firm established Maison Deutz in this area and planted vineyards there; the firm released its first *méthode champenoise* sparkling wines in 1986. Talley Vineyards, a winery that emphasizes Chardonnay and Pinot Noir, also has vineyards in Arroyo Grande, as does Saucelito Canyon Vineyard, known for its Zinfandel.

Santa Barbara

Virtually all of Santa Barbara County's nine thousand acres of vineyards have been planted since 1970. Most of the acreage consists of white-wine grapes, with Chardonnay representing more than half the total; Pinot Noir and Cabernet Sauvignon account for fewer than a thousand acres each, and there are also lesser amounts of Sauvignon Blanc and Johannisberg Riesling. The county includes two viticultural areas, the Santa Maria Valley, where most of the vineyards have been planted, and the Santa Ynez Valley, where most of the wineries are located. The Santa Maria Valley extends from the border of San Luis Obispo southeast along the Santa Maria river for about fifteen miles; cooled by ocean breezes, it is best known for Chardonnay and Pinot Noir. Two large vineyards in the Santa Maria Valley, Bien Nacido and Sierra Madre, provide grapes to many wineries and are often designated on labels. The Santa Ynez Valley, which contains the towns of Santa Ynez, Solvang, Los Olivos, and Buellton, is warmer and its vineyards include more of the Bordeaux varieties—Cabernet Sauvignon, Merlot, Cabernet Franc, Sauvignon Blanc, and Sémillon.

One of the best-known wineries of the Santa Ynez Valley is Firestone Vineyard, which began producing a range of classic varietal wines in the mid-1970s from 265 acres of vineyards and has had particular success with its Johannisberg Riesling (also made in a late-harvest version); the Firestone family also own Carey Cellars, best known for Chardonnay and for the Cabernet Sauvignon from the La Questa vineyard. Sanford Winery, established by Richard and Thekla Sanford, produced its first wines in 1981; its emphasis is on Pinot Noir and Chardonnay, special lots of which are labeled Barrel Select. Brander Vineyard, which made a reputation for its Sauvignon Blanc in the late 1970s, also produces Chardonnay and a Cabernet-Merlot blend labeled Bouchet. Austin Cellars offers several wines, including Chardonnay, Pinot Noir, and late-harvest Johannisberg Riesling. Zaca Mesa Winery, established in the 1970s, has undergone a number of changes over the years; it now focuses on Chardonnay, Pinot Noir, Syrah and other Rhône varieties. Santa Barbara Winery, noted for its Chardonnay and Pinot Noir, also makes a fruity, *nouveau*-style Zinfandel labeled Beaujour. Mosby Winery produces a number of wines, some of which are marketed under the Vega Vineyards label. Fess Parker Winery, established by the actor best known for his television portrayals of Davy Crockett and Daniel Boone, produces Johannisberg Riesling, Chardonnay, and Syrah. Other Santa Ynez Valley wineries include Babcock Vineyard, Gainey Vineyards, and Santa Ynez Winery.

Among the wineries in the Santa Maria Valley, Au Bon Climat is known for its Chardonnay and Pinot Noir, which are also produced in single-vineyard bottlings; wines made from such Italian varieties as Nebbiolo, Barbera, and Tocai Friulano are marketed under the name Il Podere dell'Olivos. Qupé has established a reputation for its Chardonnay and for wines made from Rhône varieties, including Syrah, Mourvèdre, Marsanne, and Viognier. The owners of Au Bon Climat and Qupé also produce Chardonnay, Sauvignon Blanc, and a Cabernet-based blend under the Vita Nova label. The Byron Vineyard, established by Byron (Ken) Brown in the Santa Maria Valley to focus on Chardonnay, Pinot Noir, and Sauvignon Blanc, was acquired by the Robert Mondavi family in 1990; Byron continues to produce those wines from Santa Barbara grapes. Jess Jackson of Kendall-Jackson, who purchased twelve hundred acres of vineyards in the Santa Maria Valley, established Cambria Winery to focus on Chardonnay and Pinot Noir. Foxen Vineyard produces limited quantities of Chardonnay and Cabernet Sauvignon. Rancho Sisquoc Winery, which owns vineyards in the Santa Maria Valley, sells most of its grapes but also produces limited amounts of wine.

Southeast of Santa Barbara, in Ventura County, Ojai Vineyard specializes in Syrah and other Rhône varieties, and Leeward Winery is best known for its different bottlings of Chardonnay.

There are also vineyards and wineries farther south, near Los Angeles and San Diego. The best-known wine region in southern California is located near Temecula, about fifty miles north of San Diego, in an area also known as Rancho California; its most famous winery is Callaway Vineyard & Winery, established in the mid-1970s. For some years, the winery has concentrated almost entirely on white wines, and has achieved particular success with a Chardonnay labeled Calla-lees, which receives no oak-aging but is aged on its lees in stainless steel tanks; other varietal wines include Sauvignon Blanc and Cabernet Sauvignon. Culbertson Winery, also in Temecula, produces a range of *méthode champenoise* sparkling wines; Maurice Car'rie is known for Chardonnay, Cabernet Sauvignon, and Sauvignon Blanc; and Mount Palomar Winery specializes in Chardonnay.

AMADOR AND THE SIERRA FOOTHILLS

The wine region now referred to as the Sierra Foothills includes vineyards, most of them at an elevation of twelve hundred to two thousand feet, on the western slopes of the Sierra Nevada mountains; the appellation includes eight counties, but in practice almost all the acreage is found in Amador, El Dorado, and Calaveras counties, about forty miles east of Sacramento. Vineyards and wineries were first established in this region, which is also called the Mother Lode, soon after the Gold Rush of 1849. By 1890 there were more than one hundred wineries there, but after Prohibition all but one, D'Agostini, had disappeared, and it was not until the early 1970s that new wineries were once again established. The impetus for the renaissance of the Sierra

Foothills region was the discovery in the late 1960s that Amador vineyards, many of them planted before Prohibition, could produce particularly flavorful and intense Zinfandels. Sutter Home and Ridge were among the first wineries to produce Zinfandels from Amador grapes.

There are now about eighteen hundred acres of vineyards in Amador, two-thirds of them planted with Zinfandel, plus new plantings of Sauvignon Blanc, Cabernet Sauvignon, and other varieties. Acreage in El Dorado and Calaveras has increased from fewer than one hundred to about seven hundred acres, most of it in El Dorado. Many small, family-owned wineries were established in the late 1970s and early 1980s, and almost all of them focus on Zinfandel as their primary grape, although most wineries actually produce considerably more White Zinfandel than the traditional red wine. In addition, the usual roster includes limited amounts of Sauvignon Blanc and perhaps Cabernet Sauvignon or a semisweet Johannisberg Riesling.

Amador County contains two adjoining viticultural areas, Fiddletown and Shenandoah Valley, both near the town of Plymouth. Amador's best-known producer is Montevina Winery, which was the first to be established in the area since Prohibition, and one that offers several varietal wines, including Zinfandel and Barbera; in 1988, the Trinchero family of Sutter Home bought the winery and planted additional acreage, some of it devoted to Italian varieties. Shenandoah Vineyards, established by Leon Sobon, produces several wines in addition to red and White Zinfandel, including Sauvignon Blanc and fortified Muscats; in 1989, Sobon acquired the D'Agostini winery and its vineyards and renamed the property Sobon Estate. Other Amador wineries include Amador Foothill Winery, Argonaut Winery, Baldinelli Vineyards, Karly Wines, Santino Winery, and Story Vineyards.

Boeger Winery was the first one established in El Dorado, north of Amador; it produces a wide range of wines, including Chardonnay, Merlot, and a proprietary wine labeled Hangtown Red, Hangtown being the original name of nearby Placerville. Other El Dorado wineries include Gerwer Winery, Fitzpatrick Winery, Granite Springs Winery, Sierra Vista Winery, and Madrona Vineyards, planted in the early 1970s at an elevation of three thousand feet, which makes it California's highest vineyard.

Stevenot Winery, founded by Barden Stevenot in 1974, was the first winery in Calaveras County. Some miles to the north, in Yuba County, but still within the Sierra Foothills region, Renaissance Vineyards was established in the mid-1970s; it has more than three hundred acres of terraced vineyards planted primarily with Cabernet Sauvignon, Johannisberg Riesling, and Sauvignon Blanc.

THE SAN JOAQUIN VALLEY

The San Joaquin Valley, also known as the Central Valley, extends for more than two hundred miles from Stockton down to Bakersfield. More than two-thirds of California's wine grapes come from this warm, fertile region, and if the table and raisin grapes used to make wine are included, the Central Valley (plus the vineyards north of Stockton) accounts for 80 percent of the wine made in the state. (Note, however, that this includes wines that are distilled to make brandy and those used as the base for fortified wines, flavored wines, and wine coolers.) There are a number of very large wineries situated in the valley; some produce wines that are shipped in bulk to other wineries throughout the state, many bottle their own wines and market them under a variety of names.

E. & J. Gallo, located in Modesto, is the biggest wine firm in the world, and accounts for more than one out of every four bottles of wine sold in this country. The company, founded in 1933 by Ernest and Julio Gallo, markets a complete range of generic and varietal table wines, dessert wines, sparkling wines, Boone's fruit-based wines, and flavored wines such as Thunderbird. Gallo's best-selling generic table wines include Hearty Burgundy, Chablis Blanc, and the Carlo Rossi jug wines; Gallo also markets a range of moderately priced varietal wines, including the popular White Grenache and Sauvignon Blanc, and selected lots of Chardonnay and Cabernet Sauvignon. The firm's sparkling wines include Tott's, Eden Roc, Ballatore, and Andre; the last accounts for more than a third of all the sparkling wines produced in California. Although Gallo crushes a substantial quantity of Central Valley grapes at several wineries—the enormous Modesto facility, which includes a glass factory, is used only for blending, aging, and bottling—the firm also owns nearly two thousand acres of vineyards in northern Sonoma and a winery in Dry Creek.

Guild, another major California producer, is now owned by Canandaigua; Guild wines are bottled at Lodi and the firm is associated with such brands as Cook's Imperial and Chase-Limogère sparkling wines, Dunnewood, Cribari, Roma, Tavola, and Cresta Blanca. Other Central Valley wineries include Delicato, Giumarra, and the Heublein facility at Madera, which bottles Almadén, Inglenook Vineyards (formerly Inglenook Navalle), Blossom Hill, the Christian Brothers, and Le Domaine sparkling wines. Franzia, which also produces the Summit and Colony brands, has been particularly successful with wines marketed in five-liter containers. JFJ Bronco was founded by the Franzia brothers, who are part owners of the Montpellier brand of varietal wines and also own the Laurier, Hacienda, and Grand Cru labels.

Extensive new vineyards have been planted in two adjoining regions situated between Sacramento and Stockton—the Clarksburg area, which includes the Merritt Island district, and the Lodi area; both of these viticultural areas are situated in the northern part of San Joaquin County and the southern part of Sacramento County. Clarksburg is best known for Chenin Blanc, and Lodi provides about a third of the total Zinfandel crop, but these two areas also produce significant amounts of Chardonnay, Cabernet Sauvignon, and Sauvignon Blanc. Bogle Vineyards is the most important winery in Clarksburg; the best-known winery in Lodi is Robert Mondavi's Woodbridge facility, which produces a range of less expensive varietal wines. Northwest of Sacramento, R. H. Phillips Vineyard produces a range of proprietary and varietal wines from its extensive acreage in the Dunnigan Hills; the wines labeled Night Harvest include Sauvignon Blanc and Cuvée Rouge, a blend of Rhône varieties.

OTHER WINES OF THE UNITED STATES

With a total wine production that has varied in recent years from 170 to 200 million cases—about a quarter as much wine as is produced in France or Italy—America usually ranks sixth in the world. In consumption, however, America ranks around thirtieth, with a per capita rate of about nine bottles a year, compared to eighty-five in France, Italy, and Portugal and more than sixty bottles per person in Argentina, Spain, and Switzerland. Nevertheless, consumption has increased almost four-fold since the early 1960s, and table wines, which once accounted for less than 20 percent of the total (which was made up primarily of inexpensive port, sherry, muscatel, and flavored fortified wines), now make up three-quarters of the traditional wine market.

Although 90 percent of the wines made in America come from California, wine is now produced in about forty-five states, and of the fifteen hundred wineries in this country, more than half are outside California. New York, Washington, and Oregon have the most wineries, and these three states, plus Ohio, Pennsylvania, Virginia, Missouri, Texas, and Michigan account for almost two-thirds of the non-California wineries. New York is second to California in the amount of wine produced, but most of that is made from native grapes and French-

American hybrids, with European *Vitis vinifera* grapes accounting for only two thousand acres (compared to 325,000 acres of wine grapes in California). There are about eleven thousand acres of *vinifera* grapes in Washington, about six thousand acres in Oregon, and significant new plantings in Texas, Virginia, Idaho, and elsewhere.

While almost all the vineyards and wineries outside California are of relatively recent origin, a number of states have a long history of winemaking. In the 1860s, for example, Missouri accounted for 40 percent of the wines made in America, more than California and New York together. Nicholas Longworth first produced Catawba wines in Ohio in the 1820s; Brotherhood Winery in New York State has been in operation since 1839; Wisconsin's Wollersheim Winery traces its origins back to 1857; two Arkansas wineries, Post and Wiederkehr, were founded in 1880.

Today, many American wineries continue to produce wines from such native grapes as Concord, Catawba, Delaware, and, in the south, Muscadine and Scuppernong; many cultivate French-American hybrids such as Seyval Blanc, Vidal, Vignoles, Aurora, Baco Noir, Chelois, Léon Millot, and Maréchal Foch; and most of the wineries founded in the past fifteen years or so produce at least some wines from *vinifera* grapes, especially Chardonnay, Cabernet Sauvignon, Merlot, Pinot Noir, Sauvignon Blanc, and Johannisberg Riesling. It's not unusual for wineries east of the Rocky Mountains to make wines from both native grapes and French-American hybrids, or from hybrids and *vinifera;* some make wines from all three. It should perhaps be added that many wineries throughout the country buy California wine in bulk to blend with their locally produced wine. In addition, a number of wineries specialize in fruit wines, ranging from pineapple wine made in Hawaii to blueberry wine from Maine.

NEW YORK STATE

New York State, which ranks a distant second to California in wine production, accounts for about 5 percent of all the wine consumed in this country. Nearly one-third of that is made up of sparkling wines, dessert wines such as port and cream sherry, and wine coolers, which are prepackaged mixtures of wine, carbonated water, and various flavors. And some of the table wines consist of simple, fairly sweet red, white, and pink wines with the pronounced aroma and distinctive taste that many people associate with fresh grapes, grape juice, and jelly. Nevertheless, New York State is very much an area in transition: three-quarters of the more than ninety wineries in the state were created since 1976; new wine regions have been established and traditional ones expanded; and there has been a significant increase in the number of fine wines—particularly whites—produced there.

The story of the rapidly evolving New York wine scene has as much to do with the kinds of grapes grown in the state as it does with the appearance of dozens of new wineries. New York is unusual in that its wines are made from native grapes, French-American hybrids, and European *vinifera* varieties, and it's not uncommon for a winery to make wines from all three types of grapes.

Grape vines had to be specially introduced into California, but the earliest settlers in the eastern United States found a number of native grapes already growing wild all along the Atlantic Coast. Encouraged by this profusion of vines, a few colonists imported cuttings of European *Vitis vinifera* varieties during the seventeenth and eighteenth centuries and tried to establish new vineyards on the East Coast. Invariably, these vines died, and we now know that this was a result of phylloxera, fungus, and very cold winter temperatures to which *vinifera* vines were not resistant. In the early nineteenth century, successful experiments were carried out with existing native varieties, notably Catawba, and native American wines began to be produced commercially in several Eastern states. These native grapes, made up for the most part of *Vitis labrusca,* impart a pungent aroma and flavor to the wines made from them, and their taste often seems strange to those who are used to European or California wines. This pronounced grapy character is most clearly demonstrated by the Concord grape—now used almost entirely for juice—which accounts for about two-thirds of the grape crop in New York State. Actually, less than half the total crop is crushed to make wine—the equivalent of about six million cases a year—but much of that still consists of such *labrusca* varieties as Concord, Catawba, and Niagara. The *labrusca* varieties that dominate the eastern vineyards are cultivated in only a few other places—such as Washington, Canada, and Brazil—and the unique wines they produce should be approached with this in mind.

Like California wines, some New York State wines still are marketed with generic place-names of European origin, such as Rhine Wine, Chablis, and Burgundy. Because *labrusca* grapes are used to make most of these wines, they bear no resemblance to wines from those French and German districts or to California generic wines, which are made from *vinifera* grapes. Nevertheless, people who enjoy the distinct flavor of certain table grapes find these wines very pleasing indeed, and their wide distribution in this country attests to their popularity. A few large wineries also produce varietal wines from native grapes, which are labeled with such names as Pink Catawba, Rosé of Isabella, Delaware, and Dutchess.

In recent years there has been a significant shift in the acreage of French-American hybrids in New York State vineyards—white wine varieties have increased as red varieties have declined. These hybrids are crossings that combine the hardiness of the American vines, specifically their resistance to disease and extremes of cold, with the more delicate flavor of the *vinifera* grape. Hybrids are named after the individuals who developed them and carry the serial number of the original seedling, such as Baco 1, Seibel 5279, and Seyve-Villard 5276. Most of these hybrids were developed in France at the end of the nineteenth century, and over the years they have acquired names that are more attractive than the original combinations of name and number. The most popular hybrids (and the names by which they are commonly known) are, among the red varieties, Baco 1 (Baco Noir), Seibel 7053 (Chancellor), Seibel 9549 (De Chaunac), and Kuhlman 188-2 (Maréchal Foch). The best-known white varieties include Seibel 5279 (Aurora), Seyve-Villard 5276 (Seyval Blanc), Ravat 6 (Ravat Blanc), Ravat 51 (Vignoles), and Vidal 256 (Vidal Blanc). French-American hybrids account for 20 to 25 percent of the wines produced in New York State; Seyval Blanc, Vignoles, De Chaunac, and Baco Noir are the most extensively planted. The wines, in which the *labrusca* flavor is considerably diminished or entirely absent, are sometimes blended with *labrusca* wines to reduce the latter's grapy taste. Many hybrids are also bottled on their own as varietal wines, especially the crisp Seyval Blanc.

The wines produced from the more than two thousand acres of *vinifera* grapes now planted in several different regions are the most dramatic development in the recent history of New York State viticulture. They are the result of the pioneering work done by the late Dr. Konstantin Frank, who had successfully cultivated *vinifera* in his native Russia before emigrating to this country. Frank first began grafting European vines on native American rootstocks in the early 1950s for the late Charles Fournier of Gold Seal, and later went on to establish his own company—Vinifera Wine Cellars—to produce and market such *vinifera* varieties as Johannisberg Riesling, Chardonnay, Gewürztraminer, Pinot Noir, and the unusual Rkatsiteli. Although *vinifera* varieties account for only 5 percent or so of New York State's vineyards, they account for 20 percent of the wine-grape acreage, and more than sixty-five wineries now produce Chardonnay, Johannisberg Riesling, Cabernet Sauvignon, Merlot, or other *vinifera*-based varietal wines.

THE NEW YORK WINE REGIONS

The Finger Lakes

The Finger Lakes district, which has been established as a viticultural area, is the biggest wine-producing region outside of California. Although it has only two-fifths of New York's thirty-five thousand acres of vineyards, the Finger Lakes produce about 80 percent of the state's wine. The region, situated three hundred miles northwest of New York City, gets its name from several elongated lakes that resemble an imprint made by the outspread fingers of a giant hand. The region is subject to great extremes of temperature, but the lakes exert a moderating influence on the microclimate of the vineyards situated along their sloping shores. Vines were first planted in this district in 1829 in a clergyman's garden in Hammondsport, at the southern tip of Lake Keuka. The first commercial winery was established in 1860, and by the end of the nineteenth century, four major Finger Lakes firms—Taylor, Great Western, Gold Seal, and Widmer's—had been established.

Over the years, each of these four major firms has become known for a somewhat different range of wines. The Taylor Wine Company is associated with sparkling and dessert wines, and with table wines marketed under the Lake Country label. (The Taylor California Cellars selection of generic and varietal wines, introduced in the late 1970s, is produced and bottled in California.) Great Western, which was acquired by Taylor in 1961, is best known for its sparkling wines and for varietal wines made from native grapes and French-American hybrids. Gold Seal, whose best-selling wines include Catawba Pink, Red, and Rosé, also established a reputation for its sparkling wines. In 1983, when the three firms came under the same ownership, production of the three brands was consolidated at the Taylor facility. Widmer's Wine Cellars, long known for its sherries and for wines marketed under the Lake Niagara label, also makes a range of varietal wines. In 1986, the Canandaigua Wine Company, one of the biggest wine producers in the country, which achieved success with such brands as Richard's Wild Irish Rose, J. Roget sparkling wines, and Sun Country wine cooler, acquired Widmer's; in 1993, Canandaigua also bought Taylor, Great Western, and Gold Seal. (The firm also produces Manischewitz kosher wines and owns the Guild Winery in California, whose brands include Dunnewood, Cresta Blanca, Cribari, and Cook's.)

Although the major Finger Lakes wineries continue to dominate sales, new legislation in 1976 changed the New York State wine industry. The Farm Winery Act gave special consideration to wineries producing no more than fifty thousand gallons a year, the equivalent of about twenty thousand cases. (The maximum limit was subsequently raised to three times that amount.) Annual fees were greatly reduced, but, more importantly, farm wineries—unlike the large, established firms that rely on national distribution to market their wines—were permitted to sell as much of their production as they wanted to directly to the public. By liberalizing the regulations governing wine sales, the bill, and subsequent amendments, encouraged grapegrowers to make wines from their own grapes, and enabled wine enthusiasts to start their own wineries. More than seventy wineries have been established since 1976, most of them specializing in varietal wines made from *vinifera* grapes and French-American hybrids.

Among the better-known Finger Lakes wineries are Hermann J. Wiemer Vineyard, which specializes in Chardonnay and Johannisberg Riesling; Glenora Wine Cellars, which makes *méthode champenoise* sparkling wines and such classic varietal wines as Chardonnay, Johannisberg Riesling, Cabernet Sauvignon, and Merlot; and Wagner Vineyards, whose more than two hundred acres of vineyards produce a wide range of wines, including Chardonnay, Johannisberg Riesling, Gewürztraminer, Seyval Blanc, DeChaunac, and ice wine from Ravat Blanc and Riesling. Other wineries include Hunt Country Vineyards, Heron Hill Vineyards, Casa Larga Vineyards, Lamoreaux Landing Wine Cellars, and, in the Cayuga Lake district, Swedish Hill Vineyard, Knapp Vineyards, and Lucas Vineyard. Vinifera Wine Cellars markets its wines under the Dr. Konstantin Frank label, and a second winery, Chateau Frank, produces *méthode champenoise* sparkling wines from Pinot Noir, Pinot Meunier, and Chardonnay.

Another well-known Finger Lakes winery is Bully Hill, established in 1970 by Walter S. Taylor, whose grandfather founded the Taylor Wine Company; Taylor specializes in wines made from French-American hybrids.

The Lake Erie district, also known as the Chautauqua region, extends for about sixty miles along the southern shore of Lake Erie, in the western part of New York State. The region contains more than half of the state's vineyard acreage, but 90 percent of that is planted with Concord grapes, which are used for juice. French-American hybrids and *vinifera* varieties are also planted, and several wineries produce wines from these grapes, as well as from native varieties. Johnson Estate wines were first marketed in the 1960s; wineries established more recently include Merritt Estate and Woodbury Vineyards. The Mogen David winery, which produces kosher wines, is also located in this region.

The Hudson River Region

The Hudson River Region, the oldest wine-producing district in New York State, and the first to be recognized as a viticultural area, extends about twenty miles east and west of the Hudson River from Newburgh north to Kingston; the region has witnessed a renewed interest in winemaking in recent years and is now home to about two dozen wineries. Most of the thousand acres of vineyard are planted with French-American hybrids, but a number of wineries produce *vinifera* varietal wines as well. The oldest vineyard is Benmarl, located near Marlboro, seventy-five miles from New York City. Owner Mark Miller, a pioneer in New York viticulture, began replanting the estate in the 1950s and produced his first wines in 1971. William Wetmore planted Cascade Mountain Vineyard in 1972, and in 1977 Ben Feder established Clinton Vineyard, whose twenty acres produce a widely acclaimed Seyval Blanc and a limited amount of Seyval Natural, a *méthode champenoise* sparkling wine. Millbrook Vineyard, established by John Dyson, is planted with Chardonnay, Cabernet Sauvignon, Merlot, Cabernet Franc, Pinot Noir, and other *vinifera* varieties, and produced its first wines in 1975. Other Hudson River Region wineries include West Park Wine Cellars, North Salem Vineyard, Walker Valley Vineyards, and Rivendell Winery. Brotherhood Winery, which traces its first vintage back to 1839, and Royal Kedem Winery, which produces a full range of kosher wines, are popular tourist attractions.

Long Island

The newest wine region in New York State, and the only one devoted entirely to *vinifera* varieties, is on eastern Long Island, about one hundred miles east of New York City. The recent history of Long Island wines dates back to 1973, when Alex and Louisa Hargrave planted seventeen acres of Chardonnay, Cabernet Sauvignon, Pinot Noir, and Sauvignon Blanc on a former potato farm near Cutchogue, on the North Fork of Long Island. The North Fork is a slender finger of land surrounded by water on three sides, and its maritime climate and long growing season are somewhat similar to those of Bordeaux. The Hargraves (who subsequently expanded their vineyard to sixty acres) produced their first wines in 1975, and a number of grape growers established vineyards on Long Island in the late 1970s, as did several people who planned to make wine. Among the wineries that produced their first wines in the early 1980s were Lenz Winery, Palmer Vineyards, Bedell Cellars, Peconic Bay Vineyards, Jamesport Vineyards, Pindar Vineyards (whose two hundred acres make it the biggest winery in the region), and Bridgehampton Winery, situated on the South Fork of the island. Since then, such wineries as Bidwell Vineyards, Gristina Vineyards, Mattituck Hills Winery, Paumanok Vineyards, and Pugliese Vineyards have introduced their wines.

There are about fourteen hundred acres of vineyards on Long Island and two appellations of origin—the North Fork of Long Island, centered around the town of Cutchogue; and the Hamptons, which includes the townships of Bridgehampton and Southampton. Virtually all the Long Island acreage is planted on the North Fork, and most of the wineries are situated there as well; the Bridgehampton Winery and SagPond Vineyards are in the Hamptons. Merlot and Chardonnay are considered particularly successful, as are Cabernet Sauvignon, Cabernet Franc, and Sauvignon Blanc; a few wineries produce Gewürztraminer and Johannisberg Riesling.

THE PACIFIC NORTHWEST: WASHINGTON AND OREGON

The vineyards of Washington and Oregon are often grouped together under the geographical designation Pacific Northwest, but an increasing number of wine drinkers now realize that the climatic conditions of these two states (most of whose vineyards are actually quite a distance from the Pacific Ocean) are not only quite different from those of California, but different from each other as well. The Cascade Range divides Washington and Oregon from north to south. Almost all of Washington's vineyards are east of the Cascades, in an irrigated desert with an average annual rainfall of less than ten inches; most of those in Oregon are west of the Cascades, in a cool area where more than forty inches of rain is not uncommon. As a result, winemakers in the two states do not focus their efforts on the same grape varieties, and they produce wines whose styles are different as well. The emergence of Washington, Oregon, and, more recently, Idaho as producers of fine wines is dramatic—in 1960 there were only a few acres of *Vitis vinifera* grapes planted and not a single winery was making *vinifera* wines; today, there are nearly twenty thousand acres of vines and about two hundred wineries.

Washington

Wines had been produced in Washington in the nineteenth century, but the current era of winemaking can be traced back to 1962, when the late Dr. Lloyd Woodburne and a few friends formed Associated Vintners (which became Columbia Winery in 1984) and planted five acres of *vinifera* vineyards. They produced their first commercial wine in 1967, the same year that the winery that was to become Chateau Ste. Michelle also made its first commercial wine. Although the first wineries were located near Seattle, so that they and their wines would be more accessible to the state's consumers, almost all the Washington vineyards are situated two hundred miles southeast of that city, in the Columbia River Basin. This area, protected from the Pacific rains by the Cascades, is a semiarid desert that has been transformed by extensive irrigation; it is now one of the nation's principal agricultural regions, known for its apples, peaches, corn, asparagus, and other crops, and now becoming famous for its wines. About eleven thousand acres of classic European varieties are cultivated in Washington, which makes that state second only to California as a source of *vinifera* wines. (In addition, more than twenty thousand acres are planted with Concord grapes, most of which are used for juice and jelly.) It was originally assumed that Washington was best suited to white varieties, and white-wine grapes, led by Riesling and Chenin Blanc, accounted for 80 percent of the total. In recent years, Washington has achieved particular success with its Merlot and Cabernet Sauvignon, and red-wine grapes—including limited amounts of Pinot Noir and Grenache—now represent about a third of acreage. Chardonnay has become the most widely planted white grape, while the acreage of Riesling and Chenin Blanc has decreased; other white varieties include Sauvignon Blanc, Sémillon, Gewürztraminer, and Muscat Canelli. There are more hours of sunlight and heat east of the Cascades than in California, which contributes to the ripening of the grapes, but the cold desert nights enable the grapes to retain their natural acidity. As a result of these special growing conditions, Washington wines, especially the whites, are characterized by a crisp, lively taste. The region east of the Cascades has now been defined as the Columbia Valley viticultural area; this large region includes vineyards planted in the basin of the Columbia River and its tributaries, the Yakima and Snake rivers, and extends from the foothills of the Cascades east to the Idaho border and south into Oregon. The smaller Yakima Valley viticultural area is contained within the Columbia Valley appellation, as is the small Walla Walla district, along the Oregon border. The Columbia Valley and Walla Walla appellations may be used by winemakers in both Washington and Oregon.

More than eighty wineries have been established in Washington, almost all of them since 1980. Chateau Ste. Michelle and Columbia Crest, separate wineries under the same ownership, are by far the biggest firms in the state, and account for more than half the wines produced in Washington. Other major wineries include Arbor Crest, Columbia Winery, Covey Run, Hogue Cellars, Preston Wine Cellars, Staton Hills Winery, and Washington Hills Cellars. Some of the smaller wineries are Barnard Griffin Winery, Kiona Vineyards, Latah Creek, Leonetti Cellar, Quilceda Creek Vintners, Waterbrook Winery, and Woodward Canyon Winery.

Oregon

The history of winemaking in Oregon goes back to the 1820s, but Prohibition and the Depression forced most wineries out of business, and until the 1970s the state's best-known wines were those made from fruits and berries. In 1961, Richard Sommer, who was primarily interested in Riesling, planted a vineyard in the Umpqua Valley, near Roseburg, about 180 miles south of Portland; two years later he produced his first wines at Hillcrest Vineyard. In 1966, David Lett, whose particular interest was Pinot Noir, planted a few acres in the Willamette Valley, the first *vinifera* grapes planted in that region since Prohibition; he produced his first wines at the Eyrie Vineyards in 1970. Other pioneers in the Willamette Valley (pronounced wil-*lam*-met) who produced their first wines in the 1970s include Richard Erath at Knudsen Erath, Richard and Nancy Ponzi at Ponzi Vineyards, Susan Sokol and Bill Blosser at Sokol Blosser, Joe and Pat Campbell at Elk Cove Vineyards, Myron Redford at Amity Vineyards, David Adelsheim at Adelsheim Vineyard, William and Virginia Fuller at Tualatin Vineyards, and the Vuylsteke family at Oak Knoll Winery, which had already established a reputation for fruit wines.

The acreage in Oregon has increased from fewer than one hundred in 1970 to more than six thousand acres today. Most of those who first established vineyards in Oregon did so because they believed the state's cool climate was more promising for Pinot Noir than the warmer climate of California, so it is not surprising that Pinot Noir accounts for about 40 percent of the total acreage; Chardonnay represents about a quarter of the vineyards; and Riesling (which in Oregon is known as White Riesling, not Johannisberg Riesling) is the third most widely planted grape, followed by Pinot Gris. These four varieties account for about 80 percent of the acreage; most of the rest consists of Gewürztraminer, Cabernet Sauvignon, Merlot, and Sauvignon Blanc. Oregon is most famous for its elegant and stylish Pinot Noir; Pinot Gris, a grape associated with Alsace, has become a specialty as well.

Three-quarters of Oregon's acreage is in the Willamette Valley, where most of the state's nearly one hundred wineries are located. The Willamette River flows north from central Oregon and joins the Columbia River near Portland; although the valley extends for more than one hundred miles, most of the vineyards are planted within a fifty-mile radius south and west of Portland, on outcropping hills and benchlands along the west side of the river. The area, which encompasses Yamhill, Polk, and Washington counties, includes the Dundee Hills, the Eola Hills, and Chehalem Mountain. the Umpqua Valley, just south of the Willamette Valley, has climatic conditions that are warmer and drier, as does the Rogue River Valley in southern Oregon. Although most of the state's acreage is situated between the Cascade Mountains and the Coast Range, which protects the vineyards from the Pacific Ocean, vineyards have also been planted in eastern Oregon, along the Columbia River, which forms the border between Oregon and Washington. In fact, both the Columbia Valley and Walla Walla appellations of Washington include parts of northern Oregon, so it's not surprising that growing conditions are similar to those of Washington and favor such varieties as Cabernet Sauvignon, Merlot, and White Riesling.

Oregon's labeling regulations are the strictest in the country. All of the grapes must come from the geographical area designated on the label, such as Oregon, Willamette Valley, Umpqua Valley, and Yamhill County. Wines labeled with varietal names must contain at least 90 percent of the variety named (except for Cabernet Sauvignon, which may be blended with up to 25 percent of such complementary varieties as Merlot and Cabernet Franc); and such generic names as Burgundy, Chablis, Champagne, and Port are not permitted.

Most Oregon wineries are relatively small, and produce fewer than five thousand cases a year; only a few produce more than forty thousand cases. Oregon wineries in addition to those already mentioned include Adams Vineyard, Bethel Heights Vineyard, Bridgeview Vineyards, Cameron Winery, Evesham Wood Vineyards, Henry Estate, Panther Creek Cellars, Rex Hill Vineyards, and Yamhill Valley Vineyards. Robert Drouhin, one of Burgundy's leading producers, planted a vineyard in Oregon and made the first Domaine Drouhin wine in

1988; in 1987, Brian Croser, a top Australian winemaker, produced his first Oregon wines—a *méthode champenoise* sparkling wine, a Chardonnay, and a dry Riesling—under the Argyle label.

Idaho's first major post-Prohibition winery was Ste. Chapelle Vineyards, which is situated between Boise and the Oregon border to the west, and whose vineyards are planted at an elevation of about twenty-five hundred feet, overlooking the Snake River, which is a tributary of Washington's Columbia River. The first Ste. Chapelle wines were made in 1976, and the winery achieved a particular reputation for its Johannisberg Riesling and Chardonnay, and, more recently, Cabernet Sauvignon and Merlot. With a production of about one hundred thousand cases, including sparkling wines, the winery is one of the biggest in the Pacific Northwest. In addition, several hundred acres of vineyards have been planted in Idaho by grape growers and a few small wine producers.

OTHER STATES

Most of the wineries situated outside California, New York, Washington, and Oregon produce limited amounts of wine that they sell locally, but a few have come to the attention of a wider audience, especially those of Texas, Virginia, and Ohio.

Texas

In 1975, Texas had one winery and only twenty-five acres of vineyard; in the early 1990s, there were nearly thirty wineries in the state and about five thousand acres of vines. The earliest plantings included native American varieties and such French-American hybrids as Vidal Blanc, Chambourcin, and Chancellor, but most producers soon focused on traditional European *vinifera* varieties, which now account for 90 percent of the total. The leading varieties are Cabernet Sauvignon, Chardonnay, Sauvignon Blanc, Chenin Blanc, and Johannisberg Riesling; others include Cabernet Franc, Merlot, Pinot Noir, Emerald Riesling, Gewürztraminer, and French Colombard. The state's principal wine regions (and their leading wineries) are the High Plains, near Lubbock (Llano Estacado and Pheasant Ridge); the Texas Hill Country, around Austin (Fall Creek Vineyards); west Texas, near Fort Stockton (Ste. Genevieve); and the area west and north of Dallas/Fort Worth.

Virginia

The first colonists produced wine from native grapes at Jamestown in the early seventeenth century, and Thomas Jefferson tried unsuccessfully to cultivate European *vinifera* varieties in the late eighteenth century, but the modern Virginia wine industry dates from the early 1970s, when Archie Smyth planted French-American hybrids and *vinifera* varieties at his Meredyth Vineyards. Today, there are more than forty wineries in Virginia and about fourteen hundred acres of vineyards, most of them planted along the eastern slope of the Blue Ridge Mountains; the leading varieties are Chardonnay, Cabernet Sauvignon, Johannisberg Riesling, Seyval Blanc, and Vidal Blanc. The best-known wineries include Barboursville Vineyards, Ingleside Plantation, Meredyth Vineyards, Montdomaine Cellars, Oasis Vineyard, Oakencroft Vineyard, Piedmont Vineyards, Prince Michel Vineyards, Rapidan River Vineyards, Shenandoah Vineyards, and Williamsburg Winery.

Ohio

Ohio was one of the earliest sources of American wines, and its Sparkling Catawba was celebrated in the 1840s. Today, the state's vineyards consist primarily of native varieties and French-American hybrids, but *vinifera* has also been planted, especially in the Lake Erie district, which stretches along the southern shore of the lake from Toledo to the Pennsylvania border. Meier's Wine Cellars, the state's leading producer, has vineyards on Isle St. George and markets a range of wines from native grapes and also from *vinifera* varieties; other wineries include Markko Vineyard and Debonné Vineyards.

Other Wineries

One of the smallest American wineries was also one of the most important in the recent history of this country's wines: Boordy Vineyards, established by the late Philip Wagner near Baltimore, Maryland. Wagner's pioneering efforts with French-American hybrids, which he first planted in the 1930s, are considered the major factor in the increased use of these varieties in other eastern vineyards.

Some other wineries around the country that have established more than a local reputation include Sakonnet Vineyards in Rhode Island; the Chaddsford Winery and Allegro Vineyards in Pennsylvania; Byrd Vineyards, Catoctin Vineyards, and Westport Rivers Vineyard in Massachusetts; Haight Vineyard and Chamard Vineyards in Connecticut; Chateau Grand Traverse and Fenn Valley Vineyards in Michigan; Chateau Elan in Georgia; Wiederkehr Wine Cellars in Arkansas; Mount Pleasant Vineyard, Stone Hill Winery, and Hermannhof Winery in Missouri; Alexis Bailly Vineyard in Minnesota; Biltmore Estate in North Carolina; and Gruet Winery in New Mexico.

THE WINES OF SOUTH AMERICA

CHILE

Santiago, the capital of Chile, was founded in 1541 by the Spanish Conquistadors, and it was they who planted the first vineyard, in 1551, more than two hundred years before vines were introduced to California and Australia. The grape they brought with them was called Pais, a relatively inferior variety that is identical to the Criolla of Argentina and the Mission of California. When the Spaniards were defeated in the War of Independence, in the early nineteenth century, and expelled from the country, the Chileans were able to exploit their own resources, and a number of families became rich from silver, copper, coal, and phosphates. Many wealthy patriarchs traveled to Europe, and several adopted the French custom of adding a vineyard to their holdings. Since the Pais grape was not suitable for fine wines, European vines, especially Cabernet Sauvignon, Sémillon, and Sauvignon Blanc from Bordeaux, were brought back to Chile starting in the 1850s, and a few families even invited French enologists to Chile to make the wines. In the ensuing decades, the original vineyards of Concha y Toro, Cousiño Macul, Santa Carolina, Santa Rita, and

Undurraga, among others, were established near Santiago, within easy riding distance of the capital.

Then, in the 1880s, the vineyards of France, and all of Europe, were devastated by phylloxera, a plant louse that destroys vine roots; eventually, Europe's vineyards were entirely replanted on phylloxera-resistant American rootstocks. The vineyards of Chile were not affected, however, and remain phylloxera-free to this day. While wine production decreased in Europe, production of Chilean wine increased to twelve million cases in 1883 and to thirty million cases at the turn of the century. But when the European vineyards were re-established, Chile's export business declined, and for most of this century its wines have been consumed primarily by its own citizens and those of other South American countries.

Chilean wine producers did not participate in the technological advances of the 1960s and 1970s, and political uncertainty discouraged winery owners from replanting vineyards or investing in new equipment. Then, in 1979, Miguel Torres, one of Spain's top winemakers, bought a vineyard and winery in Chile, renovated the winery and introduced the use of temperature-controlled stainless steel fermentors and small oak barrels for aging. These innovations, and the realization that wine exports were a potential source of dollars, encouraged other wineries to update their methods and equipment to compete in the export market. The owners of California wineries established joint ventures with Chilean producers and, to make the cycle complete, Bordeaux château owners, who had been the inspiration for the vineyards planted in the last century, now came to Chile to participate in the transformation of its wine industry. In 1988, Baron Eric de Rothschild of Lafite-Rothschild bought a half interest in the Los Vascos winery; and in 1993 Bruno Prats, owner of Château Cos d'Estournel, and Paul Pontallier, director of Château Margaux, produced their first Cabernet Sauvignon in Chile.

Chile, which extends for more than twenty-six hundred miles from the Atacama Desert in the north to Tierra del Fuego at its southern tip, is squeezed between the Andes Mountains, which form the border with Argentina, and the Pacific Ocean. The melting snow from the Andes, which flows west to the ocean, has formed a number of river valleys, and it is in these valleys that most of Chile's best vineyards are situated. The water provides abundant irrigation, and the vineyards are cooled by mountain air flowing down the valleys. In addition to the vineyards planted between the Andes and the Cordillera, the coastal range that lies between the Andes and the sea, there are also districts, such as Rapel and Casablanca, that are west of the coastal range and closer to the sea, which provides rainfall and cool breezes.

Although some fine vineyards are planted north of Santiago, in the Aconcagua Valley, most of the wines we see here come from vineyards south of Santiago. The best-known region is the Maipo Valley; traveling south, other regions include Rancagua, Rapel, and Colchagua. About 120 miles south of Santiago, vineyards are extensively planted near the towns of Curico and Lontué, an farther south in the Maule Valley. Casablanca is a newly developed region west of Santiago whose long, cool growing season makes it especially suitable for white wines. Each of these names may be seen on Chilean wine labels, but most producers admit that it is still difficult to define appellation character—the districts have not been officially defined, and there are so many changes taking place in grape-growing and winemaking that the name of the producer is still more important than the source of the grapes.

Accurate statistics are difficult to come by in Chile, but annual wine production seems to vary from thirty to forty million cases and it is likely that there are about 150,000 acres of wine grapes. (Chile is also known for its excellent table grapes.) Pais is still the most widely planted variety, but the principal fine-wine grapes are Cabernet Sauvignon, Sauvignon Blanc, Sémillon, and, increasingly, Chardonnay. Merlot is also being widely planted, and some producers are making Pinot Noir, Riesling, and Gewürztraminer.

Although Cabernet producers in California, Bordeaux, and elsewhere use Merlot to soften the tannic austerity of Cabernet, such blending is not widely practiced in Chile, whose Cabernet is relatively soft and supple. As a result, most wineries are using Merlot as a varietal wine on its own, rather than as a blending wine with Cabernet.

Chilean growers take particular pride in the fact that their vineyards have never been affected by phylloxera, and therefore vines are planted on their own roots, rather than grafted onto American rootstocks, as is the case throughout Europe, California, and almost everywhere else in the world. When vines are brought in from California or France, for example, they must undergo a period of quarantine and observation—the new vines must be planted two hundred to five hundred yards from the nearest vineyard and monitored for at least two years before they can be propagated elsewhere.

Increased plantings of classic grape varieties and the discovery of new districts with favorable microclimates have improved the quality of Chile's wines, but the top producers also recognize that an important factor affecting the quality of those wines is overproduction. The benefits of ample water for irrigation include the possibility of high yields. In most fine wine regions, for example, growers produce two and a half to five tons an acre; in Chile, yields of eight to ten tons an acre are not uncommon for Sauvignon Blanc and Cabernet Sauvignon. The resulting wines are likely to be light and pleasant at best, or weak and washed out. These large yields, in combination with inexpensive land and low labor costs, have enabled Chilean firms to sell their wines at low prices. But the French and California enologists who are now working in Chile insist, as do the conscientious winemakers of Chile, that reducing yields is a key factor in improving the quality of Chilean wines.

The taste of traditional Chilean wines, still preferred by an older generation of Chilean consumers, is based on extended aging in large casks made from *rauli,* or beech. The whites are dark, lacking in fruit, and may be slightly oxidized; the better reds can be soft and polished, others may be faded and dried out. Although there is still a market for such wines in Chile and throughout South America, they cannot compete in export markets with the fresh, lively whites and flavorful, well-structured reds that are now the norm.

The example set by Miguel Torres, using techniques and equipment that he had already introduced to his family winery in the Penedés region of Spain, was an important factor in the transformation of winemaking in Chile. Others were the visits of enologists from California and France, some of whom began to advise the Chilean firms. (Since the harvest in Chile takes place in March, American and European winemakers can participate in the harvest south of the equator without missing their own.) And, of course, Chile's own enologists began to travel and bring back cellar techniques they had observed elsewhere. None of this would have been possible, however, without the willingness of the owners, or their new foreign partners, to invest in stainless-steel fermenting tanks and small oak barrels. To understand just how new such innovations are, especially compared to cellar practices in Australia and California, note that temperature-controlled stainless-steel tanks were first used by several leading Chilean wineries as recently as the early 1990s; before that, Chilean wineries fermented their white wines in epoxy-lined concrete tanks, which are not as effective in retaining the fruit and delicacy of white wines. And the use of small French and American oak barrels was not widely practiced until the late 1980s.

One curious aspect of the wine business in Chile is that the difference in style between the traditional wines for the South American market and those made for export is so pronounced that several firms now have two separate wineries, one with stainless-steel and small oak barrels, the other with large *rauli* vats and casks.

Most Chilean wineries now focus virtually all their attention on four varietal wines—Cabernet Sauvignon, Merlot, Chardonnay, and Sauvignon Blanc—and many firms market these wines in two or three quality categories. For example, a winery might produce a line of varietal wines that are not aged in wood at all, for early sale and consumption. One step up, a proportion of the Chardonnay and Merlot, and all of the Cabernet, might be aged for several months in American oak barrels. The most expensive wines might include a barrel-fermented Chardonnay, an oak-aged Sauvignon Blanc, and Cabernet and Merlot that had been aged for a year or so in French oak barrels.

Concha y Toro, the biggest wine firm in Chile, has more than five thousand acres of vineyards planted in several districts; they offer a full range of varietal wines, from inexpensive magnums to those labeled Casillero del Diablo and Marqués de Casa Concha, and also produce the wines sold here under the Walnut Crest label. Cousiño Macul is a well-known family firm that produces estate-bottled wines from 650 acres in the Maipo Valley; it is best known for its Antiguas Reservas Cabernet Sauvignon. Los Vascos, whose vineyards are in the Cañeten Valley, in Colchagua, is in partnership with the Domaines Rothschild of Bordeaux. Errazuriz, whose best-known wine is the Don Maximiano Cabernet Sauvignon, also produces the varietal wines sold under the Caliterra label. Torres, whose first harvest was in 1980, produces a range of varietal wines from 450 acres of vineyards near Curico. Santa Rita, founded in 1880 and revitalized in the past decade, produces wines under the "120," Reserva, and Medalla Real labels. San Pedro, whose best-selling wines are Gato Blanco Sauvignon Blanc and Gato Negro Cabernet Sauvignon, also offers wines under the Castilla de Molina label. Other Chilean wineries that produce a range of varietal wines include Undurraga, Santa Carolina, Canepa, Santa Monica, Carta Vieja, and the Mitjans firm, whose wines are marketed under the Valdivieso and Saint-Morillon labels.

ARGENTINA

With 500,000 acres of vineyards and an annual production of 150 to 220 million cases, Argentina is the most important wine-producing country of South America and one of the half-dozen biggest in the world. Exporting very little and importing even less, Argentina drinks her own wines at the per capita rate of some seventy-five bottles a year. The vineyards are planted along the foothills of the Andes, not far from the Chilean border, about six hundred miles west of Buenos Aires. Three-quarters of the acreage is in the state of Mendoza, with additional plantings in San Juan and a limited amount in Rio Negro. The Criolla grape, similar to the Mission of California, is the most widely planted variety, but there is considerable acreage of French varieties, first introduced in the mid-nineteenth century. Malbec is the most extensively planted of the better varieties, followed by Cabernet Sauvignon; Chardonnay, Sauvignon Blanc, Chenin Blanc, Sémillon, Merlot, and Pinot Noir have been planted as well.

In recent years, a number of Argentine producers have begun to export their wines to this country, and although some are labeled with generic or proprietary names, most bear varietal names. Argentine wines suffered in the past from old-fashioned winemaking methods and excessive aging in wood, which often resulted in faded reds and oxidized whites. In an effort to increase their exports, a number of wineries have adopted modern vinification techniques and are now producing more attractive wines. Among the firms that export to this country are Bianchi, Etchart, Flichman, Navarro Correas, Orfila, Toso, Weinert, and Trapiche (produced by Peñaflor, the country's biggest winery).

In the past, the wines produced in Brazil, made primarily from *Vitis labrusca* and French-American hybrid grape varieties, were rarely seen here. In recent years, a number of American and European wine companies have invested in Brazil, and new vineyards have been planted with *Vitis vinifera* grapes. The best-known brand is Marcus James, whose labels bear such varietal names as White Zinfandel, Chardonnay, and Cabernet Sauvignon.

VARIOUS OTHER WINES

AUSTRALIA

There are interesting parallels to be drawn between the history of viticulture and winemaking in Australia and the United States, especially California. Viticulture in both countries began about two hundred years ago—vines were first planted in Australia in 1788, near Sydney—and commercial winemaking began at about the same time in each country—the 1830s—and developed in several different regions rather than in a single area. Fortified wines were made in far greater quantities than table wines, and only in the past three decades has each country reversed that trend. As recently as the early 1960s, sherry- and port-type wines accounted for 80 percent of Australia's total wine production, and the demand for fortified wines and brandies was such that more than half the grape crop was distilled. Today, table wines and sparkling wines dominate, fortified wines account for less than 10 percent of production, and very little wine is distilled. Per capita wine consumption in Australia has more than tripled in twenty years and, in fact, is more than twice that in the United States.

James Busby, a Scottish-born educator and French-trained winemaker, is often referred to as the father of the Australian wine industry, and his role seems to have been quite similar to that of Agoston Haraszthy in California. Busby brought a great many European vine cuttings into Australia in 1831, distributed them to a number of growers in the Hunter Valley, north of Sydney, and also wrote a treatise on viticulture to aid new winemakers. Today, there are about 150,000 acres of grapes in Australia; about two-thirds of the crop is made into wine (whose production varies from thirty-five to forty-five million cases a year), the rest is sold as raisin grapes and table grapes. The Sultana grape, identical to the Thompson Seedless of California, represents a quarter of the acreage and almost all of the raisin and table grape category.

The traditional red-wine grapes in Australia are Shiraz (the Syrah of the northern Rhône), Grenache, and Mataro, and as recently as the late 1960s these three varieties accounted for more than 90 percent of the red-wine crop. Shiraz continues to be an important variety, cultivated in most of the country's wine regions, and capable of producing excellent wines. Penfolds Grange Hermitage, Australia's most famous wine, is made from Shiraz. (Hermitage is another name for Syrah, and the wine, which often includes a component of Cabernet Sauvignon, originally came from the Grange estate, near Adelaide.)

Although Cabernet Sauvignon was not much seen until the 1960s, it has been cultivated in Australia since the nineteenth century and was being produced in the 1950s by such wineries as Hardy's in McLaren Vale and Wynns and Rouge Homme, both in Coonawarra. In the Hunter Valley, Cabernet Sauvignon was first produced as a varietal wine in the mid-1960s by Max Lake, who established the Lake's Folly winery. The recent success of this variety in Australia is such that it is now the most widely planted red-wine grape in the country. The complementary Bordeaux varieties Merlot, Cabernet Franc, and Malbec, which were virtually nonexistent in the early 1980s, have also been widely planted, and the acreage of Pinot Noir has increased more than tenfold in less than a decade as growers have established new vineyards in cooler regions.

The most widely planted white-wine grapes in Austra-

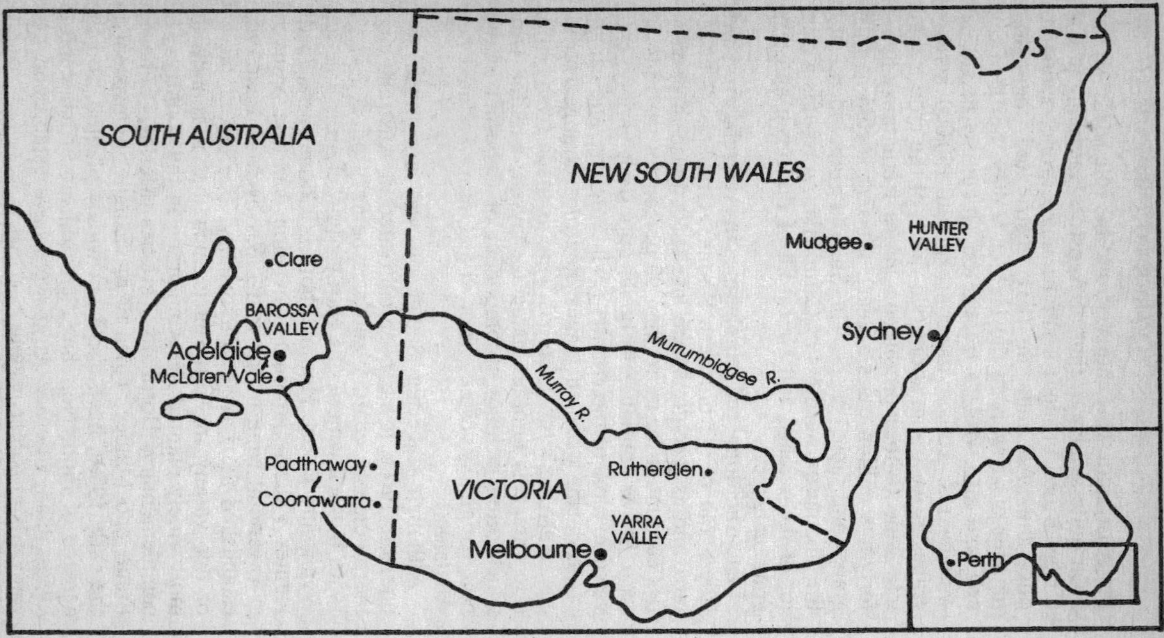
SOUTH AUSTRALIA
NEW SOUTH WALES
VICTORIA
Clare
BAROSSA VALLEY
Adelaide
McLaren Vale
Padthaway
Coonawarra
Mudgee
HUNTER VALLEY
Sydney
Murrumbidgee R.
Murray R.
Rutherglen
YARRA VALLEY
Melbourne
Perth

AUSTRALIA

lia were Rhine Riesling and Sémillon, which are holding their own. Chardonnay, which began to emerge as a varietal wine in the early 1970s, is now the most widely planted white-wine grape, and the acreage of Sauvignon Blanc has increased as well.

A varietal wine must contain a minimum of 80 percent of the variety named on the label, but Australian winemakers often blend two varieties to produce a more drinkable wine and both varieties will then be named on the label. Cabernet Sauvignon-Shiraz is one combination; Cabernet adds structure and backbone, Shiraz softens and rounds out the blend. As the acreage of Merlot and Cabernet Franc has increased, these varieties, too, are now blended with Cabernet Sauvignon. Many wineries produce a Sémillon-Chardonnay blend; depending upon how the wines are vinified, Chardonnay may add acidity to a fuller-bodied Sémillon, or a light, lean Sémillon may be enriched by a riper style of Chardonnay.

Varietal names are used almost exclusively for the wines that are shipped to this country, with particular emphasis on Chardonnay, Cabernet Sauvignon, Sauvignon Blanc, and Shiraz. But within Australia, there has been a widespread use of generic names for less expensive wine—Claret, Burgundy, White Burgundy, Chablis, Rhine Wine, and Sauternes are some examples, although these names are now less often seen than in the past. More than half of the wines produced in Australia are sold in what is known as bag-in-the-box or soft-cask containers, most of which hold four liters, the equivalent of about five regular bottles; these are packaged in a box lined with inert plastic and foil or other materials that are meant to be impermeable to air, and which collapse as the wine is drawn out through a spigot, thus preventing spoilage as the container is depleted.

There are other categories of wine that have also achieved particular success in Australia. One is late-harvest wines, affected by *Botrytis cinerea,* as in the Sauternes region of France, and noted for their rich, honeyed, lingering flavors; the Australian versions are made from both Sémillon and Riesling. A few wineries in North East Victoria also specialize in fortified Muscats and Tokays, intensely concentrated, barrel-aged wines that are among the finest dessert wines produced anywhere. The Tokays are made from the Muscadelle of Bordeaux; the Muscats are based on the Muscat de Frontignan. In addition, the Muscat of Alexandria is widely planted in Australia, where it is called Muscat Gordo Blanco and, occasionally, Lexia.

There are more than seven hundred wineries in Australia, but a few large firms dominate the wine scene. The Penfolds group includes Lindemans and Seppelts as well as Rouge Homme, Leo Buring, Wynns, Kaiser Stuhl, and Hungerford Hill, among others. Hardy's is associated with Berri-Renmano, Houghton, and Stanley Leasingham; Mildara is associated with Wolf Blass, Krondorf, Balgownie, and Yellowglen; and Orlando is associated with Wyndham Estate, Montrose, and Richmond Grove. Yalumba and McWilliam's are the biggest privately owned firms. These firms, and many others, often emphasize proprietary brands, such as Jacob's Creek, Oxford Landing, Long Flat Red, and Nottage Hill.

The state of South Australia (whose capital is Adelaide) produces about 60 percent of the country's wines; New South Wales (whose capital is Sydney) and Victoria (whose capital is Melbourne) produce almost all the rest. Note that more than half of Australia's vineyards and grape crop, including most of what is used for inexpensive wines, comes from an area that overlaps the three states and that is irrigated by the Murray River and its tributary, the Murrumbidgee; this extensive region is known as the Murrumbidgee Irrigation Area and Riverina in New South Wales; Riverland in South Australia; and Sunraysia and the Murray River area in Victoria. Note, too, that a wine labeled South Eastern Australia may be blended from vineyards located almost anywhere in the country except Western Australia (whose capital is Perth).

Many of Australia's major wine districts were established in the early and mid-nineteenth century; others, especially those in cooler districts and on hillsides, were first planted in the 1960s and 1970s. Although Australia does not have officially defined appellations of origin, legislation known as the Label Integrity Program was introduced in the early 1990s. Wineries must maintain records that will validate any claims made on the label—

based on current minimum requirements—concerning vintage (95 percent of the vintage indicated), grape variety (80 percent), and region of origin (80 percent). Increasingly, the names of specific districts appear on wine labels. What follows is a description of the most important wine regions, which lie along a two-thousand-mile crescent from the Hunter Valley, north of Sydney, to the Margaret River district, south of Perth.

New South Wales

First planted in the 1820s, the Hunter Valley, situated about one hundred miles north of Sydney, is the oldest wine region in Australia, and perhaps the most famous; it has long been known for its Shiraz and Sémillon, both of which acquire richness and complexity with extended bottle-aging. (Until recently, Sémillon was often labeled as Hunter River Riesling.) In 1967, there were only eight hundred acres of vineyard and six firms in the Hunter Valley; Chardonnay and Cabernet Sauvignon were extensively planted in the late 1960s and early 1970s, as was Sauvignon Blanc, and by the late 1970s there were thirteen thousand acres of vineyard. Much of this, planted in unsuitable areas, was abandoned, and new vineyards planted elsewhere; there are now about sixty-five hundred acres of vines. Shiraz and Sémillon are still important, as are Chardonnay and Cabernet Sauvignon; there are also increased plantings of Pinot Noir, Merlot, and Cabernet Franc. Hunter Valley wineries include Lindemans, McWilliam's Mount Pleasant, Wyndham Estate, Richmond Grove, Tyrrell's, Rothbury Estate (one of whose founders is Len Evans, Australia's most famous wine personality), Brokenwood, Hungerford Hill, and Sutherland.

In the late 1960s and early 1970s, several new vineyards and wineries were established in a region known as the Upper Hunter, about forty miles northwest of the original district, now sometimes referred to as the Lower Hunter. Rosemount Estate, which produced its first wines in the mid-1970s, is the best-known winery in the Upper Hunter.

Mudgee is a small district about sixty miles west of the Hunter Valley; wine has been made here since 1858, and Chardonnay was first planted as long ago as the 1930s. The cool climate of this district, situated at an elevation of about fifteen hundred feet, has resulted in excellent Chardonnays and intensely flavored Cabernet Sauvignon and Merlot. Montrose is the district's best-known winery; others include Botobolar, Huntington Estate, and Miramar. The Cowra district, about 150 miles west of Sydney, is becoming known for its Chardonnay, and extensive new plantings are taking place there.

The most extensive vineyard area in New South Wales is the Murrumbidgee Irrigation Area, known as MIA, whose eleven thousand acres of vineyards produce a great deal of inexpensive table wines and fortified wines; McWilliam's has pioneered the production of better table wines and De Bortoli has become known for its late-harvest Sémillon.

South Australia

The biggest and best-known wine region in South Australia is the Barossa Valley, situated about thirty-five miles northeast of Adelaide. The vineyards, established in the 1840s, combine traditional varieties with those introduced more recently: Shiraz and Grenache dominate the red-grape acreage, but Cabernet Sauvignon is also widely planted; among the white-wine grapes, Riesling and Sémillon are still important, but the acreage of Chardonnay continues to increase. Several of Australia's biggest wineries have their headquarters here, including Orlando, Penfolds, Seppelts, and Yalumba; other Barossa Valley wineries include Krondorf, Peter Lehmann, and Wolf Blass.

The Coonawarra district, considered by many to be the country's finest for red wines, is situated about 230 miles southeast of Adelaide. About nine miles long and no more than a mile wide, Coonawarra (the name is derived from the aboriginal word for honeysuckle) is noted for its cool climate and unusual *terra rossa,* or red soil, actually a layer of red clay on a bed of limestone. First planted in the 1840s, the district began to achieve its present reputation only in the late 1950s, first for Shiraz and, more recently, for Cabernet Sauvignon. Many firms have planted vines in Coonawarra and crush the grapes elsewhere; wineries in Coonawarra include Lindeman's Rouge Homme, Mildara, Penfolds, Redman, and Wynns.

The Padthaway district, previously referred to as Padthaway/Keppoch, is about fifty miles north of Coonawarra; vines were first planted there in the early 1960s, notably by Lindemans, Hardy's, and Seppelts. Just as Coonawarra is known for its red wines, Padthaway has been particularly successful with such white varieties as Chardonnay and Rhine Riesling.

Several firms have planted vineyards in the cool Adelaide Hills, east of the city, near the towns of Eden Valley and Springton, with particular emphasis on Chardonnay, Pinot Noir, and Rhine Riesling. The Petaluma winery, under the direction of Brian Croser, is well-known, as are the wines made by Henschke, Hill-Smith, and Mountadam.

Wines produced in the Southern Vales district, south of Adelaide, are usually marketed with the appellation McLaren Vale, which is the name of a town. Hardy's, which owns Chateau Reynella, is the leading firm; others include Pirramimma, Ryecroft, and Wirra Wirra. The Clare Valley, about sixty miles north of Adelaide, is a cool district best known for its Rhine Riesling; wines labeled simply Clare Riesling are made from the lesser Crouchen variety. The Riverland region, situated along the Murray River, is an extensive region known primarily for its inexpensive table wines; two leading cooperative cellars, Berri Estates and Renmano, combined their operations in 1982.

Victoria

There are wine districts throughout the state of Victoria, but none are as well known, or as clearly defined, as Hunter Valley and Barossa Valley. About twenty miles east of Melbourne, the cool Yarra Valley has become known for its Chardonnay, Pinot Noir, and Cabernet Sauvignon. Domaine Chandon is a leading producer of sparkling wines, and other wineries include Tarrawarra, Yarra Yering, and Coldstream Hills, established by wine writer James Halliday. Vines are also planted on the Morningstar Peninsula, southeast of Melbourne.

In northeastern Victoria, the Brown Brothers have been associated with the town of Milawa, near Rutherglen, since the late nineteenth century. The region is also famous for its fortified Muscats and Tokays from such producers as Bailey's of Glenrowan and Morris of Rutherglen. The Goulburn Valley, north of Melbourne, encompasses such wineries as Chateau Tahbilk, founded in 1860, and the up-to-date Mitchelton, established more than a century later. Other wineries in Victoria include Balgownie, Bannockburn, and Taltarni, the last situated in the Pyrenees area, about 120 miles northwest of Melbourne. Seppelt's Great Western, Chateau Remy, and Yellowglen are known for their sparkling wines. The extensive Murray Valley area (which becomes Riverland when the Murray River crosses over to South Australia) produces large quantities of inexpensive wine; Mildara, Lindemans, and McWilliam's have large wineries in this region.

Western Australia

Wines were being produced in the Swan Valley, just outside Perth in Western Australia, in the 1830s, but until recently, this warm region was known primarily for its fortified wines and full-bodied reds. Today, most wineries have installed modern vinification equipment to produce a full range of table wines and are likely to obtain grapes from cooler districts within the state. Houghton, the biggest firm in Western Australia, has vineyards in the Frankland River district and in Moondah Brook, about fifty miles north of Perth; Sandalford is another leading winery in the Swan Valley.

The most promising district in Western Australia is Margaret River, about 150 miles south of Perth; the region, whose principal towns are Margaret River and Willyabrup, extends for about fifty miles along the Indian Ocean. First planted in the 1960s, this area has produced a range of fine varietal wines from Cabernet Sauvignon, Chardonnay, Sauvignon Blanc, and Rhine Riesling, as well as from Sémillon and Pinot Noir. The best-known wineries include Cape Mentelle, Cullens, Leeuwin Estate, Moss Wood, and Vasse Felix.

The area known as Mount Barker/Frankland River, located about 240 miles southeast of Perth, produced its first wines in the 1970s; Plantaganet is its best-known winery.

The island of Tasmania, south of Melbourne, whose cool climate makes it suitable for such varieties as Rhine Riesling, Chardonnay, and Pinot Noir, produces a limited amount of wine. Vineyards are also planted in the Granite Belt region of Queensland, near the New South Wales border.

NEW ZEALAND

The first grapevines were planted in New Zealand in 1819, but wines were not made until the 1830s, after the arrival of James Busby, who had previously pioneered winemaking in Australia. The combination of phylloxera and a strong temperance movement prevented winemaking from taking hold in the nineteenth century, but, at the turn of the century, an influx of immigrants from Dalmatia, in Croatia, resulted in extensive new plantings near Auckland; the new vineyards consisted primarily of phylloxera-resistant French-American hybrids. In the 1960s, Müller-Thurgau was widely planted in New Zealand to produce an inexpensive, semisweet white wine as an alternative to the fortified wines that were then popular. Vineyards were cultivated in Auckland; at Hawke's Bay, on the east coast of the North Island; and at Gisborne, just north of Hawke's Bay. Then, in 1973, the Montana wine company planted vineyards in the Marlborough district, on the northeast corner of the South Island. In time, these cool-climate vineyards, with their long growing season, produced excellent Sauvignon Blancs and Chardonnays, which brought New Zealand wines to the attention of wine drinkers in England and Australia. The success of these wines in the early 1980s was such that Marlborough has become the biggest wine region in New Zealand, with Gisborne and Hawke's Bay making up almost all the rest of the acreage.

There are now about fifteen thousand acres planted in New Zealand (compared to fewer than one thousand acres in 1960), producing four to five million cases a year. Müller-Thurgau, long the most widely planted variety, was overtaken by Chardonnay in the early 1990s; the two varieties account for about 40 percent of the total acreage. Sauvignon Blanc, Cabernet Sauvignon, and Pinot Noir are also well represented; other varieties include Rhine Riesling, Sémillon, Gewürztraminer, Merlot, and Cabernet Franc. About 90 percent of the wines produced are white, and Chardonnay and Sauvignon Blanc are still widely acclaimed, but Cabernet Sauvignon and Cabernet-Merlot blends have become increasingly successful.

Montana and Corbans (which owns Cooks) are the largest New Zealand wineries; others include Babich, Cloudy Bay (under the same ownership as Cape Mentelle, in Australia's Margaret River district), Delegat's, Hunter, Kumeu River, Morton Estate, Nobilo, Selaks, Te Mata, and Villa Maria.

SOUTH AFRICA

Wines were first made on the Cape of Good Hope in 1659, from vines planted by the earliest Dutch settlers. At the end of the seventeenth century, a number of French Huguenot families settled on the Cape and established vineyards around Paarl, Stellenbosch, and Franschhoek, about twenty-five to fifty miles inland from Cape Town and the Atlantic Ocean. At about the same time, the Groot Constantia estate was created just south of Cape Town, and its rich, sweet wine—thought to be a fortified Muscat—became famous throughout Europe. The legendary Constantia disappeared in the late nineteenth century, when all the Cape's vineyards suffered from declining exports and the ravages of phylloxera. In the early twentieth century, overproduction and low prices led to the creation, in 1918, of a Cooperative Winegrowers' Association, the KWV, whose role was to supervise the entire South African wine industry by controlling production and setting minimum prices for grapes and wine, which it did until the early 1990s.

For most of this century, South Africa was best known for its brandies and fortified wines in the style of sherry and port. Even today, when the country's 250,000 acres of vineyards—virtually all of them situated in the Cape region, in the southwest corner of the country—produce the equivalent of 100 million cases of wine, about half is distilled to produce brandies and fortified wines or made into grape concentrate. Cooperative cellars account for about 80 percent of the grape crop, but only a third of their production is eventually consumed as wine—the rest is distilled or sold as grape juice.

The most widely planted grape variety in South Africa is Steen, which is identical to Chenin Blanc, and which accounts for about a third of the acreage. Sultana (which is the Thompson Seedless) and White French (which is actually the Palomino of Spain) make up almost 20 percent of the vineyards. Other varieties that are well represented on the Cape include such white-wine grapes as Colombard, Hanepoot (Muscat of Alexandria), Cape Riesling (the Crouchen of France), and Clairette Blanche; the most widely planted red is Cinsault. Given the varieties that make up most of the country's acreage, it's not surprising that the best-selling wines have traditionally been blends marketed with such proprietary names as Lieberstein, Cape Bouquet, Bonne Esperance, Baronne, Stellenrood, Rooderberg, and Chateau Libertas or with such generic names as Dry Red, Blanc de Blanc, and Premier Grand Cru. Lieberstein, a light-bodied, semisweet white wine introduced in 1959, achieved sales of more than three million cases within five years, and marked a turning point in the increased consumption of table wines in South Africa.

In recent years, however, the German style of wine-making, which produced semisweet whites made from Chenin Blanc and Cape Riesling and light reds made from Cinsault, has given way to a French influence, which has resulted in fuller-bodied dry red and white wines. There has been a greater emphasis, especially for export markets, on varietal wines made from Cabernet Sauvignon (increasingly blended with Merlot and Cabernet Franc), Chardonnay, and Sauvignon Blanc, as well as Pinot Noir, Rhine Riesling, and Shiraz (the Syrah of the northern Rhône). Pinotage, a variety unique to

South Africa, is a cross of Pinot Noir and Cinsault (which was known locally as Hermitage); it produces a red wine that can be light and fruity or rich and full-bodied, depending on the way it is vinified.

In 1973, appellations of origin—known as Wine of Origin, or WO—were established. The names most likely to be seen on labels are the Coastal Region and its inner districts of Paarl, Stellenbosch, and Constantia; and the Breede River Valley, which encompasses the districts of Worcester and Robertson. This legislation established the use of neck strips to authenticate the origin, grape variety, and vintage of a wine, if these appear on the label; the minimum requirement for variety and vintage is 75 percent.

Although South Africa's wine history goes back more than three centuries, the quality and diversity of its wines were hampered by two factors. One was the tight control over vineyards and grape varieties exercised for so many decades by the various governing bodies. This made it difficult for growers to establish new vineyards, especially in districts that were not already planted; thus, the expansion of vineyards into cooler regions more suitable for fine wines was slow. Also, a rigid quarantine system made it difficult to import vine cuttings of varieties that were not well represented in the country, such as Chardonnay, Merlot, and Cabernet Franc, or to experiment with better clones of varieties that were already cultivated, such as Pinot Noir and Cabernet Sauvignon. As a result of recent changes in these laws, Chardonnay plantings, for example, have increased from fewer than five hundred acres in the early 1980s to more than five thousand acres today, and there are increased plantings of Cabernet Sauvignon, Merlot, Cabernet Franc, Sauvignon Blanc, and other classic varieties as well.

The other factor that hampered the country's winemakers was the imposition of economic sanctions in 1986, which prevented them from exporting their wines to many countries, including the United States. When these were lifted in 1991, winemakers had a greater incentive to style their wines to an international taste and more opportunity to visit wine regions in Europe and California. Just as few estates produced a Chardonnay before 1989 or 1990, few aged their wines in small French oak barrels before the late 1980s. Today, many producers use such techniques as barrel-fermentation for their Chardonnay and French-oak aging for their Cabernet Sauvignon, Sauvignon Blanc, and Pinotage. In addition, many winemakers offer a proprietary red that is a blend of Cabernet Sauvignon with Merlot and Cabernet Franc, or of Cabernet with Shiraz.

The number of Cape wines found here expands every year, and includes selections from the largest producers as well as from smaller estates. The KWV group offers wines under the Cape Country, Springbok, and Cathedral Cellars labels, as well as fortified wines under its own name. The Stellenbosch Farmers' Winery, which is the country's largest wine marketer, offers a wide selection of wines under the Zonnebloem label; it also owns the famous Nederburg estate, known for its wines and also for the wine auction that has taken place there every year since 1975. The Bergkelder group markets wines under the brand names Fleur du Cap and Stellenryck and also represents about twenty individual estates, including Meerlust, Uitkyk, La Motte, Alto, and L'Ormarins.

An unusual aspect of the South African wine scene, which is dominated by cooperative cellars, a few major firms, and well-established brand names, is that there are five thousand grapegrowers but fewer than one hundred estates that produce and bottle their own wines; some of these are quite large, and several have six hundred acres or more of vineyards. Although many estates can trace their origins back a century or two, most were revitalized, and their vineyards replanted, in the 1970s and 1980s; several did not produce their first wines until the 1980s. The Groot Constantia estate, for example, which was established in 1685, installed a new winery as recently as 1982; and its two neighbors in the Constantia district, Klein Constantia and Buitenverwachting, produced their first wines in the mid-1980s. Some of the country's best-known estates and wineries, in addition to those already cited, are Backsberg, Blaauwklippen, Boschendal, Bouchard Finlayson, Clos Cabrière, Delheim, De Wetshof, Glen Carlou, Hamilton Russell, Kanonkop, Lievland, Mulderbosch, Neethlingshof, Neil

Ellis, Rustenberg, Rust-en-Verde, Simonsig, Thelema, Twee Jongegezellen, Villiera, and Warwick.

CANADA

As recently as the 1960s, most of Canada's wine production consisted of such fortified wines as port and sherry; today, table wines account for more than three-quarters of the total, with increasing emphasis on such *vinifera* varieties as Chardonnay, Riesling, Pinot Noir, and Cabernet Sauvignon. As it happens, Canadian firms are permitted to supplement their own production with wine, grapes, and unfermented juice imported from other countries—primarily the United States (California and Washington), Chile, France, and Italy—and these imports continue to make up an important part of all the wines bottled in Canada. In recent years, however, more firms are making wine entirely from grapes grown in Canada. About 90 percent of Canada's own wines are produced in the province of Ontario, primarily on the Niagara Peninsula, situated between Lake Ontario and Lake Erie, west of Niagara Falls. There are now about four thousand acres planted with French-American hybrids, primarily such white-wine varieties as Seyval Blanc and Vidal (which has achieved particular success when made into ice wine), plus lesser amounts of such red-wine grapes as Baco Noir and Maréchal Foch. Since the late 1980s, many growers have been uprooting French-American hybrids—as well as such native grapes as Concord and Niagara, which may no longer be used for table wines—and most of the new plantings consist of *vinifera* varieties, which now account for about four thousand acres. Chardonnay and Riesling are the leading white varieties, and the reds include Pinot Noir, Cabernet Sauvignon, Cabernet Franc, Merlot, and Gamay.

The Vintners Quality Alliance (VQA) was established in Ontario to define appellations of origin, which include Niagara Peninsula, Pelee Island, and Lake Erie North Shore, and to specify permitted grape varieties. VQA wines labeled Ontario must be made entirely from grapes grown in Ontario, only from *vinifera* or French-American hybrids, and must contain at least 75 percent of the variety named on the label; wines labeled with one of the three viticultural areas may be made only from *vinifera* grapes, and must contain at least 85 percent of the named grape. Pelee Island and the Lake Erie North Shore districts are relatively small, and their combined acreage amounts to fewer than five hundred acres; the Pelee Island Winery is the best known producer. Inniskillin led the way on the Niagara Peninsula when it obtained its wine permit in 1975, the first new permit issued in Ontario in nearly fifty years; it produces several *vinifera* varietal wines and is also known for its ice wine made from Vidal. Other Niagara Peninsula wineries that focus on premium varietal wines include Cave Spring Cellars, Chateau des Charmes, Henry of Pelham, Hillebrand Estates Winery, Konzelmann, Marynissen, Reif Winery, Stoney Ridge, and Vineland Estates. Historically, the three biggest wineries in Ontario were Andres, Brights, and Cartier (formerly Chateau Gai); in 1993, Cartier and Inniskillin merged, and that firm subsequently merged with Brights.

The other important wine-producing region of Canada is British Columbia, most of whose vineyards are just north of the state of Washington. The large wineries continue to bottle inexpensive blends made entirely or primarily from imported wines, but an increasing number of smaller wineries are producing Canadian wines from French-American hybrids and *vinifera* varieties. The most important region defined by the Vintners Quality Alliance is the Okanagan Valley; the others are the Fraser Valley, Similkameen, and Vancouver Island. The four hundred acres of hybrids consist primarily of Verdelet, Vidal, Seyval Blanc, and Maréchal Foch. *Vinifera* varieties, led by Chardonnay, Riesling, and Pinot Blanc, now account for more than fifteen hundred acres; other varieties include Pinot Blanc, Ehrenfelser, Gewürztraminer, Pinot Noir, Merlot, Müller-Thurgau, and Bacchus. Among the British Columbia wineries are CedarCreek, Gray Monk Cellars, Gehringer Brothers, Hainle Vineyards, Quails' Gate Vineyards, Sumac Ridge, and Summerhill, best known for its Cipes Brut.

ISRAEL

Wine has been made in what is now Israel since the beginning of recorded history, but that country's wine industry originated little more than a century ago. In 1882, with the financial backing of Baron Edmond de Rothschild, vines were planted and a winery constructed at Rishon-le-Zion, southeast of Tel Aviv; most of the real progress in winemaking, however, dates from 1948, when Israel became an independent state. There are now nearly six thousand acres of vineyards, producing about three million cases a year. As recently as the 1950s, 90 percent of Israel's wines were sweet and fortified; today, dry and semidry table wines account for 80 percent of the total. The earliest plantings consisted primarily of such red varieties as Carignane, Grenache, and Alicante-Bouschet, with lesser amounts of such white grapes as Sémillon, Muscat of Alexandria, and Clairette (Ugni Blanc). Subsequently, Emerald Riesling, Chenin Blanc, French Colombard, and Petite Sirah were introduced; more recently, there have been important new plantings of Sauvignon Blanc, Chardonnay, and Cabernet Sauvignon, as well as limited amounts of Merlot and Zinfandel.

The principal vineyard regions include Samson, southeast of Tel Aviv, on the western slopes of the Judean Hills, which encompasses the Dan and Adulam districts; Shomron, which includes the Sharon district; and the cooler Galil, or Golan Heights, district, north of the Sea of Galilee. As a result of new plantings, an increasing market for dry kosher wines, and improved technology in the wineries, Israel now produces a range of crisp, distinctive whites, flavorful, dry reds, and appealing, off-dry rosés, many of which are marketed with varietal names. The range of varietal wines includes Cabernet Sauvignon. Sauvignon Blanc, Chardonnay, Chenin Blanc, Emerald Riesling, French Colombard, Shiraz, Petite Sirah, and such pink wines as White Zinfandel, Grenache Rosé, and Cabernet Blanc.

There are about a dozen wineries in Israel, the most important of which is Carmel; this cooperative, founded in 1905, with wineries at Rishon-le-Zion and Zichron Ya'akov, accounts for about three-quarters of the country's production. The Golan Heights winery, which produced its first wines in 1983, has achieved particular success with its Sauvignon Blanc, Cabernet Sauvignon, and Chardonnay from new plantings in the Galil district; its wines are sold under the Yarden, Gamla, and Golan labels.

ALGERIA

Not long ago, Algeria was a relatively important producer of wines; today, its production is only a fraction of what it was in the 1950s. Algeria is a Muslim country, and Muslims are not permitted to consume alcoholic beverages, so Algeria is in the paradoxical situation of maintaining an industry whose product cannot be marketed within its own borders, except to tourists. Robust Algerian wines, almost all of them red, made from such varieties as Cinsault, Carignane, and Grenache, were traditionally shipped to France to add color, body, and alcohol to the lighter *vin ordinaire* produced in the Midi region. After Algeria obtained its independence from France in 1962, shipments to France decreased, and when the European Community was established, French wine firms realized that it was economically more advantageous to import blending wines from Italy than from Algeria. In recent years the biggest customer for Algerian wines has been Russia.

At one time, a dozen Algerian wines were entitled to the French V.D.Q.S. appellation. More recently, Algeria set up its own appellation laws for seven of these wines: Medea, Dahra, Coteaux de Mascara, Coteaux du Zaccar, Coteaux de Tlemcen, Monts du Tessala, and Aïn Bessem-Bouïra. Their labels bear the phrase *Appellation d'Origine Garantie,* and some of them, such as Dahra and Medea, are shipped here.

LEBANON

Lebanon has achieved a place on the world's wine map because of a single wine, Château Musar, a long-lived red made primarily from Cabernet Sauvignon and Cinsault. The winery, located fifteen miles north of Beirut, was established in the 1930s by Gaston Hochar; since 1959 it has been under the direction of his son, Serge, who studied enology in Bordeaux.

The vineyards that produce Château Musar are in the Bekaa Valley, forty miles south of Beirut; its 320 acres are planted with Cabernet Sauvignon and Cinsault, as well as small amounts of Merlot, Syrah, and Pinot Noir. About a third of the wine from these vineyards is sold as Château Musar, which contains about equal proportions of Cabernet Sauvignon and Cinsault. The rest of the crop is labeled Tradition (formerly Cuvée Musar), a lighter wine that contains more Cinsault than Cabernet Sauvignon. Because of the wars that have been fought in and around Beirut in recent years, certain vintages have been harvested under dangerous conditions, and, in fact, the 1984 crop could not be picked.

CHAMPAGNE AND SPARKLING WINES

It has been said that you can have too much champagne, but you can never have enough. The most festive of wines, champagne adds gaiety and distinction to any occasion at which it is served. Unfortunately, most of us drink champagne only at crowded receptions, where we enjoy its convivial effect without the chance to appreciate its quality. It's a pity that most people consider champagne so special that they reserve it for infrequent celebrations. Although fine champagne is never cheap, it is no more expensive than a good bottle of Bordeaux, Burgundy, or California Chardonnay; and the appearance of a bottle of champagne at any gathering is greeted with pleasure and enthusiasm.

Because almost all champagne is marketed with the name of the producer, rather than that of an individual vineyard, it is not a difficult wine to buy. It's a wine, nevertheless, that is made in a fairly exacting way, and a visitor to any of the famous champagne houses in Reims, Epernay, or Ay invariably leaves with the impression that champagne is not expensive considering the number of complex steps necessary to produce it.

There are a great many sparkling wines produced in France and throughout the world (these will be discussed separately), but true champagne is made only within the delimited Champagne region situated about ninety miles east of Paris. Although wine has been made there for more than fifteen hundred years, until the late seventeenth century that wine was still, not sparkling, and pale red in color. In the second half of the seventeenth century, members of the French and English courts developed a preference for light, sparkling wines, and producers in the Champagne region began to transform their wine into the product we know today. They had noted that the wines of Champagne often developed a sparkle in the spring following the vintage. In effect, not all of the natural grape sugar had been transformed into alcohol at the time of the harvest, because the early winters of northern France tended to stop fermentation before it ran its course. When warmer weather returned in the spring, the remaining traces of sugar began to referment, and the wines in barrel took on a natural effervescence. Dom Pérignon, a Benedictine monk who was the cellar master at the Abbey of Hautvillers, is credited with having invented champagne, but what he may have done was to help devise a better way of creating and retaining its natural sparkle. He also seems to have realized that a more harmonious sparkling wine was obtained if the grapes from various Champagne vineyards were blended together. He thus established the concept of a *cuvée,* or blend, which has enabled the champagne shippers (who now blend wines, not grapes) to maintain a consistent style year after year. It is this fact that makes champagne unusual among fine wines, for unlike the best Bordeaux and Burgundies, which owe their distinction to the soil and exposure of a specific vineyard and to the characteristics of a particular vintage, champagne is a wine blended from different grape varieties, different vineyards, and, for the most part, different vintages. It is in blending that champagne achieves its quality and personality. One confirmation of this is the number of champagne firms in existence, each producing a slightly different champagne by blending available wines in different proportions.

The Champagne vineyards are divided into three principal districts: the Valley of the Marne, the Mountain of Reims, and the Côte des Blancs. About three-quarters of the Champagne region's eighty thousand acres are planted in black grapes, Pinot Noir and Pinot Meunier; Pinot Noir is, of course, the variety used to make the great red Burgundies. The white Chardonnay grape makes up the rest of the plantings, and is predominant in the Côtes des Blancs.

The shipping houses market about two-thirds of the region's wines, but they own less than 15 percent of the vineyards; most of the vineyards are in the hands of thousands of small proprietors. At vintage time, those farmers who are not members of the more than 125 co-operative cellars in Champagne, or who are not among those who estate-bottle the wine made from their own grapes, sell their grapes to the shippers—who cannot rely on their own acreage alone to maintain their stocks of wine—at a price per kilo that is negotiated each year just before the harvest. The established price of the grapes is then multiplied by the official rating of the soil from which each particular load comes. There are nearly twenty villages whose vineyards are rated at 100 percent quality, including Ay, Cramant, Bouzy, Sillery, and Avize. Others are rated on a sliding scale that goes down to 80 percent. About one-third of the wines produced in Champagne come from soil rated 90 percent or higher.

Because most of the grapes harvested are Pinot Noir and Pinot Meunier, and because the color of red wines comes from pigments on the inside of the skin that dissolve in fermenting must, it is essential that the red grapes be pressed and separated from their skins as quickly as possible. For this reason the shipping houses maintain presses at strategic locations throughout the vineyards, so that the journey from vine to press is kept to a minimum. It is to these press houses that the growers take their grapes, which are then loaded in lots of four thousand kilos, or nearly nine thousand pounds. The traditional presses are wide and flat, rather than high, so that the grapes can be spread out and the juice can run out of the presses quickly. Two or three fast pressings produce the equivalent of ten barrels, each holding 205 liters, about fifty gallons. This is known as the *vin de cuvée,* or first pressing (although actually more than one pressing is needed to produce this much wine). Further pressing produces three more barrels of wine, called *tailles,* and this too can be made into champagne, although this wine is worth much less. These days, large presses can accommodate eight thousand kilos, but the proportion of *vin de cuvée* remains the same. Also, since 1992, the equivalent of only the first two barrels of *tailles* is allowed to be used to make champagne.

The pressed juice is transferred from the fields to the cellars of the shippers or the cooperatives, and there the fermentation begins that will transform the must into a still, dry white wine.

In January or February the tasting of the new wine begins, so that a *cuvée* may be made up for bottling. Each of the top shipping houses has, as always, obtained grapes from throughout Champagne to give itself flexibility in making up its usual blend. Tasting the new wines may take four or five weeks, and might take the following form. First the wines of each pressing are tasted and compared to other lots from the same district. Then the wines of different districts within Champagne are compared, and their respective qualities noted. One village may produce wine known for its bouquet, another for its body, a third for its delicacy and finesse, and so on. Each shipper also decides on the proportion of Pinot Noir, Pinot Meunier, and Chardonnay wines to be used. Some shippers may use 40 or 50 percent of Chardonnay for elegance, others prefer a richer wine with more Pinot Noir in the blend. The proportion will vary to some extent from year to year, and is likely to be different for a firm's vintage and nonvintage wines.

Finally, wines kept back from previous vintages, called reserve wines, are tasted to determine in what proportion they should be used. Remember that nonvintage champagne (and this accounts for more than 80 percent of the total) is made up of wines of more than one harvest. Certain years may produce rather thin wines, others rich wines that lack elegance. The characteristics and flaws of each vintage can be adjusted by the use of reserve wines, which may account for 15 to 30 percent of a *cuvée*. This complicated and delicate blending process, in which a dozen to fifty different lots of wine may eventually be combined, is the key to determining and maintaining a house style, upon which the reputation of each firm rests.

When a shipper considers that a particular vintage is

especially successful, he will make—in addition to this nonvintage blend—a *cuvée* entirely, or predominantly, from grapes harvested that year, and the bottles will display the vintage year on their labels. Shippers do not always agree on the quality of the wines produced in any given vintage, and the years in which vintage champagne is produced will vary from one shipper to another. Paradoxically, a vintage champagne made entirely from the wines of a single harvest may not be typical of a shipper's traditional style, since the *cuvée* is not balanced by the use of reserve wines. The laws governing the production of vintage champagne do not prohibit the use of reserve wines, however, and in practice a certain amount of reserve wine may sometimes be used even in vintage champagne.

Once the sample *cuvée* has been made up, the wines are blended accordingly and bottled, usually between March and May of the year following the harvest. A little bit of sugar syrup—*liqueur de tirage*—is added to the wine, along with yeast, to provide the elements necessary for a second fermentation. The bottle is then firmly stoppered with a temporary cork—most firms now use a crown cork similar to that previously used for soft drinks—and is placed on its side. Fermentation will now transform the sugar into alcohol and carbon dioxide gas, and because the bubbles are imprisoned in the bottle, they combine with the wine. The artificially induced second fermentation in individual bottles, which is the essence of the *méthode champenoise,* takes two or three months.

It was 150 years after Dom Pérignon first conducted his experiments that the key step of bottle fermentation began to be adequately controlled. (For that matter, it was not until several years after Dom Pérignon's death that producers in the Champagne region were first permitted to ship their wines in stoppered flasks, rather than wooden casks.) A French chemist devised a way to measure any residual sugar left in the still wine after blending, as well as a method for calculating how much additional sugar had to be added to the wine to produce the desired amount of gas pressure in the bottle. Until then, making champagne was a fairly hazardous undertaking, as the pressure resulting from a second fermentation could not be controlled, and the bottles of the day were not uniform. It was not unusual for half the contents of a cellar to be destroyed by a series of bottle explosions.

After the second fermentation, the bottles, now filled with sparkling wine, are piled up and left to mature. The extraordinary underground cellars of Champagne are carved out of the chalky subsoil of the region, and enable the champagne producers to maintain their enormous stocks—which in recent years have varied from 600 to 900 million bottles—at a constant low temperature. The bottles are said to be resting *sur lie,* that is, on the lees, the dead yeast cells thrown off as a by-product of fermentation. The interaction between the sparkling wine and the lees, known as autolysis, adds complexity and character to the bouquet and taste of the wine; long aging *sur lie* is an important factor in the quality of fine champagne. A nonvintage champagne must be aged *sur lie* for a minimum of one year. A vintage-dated champagne cannot be sold until three years after the harvest, which means it may age *sur lie* less than three years. In practice, most major firms age their wines *sur lie* well beyond the legal minimums.

Although the lees add to the flavor of champagne, the presence of this cloudy deposit makes the bottle unsalable to today's consumers. A series of complicated steps, first introduced in the eighteenth century, now takes place; its sole purpose is to rid each bottle of its deposit without losing the imprisoned bubbles. The bottles are put into *pupitres,* known in this country as riddling racks, A-shaped wooden boards with holes in which each bottle can be separately manipulated. A highly skilled *rémueur* now takes each bottle, which is at a slight downward slant, and gives it a little twist to dislodge the sediment, at the same time tipping the bottle over slightly to lower the corked end. This delicate process goes on every day for several weeks, and ends with each bottle standing upside down—*sur pointe*—with all of its sediment lying against the cork. Today, a number of champagne firms have installed labor-saving riddling bins that each hold about five hundred bottles. The bins can be manipulated, little by little, the way individual bottles are—imagine a cube on its side being gradually turned and raised until it rests on one of its corners—and each load of bottles ends up *sur pointe* in less than two weeks. The latest versions of these bins are fully automated and can be programmed by a computer.

The bottles are now ready for the *dégorgement*, or disgorging process. Still upside down, they are put on a conveyor and their necks dipped in a cold brine solution, which freezes the sediment to the temporary cork. The cork is then popped off, the pellet of sediment is disgorged, and the familiar champagne cork is inserted under great pressure.

Just before this cork is inserted, however, some sugar syrup is added to each bottle, along with as much champagne as is needed to replace whatever was lost when the sediment was expelled. This *liqueur d'expédition*, also referred to as the *dosage*, is what determines the relative dryness of a champagne. The driest of all champagne is Brut, which receives the least amount of *dosage*—it contains no more than 1.5 percent sugar, usually less. Extra Dry or Extra Sec, the next-driest style, may contain 1.2 to 2 percent of sugar. Dry or Sec is somewhat sweeter and, in fact, not really dry; and Demi-Sec, with 3 to 5 percent of sugar, is the sweetest champagne that most firms market. A few shippers occasionally market a champagne with no *dosage* at all, but such bottles are rare. A champagne that contains no more than .6 percent sugar may be labeled Extra Brut. Because the relative sweetness of champagne is determined only when the final cork is inserted, it is not difficult for any shipper to make up a champagne that will conform to his customers' demands.

One aspect of a Brut champagne that deserves mention is that the less sweetening is added, the better the wine has to be, as its quality cannot be masked. Also, a Brut does not taste at its best when served at the end of a meal, with dessert. The richness and sweetness of most desserts make the dry, delicate wine taste somewhat thin and sharp by contrast.

It's worth noting that the bottle-fermentation method described is used only for bottles, magnums (which hold two bottles), and usually, but not always, for half-bottles. Other sizes are produced by decanting bottles of Champagne into six-ounce splits and into larger sizes such as the jeroboam (four bottles), rehoboam (six bottles), and methuselah (eight bottles). Obviously, splits have the greatest chance of going flat, and are in any case poor value, ounce for ounce, compared to a half-bottle or bottle.

In addition to marketing nonvintage Brut, vintage Brut, and Extra Dry champagnes, a number of firms have also created luxury champagnes that are two or three times the price of a nonvintage Brut. Moët & Chandon's Dom Pérignon is perhaps the most famous of these deluxe champagnes, which are known as *cuvées speciales;* others include Taittinger Comtes de Champagne, Louis Roederer Cristal, Krug Grande Cuvée, Bollinger R. D., Dom Ruinart Blanc de Blancs, Veuve Clicquot La Grande Dame, Mumm Grand Cordon, Laurent Perrier Grand Siècle, and Perrier-Jouët Fleur de Champagne (known as Belle Epoque in France). The *cuvées* for these champagnes are prepared with particular care, the wines are usually aged longer on the lees, and most of them are marketed in distinctive, specially designed bottles.

Some champagne are labeled Blanc de Blancs, which indicates that the wine has been made entirely from white Chardonnay grapes. A Blanc de Blancs tends to be lighter and more delicate, and there are many who prize its particular elegance. Note that this phrase has a very specific meaning in Champagne, where most of the vineyards are planted with black grapes. But when the phrase is used on white-wine labels from other districts or other countries, it usually has no meaning, because white wines are made from white grapes as a matter of course. A champagne labeled Blanc de Noirs has been made entirely from black grapes without the use of Chardonnay in the *cuvée*.

Many firms now market a rosé champagne, almost always made by adding a small amount of red wine to the *cuvée*, just enough to give the blend the desired pink color. The wine is not easy to make, because after the bottle fermentation takes place, the color may fade or turn brown. Although pink champagne has a frivolous reputation, perhaps because of the many cheap versions made elsewhere, the best examples combine elegance with body and flavor.

Some shippers market a *crémant,* which is a wine that does not have the full sparkle of a champagne, but rather a more delicate *pétillance*. *Crémant* should not be confused with Cramant, which is a village in the Côte des Blancs whose wines are occasionally marketed under its own name.

A limited quantity of nonsparkling wine is also produced in the Champagne district from the same vineyards and the same grapes as champagne. Of course, all champagne begins as a still wine, but these go to market as such. Until 1974, the still wines of the Champagne region were labeled *Vin Nature de la Champagne*. They were almost never exported and were difficult to find even in France. In 1974, the name of the still wines of the Champagne region was changed to Coteaux Champenois, and for several years what was then an excess of production was bottled as a nonsparkling white wine—one that was light-bodied and relatively acid. In recent years, even though the crops in Champagne have increased substantially—twenty to twenty-five million cases is not uncommon—the demand for champagne has been such that shippers once again transform virtually all their wines into champagne, and nonsparkling wines from this region have become relatively rare. (There is also some still red wine produced in Champagne and bottled as such, the best known of which comes from the village of Bouzy.)

Here is an alphabetical list of most of the champagne firms whose wines can be found in the United States; there are, of course, other shippers doing business here.

Henri Abele	Jacquart
Ayala	Krug
Besserat de Bellefon	Lanson
Billecart-Salmon	Laurent Perrier
Bollinger	Moët & Chandon
Bricout	Mumm
Charbaut	Perrier-Jouët
Veuve Clicquot-Ponsardin	Piper-Heidsieck
De Venoge	Pol Roger
Deutz	Pommery
Gosset	Louis Roederer
Heidsieck Monopole	Ruinart
Charles Heidsieck	Salon Le Mesnil
Henriot	Taittinger

OTHER SPARKLING WINES

Although the Champagne region of France produces, by general accord, sparkling wines with the greatest style, complexity, and finesse, a number of other sparkling wines are made in France and, of course, throughout the world. Many of them are produced by the bulk process of tank fermentation, called *cuve close* in France, and also known as the Charmat process, after the Frenchman who first developed the technique about eighty years ago. The second fermentation of the base wine takes place in large sealed tanks rather than in individual bottles. The resulting sparkling wine is then drawn off under pressure and bottled. This method is obviously much quicker and cheaper than bottle fermentation: using the Charmat process, tanks of still wine can be transformed into bottles of sparkling wine in three weeks or less.

Another technique, called the transfer process, is often used—except in Champagne—to lower the cost of bottle-fermented sparkling wines. After the second fermentation has taken place and the wines have aged for some months, the bottles of sparkling wine are emptied, under pressure, into tanks, where the appropriate *dosage* is added. The wines are then filtered and rebottled. The transfer process is obviously cheaper than having to disgorge each bottle separately, and its use accounts for the fact that the labels of many sparkling wines—especially in the United States—carry the phrase "individually fermented in the bottle" while others, made by the *méthode champenoise,* are labeled "individually fermented in this bottle."

In France, all sparkling wines not produced in Champagne have always been called *mousseux,* no matter how they are made. There are *mousseux* produced along the Loire, notably in Saumur, Vouvray, Touraine, and Anjou, primarily from Chenin Blanc; many are made by the *méthode champenoise.* Familiar labels include Bouvet, Gratien & Meyer, Ackerman Laurance, Blanc Foussy, Rémy-Pannier, Monmousseau, Veuve Amiot, and Langlois-Château. A great deal of *mousseux* is produced in Burgundy, both red and white; Kriter, owned by Patriarche, is the best-known brand. Because the word *mousseux* may be used both for bottle-fermented sparkling wines and for less distinguished ones, new appellations were created in 1975 for certain *méthode champenoise* wines from *Appellation Contrôlée* regions. Crémant de Loire, Crémant de Bourgogne, and Crémant d'Alsace are names that can now be used for sparkling wines from these regions if they conform to certain regulations concerning the grape varieties used, minimum aging *sur lie,* and other aspects that affect quality. Other French sparkling wines that are only occasionally seen here include Saint-Péray, a dry *mousseux* from the Rhône made primarily from the Marsanne grape; Clairette de Die, also from the Rhône, which may be a dry wine made entirely from the Clairette grape, or a semisweet wine that contains a substantial proportion of Muscat; and the slightly sweet Blanquette de Limoux, produced near Carcassonne. Sparkling wine is also made in the village of Seyssel in the Haute-Savoie, in the Jura, and in Bordeaux.

The sparkling wines of Italy—dry and sweet, white and red—are labeled *spumante.* The most famous is Asti Spumante, produced in northern Italy around the village of Asti. Made from the distinctive and aromatic Muscat grape, Asti Spumante has a unique, intense bouquet reminiscent of ripe grapes and a sweet pronounced taste that many people find delicious with fruit and dessert. Asti Spumante is relatively low in alcohol—under 9 percent—and contains between 7.5 and 9 percent sugar. Virtually all of it is made by the Charmat process, called *autoclave* in Italy. Well-known producers of Asti Spumante include Gancia, Martini & Rossi, and Cinzano (each of which also produces dry sparkling wines).

Italians are among the leading consumers of French champagne (in fact, for several years in the 1970s, Italy was the Champagne region's most important export market), so it is not surprising that an increasing number of bone-dry *méthode champenoise* sparkling wines are now produced by the Italians themselves. The best of these, which come from the regions of Trentino, Alto Adige, Franciacorta, and the Oltrepò Pavese, are made from such varieties as Chardonnay, Pinot Bianco, Pinot Nero, and Pinot Grigio. The best-known producers of these bottle-fermented wines, which may be labeled *metodo classico,* include Ferrari and Equipe 5 of Trentino and, in the Franciacorta district, Ca' del Bosco, Berlucchi, and Bellavista. Many Italian wine firms now make Brut, or dry, *spumante,* some by the *méthode champenoise,* others by the Charmat process; producers include Antinori, Cavit, Fontanafredda, Frescobaldi, and Venegazzù. The Prosecco grape, planted in the hills around the towns of Conegliano and Valdobbiadene in the Veneto region, makes a dry sparkling; Carpenè Malvolti is the leading producer. In addition, a number of well-known red and white wines may, on occasion, be transformed into sparkling wines. These include Soave, Verdicchio, and Frascati among the whites, and such reds as Freisa and Nebbiolo.

Sekt is the generic name for German sparkling wines, which are produced in tremendous quantities. Historically, the thin, acid German wines of poor years were used as the base for Sekt, but demand has become so great that most of the still white wine transformed into Sekt is now imported from neighboring countries, primarily Italy and France. Today, much more sparkling wine is made in Germany than in Champagne, although almost all Sekt is produced by the Charmat process. Sekt can be an agreeable wine, and is characterized by a fruity taste and, more often than not, a slight sweetness. Henkell and Deinhard Lila Brut are among the best-known brands in this country; Kupferberg Gold is another popular label.

The sparkling wines of Spain—dry, well made, and moderately priced—have become increasingly popular in the United States in recent years. Almost all of Spain's *espumosos* are produced in or near San Sadurní de Noya, about twenty-five miles west of Barcelona, in the Penedés region. Most of the firms situated there use the traditional *méthode champenoise,* or *método tradicional,* and such wines may be labeled *cava.* The popularity of *cava* is such that production has increased from about one million cases in the 1960s to more than fifteen million cases. The first bottle-fermented sparkling wines were produced in the Penedés region more than a century ago; in 1986, *cava* was officially granted a *Denominación.* The principal grape varieties are Xarello, Macabeo, and Parellada; Chardonnay has also been planted, and is now used by several firms. It was in San Sadurní de Noya that automatic riddling machines, called *girasols*, were first used on a commercial basis to replace the time-consuming process of *rémuage* by hand. Codorníu and Freixenet (which owns Castellblanch, Segura Viudas, and Conde de Caralt) are the leading *cava* firms, and account for more than 80 percent of total production; other brands include Juvé y Camps, Marqués de Monistrol, Lembey of Domecq, and Paul Cheneau.

Despite the fame of champagne and the increasing popularity of other imported sparkling wines, about three-quarters of all the sparkling wines sold in this country are made here, almost all of them in California. To the dismay of the French, the word *champagne* may legally be used on the labels of American sparkling wines as long as it is preceded by an indication of its origin: California, New York State, America. Most American sparkling wines are made by the Charmat, or bulk, process. Actually, one such wine—André, produced by Gallo—accounts for more than a third of all the sparkling wines produced in California; other labels include Tott's and Eden Roc (both made by Gallo), Cook's, Le Domaine, and Weibel.

Although moderately priced, Charmat-process sparkling wines continue to dominate the market, there has been a dramatic increase, in recent years, in the number of California wineries producing fine sparkling wines by the *méthode champenoise*. Korbel, located in Sonoma County, has been making such wines since 1882, and they continue to be popular with consumers. But Schramsberg, a small Napa Valley winery created by Jack and Jamie Davies in 1965, was the first to specialize in *méthode champenoise* wines made from the classic Chardonnay and Pinot Noir grapes of Champagne, rather than such grapes as Chenin Blanc and French Colombard, which produce agreeable but neutral and undistinguished sparkling wines. Other wineries followed suit, combining the use of the classic varieties with extended bottle-aging on the lees to produce California sparkling wines with more finesse and complexity.

In 1973, the French firm Moët-Hennessy bought land in the Napa Valley and soon after began construction of a sparkling wine facility, Domaine Chandon; they released their first wines in 1977. Piper-Heidsieck created the Piper-Sonoma winery in Sonoma County and produced their first wines in 1980. Other French-backed wineries producing *méthode champenoise* sparkling wines in California include Mumm Napa Valley; Roederer Estate, in Mendocino's Anderson Valley; Maison Deutz, in the Arroyo Grande district between San Luis Obispo and Santa Maria; and Domaine Carneros, created by Taittinger in the Carneros district of Napa. The two leading producers of *méthode champenoise* wines in Spain have also established wineries in the Carneros district—Freixenet created the Gloria Ferrer facility in Sonoma, and Codorníu built the Codorníu Napa winery. In addition, such firms as Scharffenberger, in Mendocino, and Iron Horse Vineyards, in Sonoma's Green Valley, are known for their sparkling wines; and a number of other wineries, including Wente Bros., Chateau St. Jean, and Jordan also make *méthode champenoise* sparkling wines. None of the French-backed firms, and few others, use the word *champagne* on their labels.

Until the mid-1960s, New York State produced more sparkling wine than did California. Although New York State champagne now accounts for less than 10 percent of all sales, it is still very popular throughout the country. The native grapes, notably Delaware and Catawba, that give New York State table wines a special grapy taste have traditionally produced a very agreeable sparkling wine with a flavor of its own. Today, many of these distinctive sparkling wines display less of the taste of native grapes than in the past, and, in fact, some producers are using a substantial proportion of French-American hybrids. The major brands of New York State champagne are Great Western, Taylor, and Gold Seal.

Sparkling wines are also made in many other states; the biggest producer of *méthode champenoise* wines outside of California and New York is Domaine Ste. Michelle, in Washington. The Gruet Winery, in New Mexico, has also established a reputation for its sparkling wines.

Champagne and sparkling wines should be opened with some care. There are few sounds that fill us with as much pleasant anticipation as the loud pop of a champagne cork, but this is usually accompanied by a wasteful explosion of foam and wine, so it's worth noting the simplest and most effective means of opening a bottle. Ideally, you should put a napkin or handkerchief between your hand and the bottle, partly to avoid warming the wine with the heat of your palm, but also as a safety measure, in case a bottle should ever crack. Then remove the foil and loosen the wiring. Try to hold the bottle so that your thumb keeps the cork in place as you twist the wiring with your other hand. In any case, make sure the bottle is not pointed toward you or anyone else, because once the wire is loosened, the cork may explode out. Then hold the cork firmly in one hand and twist the bottle away from the cork with the other. The cork should come out easily, but if it doesn't, try to work it loose without shaking the bottle excessively. The bottle should be at a 45-degree angle, so that a larger surface of wine is exposed to the atmosphere when the cork comes out, which reduces the pressure in the narrow neck of the bottle. This procedure may be a bit too deliberate for celebrating a sports victory in a locker room, but you'll find it easy enough to manage in your home.

The so-called champagne glasses often used at receptions—wide, shallow, sherbet-type—are in fact the worst of all. Their flat, wide bottoms dissipate the bubbles very quickly, and they are awkward to drink from. Either a tulip-shaped glass, tapering to a point where the bowl joins the stem, or a traditional flute in the shape of an elongated V is a better choice, and both are preferable to an all-purpose U-shaped glass because if the bubbles rise from a single point, they will last longer and present a more attractive appearance.

FORTIFIED WINES

Fortified wines are those to which a certain amount of brandy has been added to bring the total alcoholic content up to 17 to 21 percent. Wine producers in this country refer to all such wines—whether they are dry or sweet—as dessert wines. Sherry and port are the most famous examples of fortified wines, and Madeira, Marsala, and Málaga are also fairly well known. Vermouth is a fortified wine that has also been flavored with a variety of herbs and spices, and traditional aperitif wines are made in a similar way.

It is common to divide fortified wines into two classes—the dry wines, which are usually served before meals, and the sweet ones, which traditionally make their appearance after dinner. In practice, however, this division has too many exceptions. Many people enjoy a sweet sherry before a meal, the French often drink a sweet port before sitting down to dinner, and both sweet and dry vermouth are often served along with cocktails.

SHERRY

Sherry is perhaps the most versatile of all wines; it can be bone-dry, mellow, or richly sweet; it can be served before or after a meal, or at almost any time of day. Its name derives from the town of Jerez de la Frontera, in the southwest corner of Spain. Until the thirteenth century this part of Spain was under Moorish domination and Jerez wås situated along the frontier (*frontera*) between the Moors and the Christians.

Jerez de la Frontera, which is the center of the sherry trade, forms a triangle with the towns of Puerto de Santa María and Sanlúcar de Barrameda, and within this triangle are found the best grape-growing districts for the making of sherry. The best soil, *albariza,* is made up of white chalk, and that district is planted entirely with the Palomino grape. A certain amount of Pedro Ximénez is also planted, and P.X., as it is called, is vinified in a special way to make very sweet wines used in the final blending of some sherries.

Sherry, virtually unique among the world's wines, is made in a rather special way. The juice is fermented into a completely dry wine, with no residual sugar, and is then stored in butts, or barrels, in the *bodegas*—high-ceilinged warehouses—of the various firms. Whereas almost everywhere else barrels of new wine are filled to the top, so that air cannot get to the wine and spoil it, in Jerez the butts are not completely filled, and exposure to air is actually encouraged. In the weeks following the vintage, each of the thousands of butts of new wine in a particular cellar develops somewhat differently. Even wines from the same vineyard, stored in adjoining butts, may not evolve into identical wines. In some, a white film of yeast cells, called *flor,* or flower, forms on the surface of the wine, and these are classified as finos. Others develop very little *flor,* or none, and may eventually be classified as olorosos. Finos and olorosos are the two basic categories of sherry. The fuller-bodied and less delicate olorosos are fortified with brandy to 18 percent, and will be used primarily to make sweet cream sherries. Finos are fortified to only 15.5 percent, so that the *flor,* which gives these wines their individuality, will not be destroyed. In time, finos are classified once again: some remain finos; others, slightly richer and fuller, become amontillados.

Although it is true that two butts of sherry from the same vineyard may turn out somewhat differently, their evolution is not quite as mysterious and unpredictable as it is sometimes made out to be. The shippers know, for example, that certain vineyards traditionally produce finos, others olorosos; that wines from severely pruned vines are likely to turn into finos; and that younger vines will probably produce olorosos. What's more, sherry producers are now able to influence the style of wine when the grapes are pressed—the light, delicate wines that are made from the juice of the first pressing will be transformed into finos, the fuller-bodied wines from subsequent pressings will be used for olorosos. After the wines are fermented, only the lighter wines selected to be finos are put into incompletely filled barrels, as in the past, so that *flor* can develop; and the *flor* itself can be induced by controlling the temperature and humidity of the cellars.

As finos and olorosos continue to age, the exact style of each butt of wine is determined, and it is earmarked to become part of a particular *solera* within the firm's *bodegas*. It is the *solera* system of blending and aging, unique to sherry, that is the heart of the production of this wine. A *solera* can be visualized as several tiers of barrels, all containing wines similar in style, with the oldest wines at the bottom. When some of the wine from each barrel in the bottom row is drawn off to be blended, bottled, and shipped, the loss is made up with wines from the second tier, which contains the next-oldest wines. These, in turn, are replaced with wines from the third tier, and so on. At each level, the older wine already in the barrel is said to "educate" the younger wine that is added. Although the entire collection of barrels is usually referred to as a *solera,* technically speaking, it is the barrels containing the oldest wines that are the *solera;* each tier that feeds the *solera* is called a *criadera,* or nursery; and the youngest *criadera* is replenished from an *añada,* a wine only one or two years old. Because the amount of wine withdrawn from a *solera* is limited to, say, no more than a third of a barrel at one time, the *solera* system enables the shipping firms of Jerez to maintain a continuity of style for each of their sherries, year after year. In practice, a *solera* system is more varied and complex than this simple visualization. A fino *solera* may consist of four tiers, or scales; an oloroso of seven or eight. Sometimes, the youngest *criadera* in an oloroso *solera* may be replenished not by a young *añada*, but by the oldest wine in another *solera,* so that the wine that is bottled may have passed through twelve or fourteen scales. Since each scale in a *solera* may consist of two or three hundred barrels, they are not actually piled one on top of another, and may even be scattered throughout several cellars.

The amount of wine drawn off from a *solera* differs depending on the style of wine. One-third of a fino *solera* may be drawn off four times a year, whereas in an oloroso *solera* only a quarter may be withdrawn twice a year. Also, to make up a particular sherry, a shipper will often combine wines from several *soleras,* so that the final blend consists of wines of slightly different styles. Since sherry is produced by a system of fractional blending that includes a number of successive vintages, and wines from many vineyards, sherry is never vintage-dated, nor is it identified by the name of an individual vineyard.

Although sherries are classified as finos and olorosos, they are marketed in four main categories. A manzanilla is a fino that has been matured in the seacoast village of Sanlúcar de Barrameda, fifteen miles from Jerez. This bone-dry wine acquires a distinctive tang, sometimes attributed to the salt air, but more likely the result of higher humidity, which produces a richer *flor.* Curiously enough, if a manzanilla is shipped back in barrel to Jerez, it gradually loses its special taste. A fino is a dry sherry, but many shippers do not emphasize this word on their labels, preferring instead to feature such proprietary brand names as La Ina or Tio Pepe. A good fino, delicate and complex, is a difficult wine to make, and some cheap examples are not even dry. An amontillado is usually described as nuttier than a fino, and since amontillados are often finos with more barrel age, they tend to be fuller-bodied. The most obvious difference between the two, however, is that most of the Amontillados shipped here are distinctively sweeter than finos. It is not difficult to find a dry amontillado in Spain, where the best of them are very much admired, but most of the popular brands available here are somewhat sweet, even those labeled as dry. As with finos, the word amontillado does not always appear on the labels of these wines. The fourth category of sherry is cream sherry, which is almost always made from olorosos. Although an oloroso is completely dry as it ages in its *solera,* its bigger body and fuller flavor lends itself to transformation into a cream sherry by the addition of specially made sweet wines during the final stages of blending. The sweetness of a cream sherry varies from shipper to shipper, but most contain 10 to 14 percent sugar. Amoroso is still used occasionally on a label to indicate a golden sherry that is between an amontillado and a cream sherry in color and sweetness. Brown sherry, rarely seen in this country, is even darker and sweeter than a cream sherry.

Dry sherries taste best chilled, and it's better to put a bottle of fino in the refrigerator than to serve it with ice cubes, which dilute its delicate flavor. An open bottle of sherry lasts longer than a table wine because of its higher alcoholic content. Nevertheless, most sherry shippers agree that once opened, a good fino will begin to lose its character within a week or two.

When buying sherry, it is the name of the shipper that is important rather than that of a village or vineyard. Furthermore, many sherry shippers have individualized certain of their wines by the use of proprietary brand names, some of which are better known than the names of the firms that produce them. Some sherry houses (and their leading brand names) are Croft (Original), Pedro Domecq (La Ina), Duff Gordon (Club Dry), Gonzales Byass (Tio Pepe), Harveys (Bristol Cream), Emilio Lustau, Osborne (Fino Quinta), Sandeman (Character, Armada Cream), Williams & Humbert (Dry Sack), and Wisdom & Warter. Two firms in Sanlúcar de Barrameda are Hidalgo (La Gitana) and Antonio Barbadillo (Solear).

About one hundred miles northeast of Jerez is the Montilla-Moriles district, whose wines are labeled simply as Montilla. The name amontillado is derived from Montilla, and these wines are similar in style to sherry. They are made primarily from the Pedro Ximénez grape, which in this region is fermented out until the wines are dry. Montilla has a natural alcohol content of about 16 percent, so finos may be bottled and shipped without being fortified with brandy.

Wines labeled sherry are also made in the United States, primarily in California and New York State. However, most American sherries are made by baking neutral white wines to age them artificially, which is a technique used in Madeira, not in Jerez. Consequently, the drier sherries are often less successful than the cream sherries, whose baked taste can be more easily masked by sweetening. A number of American wineries age at least some of their sherries in small barrels, but the traditional *solera* system of blending is not practiced here. Many wineries now use a submerged *flor* process: *flor* yeast is mixed with dry white base wines, the mixture is put into large pressurized tanks in which oxygen circulates, and after one to four weeks, the wine is drawn off the yeast and aged in barrels. There is a difference, however, between wines exposed to *flor* for a short time and those that react with *flor* for many years. Furthermore, many California *flor* wines are later blended with baked wines before bottling. Although sherries produced in the United States generally lack the distinctive nutty quality and complexity of taste typical of Spanish sherry, many of them are soundly made and the best of them are a good value.

PORT

Port is a sweet, red, fortified wine made along a delimited section of the Douro River in northern Portugal. (White port has also been made for a hundred years, but most of it is used for blending.) Port takes its name from the town of Oporto, at the mouth of the Douro, although the offices and warehouses of the famous port shippers are located across the river in Vila Nova de Gaia. Port has long been popular in Great Britain and was, in fact, specifically developed for the British market, but it has been slow to catch on in this country. Perhaps the image of cheap American port has discouraged consumers from discovering how good authentic port can be, or it may be that our drinking habits don't lend themselves to the appreciation of a sweet red wine that is usually served after a meal.

In 1968, in an effort to distinguish true port from imitations produced in this country, the Portuguese government took the unusual step of declaring that port shipped from Portugal to the United States must be labeled porto. Although wines bottled in Portugal now carry the phrase Vinho do Porto, many shippers continue to feature port, rather than porto, on their labels, and despite the ruling, the wine continues to be called port by both shippers and consumers alike.

The red wines of the Douro were known as unexceptional table wines until the early eighteenth century, when political considerations made it cheaper for the English to import wines from Portugal than from France. As more Portuguese wines were exported to England, some shippers began to add brandy to the wines to fortify them for the long voyage, and port as we now know it gradually evolved. Today port continues to be popular in England, but surprisingly enough, France now imports four times as much of this wine as does England. The French drink port before the meal, as an aperitif.

Port is produced along the upper Douro River on steeply terraced vineyards planted with more than a dozen different grape varieties. Today, grapes are crushed by mechanical means, but as recently as the 1950s all the grapes used for port were crushed by foot in large cement troughs, and some firms still use this old-fashioned treading for selected lots of grapes. The purpose of treading is not to squeeze juice from the grapes, which can be done more effectively with a press, but to extract as much color and tannin as possible from the skins in the relatively short time that they are in contact with the fermenting juice. As the grapes are crushed, fermentation begins, converting the sugar in the juice into alcohol. At a certain point, brandy is mixed with the incompletely fermented wine. This sudden dose of alcohol stops the fermentation completely, and the resulting fortified wine contains 9 or 10 percent unfermented grape sugar and about 20 percent alcohol. White port is made in the same way and mostly used for blending with reds, although some is fermented out until it is dry and marketed as an aperitif wine. In the spring following the vintage, the new wine is transported from *quintas,* or vineyard estates, along the Douro to shippers' cellars, called lodges, in Vila Nova Gaia. There the wine is aged in wooden casks, called pipes. A pipe of port, the traditional measure in that region, holds the equivalent of a little more than seven hundred bottles.

Young port is a deep red-purple wine, quite fruity and grapy, which has not yet absorbed the brandy with which it was mixed. It is not a harsh or unpleasant wine—its sweetness masks its tannin and alcoholic content—but it is not fine or complex, and has yet to develop its character. Almost all port is wood port, that is, aged for several years in cask before being bottled. (The exception is vintage port, which will be discussed further on.) The two basic styles of wood port are ruby and tawny. Ruby port is darker in color, more fruity and vigorous in style. Tawny port is lighter in color, as its name suggests, generally older, softer, more delicate, and often more complex. This distinction is blurred by the fact that the only requirement of wood ports is that they be aged two or three years before being shipped. It takes six or seven years for a young port to develop into a tawny, and fine tawnies are aged considerably longer. Aging wines is expensive, of course, and consequently many tawnies on the market are simply rubies to which a certain amount of white port has been added to lighten the color and soften the taste. It is a mistake, therefore, to assume that an inexpensive tawny is necessarily older than a ruby from the same firm. An authentic aged tawny can be a very fine example of mature port, subtle, polished, and complex. Note that most shippers do not feature the words *ruby* and *tawny* on the labels of their best bottlings, but prefer to use such proprietary names as Special Reserve, Bin 27, Distinction, and Boardroom. In recent years, another category of tawny port has appeared in which an indication of the years spent in wood may be shown on the label. Such tawnies may be labeled specifically as ten, twenty, thirty, or forty years old, and several shippers now offer a full range of these four types of mature port. All wood-aged ports, whether young rubies or old tawnies, are ready to drink when bottled.

Although wood ports account for virtually all of the seven to nine million cases of port produced annually, the most famous and glamorous wine of the region is undoubtedly vintage port. It is a wine made entirely from the grapes of a single harvest and bottled after about two years in wood, so that it matures in bottle rather than in cask. Like champagne, it is a blend of different vineyards and grape varieties. A shipper "declares" a vintage only when he thinks the quality of the wine exceptional enough to warrant it, and this usually occurs only three or four times in a decade. The decision is not made until the second spring after the vintage, in case the second of two consecutive vintages turns out better than the first, and every shipper decides for himself whether or not to declare a vintage. For example, more than thirty shippers made a vintage port in 1960, only seven in 1962, about thirty in 1963, twenty-odd in 1966, only a dozen in 1967, about forty in 1970, only five in 1972, nearly thirty in 1975, and about twenty in 1977 and 1980; a number of firms declared the 1982 vintage, others preferred to bottle their 1983s, and virtually every firm declared a 1985. The next generally declared vintage was 1991. Even in a year when a shipper declares a vintage, only a very small part of his production, perhaps 5 percent, is set aside to be bottled as vintage port. The rest is needed to maintain the quality and style of his wood ports. The total amount of vintage port produced in a given year rarely exceeds 250,000 cases, and even in an abundant vintage, few firms are likely to bottle more than twelve to twenty thousand cases each.

Vintage port is unquestionably one of the finest wines made, and since it is bottled only in good vintages it is perhaps the most dependable of all fine wines. Wine ages in bottle much more slowly than in wood, however, and since the wines begin as exceptionally tannic and intense examples of port, most shippers suggest that a vintage port needs a minimum of ten or fifteen years to be drinkable. Since vintage port throws a heavy deposit as it ages, careful decanting is a necessity.

Although the classic examples of vintage port are those produced by the top firms in the best years, many shippers are now bottling vintage ports made from a single *quinta*, or estate, usually the one that makes up the core of the firm's vintage port blend. Single *quinta* ports are treated just like vintage ports, bottled after two years, and meant to mature in bottle. They are made when there is not enough top wine available to declare a vintage or in a vintage that is very good but not quite up to a firm's vintage port standards. Among the best-known *quintas* are Taylor Fladgate's Quinta de Vargellas, Croft's Quinta da Roeda, Dow's Quinta do Bomfim, and Graham's Quinta de Malvedos.

In addition to vintage port, there are two other styles of port on whose labels the word vintage may appear. Late-bottled vintage ports, known as LBV, are, like vintage ports, produced from wines of a single vintage but are bottled only after four to six years in wood. (The year of bottling appears on the label.) Some shippers use the wines of a generally declared vintage year; most use intermediate years. They are meant to combine the character of vintage port with additional barrel age and are, in a manner of speaking, specially selected aged rubies. A shipper's LBV will be a richer and more intense wine than his ruby, but more evolved than a vintage port of about the same age. They can be drunk when they are bottled, and, with one or two exceptions, are not meant to improve with age.

There are also bottles to be found labeled port of the vintage rather than vintage port. These wines, also known as *colheitas,* have nothing whatever to do with vintage port, but are simply old tawnies from a specific year, often refreshed with younger wines and bottled after a minimum of seven years in wood. (The date of bottling must now appear on the label.) These wines are often overpriced, and often misleadingly advertised as if they were vintage ports.

Some port shippers whose wines are found in this country (and their best-known proprietary brands) are Cálem, Cockburn (Special Reserve), Croft (Distinction), Delaforce (His Eminence's Choice), Dow (Boardroom), Fonseca (Bin 27), Graham (Six Grapes), Harveys (Gold Cap, Directors' Bin), Hoopers, Niepoort, Ramos-Pinto, Robertson (Dry Humour), Sandeman (Founders Reserve), Smith Woodehouse, Taylor Fladgate (First Estate), and Warre (Warrior, Nimrod). Most of these firms also ship vintage ports, as do Ferreira, Gould Campbell,

Forrester (labeled Boa Vista), Quarles Harris, Rebello Valente, and Quinta do Noval, among others.

California ports are produced by a great many wineries and vary widely in quality. Most of them are full, fruity, mellow wines that nevertheless lack the subtlety and complexity of the wines from the Douro. There are, however, a few small California wineries that specialize in port. Ficklin Vineyard, near Madera, has been producing port from traditional Douro varieties since 1948. Andrew Quady, whose winery is in Madera, has been making limited quantities of vintage-dated port from Amador County Zinfandel grapes since 1975; he also produces two other fortified wines—an Orange Muscat labeled Essensia and a Black Muscat labeled Elysium. Port made in New York State tends to retain more of the native *labrusca* flavor than does New York State sherry.

MADEIRA

Madeira is a small Portuguese island off the coast of North Africa whose distinctive fortified wines range from fairly dry to very sweet. In colonial times, Madeira was probably the most popular wine in America, and was specially imported by connoisseurs in Boston, New York, and Charleston. Only a small quantity is imported today. The vineyards of Madeira were devastated by two plagues in the second half of the nineteenth century, first the fungus oïdium, then phylloxera, and its production has never regained its former size.

As is the case with port, the fermentation of Madeira was traditionally stopped by the addition of brandy at a point determined by just how sweet the finished wine was meant to be. Although this technique is still occasionally used, most Madeira is now fermented out until it is dry, just like sherry. In the past the fortified wines were then put in rooms called *estufas,* or ovens, and the wines slowly baked for several months. Today, large concrete vats heated by internal pipes are used to bake the wines. The wine must be baked for a minimum of ninety days at a temperature no higher than 122°F. This concentrated aging process is meant to approximate the beneficial effects of a long sea voyage, as it was discovered in the eighteenth century that the voyages to which all cargo was subjected seemed to improve the wines of Madeira.

Madeira has a special pungent taste that comes from the volcanic soil in which the vines are planted, a relatively high acidity, and a distinctive cooked or burned taste that it acquires in the *estufas*. At the time of bottling each lot of wine is sweetened to produce the appropriate style of wine. Sercial is the driest of all Madeiras, Verdelho the next driest; Malmsey is the sweetest, and Bual, or Boal, is medium-sweet. Although these four names are those of specific grape varieties once cultivated on the island, the wines are no longer from the grape with which each is labeled. In fact, only Bual and Sercial are still cultivated in more than token amounts; a variety called Tinta Negra Mole accounts for about 80 percent of Madeira production today. The grape names are now used simply to indicate the relative style and sweetness of each wine. Some shippers also market their wines with proprietary brand names such as Island Dry, Saint John, Duke of Clarence, and Viva. Rainwater Madeira, typically pale in color, is a generic name for a medium-sweet wine. Madeira is among the longest-lived of all wines, and it is still possible to find fifty- or one-hundred-year-old single-vintage Madeiras (as opposed to vintage-dated *solera* wines, which are actually blended from many vintages): good examples are by no means faded, and offer a remarkable tasting experience.

One of the principal shippers on the island is the Madeira Wine Company, which produces and markets such brands as Blandy's, Cossart Gordon, Leacock, and Rutherford & Miles. Other shippers include Barbeito, Borges, Henriques & Henriques, and Justino Henriques.

Marsala is a fortified wine made in Sicily. As is the case with sherry, the wine is completely fermented until it is dry, then later fortified and sweetened. Even dry Marsala is not completely dry. Most firms market not only a sweet Marsala, but specially flavored Marsalas as well, using egg yolks, almonds, oranges, and so forth.

The city of Málaga, situated along the southern coast of Spain, gives its name to a sweet, fortified wine made primarily from Muscatel and Pedro Ximénez grapes. Málaga is rarely encountered here.

VERMOUTH AND APERITIFS

Vermouth, both sweet and dry, is most often used in mixed drinks, but it is also popular as an aperitif, and is usually served with ice and a twist of lemon peel. Vermouth has a wine base, and is fortified, sweetened, and flavored with various herbs, spices, and, increasingly, flavor extracts, according to each firm's secret recipe. Traditionally, Italian vermouth is red and sweet, while French vermouth is pale and dry, but both types are made in each country, and two-thirds of the vermouth consumed here is made in this country. The French town of Chambéry, near the Swiss-Italian border, has given its name to a distinctive pale and dry vermouth.

Anything that is drunk before a meal—sherry, vermouth, white wine, champagne, or even a cocktail—could properly be described as an aperitif, but the term "aperitif wine" usually refers to certain proprietary brands, such as Dubonnet, St. Raphaël, Byrrh, and Lillet. They can be red or white and some are made primarily from *mistelle*, must whose fermentation has been arrested by the addition of alcohol, thus retaining a high proportion of grape sugar. Most aperitifs have a more pronounced and distinctive flavor than vermouth because they are meant to be drunk by themselves, with ice and perhaps a splash of soda water. Quinine or an equivalent flavoring agent is a traditional ingredient that contributes a slightly bitter aftertaste to temper the sweetness of the aperitif.

Pineau des Charentes is an unusual aperitif produced in the Cognac region of France. It is a blend of sweet, unfermented grape juice and young cognac, and is bottled with about 17 percent alcohol. Floc de Gascogne is a similar product made with Armagnac in the region of Gascony.

COGNAC AND
OTHER BRANDIES

Although this book is primarily concerned with wine, a meal at which good wines are served often ends with a glass of brandy, which is, almost always, distilled from wine. The word is derived from *brandewijn*, a Dutch word for burned (distilled) wine. Wherever grapes are grown and fermented into wine, brandy of some kind is also made. The most famous and most highly regarded of all brandies is cognac, which is distilled from wine produced in a specifically delimited area in southwest France, about sixty miles north of Bordeaux. All cognac is brandy, but there is only one brandy that can be called cognac.

It was in the early seventeenth century that the white wines produced in the region near the Charente River were first distilled to make a *vin brûlé*, presumably to provide an alcoholic beverage for export markets that would be less bulky to ship than wine. The city of Cognac, which lies on the bank of the Charente, gave its name to this brandy in the eighteenth century, and only a hundred years ago did the various cognac producers first begin to bottle and label their brandy in their own cellars, thus establishing the brand names by which almost all cognac is marketed today.

We have seen how important soil is to the quality and

characteristics of various wines, and this is equally true for the wines used to make cognac. There are six clearly defined districts whose wines are permitted to be distilled into cognac. The two most important inner districts are called Grande Champagne and Petite Champagne, but these names bear no relation to the sparkling wines of Champagne. *Champagne* in French means open fields, a distinction made even clearer by the name of the four other districts, three of which refer to *bois*, or woods: Borderies, Fins Bois, Bons Bois, and Bois Ordinaires. These legally delimited areas were established when it was discovered that the wines from each district, when distilled, produced cognacs with marked differences in quality. The very best cognacs come from Grande Champagne and Petite Champagne, which now account for about 40 percent of the total production of cognac.

A cognac labeled Grande Champagne or Grande Fine Champagne has been distilled entirely from wines made from grapes grown in the Grande Champagne district, and this is the highest appellation possible. More familiar is Fine Champagne Cognac, which indicates that the brandy comes from both Grande and Petite Champagne, with at least 50 percent from Grande Champagne. Because of the importance attached to these appellations, some cognacs are labeled Fine Cognac or Grande Fine Cognac, phrases as meaningless as they are misleading.

There are three grape varieties used to make Charente wines, but it is the Saint-Emilion (also known as the Ugni Blanc, and unrelated to the Bordeaux wine district) that has almost totally replaced the Folle Blanche and the Colombard. The white wine of the Charente is thin and sour, usually 7 to 10 percent alcohol, and unattractive to drink. Oddly enough, the wine produced in Grande Champagne from its predominantly chalky soil tastes even worse than the rest, and yet it produces the finest cognac. There are no quantity limits per acre to the wines produced in the Charente, but the growers must vinify their wines carefully, because any off-taste or defect in the wine will show up even more strongly in the distilled brandy. Much of the annual wine crop is sold directly to big distilling houses that are owned by or under contract to the biggest cognac shippers, but thousands of small growers also distill their own cognac, to be sold later to the shippers.

Once the wine has been made, distillation takes place in old-fashioned pot stills, which resemble giant copper kettles, and proceeds for several months on a twenty-four-hour schedule. Cognac is unusual in that it is doubly distilled. The first distillation produces a liquid of about 60 proof (or 30 percent alcohol), called *brouillis*. This is redistilled to make the raw cognac, known as the *bonne chauffe*, which comes out of the still at 140 proof. It takes about ten barrels of wine to make a barrel of cognac. Distillation is deliberately slow, so that the characteristics of the wine are imparted to the brandy. The congeners, or flavoring elements, retained during distillation give cognac its particular character, whereas a fast, high-proof distillation would result in a relatively flavorless alcohol.

The new cognac, which is colorless, is then aged in oak barrels. These barrels were traditionally made of Limousin oak, but the forest of Limousin can no longer supply all the needs of the cognac shippers. Today, about half the barrels in the cellars of Cognac are made of Tronçais oak, from a forest about two hundred miles away. It is the interactions between oak and brandy, as well as the continual oxidation that takes place through the porous wood, that gives cognac its superb and distinctive flavor. The basic elements are present in embryonic form in the new cognac, but it is barrel-aging (during which the brandy also picks up color and tannin from the oak) that refines a harsh distillate into an inimitable beverage. Cognac, like all brandies, ages only as long as it remains in wood, and undergoes no further development once it is bottled. It is not the vintage that matters, as with wine, but the number of years spent in wood.

Aging is expensive, however, not only because the nearly one million barrels of cognac lying in the warehouses of the big shippers and in small cellars throughout the countryside represent an enormous capital outlay, but also because cognac evaporates as it ages, at the rate of about 2 percent a year (the equivalent of nearly twenty million bottles at 80 proof). This explains not only why fine cognac is expensive, but also why most cognacs on the market are considerably younger than consumers imagine.

The finest cognacs will continue to improve in barrel for about forty years, after which there is a danger that they will dry out and take on a woody or stalky flavor. Very old cognacs are therefore stored in glass demijohns or in old barrels that will not alter the brandy's flavor. Cognacs from lesser districts, on the other hand, will mature and mellow for only a few years, at which time they are already quite pleasant. They can naturally be improved by being combined with older cognacs from other districts, and it is at this point that the blender's skill comes into play. Apart from cognacs that may have been distilled especially for them, all the cognac houses constantly buy young cognacs from the thousands of grower-distillers in the region. Tremendous stocks of different cognacs of various ages must be maintained by the shippers in order to make up their respective house styles on a continuous basis.

As cognac ages, its alcoholic content diminishes slowly, but it is obviously not possible to age every cognac until it arrives at a marketable strength—usually 80 proof—and the shippers must therefore add distilled water to their final blends to achieve the desired proof.

Note that color is irrelevant as an indication of the age or quality of a cognac: a cognac aged in new wood for only two or three years may be darker than one aged in old wood for ten, and it's common practice at most firms to adjust the color with caramel to ensure continuity from one shipment to the next.

There are a number of markings—stars, initials, and phrases—that traditionally appear on cognac labels, and some of these are more meaningful than others. Most of the cognacs marketed here fall into two basic categories—those labeled Three Star, Five Star, VS, or VSP, and those labeled VSOP (Very Superior Old Pale). The number of stars on a bottle of cognac is completely meaningless, except to place the brandy in the youngest age category. By French law a cognac must be aged at least eighteen months, but our federal laws stipulate that all brandy must be at least two years old. Because stars have no legal meaning, and because so many other brandies have now adopted the star system that originated in Cognac, a few shippers dropped this designation from their labels and introduced proprietary brand names such as Régal, Célébration, and Gold-Leaf. Today, most shippers have replaced stars and proprietary names with the initials VS or VSP, but neither of these designations has any particular significance with respect to the age of the cognac.

VSOP, however, does have a special meaning: any cognac so labeled must be at least four years old. Clearly, the increasing use of the initials VS and VSP is an attempt not only to get away from the meaningless star system, but also to blur the distinction between younger cognacs, which account for perhaps 80 percent of sales, and the VSOPs. Fantastic claims to the contrary, it's safe to say that virtually all VSOPs consist primarily of four- or five-year-old cognacs, with very small amounts of older reserves added to the blend to enrich it.

A cognac labeled Napoléon—the next higher step in quality—must be at least six years old, as must one labeled Extra or XO. Six years is the maximum age that is officially controlled by the Cognac Bureau (it was five until 1978). Consequently, the actual age of older cognacs is determined by each shipper—one firm's Napoléon may be only six years old, another's fifteen years or more; the same applies to Extra or XO. Some shippers market their older cognacs with these designations, others use such proprietary names as Cordon Bleu, Triomphe, Très Vénérable, and Paradis. Anyone who has occasion to compare some of the more expensive cognacs—at a well-stocked bar, for example—will discover not only that they are noticeably older and finer than the VSOPs, but that each shipper has developed an individual style that brandy connoisseurs can distinguish and appreciate.

Finally, a word about Napoléon cognacs that supposedly date from the days of the emperor. Even if you came across an authentic bottle dated, say, 1812, you would have no way of knowing how long the brandy had spent in wood. If the cognac had been bottled in 1813, it would simply be a one-year-old cognac, for once in bottle brandies no longer improve. As it happens, bottles of 1811 Napoléon Cognac regularly show up at London auctions. Some experts believe that they were bottled at the turn of the century, and they have the heavy, somewhat caramelized taste that was preferred at the time. No one really believes that they have anything to do with 1811 or with Napoléon.

Cognac is most often served in special brandy glasses, which are available in a variety of sizes. It is traditional to cup the bowl with your palm, so that the applied warmth releases the brandy's bouquet. For this reason very small and very big glasses are less comfortable than those with a bowl whose size is somewhere between that of a tangerine and an apple. Good cognac is noted for its complex and refined bouquet, and in fact brandy glasses are also known as snifters. A professional cognac taster actually relies more on his nose than on his palate when buying young cognacs or making a final blend, and if you pause a moment to inhale cognac before tasting it, you'll be surprised at how much this will tell you about its style and quality.

The best-known cognac firms, listed alphabetically, are:

Bisquit	Hine
Camus	Martell
Courvoisier	Otard
Delamain	Polignac
Denis-Mounité	Prunier
Gaston de Lagrange	Rémy Martin
Hennessy	Salignac

Smaller firms and estates whose cognacs may also be found here include Pierre Ferrand, Château de Fontpinot, A. de Fussigny, and Marcel Ragnaud.

Cognac may be the most famous of all brandies, but there are quite a few others that serve admirably to round out a meal. After cognac, the best-known of all French brandies is Armagnac, which is somewhat richer and fuller in taste than cognac. If it lacks the finesse and distinction of cognac at its very best, Armagnac nevertheless offers good value for those who enjoy its more direct taste: Armagnac of a given age is likely to be less expensive than a cognac of equal age.

Armagnac is produced in the region of Gascony, in a delimited area situated within a triangle formed by

Bordeaux, Toulouse, and Biarritz. First made in the fifteenth century, it predates cognac by nearly two hundred years. But unlike the Cognac region, which is about 120 miles to the north, the Armagnac region is a relatively inaccessible place, which is one reason that its brandy is still unfamiliar to many consumers. Almost all of the fifty thousand acres of vineyards whose wines can be distilled into Armagnac are situated in the two districts of Bas-Armagnac and Tenarèze. The former is considered the best source of fine brandies, and its name sometimes appears on a label. A third district, Haut-Armagnac, is less well thought of, but virtually no Armagnac is currently produced there.

A number of grape varieties, including Ugni Blanc, Folle Blanche, Colombard, and Baco 22A, a French-American hybrid, are planted in the Armagnac region. As in Cognac, the wine is thin, acid, and low in alcohol. The traditional difference between the two brandies has been in the way each is distilled. In Armagnac, wine is transformed into brandy by a continuous still—the wine goes in at one end, the colorless brandy trickles out at the other at 104 to 112 proof. (Cognac is twice-distilled and emerges at 140 proof.) The higher the proof, the fewer flavoring elements, known as congeners, are found in the distillate. That's why Armagnac has more flavor than cognac, which is, in turn, characterized by more finesse.

Not so many years ago, many small farmers in this region had barrels of old Armagnac aging in their cellars or behind the barn. These farmers are able to produce brandy, despite their lack of facilities, because it was the custom for portable stills to be transported throughout the region from November through the following April, transforming wine into Armagnac. These portable stills, which resemble small locomotives, are less frequently seen today, and about a quarter of the region's production now comes from cooperative cellars.

To accommodate certain European Community requirements, new regulations were introduced in 1972 that permit Armagnac producers to distill as high as 144 proof. Those regulations also permit the use of the traditional cognac pot still to produce Armagnac, and a few firms, notably Janneau and Samalens, now use both the continuous still and the pot still. The advantage of the pot still is that it produces a lighter and more refined brandy that matures more quickly in wood and is therefore useful for less expensive blends of younger Armagnacs.

Armagnac is aged in barrels made of the local Monlezun oak and, increasingly, in Limousin and Tronçais oak as well. Like cognac, Armagnac shipped to this country must be aged a minimum of two years. Those labeled VO, VSOP, or Réserve must be aged no less than four years; and five years in oak is the minimum for Armagnacs labeled Napoléon, Extra, Hors d'Age, or Vieille Réserve.

Armagnac producers have one important advantage over Cognac producers—they are permitted to market vintage-dated brandies. This privilege has often been abused in the past, and it's a rare restaurant in France that does not have a bottle of "1893" Armagnac for sale. Nevertheless, authentic examples of vintage-dated Armagnacs do exist, and are worth seeking out.

Many Armagnacs are marketed in the distinctive, flat-sided *basquaise* bottle. Well-known names include Marquis de Caussade, Marquis de Montesquiou, Samalens, Janneau, Sempé, Larressingle, Clès des Ducs, de Montal, and Loubère.

A brandy that provokes strong feelings pro and con is marc (pronounced *mar*). Called pomace in America, marc is the residue of skins, pits, and stalks from which wine has been pressed out. Water is added to the marc, which still contains enough sugar so that fermentation takes place, and the low-alcohol result is then distilled to produce a very pungent and distinctive brandy. The best-known marc is Marc de Bourgogne, although the brandy is also produced in Champagne, the Rhône Valley, and Alsace, where an unusual Marc de Gewürztraminer is made. Marc, which has a strawlike bouquet and somewhat leathery taste, is occasionally made from pressings of an individual vineyard and so labeled, such as Marc de Chambertin.

Brandies from France, labeled simply French Brandy, are widely available here, but they are the cheapest and least interesting group of all. All French brandy is purchased by the shippers from the French government, which distills a certain amount of cheap wine each year. Despite this anonymity of origin, many French brandy labels bear such designations as Napoléon, VSOP, Ten Star, and Grande Réserve, none of which has any legal meaning at all. In fact, several of the brands available here are shipped in bulk and bottled in this country.

Spanish brandies, noted for their fullness rather than their finesse, are sweet compared to the brandies of France, and this mellowness must certainly contribute to their popularity here. Most Spanish brandies are distilled from the wines of La Mancha, which are made primarily from the unfamiliar, but productive, Airén grape. The best-known brandies are then aged, blended, and bottled in Jerez, because a number of sherry firms are important brandy producers as well. These brandies are matured in used sherry casks made of American oak, and their aging is based on the solera system of fractional blending, by which younger brandies are added to older ones. A new appellation, Brandy de Jerez, has been established, and it encompasses three categories—Solera (which must be aged a minimum of six months), Reserva (one year), and Gran Reserva (three years). Fundador of Pedro Domecq and Soberano of Gonzalez Byass are two of the most popular Spanish brandies; premium brandies include Carlos I, Lepanto, Cardenal Mendoza, Gran Garvey, Terry Primero, Conde de Osborne, and Gran Duque de Alba.

Italy, which produces a number of wood-aged brandies modeled on cognac—including Stock "84" and Vecchia Romagna of Buton—has also established a particular reputation for grappa, made from the residue of skins and pits that is left after the wines have been pressed out. Unlike the French marc, however, grappa is not aged in wood and is bottled as a clear, pungent distillate. In recent years, a number of top wine producers have been marketing grappas made from specific appelations, such as Barbaresco, Barolo, Verdicchio, and Gavi; from individual grape varieties, including Nebbiolo, Brunello, Barbera, Moscato, and Picolit; and even from single vineyards. Some of these grappas are sold in specially designed bottles, and several of these unusual brandies have become fashionable and expensive.

Asbach Uralt is the best-seller here among German

imports; it is a dry, delicate, and attractive brandy in the French style.

The United States produces two-thirds of the brandy consumed in this country, and virtually all of it comes from California. California brandies are very slightly sweetened, but they also have a distinctive, spicy, wood-fruit flavor that gives them a complexity of taste lacking in brandies that are merely sweet. California brandy is made primarily from raisin and table grapes, and the wines are distilled at 160 to 170 proof, producing a brandy that is relatively light, clean, and fairly neutral and does not require much aging. California brandies are inexpensive, and many of them are appealing, but they are often marketed as an alternative to whiskey and other traditional spirits in mixed drinks and highballs, rather than as a brandy to be drunk from a snifter. The E&J label of Gallo accounts for about half the California brandy made; other brands include the Christian Brothers, Korbel, Paul Masson, and Coronet. Two small California firms with ties to the Cognac region of France produce limited amounts of pot-still brandy: RMS Special Reserve is the label used by the Carneros Alambic Distillery, owned by the Heriard-Dubreuil family, directors of Rémy Martin; Germain-Robin brandy is made by Hubert Germain-Robin, of Cognac, and Ainsley Cole, Jr., at a distillery in Mendocino.

There are also a few well-known brandies that are made from fruits other than grapes. The most unusual, often the most expensive, and to some palates the finest of all brandies are those distilled from wild fruits in Alsace, Switzerland, and the Black Forest of Germany. *Kirsch* (wild cherry), *framboise* (wild raspberry), *mirabelle* (yellow plum), *quetsch* (purple plum), and *poire* (pear) are the best known, and because they are colorless, they are known generically as *alcools blancs,* or white alcohols. Actually, all distillates are colorless when they come from the still, but most are aged in wood and are pale brown when bottled. (Vodka and gin are obvious exceptions.)

The *alcools blancs* are made in a special way. In the case of pears, cherries, and plums, clean, ripe fruit is crushed and allowed to ferment. The mash, called *marmalade,* is then distilled. Berries have too little sugar to ferment easily, so they are macerated for a month in high-proof alcohol distilled from wine, and that alcohol is then redistilled. Whatever process is used, the result is a colorless distillate that concentrates the essence of the fruit. A great deal of fruit is needed to produce a bottle of brandy—25 to 35 pounds of Williams pears for a bottle of *poire*, up to 30 pounds of raspberries for a bottle of *framboise*—which is one reason these brandies are so expensive.

Although the labels of most fruit brandies sold here state that the brandy "is a finished product when it leaves the still and does not require mellowing in oak to perfect quality," the fact is that many fruit brandies are aged for two or three years, sometimes even longer. The aging takes place in glass demijohns or, increasingly, in glass-lined tanks so that the brandies do not acquire any color. The bouquet develops finesse through subtle oxidation without taking on color. It is the delicate and fragrant bouquet of these white alcohols, each reminiscent of the original fruit in its ripe and undistilled state, that makes the best of these brandies so remarkable and so different from grape brandies.

Fruit brandies are distilled at about 140 proof and sold at about 90 proof: for all their haunting bouquet they are by no means bland. These *alcools blancs*, which are completely dry, bear no relation to various fruit-flavored brandies, such as blackberry brandy or apricot brandy, which are made in an entirely different way, appropriately colored, and quite sweet.

Dry, colorless fruit brandies similar to those produced in Alsace and Switzerland are now made in the United States from such fruits as pears, raspberries, and cherries; the best-known producers are St. George Spirits, in California, and Clear Creek Distillery, in Oregon.

Another famous fruit brandy is Calvados, made from apples in France's Normandy region. The name dates back, indirectly, to 1588 and the Spanish Armada, one of whose ships, *El Calvador*, ran aground on the Normandy coast. An area along the coast became known by a corruption of that name, Calvados, and in the nineteenth century the name also began to be used for the apple brandy that had been distilled in the Normandy region since the sixteenth century.

The apple harvest takes place in the last three months of the year. The appellation laws recognize over a hundred varieties of apples as acceptable for Calvados, although about a dozen—none of them eating apples—account for most of the total harvested. The apples are grated, crushed, and pressed; the resulting juice is then left to ferment for at least a month. Cider for distillation usually contains about 5 or 6 percent alcohol—it is dry, high in acid, cloudy, and disagreeable to drink. The fermented cider is then distilled and emerges colorless from the still at 140 proof (70 percent alcohol).

There are two methods of distillation permitted in the eleven Normandy districts that produce Calvados. In ten of them, the brandy is produced in a continuous still and is usually labeled simply *Appellation Réglementée,* without the name of the specific district from which it comes, such as Contentin, l'Avranchin, Domfrontais, Pays de la Risle, and so on. Calvados from the Pays d'Auge district, a delimited area south of Deauville and Honfleur, between Rouen and Caen, is twice distilled in a traditional pot still similar to that used in the Cognac region. It is the only Calvados district entitled to *Appellation Contrôlée* status, and Appellation Pays d'Auge Contrôlée will always appear on the label.

Calvados from the Pays d'Auge—which accounts for only 25 percent of all Calvados, but for most of what is shipped to the United States—is considered the finest apple brandy, partly because of the way it is distilled, partly because of the soil and the particular mix of apples grown there. A well-made Calvados from outside the Pays d'Auge district may be more appley when young, and quite appealing, but a Pays d'Auge, even when young, already displays more richness and depth. As the brandies age in cask, the Pays d'Auge will acquire more complexity and length of flavor than one from outside the district, which will almost always remain relatively simple.

As is the case for cognac and Armagnac, there are minimum age requirements for Calvados, and these are reflected in the rather extensive list of letters and phrases that may appear on labels. Any Calvados shipped here must be aged at least two years in barrel; those labeled Vieux or Réserve must be aged a minimum of three years; VO or Vieille Réserve, four years; VSOP, five years; and Extra, Napoléon, Hors d'Age, and Age Inconnu, six years. In practice some firms use one or more of these designations for their different bottlings, others use none, preferring such undefined terms as *fine, grand fine,* Prestige and so on.

Leading Calvados producers whose brandy can be found here are Boulard and Busnel; other labels include those of Bizouard, Ducs de Normandie, La Pommeraie, Montgommery, and Père Magloire.

THE ENJOYMENT OF WINE

STARTING A CELLAR

In the English translation of a French guide to wine, the 1945 Bordeaux vintage is described as "exceptionally great ... full and round ... wines to lay down with." Not all of us are prepared to look after our wines quite so conscientiously, but anyone who enjoys wine recognizes the advantages of setting aside at least some storage space in an apartment or a house.

Among the reasons for maintaining a cellar, even if it consists of only half a dozen bottles, are that you needn't make a trip to the store whenever you want a glass of wine, and you are spared the awkwardness of running out of wine halfway through a meal with guests. Then there's the chance to save money: if you have storage space you can take advantage of wine sales, and you can also benefit from the discount offered by many stores when you buy a full case of twelve bottles. If you have a larger collection you can easily arrange an interesting comparison when friends stop by—two different California Zinfandels, the wines of two adjoining vineyards in Bordeaux, or two vintages from the same producer. Also, fine red wines that have thrown a deposit may need a few days' rest if they have been badly shaken up.

If such bottles are already resting in your cellar, you'll be sure of getting the most they have to offer. Finally, don't underestimate the real pleasure of being able to choose a wine from your own collection—red, white, or rosé—that suits your dinner and your mood.

The wine cellar itself can be as simple as a whiskey carton turned on its side, and the guides to maintaining a store of wines are simple and logical. The first rule, of course, is to lay a wine bottle on its side, so that the cork is kept moist and expanded, preventing air from entering the bottle. Ideally, wines should be kept at a constant cool temperature, away from daylight and vibrations. To keep wines in a home or apartment, you should remember that evenness of temperature is at least as important as the temperature itself, within limitations, because constant fluctuations of heat and cold will hasten a wine's evolution and eventual decline. Therefore, keep wines away from boiler rooms, steam pipes, or kitchen ovens. Don't store wines in a place where they will be subject to a lot of knocking about, such as the closet where the brooms and vacuum cleaner are kept. And keep wines away from direct exposure to sunlight, which seems to decompose them in a short time (whether in your house or in a retailer's window). If the temperature of your storage area stays much above 70°, you should limit yourself to no more than a year's supply of wines or, in the case of sturdy reds, two years. With these general rules in mind, you should be able to figure out a good place to store a few bottles.

If you intend to put aside good bottles for more than two years, your storage space must be temperature-controlled and maintained at a steady 55° to 60°. An air-cooled closet, an air-conditioned basement or storage room, a prefabricated walk-in cellar, or, in some cities, public warehousing are some possibilities. Another is to purchase one of the refrigerated units that function as a self-contained cellar. These wine vaults, which can accommodate anywhere from a few dozen up to several hundred bottles, are fairly expensive, but they are useful to store the finest bottles in a collection—those you expect to keep for several years. If the initial cost of an ideal cellar seems expensive, you may be able to get two or three wine-minded friends to share the expenses and the space.

Wine racks are available from most department stores and, in many states, from liquor stores. Many of these racks are designed to be stacked, and those are the ones you should look for, so that you can expand the capacity of your cellar. Never store fine red wines in racks in which the bottles lie at a downward angle, neck lowest. The cork will be kept moistened, but any sediment present in such wines will slide toward the cork and may adhere to it. You will thus drink cloudy wine from your first glass. It's also a good idea to store wine bottles with their labels facing up. This makes it easier to locate any bottle without having to twist it around, and, in the case of red wines with sediment, you'll know that the deposit always lies along the side opposite the label.

As you determine the wines you like most, you will want to increase the size of your collection. Before buying a substantial amount of wine, however, you should adopt a buying strategy that conforms to the way you actually consume wine. This means noting, for example, the ratio of fine wines to moderately priced ones; whether you serve more red or white wine; whether you usually serve a wine before dinner; and whether you tend to have larger dinner parties, at which many bottles of one or two wines are served, or small wine dinners, at which one bottle each of several wines are compared.

There are sound reasons for buying wines to be consumed in the future. Certain wines, such as red Bordeaux and vintage port, are usually least expensive when they first appear on the market, and then gradually increase in price. Other wines, such as Burgundies, the best of California, and a number of fine Italian wines, are often produced in such limited quantities that they disappear from retail shelves within a few months or a year. Those who purchase such wines early will have the satisfaction of knowing that their cellars include bottles that have become much more expensive or that are virtually unobtainable.

A certain amount is written about wine as a financial investment. To begin with, only long-lived wines with established reputations are appropriate for this purpose, which limits your purchases to the finest red wines in the best vintages. Such wines will almost certainly increase in value over the years, but whether that appreciation will be greater than what can be achieved by investing your capital in other ways is not certain. Furthermore, it's illegal for a consumer to resell wine without the necessary licenses, which most people find complicated and impractical to obtain. And even if you can find a retailer willing to buy your wines, you will not get the current market price, since he must allow for his profit margin. Another way to resell your wines is at one of the wine auctions that occasionally take place in this country, but you will have to ship your wines to the site of the auction. Unless you are prepared to follow the wine market carefully, however, it may be wiser to think of your wine purchases as an investment in future pleasure, rather than as a way of making a profit.

Buying and drinking wine is easy. The one onerous task connected with a varied collection of wines is to maintain an inventory. Even a collection of only twenty randomly chosen bottles almost always includes four or five that are past their prime. A cellar full of wine will invariably include quite a few that should be drunk up, and without an inventory they are likely to be forgotten for months at a time. Also, if you keep a record of your wines, you are less likely to overlook special bottles when the appropriate occasion arises; you'll be able to match specific bottles with the guests who'll enjoy them most; and you can more easily plan a wine evening at which a number of carefully chosen bottles will be served.

An inventory can be kept in a notebook, on cards, or even on a home computer. One simple method is to ask for legible invoices whenever you buy wines, make photocopies of the invoices so they are all on a standard page size, and keep the sheets together as a "cellar book" in which you can make appropriate comments in the margins as you consume the wines.

SERVING WINES

Serving wine—or more specifically, drinking wine—is certainly not very complicated and can be briefly summarized: chill white wines and rosés; serve red wines at cool room temperature; use large, stemmed glasses that are slightly curved in at the top, and fill them only half-way. This covers the subject in a general way and gets you started as a wine drinker. There is so much conversation and snobbism about the proper way to drink wines, however, that it might be useful to describe the various steps in serving a wine. What follows is not meant to discourage anyone by its attention to detail, but rather to suggest, for reference, the most logical way to get a wine from the cellar into your glass. The degree of special efforts to be made will depend on the wine and the occasion: a sandwich doesn't require special presentation, nor is an elaborately prepared dish shown to best advantage on paper plates.

Temperature

Red wines are supposed to be served at room temperature, which is to say, not at the cooler temperature of the ideal cellar. Because few of us have real cellars, the bottle has presumably been lying in a closet or in a rack along the wall, so the wine is already at room temperature. Remember that the concept of serving wines at room temperature originated before the days of central heating. Actually, red wines often taste dull, flat, and alcoholic if served too warm, much above 70°, say, no matter what the temperature of the room is. In the summer, it's advisable to cool down a light red wine (Beaujolais, California Pinot Noirs, Valpolicella) by putting it in the refrigerator for an hour or so. This will give the wine an agreeable freshness and actually seems to improve its flavor. A complex red wine, however, should never be chilled; the wine will be numbed and the puckerish taste of tannin will become more pronounced.

Since almost all whites and rosés are less complex than most reds, their basic appeal has more to do with their refreshing qualities than with nuances of taste and texture. Such wines are more enjoyable and thirst-quenching when properly chilled, just as water, juice, and soft drinks are considered more appealing served cold or cool than at room temperature. Two or three hours in the refrigerator will do the job. If you want to chill a bottle of white wine or rosé on short notice, or need a second bottle to serve with a dinner in progress, empty one or two ice trays into a tall container, fill it with water, and put in the bottle. It should be cool in fifteen or twenty minutes. The trouble with most wine coolers and ice buckets is that they are too shallow and chill only half the bottle. Chilling a wine in ice and water is actually quicker than putting the bottle in the freezer; and if you forget about a bottle in the freezer, it may be frozen by the time you remember to take it out. The colder a wine is, the harder it is to taste, and some people use the trick of overchilling a bottle of poor white wine to mask its defects. For the same reason, a bottle of fine white wine should not be chilled too much, or you will deaden the qualities for which you have paid.

Corkscrews

A corkscrew is really the only piece of equipment that a wine drinker needs, and as it will last for years, it pays to look for a good one. In the first place, the screw part, called the bore, should be at least two inches long. Because good wines are long-lived, they are bottled with long, strong corks, and a poor corkscrew will often break the cork of an expensive bottle of wine. Second, the bore should be in the form of a true coil, not a wiggly line. A coil will get a real grip even on an old cork, whereas a wiggly line will just bore a hole in it. Finally, get a corkscrew that gives you leverage. A simple T-shaped corkscrew, even with an excellent bore, requires too much tugging, and you will find yourself gripping the bottle between your feet or your knees, which can lead to messy accidents.

To open a bottle of wine, first remove the capsule that covers the cork and part of the neck. Because the capsule may impart an unpleasant taste, cut it off well below the lip of the bottle, so that the wine will not be in contact with the capsule when it is poured. (Note that since the beginning of 1992, capsules may no longer be made of lead foil; most capsules today are made of tin, plastic, or aluminum and plastic polylaminates.) Wipe off the top of the cork and insert the corkscrew into the center of the cork. Remember to pull the cork gently, because if you give it a sharp tug, the vacuum that is

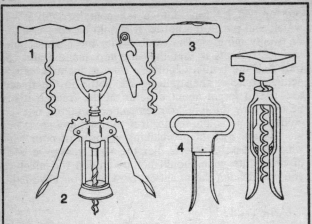

CORKSCREWS

A good corkscrew should have a bore at least two inches long with smooth edges, so that it can completely penetrate a long cork without crumbling it. The bore should also be in the form of a real coil, rather than having an awllike solid core: a corkscrew must be able to grip an old cork, not drill a hole in it. The simplest corkscrew (1) may require some awkward tugging; a corkscrew with leverage (such as 2) is more convenient. This model is popular, easy to use, and usually effective, but note that it does not have a true coil, nor is the bore long enough to penetrate long corks. The folding corkscrew (3), which usually has a long bore in the form of a true coil, is favored by waiters because it can be carried in a pocket, has a knife with which to cut the capsule, and has good leverage. The two prongs of this popular corkpuller (4) are inserted between the cork and the neck of the bottle, and the cork is then twisted out. The very effective Screwpull (5) has a long bore in the form of a true coil that is coated with an antifriction substance for easy insertion. As the handle is twisted continuously in one direction, the cork climbs the bore without having to be pulled out.

momentarily created between the wine and the rising cork may cause some wine to splash out of the bottle.

If you break the cork—and this occasionally happens even with a bottle of sound wine—reinsert the corkscrew at an angle to get a grip on the remaining piece. If the cork crumbles, you can simply strain the wine into another container, or directly into wine glasses, through a clean tea strainer.

Incidentally, you should never wrap a wine bottle in a napkin: it's considered bad manners not to let your guests see what is being poured into their glasses. If you're worried that a few drops of wine may spill onto the tablecloth, you can tie a small napkin around the neck of the bottle.

Breathing

Most wine drinkers believe that red wine should be uncorked half an hour or an hour before it is to be served because this exposure to air, called breathing, will develop the wine's bouquet and soften the tannic harshness of a young wine. A number of enologists have tested this theory and feel that the surface of wine exposed to air in the neck of the bottle is too small to have any effect on the taste of the wine, even after several hours. It seems reasonable to assume that if exposure to air is beneficial to a red wine, a more effective way of letting a wine breathe would be either to pour it into a carafe or to pour it into large glasses fifteen or twenty minutes before starting to drink it. Many people assume that letting a wine breathe is synonymous with uncorking it, but there are obviously more efficient ways to achieve whatever improvements aeration may accomplish.

As to the concept of letting wines breathe, there are a number of professional wine people who believe that unnecessary exposure to air actually diminishes the quality of a wine. Older wines, which are often fragile, will fade in the decanter; younger wines will lose some of their intensity and definition without achieving any improvement in bouquet or flavor. Occasionally you may come across a wine, either red or white, that has an off-odor, and this may be dissipated by swirling the wine in your glass for a few moments. Also, wines that have experienced several years of bottle age may require a few minutes in the glass for their bouquet and flavor to show themselves. Extended exposure to air, however, may well be an error. One exception to the view that wines should simply be opened and poured is in the case of older red wines that have thrown a deposit. Such wines should always be decanted (as described below) so that the sediment does not spoil one's enjoyment of the wine, but the decanting should take place just before the wine is to be served, which is usually not the same thing as decanting before the start of the meal.

The observation that wines are not improved by being allowed to breathe is a controversial one, but it's one that you can easily test for yourself. Next time you plan to serve two bottles of the same red wine, whether it be a young, vigorous one or an older, mature one, simply decant one bottle an hour ahead of time, and then compare a glass of that wine with one from a bottle that has just been opened. After a few experiments of your own, you can decide whether or not you prefer the taste of wines that have been allowed to breathe.

Decanting

Decanting red wines may seem complicated or affected, but it's very simple and very useful. The sediment that red wines develop after ten years or so, although harmless, has a bitter taste and is also distracting when it appears in the last two or three glasses that are poured. Decanting a wine, which simply involves transferring it from its original bottle to another container, permits you to serve a wine that is completely brilliant and unclouded to the very end, and at the sacrifice of only an ounce or two of wine. First, you must stand the bottle up for half an hour or so to allow all the sediment to fall to the bottom. Your decanter can be any clean container, whether it's a crystal wine decanter, an inexpensive carafe, or a glass pitcher. Hold the decanter firmly (remember, it will soon contain a full bottle of wine) and transfer the wine slowly in one continuous motion—otherwise the sediment will wash back and forth. Traditionally, the shoulder of the wine bottle is held over a candle, so that you can see when the sediment begins to approach the neck of the bottle and can stop pouring at that moment. Because we now have electricity and because the heat of a candle is not going to do an old wine any good, you may find it easier to use a flashlight standing on end.

If you are worried about decanting an expensive bottle of wine, decant the very next wine you drink, whatever it is, just to get the hang of it. Decanting is really the only way to get your money's worth out of older wines, when you can afford them. A decanter of wine on a dining table is also a most attractive and appropriate sight and enhances the enjoyment of wine. If you're concerned that a good wine will go unnoticed because it's unlabeled, you should know that it's customary to put the empty bottle alongside the decanter, so that your guests will know what they're drinking.

There is one other point about decanting, which may seem finicky, but remember, you've got an old, expensive bottle, and you want to get the most out of it. Because these bottles don't come our way very often, the decanter may be musty or have an off-odor from whatever was in it last. Therefore, you might first pour a few drops of wine into the decanter, swirl, and pour it out. This will not only remove any odor that may be in the decanter, but will give the decanter the bouquet of the wine that's about to go into it.

Wineglasses

Wineglasses have been discussed earlier, in the chapter on tasting, but to summarize: use a stemmed, clear glass with a bowl that is slightly tapered at the top to retain the wine's bouquet, and with a capacity of at least eight ounces. Small glasses seem stingy and don't permit a wine to be swirled to release its bouquet. Glasses with tall stems and colored bowls are sometimes recommended for German wines, but they only hide the delicate golden colors of a fine Moselle or Rhine wine. These glasses originated when winemaking techniques had not been perfected, and a bottled wine was apt to turn cloudy. Colored bowls hid this defect.

Almost every major wine region has its traditional

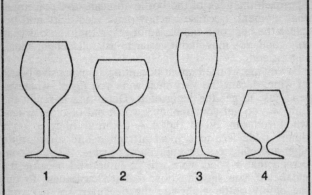

WINEGLASSES

The ten-ounce all-purpose wineglass (1) can be used for all table wines, as well as for sherry and port, if need be. It should be filled only about halfway, so that the wine can be swirled to release its bouquet. The first glass is in the traditional Bordeaux shape; the second all-purpose glass (2) is in the traditional Burgundy shape. The classic champagne glass (3) displays bubbles more attractively and releases them more slowly than does the familiar wide-bottomed saucer-shaped glass. The traditional brandy glass (4) may vary in total capacity from about six to twelve ounces: a much smaller or much bigger glass is difficult to cup in one's hand, as is done to release the brandy's bouquet.

glass, just as it has its traditional bottle, but it is completely unnecessary to have different glasses to serve and enjoy wine properly. When two or more wines are served at a meal, it does dress up the table to use differently shaped glasses, but even here an all-purpose wineglass is perfectly acceptable. If you do use glasses of two different sizes, the smaller one is traditionally used for white wines, the larger for reds. If you serve two reds, the better wine should be poured into the bigger glass.

Leftover Wine

As a general rule, expensive red wines will not keep a second day, and you had better plan to drink them when opened. Their flavor tends to become somewhat dulled and indistinct, at best, and may taste rather sharp and vinegary at worst. Almost all white wines can usually be kept in the refrigerator for several days and are only slightly the worse for wear. Inexpensive red and white wines, especially those from California, will keep much better, perhaps because they are less complex to begin with. It doesn't hurt to keep even red wines, once opened, in the refrigerator, just as you would milk or any other perishable product.

The most useful point to remember about leftover wine is to cork it up as soon as possible. It is excessive exposure to air that spoils a wine, and it doesn't help a half-empty bottle to be left open an extra hour or two.

When you put the cork back into a bottle for any reason, remember not to put the top, which is usually dirty, in contact with the wine. If the bottom of the cork has expanded, once pulled, and cannot be easily replaced, the simplest solution is to slice a quarter inch off the top and then reverse it.

If you do find yourself with leftover wine that has lost some of its flavor but is still drinkable, there are several ways it can be used. You can use red wine to make *sangría,* a cold wine punch, by adding sugar or sugar syrup (which disguises the tartness of leftover or inexpensive wine), a couple of slices of lemon and orange, and ice cubes. When you pour out the *sangría,* add a splash of club soda to give it zest. You can use white wine to make a spritzer by adding club soda—it's a refreshing aperitif. And finally you can make your own wine vinegar. Although wine that's been left out for a while will be attacked by the vinegar bacteria and will soon taste sour, it will not actually turn to vinegar by itself. You must add a quantity of good vinegar to the leftover wine to start the process properly.

The amount of wine needed for a dinner will naturally vary depending on the occasion, the menu, and the extent to which each of your guests enjoys wines. Even assuming that we are talking about people who normally drink wine with their meals, the amount of wine you should serve seems to increase in an almost geometrical proportion to the number of people present. Two people having a light supper may be happy to share a half-bottle. Four people can easily drink two bottles, and six people at a leisurely dinner might consume four bottles without any signs of overindulgence, especially if more than one kind of wine is served. The simplest approach is to have on hand—unopened—an extra bottle or two of whichever wine you're serving.

WINE AND FOOD

The question of which wine to serve with which food is one that seems to intimidate many people. Some respond by following charts that dictate the right wine for every dish. Others democratically maintain that any wine goes with any dish if it pleases you, an attitude that is perfectly acceptable if everyone shares your taste. The best approach to this subject is one that combines an experimental attitude with some understanding of the elements that create harmony between a dish and its accompanying wine.

The three basic tastes found in wine are acid, bitter, and sweet—with this in mind, it's easier to understand how the interaction between food and wine can diminish a wine or enhance it. To take a common example, the vinegar in a salad dressing will alter a wine's taste by suppressing its acidity. That is, the intense acidity of vinegar makes it difficult to taste the less intense acid that is actually present in a wine, and makes the wine taste flabby. When you realize why the wine's taste is altered, you can see that substituting lemon juice for vinegar in the dressing does not solve the problem. The simplest solution is not to drink wine while eating salad (which is why serving salad and cheese together is unwise if you plan to serve an interesting wine as well), but if the main course is a salad or a dish that features a vinegar-based sauce, then you should choose a wine with high acidity, such as a Sancerre, or a pungent California Sauvignon Blanc.

An example of the way a dish can enhance a wine occurs whenever meat, poultry, or cheese accompanies a young, tannic red wine. Just as the protein in milk combines with, and diminishes, the tannin present in strong tea, so the protein in many foods diminishes the tannic harshness of, say, a young red Bordeaux or California Cabernet Sauvignon, and makes the wine taste softer and more attractive than if it were drunk without food.

Different foods alter the taste and texture of wine in different ways. Anything oily, such as mayonnaise, will emphasize a wine's acidity; a rich cream sauce is likely to rob a wine of some of its body and may make a light-bodied wine taste thin, as will fatty dishes, such as pâté; egg yolks, which appear in such popular brunch dishes as eggs Benedict, will dull the taste of any wine; dry wines drunk with sweetened sauces—as in *canard à l'orange*, for example—will taste thin and sharp; and foods prepared with mustard or peppercorns will overwhelm delicate wines. Chocolate tends to overwhelm wine, even the sweet white wines that sometimes accompany chocolate desserts. Spicy foods also overwhelm wine, and beer is a more appropriate accompaniment for curries and highly seasoned Oriental dishes. Generally speaking, red wines do not taste right with fish. The oiliness of most fish seems to give red wines a somewhat bitter and unpleasant taste, and the refreshing quality of a chilled white wine is much more enjoyable. It must be added, however, that a number of restaurateurs and gastronomes in France consider a light-bodied, chilled red wine such as Beaujolais to be a suitable accompaniment to many fish dishes.

Perhaps the most practical rule to follow in choosing

wines is, the richer the dish, the richer the wine. Just as there are differences in weight between skim milk and cream, and in texture between, say, poached fish and steak, so there are similar, if less obvious, differences between wines. Whether a wine is light and delicate or rich, robust, and chewy is an important consideration when trying to match it with a specific dish, as is its intensity of taste.

Very often, when choosing a wine to accompany a particular dish, the primary consideration is not the basic ingredient, but how it's prepared. Pasta, chicken, and veal, for example, can be prepared in ways so varied that the most appropriate wine can range from a light, crisp white to a robust red. A plain rack of lamb will show off a subdued, mature red; lamb Provençal, with tomatoes and garlic, is best accompanied by a younger, more vigorous red, just as the balanced Bordeaux or mature Cabernet that accompanies a grilled steak might be replaced by a flavorful Zinfandel if the meat is served with a peppercorn sauce.

Choosing wines to accompany specific dishes or meals means, therefore, focusing on a wine's taste, weight, and texture, rather than its place of origin. In any case, it's always more fun to experiment, guided by your own common sense, than to stick to a few safe but unimaginative rules.

The Sequence of Wine

So far we have been matching a dish with a wine, but for more elaborate dinners you may want to serve more than one wine. There is certainly nothing unusual or particularly fancy about serving two or three wines with a meal, and it can be more fun than serving two or three bottles of the same wine, especially when you have several enthusiastic wine drinkers at the dinner table. There are some traditional guidelines concerning the service of more than one wine: white before red, dry before sweet, young before old.

White before red simply conforms to the normal sequence of food, assuming you are having a light appetizer, or shellfish, or even a cooked fish dish, before a main dish of meat. Also, because red wines are usually richer and more complex than white wines, serving a dry white wine second would diminish its qualities by comparison. Dry before sweet is traditional because sweet foods dull our taste buds (and our appetite) for the more delicate foods to follow (which is why dessert is served last). This rule supersedes the previous one in that a sweet white wine such as Sauternes or a German Auslese is usually served at the end of the meal, and therefore after the red wine.

Young before old is a traditional rule in most wine regions, and indicates that similar wines are usually served in order of increasing age and interest, to avoid an anticlimax. For example, if you are serving two red Bordeaux or two California Cabernet Sauvignons, the older one, presumably more mature and distinguished, will be preceded and, so to speak, introduced by the younger wine. If you are not serving different vintages of the same or similar wines, however, you may find it more appropriate to serve the best wine of the evening with the main course. You can then continue with a completely different wine that need not be older and finer, but that should be interesting enough to follow the previous bottle.

Champagne is often suggested as the one wine (along with rosé, I suppose) that can be served throughout a meal. Although this is a generous gesture and will be greeted with enthusiasm, champagne does not complement all foods, especially full-flavored meats, and its taste may pall at the end of an evening. One alternative is to serve champagne as an aperitif before the meal and then with the first course as well. Another is to serve it with dessert, but in that case choose an Extra Dry or Demi-Sec rather than the drier Brut.

Cheese and wine are traditional partners, although a cheese course is not as common here as in Europe. Even restaurants of the highest caliber, for example, will rarely present a cheese tray that is adequate. At a dinner party, a cheese course, which precedes the dessert, gives the host or hostess the opportunity of serving a fine old wine. Although cheese is considered an ideal accompaniment to wine, many cheeses actually overwhelm mature and subtle wines. If you decide to bring out a good bottle at this point, select the cheeses carefully so that they enhance the flavor of a delicate wine. If you prefer rich, creamy cheeses, tangy goat cheeses, or strongly flavored blue cheeses, it may be best to choose a younger and more vigorous wine.

Sweet white wines such as Sauternes, Barsac, and German Auslese are not often served these days, but if they are, they usually accompany dessert. Actually, the sweetness of most desserts diminishes the richness and concentration of flavor that characterizes the best sweet white wines, thereby depriving you of the qualities that make these wines so distinctive. German winemakers, for example, prefer to serve Auslese and Beerenauslese wines by themselves, without food, and in Bordeaux most vineyard proprietors in Sauternes and Barsac prefer not to serve their wines with rich desserts. You might consider serving Sauternes, German Auslese wines, and late harvest Johannisberg Rieslings from California as an alternative to dessert, or perhaps with nothing richer than plain cake or ripe fruit. Because sweet wines are not consumed in large quantities, it's not inappropriate to open just a half-bottle for three or four people at the end of a meal.

Calories and Wine

A myth about wine that is of particular interest to diet-conscious consumers is that white wines have fewer calories than reds. This misconception may stem from the fact that most white wines are light, refreshing, and easy to drink, whereas many reds are sturdy, full-flavored, and have a tannic astringency that makes them, for some people, less appealing. Actually, the caloric content of a red or white wine is based on two of its components—alcohol and, if there is any, sugar. Each percent of alcohol in wine accounts for about 40 calories per standard 75-centiliter (25.4 ounce) bottle. Thus a bottle of dry wine with 12 percent alcohol contains about 500 calories. (Certain extracts found in all wines contribute another 30 to 45 calories a bottle.) The caloric difference between one dry wine and another depends on its alcohol, not its color—a delicate red Gamay with 11 percent alcohol would have about 120 calories fewer per bottle than a rich white Chardonnay with 14 percent alcohol. It would be a mistake, however, to try to calculate the exact caloric content of a wine from the alcohol percentage listed on its label because federal law permits that figure to vary by 1.5 percent either way as long as the actual alcohol content does not exceed 14 percent. (If it does, the label must show this.)

But even if the alcohol content is accurately stated, it's not the only element that contributes calories; the other is sugar. One percent of sugar adds about 30 calories to a bottle of wine, so a German Liebfraumilch or a California Chenin Blanc with 2.5 percent of sugar would each have about 75 calories a bottle from sugar alone. And since there are many more white wines that are semisweet than reds, the extra calories contributed by sugar are more often to be found in whites than in reds. It must be added, however, that a number of appealing, semidry whites are comparatively low in alcohol—10 or 11 percent is not uncommon.

What all this means is that a five-ounce serving of wine—whether a simple jug wine, a fine Bordeaux, a delicate Moselle, or a vintage-dated champagne—probably contains between 100 and 110 calories. (Dessert wines, of course, are significantly higher in calories. A fine Sauternes contains about 160 calories per five-ounce glass, vintage port, about 200, and cream sherry, 220 or more.)

Cooking with Wine

There is a product called Cooking Wine sold in food stores that are not licensed to sell wine. It contains an excessive amount of salt to render it unpalatable as a beverage, which, of course, makes it unattractive as an ingredient in a prepared dish. The term "cooking wine" is more often used to describe a cheap wine that can be used in recipes, but it's a mistake to imagine that you can cook with a wine that you wouldn't want to drink. Most of the alcohol in wine will evaporate during cooking, and what's left is its flavor. It's not necessary to use an expensive bottle of Chambertin to make a *boeuf bourguignon* or a *coq au vin,* but if you try to economize by using a poor wine, all of its defects will be concentrated in the sauce.

Furthermore, it is actually uneconomical to buy cheap wine for cooking. Say that an elaborate lobster dish calls for a spoonful or two of sherry to heighten its flavor. A cook who runs out to buy a bottle of cheap sherry will diminish the taste of an expensive and time-consuming dish with a quarter's worth of wine. What's more, because the wine is a poor example of its type, it may not be enjoyable to drink, so the spoonful of wine has, in fact, cost the full price of the bottle.

WINE IN RESTAURANTS

Most of the elements of service that apply in the home are equally valid in restaurants. There are some aspects of wine service, however, that are more relevant to restaurants, and these are reviewed here briefly. If you plan to have wine, ask for the wine list while you are looking at the menu; otherwise you may be subjected to a long wait between the time you order your meal and the moment when a wine list is finally put into your hands. Once you've ordered a wine, make sure that it is brought to the table and uncorked as soon as possible, to avoid the possibility of a forgetful waiter opening the bottle long after he has served the dish that the wine was meant to accompany. Getting wine brought to the table in time is particularly important if you plan to have a bottle of wine with the first course, which is often prepared ahead of time and brought to your table minutes after you've ordered it.

White wine should be chilled, of course, but not too cold. If a wine is placed in an ice bucket at the beginning of a meal, and then served with the main course, it may well be overchilled and have lost almost all its taste. Don't hesitate to take the bottle out of the cooler and stand it on the table. Also, note that many restaurants use ice buckets that are not deep enough for a bottle of wine, especially German or Alsatian wines. The easiest solution is to recork the bottle and then turn it upside down for a moment before the first glass is poured: this may look odd, but the alternative is to drink the first two or three glasses of white wine at room temperature.

When you've ordered a wine, the waiter or captain

should always show you the bottle before he opens it to make sure the wine is exactly the one you ordered, and of the vintage specified on the wine list (or at any rate, one acceptable to you). If it's a better-than-average wine that you've ordered, especially an older one, be sure that there is no more than the usual space between cork and wine: older wines sometimes develop too great an air space, and this may in turn affect the wine adversely. If you note too much ullage, as this is called, draw it to the waiter's attention to let him know that you'll be on your guard against an oxidized wine.

After opening the bottle, the waiter may show you the cork, or even hand it to you: the cork should be sound and the wet end should smell of wine, not of cork. You can give the cork a squeeze and a sniff if you want, but the wine in the glass is what's really important. The waiter will then pour some wine into the glass of whoever chose it, so that he or she can determine whether or not it is defective in any way. If you happen to be eating your first course when the red wine is poured, don't try to judge the wine against smoked salmon, tomato salad, creamed herring, vichyssoise, or whatever may be in your mouth. Take a piece of bread first, or else tell the waiter that you'll taste the wine a little later, at your convenience. If a wine is corky (that is, contaminated by a faulty cork with a distinctly moldy bouquet and taste) or spoiled (an oxidized white, a vinegary red), it should naturally be sent back. Some restaurants will do this more gracefully than others. Even the most accommodating restaurateurs will privately complain, however, that some of the wine that is sent back is perfectly sound—either the customer was trying to show off, or he had made an uninformed choice and mistakenly expected the wine to have a different taste. Remember that the reason you taste a wine in a restaurant is not to evaluate its quality, but simply to determine whether or not there is anything wrong with the bottle in front of you.

Wineglasses in restaurants are often too small, and those ubiquitous five- and six-ounce glasses are inappropriate not only because they don't permit a good wine to be swirled and sniffed, but also because using a small glass seems such a stingy way of drinking wine. The simplest solution is to ask for empty water goblets and fill them only a third. You can expect five or six glasses of wine from a bottle, depending on how generously the waiter pours. It's a pity to run out of wine halfway through a meal, and if a second bottle seems too much, an extra half-bottle might be the answer.

These general observations aside, the most important question is, Which wine to order? This will naturally depend on the kind of restaurant you're in, the food you plan to eat, and the variety and prices of the wines offered. Today, many people simply order a glass of the red or white house wine. This is likely to be an acceptable but neutral jug wine from California, Italy, or France. Since many restaurants now charge as much for a five-ounce glass of wine as for a cocktail, you may end up paying a rather high price for thirty or forty cents' worth of wine. If the house wine is available by the carafe, it's usually a better value, especially if the restaurant uses liter carafes, which hold thirty-three ounces.

An increasing number of restaurants now offer a choice of several wines by the glass, and many have installed a Cruvinet or similar machine, which replaces the wine drawn out of a bottle with inert gas, thus preventing the wine left in the bottle from oxidizing. This device permits a restaurant to offer fine red and white wines by the glass without having to worry that the remaining wine will spoil before the bottle is depleted.

There are now a great many restaurateurs around the country who take a particular pride in their wine lists, and a selection of a hundred or more wines is no longer as unusual as it was only a few years ago. Unfortunately, many wine lists are still inadequate. Far too many neglect to indicate the producer or shipper of a wine, or the vintage. This gives the restaurateur some flexibility in replacing a wine if his supplier runs out, but it also makes it difficult for his patrons to make an intelligent choice. Vintages do matter, if only to indicate the age and relative freshness of the many popular wines meant to be consumed young. And when you turn to the pages listing more expensive wines, vintages naturally matter a great deal with respect to both quality and value. One response to an incomplete wine list is to pick out two or three potentially interesting wines and ask the waiter to bring the bottles to your table. After you examine the labels for producer and vintage, you can choose one and send the others back.

Fortunately, many restaurateurs do list producer and vintage and are also committed to reprinting or rewriting their wine lists at frequent intervals. Others, with smaller budgets, have adopted the sensible policy of using well-designed typewritten or computer-generated lists that are easy to read, contain the relevant information about each wine, and are easily updated. These lists are a welcome change from the cumbersome leather-bound books that, as often as not, offer a limited choice.

When looking over a list, remember that the least expensive wine is often a poor value, since its price is based not on its cost but on what the restaurateur feels is the minimum he or she should charge for a bottle of wine. Usually, if you spend two or three dollars more, you are likely to get a wine whose price more accurately reflects its value.

Just as it is usually a bad idea to order the least expensive wines, so should you avoid the most expensive red wines, whatever your budget. Even if, for example, fine red Bordeaux châteaux are listed, they are likely to be of recent vintages and therefore too young to drink. It's a waste to pay what is inevitably a great deal of money for glamorous wines that are not yet showing the qualities for which they are famous. As for ordering older fine red wines that are mature, if you can find them, remember that they are likely to contain sediment, so you must make sure that the waiter or captain is knowledgeable about old wines and is prepared to decant the wine carefully for you.

Looking through a wine list can often be a frustrating experience, and there are times when you find yourself not so much making a choice as resigning yourself to ordering the least objectionable wine. Nevertheless, varied and fairly priced wine lists are now much more common than they were, and there are a growing number of restaurants throughout the country that are even better known for their wine cellars than for their kitchens.

VINTAGES

For some reason, many people who are relatively unfamiliar with wines are nevertheless unduly concerned about vintages. Some pontificate about what they imagine to be the best vintage years, others simply become uneasy about whether or not a particular wine represents a good year. It seems to me that a wine's vintage is almost always the last fact to consider when deciding what to drink with dinner: the primary consideration should be the kind of wine that you would like. Often enough, its vintage will turn out to be of little importance. After all, more than three-quarters of all the wine produced in the world is meant to be consumed within a year of the harvest, and a great deal of what we drink is at its best within two years. Since the chief attribute of many wines is their freshness, the vintage date is often more useful as an indication of the wine's age than of its quality.

The importance given to vintages is of relatively recent origin. For centuries new wines were poured into goblets directly from the barrel. If bottles were used as an intermediate step, they were loosely stoppered up with oil-soaked rags or a wooden peg. In the eighteenth century, when an effective cork made of bark first became generally available, it was discovered that port improved with a certain amount of bottle age. In consequence, the port bottle evolved during the eighteenth century from a squat shape to the kind of bottle that we see today. What emerged was the binnable bottle—a bottle that could be stored on its side, thus keeping the cork wet and expanded, and preventing air from entering the bottle and spoiling the wine. It is possible that the first Bordeaux to be bottled and stored away was Lafite 1784, and a few bottles of 1797 are still displayed today at the château. The effects of bottle age became so greatly admired that in the second half of the nineteenth century red Bordeaux was vinified in such a way as to retain its qualities for forty or fifty years, and these wines were rarely drunk before they were fifteen or twenty years old.

The concept of vintage year or a vintage wine is often misunderstood. A vintage, or harvest, occurs every year in all of the world's vineyards. Consequently, every year is a vintage year, although some are better than others. Now, in the case of port and champagne, it is traditional to blend together the wines of several years. When an exceptionally good growing season results in better-than-average wines, however, the producers may decide to bottle part of that crop without blending in wine from other years, and the resulting wine bears on its label the year in which the grapes were harvested. In all other wine-producing regions, however, the words "vintage year" or "vintage wine" have no special meaning.

There are a number of factors that make one vintage better than another in a particular region, but the most important is the amount of sunshine and heat between the flowering of the vines in June and the harvest in late September or early October. (In the southern hemisphere the seasons are reversed, of course, and the harvest takes place in March.) As grapes ripen in the sun, their natural acidity decreases and their sugar content increases. Ideally, the vintage takes place when the sugar/acid balance is in correct proportion. The wine will consequently have enough alcohol (from the sugar in the grapes) to be stable, and enough acidity to be healthy and lively. Cold and rainy summers result in unripe grapes that produce less alcohol, more acidity, and for red wines, less coloring matter in the skins. The wines are therefore weak, tart, and pale. In general, there are more good vintages for white wines than for reds—within a given district—because white wine grapes normally ripen earlier and do not require as long a growing season as do red grapes, and they make fine wine at lower levels of sugar. In addition, color is not as important to the appearance of white wines, extra acidity does less harm to their taste, and they do not need the depth of flavor that is expected of red wines.

The quantity produced in a vintage may be affected by poor weather during the flowering, which will diminish the crop, or by brief summer hailstorms, which can destroy part of a vineyard's production in minutes. A sudden frost in the spring may kill the new growth on the vines and can drastically reduce the crop in a wine region overnight. Many growers in northerly vineyards are now using modern frost-control devices to protect their vines during cold spells, but frost is still a danger.

Although it is axiomatic that a wine cannot be judged before it is made, it is not uncommon for a vintage to be publicized as excellent—by the wine trade and by the press—before the grapes have even been picked. Unfortunately, even an excellent growing season that gives every promise of producing fine wines can be marred by bad luck. Rain just before a harvest can swell the grapes and dilute the intensity of the wine, and continued rain can transform ripe grapes into rotten ones. Rain during the vintage means that the pickers are harvesting water along with grapes, which may result in weak wines lacking in flavor. Although the personality of a vintage can be determined once the wines have finished fermenting, many winemakers and professional tasters prefer to reserve judgment until the following spring, when the wines have become more clearly defined. This suggests that the first impression of a vintage, even a good one, may not be completely accurate, but by the time knowledgeable wine people have determined the character of an overpublicized vintage, consumers may have already heard and read too much about it for their impression to be corrected, much less reversed.

Any discussion of vintage years must take into account two basic factors: How accurate is the vintage date on the label? How useful is it?

The first question is basic, because if vintage dates are inaccurate, than it's obviously a mistake to attach too much significance to them. California wines must be made 95 percent from grapes harvested in the year shown on the label. German wines can be blended with up to 15 percent of wines from a vintage other than the one shown. French wines must come entirely from the vintage indicated, but since vintage years are not part of the *Appellation Contrôlée* laws, but another set of laws, it is possible that the labels of some blended wines are not as accurate as those of single-vineyard wines. In many other countries, vintage years are not taken seriously except for the finest wines, and even then it is not unusual for wines that undergo long barrel aging to be refreshed with younger wine.

Even when vintage dates are accurate, how useful is the information? Although many consumers have at least some acquaintance with the best recent vintages in Bordeaux, Burgundy, and perhaps along the Rhine and Moselle, what do most of us know about good and bad vintages for Barolo, Valpolicella, or Chianti; for Rioja; for Hungarian Tokay, Austrian Gumpoldskirchner, or Romanian Cabernet; or for the wines of Chile, Argentina, Australia, or South Africa (where their harvest takes place in our spring)? For that matter, what are the best recent years for Napa Cabernet Sauvignon, Sonoma Zinfandel, and Monterey Chardonnay?

There are, however, many wines whose vintages are both accurate and important. These include most of the world's fine wines, and as a general rule, the more you pay for a bottle, the more important its vintage becomes. Most fine wines are made in regions where hot and sunny summers cannot be taken for granted, and where wide variations exist from one year to the next. Furthermore, in such regions as Bordeaux and Burgundy and along the Rhine and Moselle, the finest and most expensive wines come from individual vineyard sites whose proprietors are not even permitted to blend together wines from neighboring vineyards or villages to offset some of the deficiencies of a lesser year. The best varietal wines of California, too, display greater variations from one year to another than many people imagine. Although the weather in California is more consistent than in Burgundy or along the Rhine, there are nevertheless differences between, say, Napa and Monterey, which are nearly two hundred miles apart. Furthermore, if a number of different grape varieties are planted side by side, the same growing season is unlikely to be equally successful for each of them.

The problem with evaluating vintages of fine wines is that knowing just a little is usually not enough, and as these wines are often expensive, mistakes can be more costly than for most other wines. Consumers generally seem to be most familiar with the best years for red Bordeaux, and the reputation of those vintages inevitably has an effect on many people's perception of vintage years in other regions. Actually, the best vintages in Bordeaux are not even the same for fine red wines and for the sweet white wines of Sauternes. Vintages for red Bordeaux and red Burgundy do not match, nor do those for red and white Burgundy. Bordeaux and Burgundy vintages do not necessarily have any relevance to the best years in the Rhône Valley or along the Loire, and of course, French vintages do not correspond with those of Germany or Italy. The best years for vintage port bear no relation to those for most other European wines, and European vintages are quite different from those for the best California varietal wines, produced six thousand miles away.

Vintage charts, with their numerical rating system, can be useful as a rough guide to recent years for the best-known wines. The system is too summary, however, to indicate much more than the comparative overall reputation of those vintages. The basic flaw in vintage charts, most of which are prepared by shippers and importers, is that they are so often self-serving, especially for recent vintages that are still currently available. Good years are rated as excellent, poor years are rarely rated as less than acceptable. It is often pointed out that not only the wines of a top-rated year are equally good, and conversely, that certain vineyards may have produced decent (and less expensive) wines in a year rated only fair. While variations naturally exist between the wines of one producer and another within a vintage, the main characteristic of poor years—those in which wines are made from unripe or even partially rotted grapes—is that they are unsound and cannot last. Even if there are a few bargains to be found, they are unlikely to maintain what little quality they possess for very long. Although vintage charts may be faulted for perpetuating the public's tendency to focus only on the best vintages, it is nevertheless true that, among fine wines, it is the best wines of the best vintages that are the most dependable and the longest-lived, and that will eventually provide the greatest pleasure.

On the other hand, an unfortunate result of the attention given even to indisputably fine vintages is that the public, anxious to buy these wines as soon as they appear, consumes the best wines of each vintage long before their prime. The wave of anticipation that accompanies a publicized vintage carries in its wake the disappointment that must inevitably occur when a good red wine is drunk too young. A fine Bordeaux or California Cabernet Sauvignon will demonstrate its quality only with the passage of years, when it has fully matured. If you drink such a wine soon after it has been bottled, you can perceive only in rough outline the particular qualities that have made it sought-after and expensive. Of all the comparative tastings that can be arranged, few are more instructive or surprising than to compare fine red wine from the same vineyard or the same winery in two good vintages that span at least three or four years. You will understand, as you taste the more mature wine, why certain wines are so highly acclaimed, and you will also realize, as you taste the younger wine, that to drink expensive red wines too young is pretty much a waste of money.

The success of a vintage is one element in a wine's quality and appeal, its ability to age is another. While it's true that all wines change during their life in the bottle, not all wines change for the better. The consideration of a vintage takes on a different dimension for wines whose virtues are charm, lightness, and fruit than for wines characterized by tannin, depth of flavor, and a slowly developing bouquet. On most vintage charts a great year is great forever, but every wine has a life cycle of its own, based on the combination of soil, grape, and climate that produced it, as well as on grape-growing and winemaking techniques that may differ from one producer to another. Some wines are at their best when they are bottled, remain good for a year or two, and then decline rapidly. Others reach maturity only after a few years in bottle, maintain their excellence for several years, and then very gradually decline. Age alone is no guarantee of quality, nor is a good vintage, in itself, a guarantee that the wine will be enjoyable today.

Finally, an observation about nonvintage wines, those on whose labels the year of the harvest does not appear. The trouble with such wines is not that they are blended from wines of more than one year, but that it is difficult for the consumer to determine just how old a particular bottle is. As most nonvintage wines are inexpensive (except for port and champagne) and meant to be drunk without any bottle age, not knowing how long such wines have been around means that you will sometimes come across faded and disappointing examples.

PRONUNCIATION GUIDE

Abboccato	ah-bo-*kah*-toe
Aglianico	ah-lee-*ah*-nee-koh
Alella	ah-*lay*-l'yah
Alentejo	ah-len-*tay*-oh
Aligoté	ah-lee-go-tay
Aloxe-Corton	ah-lox cor-tawn
Alto Adige	*ahl*-toe *ah*-dee-d'jay
Amabile	ah-*mah*-bee-lay
Amarone	ah-ma-*roe*-neh
Amontillado	ah-mon-tee-*yah*-doe
Anjou	ahn-joo
Arneis	ahr-*nay*'ss
Auslese	*ow*-slay-zuh
Auxey-Duresses	oak-say duh-ress
Baco	bah-coe
Barbaresco	bar-bah-*ress*-coe
Barbera	bar-*bear*-ah
Bardolino	bar-doe-*lee*-no
Barolo	bar-*oh*-loe
Barsac	bar-sack
Batârd-Montrachet	bah-tar mon-rah-shay
Beaujolais	bo-jo-lay
Beaumes-de-Venise	boh-'m-duh-veh-*neez*
Beaune	bone

Beerenauslese	*beer*-en-*ow*-slay-zuh
Bereich	buh-*rye'k*
Bernkastel	bearn-castle
Blanc de Blancs	blahn duh blahn
Blanc Fumé	blahn foo-may
Bocksbeutel	box-boyt'l
Bodega	bo-*day*-gah
Bonnes Mares	bon mar
Bordeaux	bore-doe
Bourgogne	boor-*gon*-yuh
Bourgueil	boor-guh'y
Brouilly	brew-yee
Brunello di Montalcino	brew-*nell*-oh dee mon-tahl-*chee*-noe
Brut	brute
Bual	boo-ahl
Buzet	boo-zay
Cahors	cah-or
Calvados	cahl-vah-dohss
Carneros	car-nair-oh'ss
Carruades	cah-roo-ahd
Cassis	cah-seece
Cave	cahv
Chablis	shah-blee
Chai	shay
Chambertin	sham-bear-tan
Chambolle-Musigny	shahm-bol moo-seen-yee
Chassagne-Montrachet	shah-sahnyuh mon-rah-shay
Chasselas	shass-lah
Château	shah-toe
Châteauneuf-du-Pape	shah-toe-nuff-doo-pahp
Chénas	shay-nahss
Chenin Blanc	shay-nan blahn
Chiroubles	shee-roobl
Climat	clee-mah
Clos de Bèze	cloh duh behz
Clos Vougeot	cloh voo-joh
Colheita	cul-*yay*-tah
Collio	col-yoh
Consorzio	con-*sorts*-ee-oh
Corbières	cor-b'yair
Cortese	cor-*tay*-zuh
Corton	cor-tawn
Cosecha	co-*say*-chah

Côte de Beaune	coat duh bone
Côte Chalonnaise	coat shah-lo-nayz
Côte de Nuits	coat duh nwee
Côte d'Or	coat dor
Côtes du Rhône	coat doo rone
Côte Rotie	coat ro-tee
Crémant	creh-mahn
Cru	crew
Cru Classé	crew clah-say
Cuvaison	coo-vay-zohn
Cuvée	coo-vay
Dão	down
Dolcetto	dole-*chet*-toe
Douro	*doo*-roe
Echézeaux	eh-shay-zoh
Edelfäule	ay-del-foil
Einzellage	*ein*-tsuh-lah-guh
Egri Bikavér	egg-ree bee-ka-vair
Entre-Deux-Mers	ahn'tr-duh-mair
Erzeugerabfüllung	*air*-tsoy-guh-*ahb*-foo-lung
Estufa	esh-*too*-fah
Fendant	fahn-dahn
Fiaschi	fee-ahss-kee
Fino	*fee*-no
Fixin	fix-ahn
Fleurie	fluh-ree
Framboise	frahm-bwahz
Frascati	frahss-*ca*-tee
Freisa	fray-zah
Frizzante	free-*zahn*-tay
Friuli	*free*-ooh-lee
Gattinara	gah-tee-*nah*-rah
Gavi	*gah*-vee
Gevrey-Chambertin	jev-ray sham-bear-tan
Gewürztraminer	guh-*vurts*-trah-*mee*-ner
Gigondas	jee-gon-dahss
Grands-Echézeaux	grahnz eh-shay-zoh
Graves	grahv
Grenache	greh-nahsh
Grignolino	gree-n'yohl-*ee*-no
Grosslage	*gross*-lah-guh
Gumpoldskirchen	goom-poles-*kir*-ken

Haut	oh
Hermitage	air-mee-tahj
Heurige	*hoi*-ree-guh
Hospices de Beaune	oh-speece duh bone
Jerez	hair-reth
Johannisberg	yoh-*hah*-niss-bairg
Juliénas	jool-yeh-nahss
Kirsch	keersh
Labrusca	la-*broos*-ca
Lacryma Christi	*la*-cree-mah *kriss*-tee
Mâcon	mah-kohn
Maderisé	mah-dair-ree-zay
Maipo	*my*-poh
Malmsey	*mahlm*-zee
Malvasia	mahl-vah-*zee*-ah
Manzanilla	man-zah-*nee*-ya
Marc	mar
Margaux	mahr-goe
Médoc	meh-dock
Merlot	mehr-loe
Meursault	muhr-soe
Mise en bouteilles	meez ahn boo-tay
Montilla	mon-*tee*-yah
Montrachet	mon-rah-shay
Morey-Saint-Denis	moh-ray san-deh-nee
Moulin-à-Vent	mooh-lahn-ah-vahn
Mousseux	moo-suh
Müller-Thurgau	*moo*-lair-*toor*-gahw
Muscadet	muhss-ka-day
Musigny	moo-see-nyee
Nahe	nah
Nebbiolo	neh-b'*yoh*-low
Neuchâtel	nuh-shah-tell
Nierstein	neer-shtine
Nuits-Saint-Georges	nwee-san-jawrj
Oechsle	*uhk*-sluh
Oloroso	oh-lo-*ro*-so
Oltrepò Pavese	ohl-treh-*poe* pah-*veh*-seh

Orvieto	ohr-vee-*ay*-toe
Pauillac	paw-yack
Pays	pay-yee
Pétillant	pet-tee-yahn
Petit	puh-tee
Phylloxera	fil-*lox*-uh-rah
Piave	pee-*ah*-veh
Piesport	*peez*-port
Pinot Grigio	pee-noe *gree*-d'joh
Pinot Noir	pee-noe n'whar
Poire	pwahr
Pomerol	pom-uh-rohl
Pommard	poh-mar
Pouilly-Fuissé	poo-yee fwee-say
Pouilly-Fumé	poo-yee foo-may
Pourriture noble	poo-ree-toor nohbl
Premier Cru	preh-m'yay crew
Puligny-Montrachet	poo-lee n'yee mon-rah-shay
Puttonyos	puh-tohn-yosh
Qualitätswein mit Prädikat	kvah-lee-*tayts*-vine mitt *pray*-dee-kaht
Quincy	kan-see
Quinta	*keen*-tah
Recioto	ray-*t'shot*-oh
Retsina	ret-*see*-nah
Rheingau	rine-gow
Rheinhessen	rine-hessen
Rheinpfalz	rine-faltz
Ribatejo	ree-bah-*tay*-oh
Ribera del Duero	ree-*bair*-ah dell d'*weh*-roh
Richebourg	reesh-boor
Riesling	*reece*-ling
Rioja	ree-*oh*-ha
Rosé	roh-zay
Rueda	roo-*eh*-dah
Ruwer	*roo*-vuh
Saar	sahr
Sancerre	sahn-sair
Sangiovese	san-joh-*vay*-zeh
Sauternes	saw-tairn

Sauvignon Blanc	saw-vee-n'yohn blahn
Scheurebe	*shoy*-reh-buh
Secco	say-co
Sekt	sekt
Sémillon	seh-mee-yohn
Soave	so-*ah*-vay
Solera	so-*lair*-ah
Sommelier	so-mel-yay
Spätlese	sh'*payt*-lay-zuh
Spumante	spoo-*mahn*-tay
Sylvaner	sil-*vah*-ner
Tafelwein	*tah*-fell-vine
Tastevin	taht-van
Tavel	tah-vell
Tenuta	ten-*noo*-tah
Terroir	tehr-wahr
Tête de cuvée	teht duh koo-vay
Tonneau	tun-oh
Traminer	trah-*mee*-ner
Trebbiano	t'reh-bee-*ah*-no
Trentino	tren-*tee*-no
Trockenbeerenauslese	*trok*-en-*beer*-en-*ow*-slay-zuh
Valdepeñas	val-day-*pain*-yass
Valpolicella	val-poh-lee-*t'chell*-ah
Valtellina	vahl-teh-*lee*-nah
Vaud	voh
Veltliner	velt-*lee*-nuh
Verdelho	vehr-*dell*-yoh
Verdicchio	vehr-*dee*-kee-oh
Vernaccia	vair-*nah*-t'cha
Vinho Verde	*veen*-yoh *vair*-day
Vinifera	vin-*if*-uh-rah
Viognier	vee-oh-n'yay
Vosne-Romanée	vohn ro-mah-nay
Wachau	*vah*-kow
Wehlen	*vay*-len
Yquem	ee-kem

INDEX

Abbazia di Rosazzo, 121
Abboccato, 107, 134
Abele, Henri, 307
Abruzzi, 137
Acacia Winery, 219
Acetic acid, 9, 17
Achaia-Clauss, 188, 189
Acquileia, 119, 121
Acidity in wine, 9, 19, 35, 197
Ackerman-Laurance, 308
Aconcagua Valley, 275
Adams Vineyard, 269
Adda, river, 114
Adelaida Cellars, 250
Adelaide Hills, 287
Adelsheim Vineyard, 268
Adler Fels, 236
AGE, 173
Aging of wine:
  in bottle, 11–12, 16, 29,
     157–158, 322, 367
  in barrel, 8, 36–37, 105–106,
     108–109, 172, 197
Aglianico, 138

Ahlgren Vineyards, 245
Ahr, river, 140
Aigle, 182
Aïn Bessem-Bouïra, 297
Airen, 171, 177
Alameda, 240–241
Alba, 108
Albana di Romagna, 136
Albariño, 171, 177
Albariza, 315
Alcamo, 139
Alcohol in wine, 3, 6–7, 8, 11,
    79–80, 83, 100, 125,
    167, 175, 262, 267
Alcool blancs, 336–337
Aldenbrook Vineyards, 231
Alella, 176–177
Alentejo, 182
Alexander Valley, 228
Alexander Valley Vineyards,
    229
Alexander's Crown, 229
Algarve, 182
Algeria, 297

Aliança, 180
Aligoté, 62
Allegrini, 117
Allegro Vineyards, 272
Almadén, 243, 256
Aloxe-Corton, 74
Alsace, 94–97
Altaire, 229
Altare, Elio, 109
Altesino, 132
Alto, 293
Alto Adige, 122–124
Alvarinho, 179
Amabile, 107
Amador, 253–254
Amador Foothill Winery, 254
Amarone, 117
Ambra, 131
Amity Vineyards, 268
Amontillado, 317–318
Amoroso, 318
Amtliche Prüfungsnummer, 156
Añada, 316–317
Anderson Valley, 238
Anderson, S., 220
André, 255, 311
Andres, 295
Anghelu Ruju, 139
Anheuser, 164
Ania, 129
Anjou, 91
Anjou Rosé, 84, 91–92
Anselmi, 117
Antinori, 128, 129, 130, 134
Antoniolo, 111
Aperitif wines, 326
Apetlon, 185
Appellation Contrôlée, 24–27,
        30–31, 66–67
Aprilia, 137
Apulia, 138
Arbois, 100
Arbor Crest, 267
Archambault, 94
Arciero Winery, 250
Argentina, 278–279
Argiano, 132
Argonaut Winery, 254

Argyle, 270
Ariel, 243
Armagnac, 332–334
Armida Winery, 233
Armigne, 183
Arneis, 112, 113
Arrowood, Richard, 236
Arroyo Grande, 251
Arroyo Seco, 247
Arvine, 183
Asbach Uralt, 335
Assemblage, 36
Assmannshausen, 161
Associated Vintners, 266
Asti Spumante, 108, 309
Aszu, 186, 187
Atlas Peak Vineyards, 221
Au Bon Climat, 252
Auckland, 289
Audubon Cellars, 241
Aurora, 260
Ausbruch, 185
Auslese, 148
Austin Cellars, 252
Australia, 280–289
Austria, 183–185
Autoclave, 309
Autolysis, 304
Auxerrois, 99
Auxey-Duresses, 77
Aveleda, 179
Avellino, 137–138
Avelsbach, 168
Avia, 190
Avignonesi, 133
Avize, 301
Ay, 301
Ayala, 307
Ayl, 167
Aziano, 129
Azienda Vinicola, 107

Babcock Vineyard, 252
Babich, 290
Bacchus, 146
Baco 22A, 333
Baco Noir, 260
Backsberg, 293

Badacsony, Mount, 187–188
Baden, 144
Badia a Coltibuono, 128, 130
Bag-in-the-box, 283
Baga, 180
Bailey's, 288
Bailly, Alexis, 272
Bairrada, 180
Balaton, Lake, 187
Balbach, Anton, 160
Balbas, Victor, 175
Baldinelli Vineyards, 254
Balgownie, 284
Banda Azul, 174
Banda Dorada, 174
Banfi, 132–133
Bandol, 97–98
Bannockburn, 288
Banyuls, 99
Barbacarlo, 114
Barbadillo, 318
Barbaresco, 109–110
Barbeito, 325
Barbera, 112, 211
Barberani, 134
Barbi, Fattoria dei, 132
Barbier, René, 176
Barboursville Winery, 271
Barca Velha, 180
Barco Reale, 131
Bardolino, 116
Barilot, 112
Barnard Griffin Winery, 267
Barolo, 108–109
Baron Philippe, 33
Barré Frères, 91
Barrel age, *see* Aging
Barrel fermentation, 3, 194
Barrique, 8, 36, 116
Barossa Valley, 286
Barsac, 57
Bartles & James, 208
Barton, Anthony, 46
Barton & Guestier, 33
Bas-Médoc, 38
Basquaise, 334
Bassermann-Jordan, 159
Bâtard-Montrachet, 77

Batasiolo, 109
Battistina, La, 113
Baxter, Phil, 226
Bay Cellars, 241
Beaucannon Winery, 226
Beaudet, Paul, 85
Beaujeu, 83
Beaujolais, 82–86
Beaujolais de l'année, 83
Beaujolais *nouveau,* 83
Beaujolais *primeur,* 83
Beaujolais Supérieur, 84
Beaujolais-Villages, 84
Beaulieu Vineyard, 221–222
Beaumes-de-Venise, 89
Beaune, 75, 76
Beaune, Hospices de, 75–76
Bedell Cellars, 265
Beerenauslese, 148, 151
Bekaa Valley, 297
Bel Arbors, 237
Bella Oaks, 224
Bellavista, 115, 310
Belle Terre Vineyard, 228
Bellerose Vineyard, 231
Bellet, 98
Belvedere Winery, 233
Benmarl, 264
Bennett Valley, 236
Benziger, 235
Bereich, 153
Bergerac, 99
Bergfeld Winery, 226
Bergkelder, 293
Beringer, 223, 250
Berlucchi, 115, 310
Bernardus Vineyards, 248
Bernkastel, 166
Bernkasteler Doctor, 165
Berres, 114
Berri-Renmano, 284
Bersano, 126
Bertani, 117
Bertolli, 140
Besserat de Bellefon, 254, 307
Bethel Heights, 269
Bianchi, 279
Bianco, 107

Bianco di Custoza, 117–118
Bianco di Pitigliano, 131
Bidwell Vineyards, 265
Bien Nacido, 251
Bienvenue-Bâtard-Montrachet, 77
Bigi, 134
Bikavér, 187
Billecart-Salmon, 307
Biltmore Estate, 272
Biondi Santi, 132
Bischöfliche Weingüter, 165
Bischöfliches Konvikt, 165
Bischöfliches Priesterseminar, 165
Bishop of Riesling, 157
Bisquit, 332
Bizouard, 339
Blaauwklippen, 293
Black Mountain Vineyard, 230
Black Tower, 156
Blanc de Blancs, 306
Blanc de Morgex, 112
Blanc de Noirs, 215, 306
Blanc Foussy, 308
Blanc Fumé, 94
Blandy's, 325
Blanquette de Limoux, 309
Blass, Wolf, 284
Blauer Spätburgunder, 140
Blaufränkisch, 184
Blaye, 57
Blind tasting, 14
Blossom Hill, 256
Blue Nun, 156
Blush wines, 231
Boa Vista, 324
Boal, 325
Boca, 111
Bocksbeutel, 144, 168
Bodega, 173, 315
Bodegas Berberana, 173
Bodegas Beroni, 173
Bodegas Bilbainas, 173
Bodegas Campo Viejo, 173
Bodegas Franco Españolas, 174
Bodegas Gurpegui, 174
Bodegas Lan, 174

Bodegas Monticello, 174
Bodegas Muerza, 174
Bodegas Muga, 174
Bodegas Olarra, 174
Bodegas Palacio, 174
Bodegas Riojanas, 174
Bodegas Santiago, 174
Boeger Winery, 254
Bogle Vineyards, 256
Bois Ordinaires, 328
Boisset, Jean-Claude, 230
Bolgheri, 131–132
Bolla, 117
Bollinger, 306, 307
Bollini, 122
Bologna Giacomo, 112
Bolzano, 121
Bonacossi, 131
Bonne chauffe, 329
Bonnes Mares, 72
Bonnezeaux, 92
Bonny Doon Vineyard, 244
Bons Bois, 328
Bonvillars, 183
Boone's, 208
Boordy Vineyard, 272
Bordeaux, 29–61
Borderies, 328
Borges, 325
Borgo Conventi, 120
Borgogno, 109
Borie, Jean-Eugène, 47
Borie-Manoux, 33
Borro della Sala, 134
Boscarelli, 133
Bosché Vineyard, 226
Boschendahl, 293
Botobolar, 286
Bottle sizes, 12
Botrytis cinerea, 58, 148, 151, 185, 206, 283
Bouchaine, 219
Bouchard Finlayson, 293
Bouchard Père & Fils, 70
Boucheron, 29
Bouchet, 52
Bouquet of wine, 16–18
Boulard, 339

Bourg, 57
Bourgogne Aligoté, 62
Bourgogne-Passetousgrain, 62
Bourgueil, 93
Boutari, 189
Bouvet, 308
Bouzy, 301, 307
Boyer, Richard, 247
Bramaterra, 111
Brander Vineyard, 252
Brandewijn, 327
Brandy, 327–339
Brandy de Jerez, 335
Brauneberg, 166
Brazil, 279
Breathing, 347–348
Bredif, Marc, 93
Breede River Valley, 292
Breganze, 118
Briarcrest, 230
Bricco, 109
Bricco Manzoni, 112
Bricout, 307
Bridgehampton Winery, 265
Bridgeview Vineyards, 269
Brights, 295
Bristol Cream, 318
British Columbia, 295
Brix, 205–206
Brolio, 128
Bronco, JFJ, 256
Brotherhood Winery, 264
Brouillis, 329
Brouilly, 84
Brown Bros., 288
Brown Forman Distillers, 237
Brown sherry, 318
Bruce, David, 244
Brunate, 109
Brunello di Montalcino, 132–133
Brusco dei Barbi, 133
Brut, 305
Bual, 325
Bucelas, 181
Buehler Vineyards, 225
Buena Vista, 234
Buitenverwachting, 293
Bukkuram, 139

Bulgaria, 189
Bühl, von, 159
Bulk process, 308
Bully Hill, 263
Burgenland, 185
Bürgerspital, 168
Burgess Cellars, 226
Buring, Leo, 284
Burgundy, 61–81
Bürklin-Wolf, 159
Busby, James, 280–281, 289
Busnel, 339
Buttafuoco, 114
Buzet, 100
Bynum, Davis, 233
Byrd Vineyards, 272
Byron Vineyard, 224, 252
Byrrh, 326

Ca' del Bosco, 115, 310
Ca' del Pazzo, 133
Ca' del Solo, 244
Cabernet d'Anjou, 92
Cabernet Sauvignon, 34–35, 99,
     106, 129–130, 209,
     265, 267, 273, 275, 281
Cabernet Franc, 34–35, 52, 92,
     209
Cabinet, 147
Cadillac, 61
Cafaro Cellars, 225
Cahors, 99–100
Cain Cellars, 221
Cakebread Cellars, 226
Calabria, 138
Calaveras, 253, 254
Calcaire, 230
Caldaro, 123
Cálem, 323
Calera, 249
California:
     table wine, 191–256
     fortified wine, 319, 324
     sparkling wine, 311–312
     brandy, 336
Calistoga, 217
Caliterra, 278
Callaway, 253

Calories in wine, 356–257
Calvados, 337–339
Calvet, 33
Cambas, 188
Cambria Winery, 240, 252
Cameron Winery, 269
Campania, 137–138
Campbell, Patrick, 236
CampoFiorin, 117
Camus, 332
Canaiolo, 125
Canandaigua Wine Co., 256, 262
Canepa, 278
Cannonau, 139
Cannubi, 109
Canon-Fronsac, 57
Cantenac, 48
Cantina sociale, 107
Caparone Winery, 250
Caparzo, Tenuta, 132
Cape Mentelle, 288
Cape Riesling, 291
Cappezana, Villa di, 131
Capri, 137
Capsules, 345
Carbonic maceration, 7
Carcavelos, 181
Carema, 111
Carey Cellars, 251
Carignan, 88, 99
Carignane, 211
Cariñena, 171, 178
Carmel, 296–297
Carmel Valley, 248
Carmenet, 235
Carmignano, 131
Carmine, 212
Carnelian, 212
Carneros, 217, 219, 234
Carneros Creek Winery, 219
Carpenè Malvolti, 310
Carras, Domaine, 189
Carruades de Lafite, 44–45
Carso, 121
Carta Vieja, 278
Cartier, 295
Cartizze, 119
Casa Larga, 263

Casa Vinicola, 107
Casablanca, 275
Casal Garcia, 179
Casal Thaulero, 137
Cascade Mountain Vineyard,
    264
Case Basse, 132
Cassis, 98
Castel Danielis, 188
Castel del Monte, 138
Castellare di Castellina, 128, 130
Castellblanch, 311
Castelgiocondo, 132
Castelli di Jesi, 135
Castelli Romani, 136
Castello d'Albola, 128
Castello di Ama, 128
Catello di Fonterutoli, 128
Castello di Gabbiano, 128
Castello di Neive, 109
Castello di Nipozzano, 129
Castello di Querceto, 128
Castello dei Rampolla, 128
Castello della Sala, 134
Castello di Uzzano, 1128
Castello di Verrazzano, 128
Castello Vicchiomaggio, 128
Castello di Volpaia, 128
Castello Ygay, 174
Catalonia, 175–176
Cataratto, 138
Catawba, 260
Catoctin Vineyards, 272
Catullo, 117
Cava, 169, 175, 310–311
Cave Spring Cellars, 295
Cavit, 122
Caymus Vineyards, 225
Cazes, 46
Cella, 136
Cecchi, 128
CedarCreek, 295
Cellar, at home, 340–343
Cencibel, 171, 177
Central Coast, 203
Central Valley, 255
Centurion, 212
Cérons, 61

Cerretto, 109
Cerro, Fattoria del, 133
Cervaro della Sala, 134
Cesare, Pio, 109
Chablais, 182–183
Chablis, 62–65
Chaddsford Winery, 272
Chai, 32
Chalk Hill, 233
Chalk Hill Winery, 233
Chalone Vineyard, 248
Châlonnais, 81
Chamard Vineyards, 272
Chambertin, 71
Chambéry, 326
Chambolle-Musigny, 72
Chamisal Vineyards, 251
Champagne, 299–307
Champigny, 92
Chancellor, 260
Chanson, 70
Chantefleur, 29
Chapelle-Chambertin, 72
Chapoutier, 88, 90
Chappellet Vineyard, 225
Chaptalization, 9–10, 127, 147
Charbaut, 307
Charbono, 211
Chardonnay, 62, 64, 81, 99, 106,
        116, 130, 175–176,
        181, 212, 275, 283, 290,
        291, 294, 301, 311
Charente, river, 327
Charmat process, 308, 309, 311
Charmes-Chambertin, 72
Charta, 162
Chase-Limogère, 256
Chassagne-Montrachet, 76, 77
Chasselas, 94, 182
Château (Bordeaux), 32
Château-bottling, 33, 37
Chateau de Baun, 233
Château de Beaucastel, 88, 249
Château de la Cassemichère, 91
Château-Chalon, 100
Chateau des Charmes, 295
Château de Cléray, 91
Château Corton Grancey, 74

Chateau Elan, 272
Château de Fonscolombe, 97
Château de Fontpinot, 332
Château Fortia, 88
Château de la Gardine, 88
Chateau Grand Traverse, 272
Château Grillet, 90
Château de Haut-Serre, 100
Château La Nerthe, 88
Château Lagrezette, 100
Chateau La Salle, 222
Chateau de Leu, 227
Château Moncontour, 93
Château de Mont-Redon, 88
Chateau Montelena, 225
Château Musar, 297–298
Château Pech de Jammes, 100
Château du Nozet, 94
Chateau Potelle, 220
Château Rayas, 88
Chateau Remy, 288
Chateau Reynella, 287
Chateau St. Jean, 236, 312
Chateau Ste. Michelle, 266, 267
Château de Selle, 97
Chateau Souverain, 222, 229
Chateau Tahbilk, 288
Château de Triguedina, 100
Château Val-Joanis, 89
Château de Vaudieu, 88
Château de Vignelaure, 97
Chateau Woltner, 220
Châteauneuf-du-Pape, 87
Châteaux of Bordeaux:
    d'Agassac, 43
    Angludet, 43
    d'Arche, 61
    Ausone, 42, 53, 54
    Avensan, 43
    Balestard-la-Tonnelle, 54
    Batailley, 40, 46
    Bauregard, 56
    Beau-Séjour-Bécot, 54
    Beauséjour-Duffau-
            Lagarrosse, 54
    Beau-Site, 43
    Belair, 54
    Bel-Air-Marquis-d'Aligre, 43

Bel-Orme, 43
Belgrave, 41
Berliquet, 54
Beychevelle, 40, 47
Bouscaut, 51
Boyd-Cantenac, 40
Branaire-Ducru, 40
Brane-Cantenac, 39, 48
Broustet, 61
Cadet-Piola, 54
Caillou, 61
Calon-Ségur, 40, 44
Camensac, 41
Canon, 54
Canon-la-Gaffelière, 54
Cantemerle, 41, 48
Cantenac-Brown, 40
Cap de Mourlin, 54
Capbern, 43
Carbonnieux, 51
Castera, 43
Certan-de-May, 56
Certan-Giraud, 56
Chasse-Spleen, 43, 48
Cheval Blanc, 42, 53, 54
Chevalier, Domaine de, 51
Citran, 43
Clarke, 43, 48
Clerc-Milon, 41, 45
Climens, 60
Clinet, 56
Clos des Jacobins, 54
Clos Fourtet, 54
Corbin, 54
Corbin-Michotte, 54
Cos d'Estournel, 39, 44
Cos Labory, 41
Coufran, 43
Couhins, 50, 51
Couhins-Lurton, 50, 51
Coutet, 60
Couvent des Jacobins, 54
Croizet-Bages, 41
Curé-Bon, 54
Dassault, 54
Dauzac, 41
Desmirail, 40, 48
Doisy-Daëne, 61

Doisy-Dubroca, 61
Doisy-Verdrines, 61
Ducru-Beaucaillou, 39, 47
Duhart-Milon, 40, 45
Dufort-Vivens, 40, 48
Dutruch-Grand-Poujeaux, 43
Fargues, de, 60
Ferrande, 51
Ferrière, 40
de Fieuzal, 51
Figeac, 53, 54
Filhot, 61
Fombrauge, 55
Fonplégade, 54
Fonreaud, 43
Fonroque, 54
Fourcas-Dupré, 43, 48
Fourcas-Hosten, 43, 48
Gazin, 56
Giscours, 40, 48
du Glana, 43
Gloria, 43, 47
Grand-Barrail-Lamarzelle-
    Figeac, 54
Grand-Corbin, 54
Grand-Mayne, 54
Grand-Pontet, 54
Grand-Puy-Ducasse, 40, 46
Grand-Puy-Lacoste, 40, 46
Gressier-Grand Poujeaux, 43
Greysac, 43
Gruaud-Larose, 39, 47
Guiraud, 60
Haut-Bages Averous, 46
Haut-Bages-Libéral, 41
Haut-Bailly, 51
Haut-Batailley, 40, 46
Haut-Brion, 39, 50, 51
Haut Marbuzet, 43
Haut-Peyraguey, 60
d'Issan, 40
Kirwan, 40, 48
La Bécade, 43
Labégorce, 43
La Cardonne, 43
La Clotte, 54
La Conseillante, 56
La Croix, 56

La Croix-de-Gay, 56
La Dominique, 54
Lafaurie-Peyraguey, 60
Lafite-Rothschild, 39, 44–45, 274
Lafleur, 56
La Fleur Pétrus, 56
Lafon-Rochet, 40, 44
La Gaffelière, 54
La Garde, 51
Lagrange, 40, 47, 56
La Grace Dieu, 55
La Lagune, 40, 48
Lalande-Borie, 47
La Louvière, 50, 51
Lamarque, 43
La Marzelle, 54
La Mission Haut-Brion, 50, 51
Lamothe, 61
Lanessan, 43
L'Angélus, 54
Langoa-Barton, 40, 46
Lapelletrie, 55
La Pointe, 56
Larcis-Ducasse, 54
Larmande, 55
Larose Trintaudon, 43
Larrivet Haut-Brion, 51
Lascombes, 39, 48
Latour, 39, 45–46
La Tour Blanche, 60
La Tour Carnet, 40
La Tour de By, 43
La Tour-de-Mons, 43
La Tour Figeac, 55
La Tour-Haut-Brion, 50, 51
La Tour-Martillac, 51
Latour-Pomerol, 56
La Tour St.-Bonnet, 43
Laville-Haut-Brion, 50, 51
L'Eglise, Clos, 56
L'Eglise-Clinet, 57
L'Enclos, 57
Léoville-Barton, 39, 46
Léoville-Las-Cases, 39, 46
Léoville-Poyferré, 39, 46
Les Ormes de Pez, 43, 44
Lestage, 43

L'Evangile, 57
Lilian Ladouys, 43, 44
Liversan, 43
Livran, 43
Loudenne, 43
Lynch-Bages, 40, 46
Lynch-Moussas, 40
Magdelaine, 54
Magence, 51
Malartic-Lagraviére, 51
Malescasse, 44
Malescot-Saint-Exupéry, 40, 48
de Malle, 61
Malleret, 43
Malmaison, 48
Marbuzet, 43, 44
Margaux, 39, 47
Marquis-d'Alesme-Becker, 40, 48
Marquis-de-Terme, 40
Maucaillou, 43, 48
Meyney, 43
Monbousquet, 55
Montrose, 39, 44
Mouton d'Armailhac, 40, 45
Mouton-Baron-Philippe, 45
Mouton-Rothschild, 39, 42, 45
Myrat, 61
Nairac, 61
Nenin, 57
Olivier, 51
Palmer, 40, 48
Pape Clément, 51
Patache d'Aux, 43
Paveil de Luze, 43
Pavie, 54
Pavie-Decesse, 55
Pavie-Macquin, 55
Pedésclaux, 41
Petit-Village, 57
Petrus, 42, 56
Peyrabon, 43
de Pez, 44
Phelan-Ségur, 43, 44
Pibran, 43
Pichon-Longueville, 39, 46

Pichon-Longueville-Comtesse
  de Lalande, 39, 46
Plagnac, 43
Pontac-Monplaisir, 51
Pontet-Canet, 40, 44, 46
Potensac, 43
Pouget, 40
Poujeaux, 43, 48
Prieuré-Lichine, 40, 48
Puy-Blanquet, 55
Rabaud-Promis, 60
Ramage La Batisse, 43
Sigalas-Rabaud, 60
Rahoul, 51
Rausan-Segla, 39, 48
Rauzan-Gassies, 39, 48
Raymond-Lafon, 60
de Rayne-Vigneau, 60
René, Clos, 57
Rieussec, 60
Ripeau, 55
Romer, 61
Rouget, 57
Saint-Pierre, 40, 47
de Sales, 57
Sigalas-Rabaud, 60
Simard, 55
Siran, 43
Smith-Haut-Lafitte, 51
Sociando-Mallet, 43
Soutard, 55
Suau, 61
de Suduiraut, 60
Taillefer, 57
du Taillan, 43
Talbot, 40, 47
du Tertre, 41
Tertre Daugay, 55
Trimoulet, 55
Tronquoy-Lalande, 43
Troplong Mondot, 55
Trottevieille, 54
Verdignan, 43
Vieux-Certan, 57
Vieux Robin, 43
Villemaurine, 55
Yon Figeac, 55
d'Yquem, 59, 60

Chautauqua, 263
Cheese and wine, 355–356
Chénas, 84
Chenau, Paul, 311
Chenin Blanc, 92, 213–214, 291
Chéreau-Carré, 91
Chevalier Védrines, 60
Chevalier-Montrachet, 77
Chevaliers du Tastevin, 73
Chevrignon, 223
Chianti, 124–130
Chianti Classico, 127–129
Chiaretto, 118
Chiarlo, Michele, 109
Chiavennasca, 114
Chile, 273–278
Chilling wine, 344–345
Chimney Rock Winery, 220
Chinon, 93
Chiroubles, 85
Christian Brothers, 222, 336
Christophe, 230
Christopher Creek, 232
Cienega Valley, 248
Cigare Volant, Le, 244
Cinnabar, 245
Cinqueterre, 115
Cinzano, 309
Cinsault, 87
Cipes Brut, 295
Cirò, 138
Clairette de Die, 309
Clare Valley, 287
Claret, 29
Clarksburg, 256
Classed growths, 33
Classico, 104
Classification of 1855, 38–42
Clear Creek Distillery, 337
Clear Lake, 239
Clerico, 109
Clès des Ducs, 334
Clicquot-Ponsardin, Veuve,
  306, 307
Climate and wine, 11, 97–98,
  307–308, 309
Climats, 67
Cline Cellars, 234

Clinton Vineyards, 264
Clonal selection, 195–196
Clos de Bèze, 71
Clos Blanc de Vougeot, 73
Clos Cabrière, 293
Clos des Mouches, 76
Clos de la Roche, 72
Clos de Tart, 72
Clos de Vougeot, 72–73
Clos du Bois, 229–230
Clos du Marquis, 46
Clos Du Val, 220
Clos Fourtet,
Clos L'Eglise,
Clos des Lambrays, 72
Clos Pegase, 226
Clos René, 57
Clos Saint Denis, 72
Cloudy Bay, 290
Cockburn, 323
Codorníu, 176, 219, 311, 312
Cognac, 327–332
Cohn, B. R., 235
Col d'Orcia, 132
Colares, 181
Colchagua, 275
Coldstream Hills, 287
Cole Ranch, 237
Colheita, 323
Collavini, 120
Colli Albani, 136
Colli Aretini, 129
Colli Berici, 118
Colli Euganei, 118
Colli Fiorentini, 129
Colli Lanuvini, 136
Colli Orientale di Friuli, 121
Colli Senesi, 129
Colline Pisane, 129
Collio, 120–121
Collio Goriziano, 120
Colony, 256
Colorino, 125
Color of wine, 6, 15–16
Coltasala, 130
Coltura promiscua, 102–103
Columbia Crest, 267
Columbia Valley, 267, 269

Columbia Winery, 266
Comtes de Champagne, 306
Conca de Barbera, 176
Concannon Vineyard, 241
Concentrate, grape, 10, 125, 127
Concerto, 130
Concha y Toro, 277–278
Concord, 260
Conde de Caralt, 311
Conde de Valdemar, 174
Condrieu, 90
Conegliano, 119
Congeners, 329
Conn Creek Winery, 225
Consenso, 221
Consorzio, 103, 105, 127–128
Constantia, 291, 292
Conterno, Aldo, 109
Conterno, Giacomo, 109
Contino, 173
Contratto, 109
Conundrum, 225
Cooks, 255
Cooking Wine, 357
Coonawarra, 286
Cooperative cellars, 103, 155,
    290, 293
Coppola, Francis Ford, 225
Corbans, 290
Corbett Canyon Vineyards,
    250–251
Corbières, 99
Cordier, 32
Corison Wines, 225
Corkscrews, 345–347
Corky wine, 17
Cornas, 90
Coronas, 176
Coronet, 336
Cortaillod, 182
Cortese, 113
Corton, 74
Corton-Charlemagne, 74
Corvina Veronese, 116
Corvo, 139
Cosecha, 173
Cosentino, 226
Cossart Gordon, 325

Costanti, Emilio, 132
Costers del Segre, 176
Costières de Nimes, 99
Côte, La, 182
Côte de Beaune, 74–77, 80–81
Côte de Beaune-Villages, 76
Côte des Blancs, 300
Côte de Brouilly, 84
Côte de Nuits, 71–74, 77–80
Côte de Nuits-Villages, 74
Côte d'Or, 65–81
Côte Rôtie, 89
Coteaux Champenois, 307
Coteaux d'Aix en Provence, 97
Coteaux de l'Aubance, 92
Coteaux du Languedoc, 98
Coteaux du Layon, 92
Coteaux de la Loire, 92
Coteaux de Mascara, 297
Coteaux de Tlemcen, 297
Coteaux du Tricastin, 89
Coteaux du Zaccar, 297
Côtes de Bourg, 57
Côtes de Gascogne, 100
Côtes de Luberon, 89
Côtes de Meliton, 188
Côtes de Provence, 97
Côtes du Rhône, 88–89
Côtes du Roussillon, 98
Côtes du Ventoux, 89
Cotnari, 190
Coulée de Serrant, 92
Cour Pavillon, La, 33
Courvoisier, 332
Cousiño Macul, 278
Covey Run, 267
Cowra, 286
Cramant, 301
Cream sherry, 318
Crémant, 306–307
Crémant d'Alsace, 95, 309
Crémant de Bourgogne, 309
Crémant de Loire, 309
Crème de cassis, 98
Crépy, 98
Cresta Blanca, 256
Creston Manor, 250
Criadera, 316–317

Cribari, 256
Crichton Hall, 225
Crimea, 190
Criolla, 278
Criots-Batârd-Montrachet, 77
Cristal, 306
Croatia, 190
Croatina, 114
Croft, 318, 323
Cronin, 245
Croser, Brian, 270, 287
Crouchen, 287, 291
Crozes-Hermitage, 89
Cru, 84, 107
Cru bourgeois, 42–43
Cru classé, 33
Cru exceptionnel, 42
Crusius, 164
Culbertson, 253
Cullen's, 289
CUNE, 173
Curico, 275
Cuvaison, 6
Cuvaison (winery), 225
Cuve close, 308
Cuvée, 300, 302–303
Cuvées speciales, 306
Cygnet Cellars, 249

DOC, 103–106
DOCG, 105–107
D'Agostini, 253, 254
Dahra, 297
Dalla Valle, 225
Daniel, John, 225
Danube, river, 185
Dão, 180
De Bartoli, 139
De Bortolli, 286
De Castris, Leone, 138
De Chaunac, 260
De Loach Vineyards, 232
De Lorimier, 230
De Montal, 334
De Moor Winery, 226
De Venoge, 307
De Wetshof, 293
Dealul Mare, 190

Debonné Vineyards, 271
Debrö, 187
Decanting wines, 348–349
Decugnano dei Barbi, 134
Dégorgement, 305
Dehlinger Winery, 232
Deidesheim, 159
Deinhard, 156, 157, 162, 310
Delaforce, 323
Delamain, 332
Délas Frères, 90
Delaware, 260
Delegat's, 290
Delheim, 293
Delicato Vineyards, 256
Délice du Sémillon, 207
Demestica, 188
Demi-Sec, 305
Denis-Mounié, 332
Denominacão de Origem Con-
    trolada, 179
Denomináción de Origen,
    169–170
*Denominazione di Origine Con-
    trollata,* 103–106
*Denominazione di Origine Con-
    trollata e Garantita,*
    105–107
Dessilani, 111
Deutscher Tafelwein, 146–147
Deutz, 251, 307, 312
Deuxième Vin, 36
Dézalay, 182
Diamond Creek Vineyards, 221
Diamond Mountain, 221
Diel, 164
Dillon, Clarence, 50
Dimiat, 189
Disgorging, 305
Doctor (Bernkasteler), 165
Dolce, 107
Dolce, 207
Dolceacqua, 1115
Dolcetto, 112–1113
Dôle, 183
Dom Pérignon, 300, 306
Dom Ruinart, 306

Domain-bottling, *see* Estate-
    bottling
Domaine Carneros, 219, 312
Domaine Chandon, 311
Domaine de Chevalier, 51
Domaine de L'Hyverniere, 91
Domaine du Nalys, 88
Domaine de la Romanée-
    Conti, 73
Domaine St. George, 232
Domaine Ste. Michelle, 312
Domaine Tempier, 98
Domaine du Vieux Télégraphe,
    88
Domecq, Pedro, 173, 311, 318,
    335
Dominus, 225
Donatien-Bahuaud, 91
Donnaz, 111
Dopff, 97
Dopff & Irion, 97
Dordogne, 30, 52, 99
Dorin, 182
Dosage, 305
Double magnum, 12
Doumani, Carl, 220
Douro, 180, 319
Dourthe, 33
Dow, 323
Draper, Paul, 243
Dri, Giovanni, 121
Drouhin, Joseph, 70, 76, 85, 269
Dry Creek Valley, 230
Dry Creek Winery, 230
Dry Sack, 318
Duboeuf, Georges, 85
Dubonnet, 326
Duckhorn Vineyards, 226
Ducs de Normandie, 339
Duff Gordon, 318
Dulong, 33
Dunn Vineyards, 220
Dunnewood, 238
Durif, 211
Dürkheim, 1159
Durney Vineyard, 248
Dürnstein, 185
Dutchess, 260

E & J, 336
Eberle Winery, 250
Echézeaux, 73
Edelfäule, 148
Edelwein Gold, 207
Edelzwicker, 95
Edes, 187
Edmeades, 240
Edmunds St. John, 241
Edna Valley, 250–251
Edna Valley Vineyard, 250
Eden Roc, 311
Edwards, Merry, 232
Egri Bikavér, 187
Ehrenfelser, 146
Einzellage, 153
Eiswein, 148–149, 152
Eitelsbach, 167, 168
El Dorado, 253, 254
Eldorado Gold, 207
Elbe River, 143
Elk Cove Vineyards, 268
Ellis, Neil, 293–294
Eltville, 163
Elysium, 324
Emerald Riesling, 213
Emilia-Romagna, 135–136
Enfer d'Arvier, 112
EnoFriulia, 120
Enologica Valtellinese, 114
Entre-Deux-Mers, 61
Equipe 5, 122
Erath, Dick, 268
Erbach, 163
Erben, 155
Erden, 166
Errazuriz, 278
Erzeugerabfüllung, 154
Eschenauer, 33
Eschendorf, 168
Eshcol, 227
Essensia, 324
Estancia Estates, 229, 248
Estate-bottling, 69
Est! Est!! Est!!!, 137
Estrella River Winery, 250
Estremadura, 180
Estufas, 324, 325

Eszencia (Tokay), 186–187
Etchart, 279
Etna, 139
Etude, 225
Evans, Len, 285
Evesham Wood, 269
Extra Brut, 305
Extra Dry, 305
Eyrie Vineyards, 268

Faberrebe, 146
Falchini, Riccardo, 131
Falco, Carlos, 175
Falcon Crest, 221
Falkenstein, 185
Fall Creek Vineyards, 271
Far Niente, 226
Fara, 111
Farm Winery Act, 262–263
Faro, 139
Farrell, Gary, 233
Fass, 155
Fassati, 133
Fattoria, 107
Faugères, 99
Faustino Martinez, 173
Faux, 231
Favonio, 138
Favorita, 113
Fazi-Battaglia, 134
Feder, Ben, 264
Feine, feinste, 155
Fellom Ranch, 245
Felluga, Livio, 120
Felluga, Mario, 120
Felsina, 128
Felton-Empire, 245
Fendant, 182
Fenestra, 241
Fenn Valley Vineyards, 272
Fermentation, 5–9
Fernandez, Alejandro, 175
Ferrande, Pierre, 332
Ferrari, 122, 310
Ferrari-Carano, 231
Ferreira, 180, 323
Ferrer, Gloria, 234, 312
Fetească, 190

Fetzer Vineyards, 237
Fiano di Avellino, 138
Fiasco, 124
Ficklin, 324
Fiddletown, 254
Field Stone, 230
Filtering, 10–11
Fine Champagne, 328
Finger Lakes, 261–263
Fining, 10
Fino, 315–316
Fins Bois, 328
Fiorano, 136–137
Firestone Vineyard, 251
First growths, 38, 39, 42
First pressing, 301
Fischer, Dr., 167
Fisher Vineyards, 236
Fitou, 99
Fitzpatrick Winery, 254
Fixin, 71
Flaccianello della Pieve, 130
Flagey-Echézeaux, 73
Fleur de Champagne, 306
Fleur du Cap, 293
Fleurie, 84
Flichman, 279
Floc de Gascogne, 325
Flor, 315–316, 319
Flora, 214
Flora Springs, 226
Floréal, 226
Fogarty, Thomas, 245
Fognano, Fattoria di, 133
Folie à Deux, 226
Folle Blanche, 214
Folonari, 117
Fonseca, 323
Fonseca, J. M. da, 181
Fontana Candida, 136
Fontanafredda, 109
Fontodi, 128
Food and wine, *see* Wine
Foppiano, 232
Forman Winery, 220
Formentini, Conti, 120
Forst, 159
Fortified wines, 314–326

Fortino, 243
Forts de Latour, Les, 46
Fournier, Charles, 261
Foxen Vineyard, 252
Framboise, 336
France;
    table wines, 24–100
    sparkling wines, 299–309
    brandy, 327–334
Franciacorta, 114–115, 309–310
Franciscan Oakville Estate,
    226, 248
Franconia, 144, 168
Frank, Konstantin, 261
Franken Riesling, 213
Frankenwein, 168
Frankland River, 288
Franzia, 256
Frascati, 136
Frecciarossa, 114
Free-run, 7
Freemark Abbey, 226
Freiherr, 155
Freisa, 112–113
Freixenet, 311, 312
French-American hybrids, 258,
    260–261, 272, 294, 295
French Colombard, 214
Frescobaldi, 129
Freidrich Wilhelm Gymnasium,
    165
Frey Vineyard, 238
Frick Winery, 231
Fritz Cellars, 231
Friuli-Venezia Giulia, 119–121
Friulvini, 120
Frizzante, 107
Frog's Leap, 226
Fronsac, 57
Frontignan, 99
Frost, 64
Fuder, 155
Fuller, William and Virginia, 268
Fumé Blanc, 212–213, 223
Fundador, 335
Furmint, 186, 187
Fürst, 155
Fussigny, A. de, 332

Gabiano, 112
Gainey Vineyards, 252
Gaja, Angelo, 109–110
Galestro, 130
Galicia, 177
Galil, 296
Gallo, E. & J., 231, 255–256
Gallo nero, 127
Gamay, 83, 62, 210
Gamay Beaujolais, 210
Gambellara, 118
Gamla, 297
Gamza, 189
Gan Eden, 233
Gancia, 309
Garafoli, 135
Garda Lake, 116, 118
Garganega, 116
Garonne, 30, 52
Garrafeira, 178
Gascony, 100, 332
Gaston de Lagrange, 332
Gattinara, 111
Gavi, 113
Gavilan Mountains, 246, 248
Gehringer Brothers, 295
Geisenheim, 163
Generic wine names, 4–5,
        198–199
Geneva, Lake, 182
Geography and wine, 3–4
Germain-Robin, 336
Germany:
    table wines, 140–168
    sparkling wines, 310
    brandy, 335–336
Gerwer Winery, 254
Gevrey-Chambertin, 71–72
Geyser Peak Winery, 230
Gewürztraminer, 95, 96, 214
Ghemme, 111
Ghiae della Furba, 131
Giacosa, Bruno, 109
Gigondas, 89
Gilroy, 243
Ginestet, 47
Girard Winery, 226
Gironde, 30

Girasols, 311
Gisborne, 289
Giumarra, 256
Giustiniana, La, 113
Givry, 81
Glasses, see Wine
Glen Carlou, 293
Glen Ellen Winery, 235
Glenora Wine Cellar, 263
Gloria Ferrer, 234, 312
Golan Heights Winery, 297
Gold Seal, 262
Goldener Oktober, 156
Gonzalez, Byass, 318, 335
Goosecross Cellars, 226
Gosset, 307
Goulburn Valley, 288
Gould Campbell, 323
Governo alla toscano, 125, 127
Gotto d'Oro, 136
Graach, 166
Graciano, 171
Graf, 155
Graff, Richard, 248
Graham, 323
Grahm, Randall, 244
Grai, Giorgio, 123
Gran Reserva, 173
Grand cru:
    Bordeaux, 38–39, 53
    Burgundy, 64, 66–67, 68
    Alsace, 96
Grand Cru, 256
Grande Champagne, 328
Grand vin, 36
Grand Fine Champagne, 328
Grand Rue, La, 73
Grand Siècle, 306
Grands-Echézeaux, 73
Grange Hermitage, 281
Granite Springs, 254
Grão Vasco, 180
Grape varieties, see Chardonnay,
        Riesling, etc.
Grappa, 335
Gratien & Meyer, 308
Grave del Friuli, 120
Graves, 49–51

Graves Supérieures, 49
Gravner, 120
Gray Monk Cellars, 295
Great Western, 262
Grechetto, 134
Greco di Tufo, 138
Greece, 188–189
Green & Red Vineyard, 226
Green Hungarian, 214
Greenwood Ridge Vineyards, 238
Green Valley-Solano, 227
Green Valley-Sonoma, 233
Grenache, 87, 211
Grenache Rosé, 211, 215
Grey Riesling, 213
Grgich Hills, 226
Grifi, 133
Grignolino, 112–113
Grinzing, 184
Griotte-Chambertin, 72
Gristina Vineyards, 265
Groenesteyn, Schloss, 162
Groot Constantia, 290, 293
Gros Plant du Pays Nantais, 91
Groslot, 91
Grosslage, 154
Groth Vineyards, 225
Gruet Winery, 272, 312
Grumello, 114
Grüner Veltliner, 183–184, 185
Guenoc Valley, 239
Guenoc Winery, 239
Guglielmo, 243
Guigal, 90
Guigone de Salins, 75
Guild, 256
Gumpoldskirchen, 184
Gundlach-Bundschu, 235
Gutedel, 146

Haardt Mountains, 158–159
Haas, Robert, 249
Hacienda, 256
Hagafen Cellars, 226
Hahn Estates, 247
Haight Vineyards, 272
Hainle Vineyards, 295

Halbtrocken, 152
Half-bottles, 12
Hallcrest, 245
Hallgarten, 163
Halliday, James, 287
Hamilton Russell, 293
Hammondsport, 262
Handley Cellars, 238
Hanepoot, 291
Hanna Winery, 233
Hanzell, 235
Haraszthy, Agoston, 193, 234
Hardys, 284
Hargrave Vineyard, 264–265
Hárslevelü, 187
Harveys, 318, 323
Hattenheim, 163
Hatzi Michalis, 189
Hauner, Carl, 139
Haut-Médoc, 38
Haut-Sauternes, 59
Hautes Côtes de Beaune, 76
Hautes Côtes de Nuits, 74
Hawk Crest, 220
Hawkes Bay, 289
Haywood Winery, 234
Heat summation, 202
Hecker Pass, 243
Heidsieck, Charles, 307
Heidsieck Monopole, 307
Heitz Cellars, 224
Henkell, 310
Hennessy, 332
Henriot, 307
Henriques & Henriques, 325
Henriques, Justino, 325
Henry Estate, 269
Henry of Pelham, 295
Henschke, 287
Hermannhof Winery, 272
Hermitage, 89
Heron Hill Winery, 263
Hess Collection, 220
Hessian State, 161
Hessische Bergstrasse, 147
Heublein, 256
Heurige, 183
Heyl zu Herrnsheim, 160

Hidalgo, 318
Hidden Cellars, 238
Hill, William, Winery, 226
Hill-Smith, 287
Hillcrest Vineyard, 268
Hillebrand Estates Winery, 295
Hine, 323
Hochar, Serge, 298
Hochheim, 163
Hock, 161
Hofstätter, 123
Hogue Cellars, 267
Honig Cellars, 226
Hooper's, 323
Hop Kiln, 233
Hospices de Beaune, 75–76
Houghton, 284
Howell Mountain, 220
Hudson River region, 264
Huet, Gaston, 93
Hugel, 97
Hungary, 185–188
Hungerford Hill, 284
Hunt Country Vineyards, 263
Hunter, 290
Hunter Valley, 285
Huntington Estate, 286
Husch Vineyard, 238
Huxelrebe, 146
Hybrids, 257–258, 260–261
Hymettus, 188

Ice-buckets, 344–345
Ice wine, 148–149
Idaho, 270
Imbottigliato, 107
Imperial, 12
Ina, La, 318
Inferno, 114
Inglenook, 222
Ingleside Plantation, 271
Inniskillin, 295
Insignia, 224
Iphofen, 168
Iron Horse Vineyards, 233, 312
Ischia, 137
Isole e Olena, 128
Isonso, 121

Israel, 296–297
Italian Riesling, 145
Italy:
    table wines, 101–139
    sparkling wines, 309–310
    brandy, 335

JFJ Bronco, 256
Jaboulet, Paul, Aîné, 88, 90
Jacob's Creek, 284
Jacquart, 307
Jadot, Louis, 70, 85
Jaeger, Inglenook, 226
Jamesport Vineyards, 265
Janneau, 334
Jardinet, Le, 29
Jekel Vineyard, 247
Jensen, Josh, 249
Jepson Vineyards, 238
Jerez de la Frontera, 315
Jermann, 120
Jeroboam, 12, 306
Johannisberg, 163
Johannisberg, Schloss, 161–162
Johannisberg Riesling, 145, 213
Johnson Estate, 264
Johnson's Alexander Valley, 230
Joliesse, 230
Jordan Winery, 229, 312
Josephshof, 165
Josmeyer, 97
Joullian Vineyards, 248
Jug wines, 12
Juliénas, 84
Juliusspital, 168
Junot, René, 29
Jura, 100
Justin Vineyards, 250
Justino Henriques, 325
Juvé y Camps, 311

KMW, 184
K.W.V. 290, 293
Kabinett, 147
Kadarka, 187
Kaiser Stuhl, 284
Kalin Cellars, 241
Kalterer, Kalterersee, 123

Kanonkop, 293
Kanzem, 167
Karakash, Domaine, 221
Karthäuserhofberg, 167, 168
Karly Wines, 254
Kasel, 168
Keenan, Robert, 221
Kékfrankos, 187
Kéknyelü, 187
Kellerei, 155
Kendall-Jackson, 239–240, 252
Kendermann, 156
Kennedy, Kathryn, 245
Kenwood Vineyards, 236
Kerner, 146
Kesselstatt, von, 165
Kettmeir, 123
Kiedrich, 163
Kionah Vineyards, 267
Kir, 98
Kirigin Cellars, 243
Kirsch, 336
Kistler Vineyards, 236
Klein Constantia, 293
Kloster Eberbach, 161
Klosterneuberg, 184–185
Knapp Vineyards, 263
Knights Valley, 231
Knudsen-Erath, 268
Kokinelli, 188
Konocti Winery, 240
Konzellman, 295
Konrad Estate, 238
Korbel, 232, 311
Kosher wines, 296
Kourtakis, 189
Krems, 185
Kreuznach, 164
Kriter, 308
Krondorf, 284
Kröver Nacktarsch, 166
Krug, 306, 307
Krug, Charles, 222
Kruse, Thomas, 243
Kumeu River, 290
Kunde Estate, 236

LBV port, 323

Labels, how to read, 2–5,
    198–206
Labrusca, see Vitis labrusca
La Cour Pavillon, 33
Lacryma Christi, 137
Ladoix-Serrigny, 75
Ladoucette, de, 94
Lady Langoa, 46
Lafond, Comte, 94
Lageder, Alois, 123
Lago di Caldaro, 123
Lagrein, 115, 123
La Ina, 318
La Jota, 220
La Mancha, 177
La Motte, 293
La Pommeraie, 339
Lake County, 239–240
Lake Erie, 263, 271
Lake's Folly, 281
Lakespring Winery, 226
Lalande de Pomerol, 57
La Mancha, 177
Lamberti, 117
Lamborn Family Vineyards, 220
Lambrusco, 135–136
Lamoreaux Landing, 253
Lancers, 178
Landmark Vineyards, 236
Landwein, 147
Langenlois, 184
Langlois-Château, 308
Languedoc-Roussillon, 98–99
Langtry, Lillie, 239
Lanson, 307
La Reina Winery, 247
Larressingle, 334
La Tâche, 73
Latah Creek, 267
Late Bottled Vintage port, 323
Late Harvest, 206–207
Latisana, 121
Latour, Georges de, 221
Latour, Louis, 70, 74, 85
Latricières-Chambertin, 72
Lauerberg, 165
Laurel Glen Vineyard, 236
Laurent Perrier, 306, 207

Lauretan, 23
Laurier, 256
Lavaux, 182
Laws, see Wine laws
Lazy Creek Vineyards, 238
Le Domaine, 256, 311
Leacock, 325
Leasingham, Stanley, 284
Lebanon, 297–298
Leeward Winery, 253
Leeuwin Estate, 289
Leányka, 187
Léognan, 50–51
Leftover wine, 351–352
Lehmann, Peter, 286
Leighton, Terry, 241
Lembey, 311
Lenz Vineyards, 265
Leon, Jean, 175–176
Leonetti, 267
Lérida, 176
Lessona, 111
Lett, David, 268
Lexia, 284
Liberty School, 225
Lichine, Alexis, 48
Lieberstein, 291
Lievland, 293
Liebfraumilch, 156
Light wines, 207
Liguria, 114–115
Lillet, 326
Limousin oak, 329
Lindeman's, 284
Lingenfelder, 159
Lipari, 139
Liqueur de tirage, 303
Lirac, 88
Lisini, 132
Lison-Pramaggiore, 118
Listrac, 48
Liter, 12
Livermore Valley, 240–241
Livingston Cellars, 225
Llano Estacado, 271
Lockwood, 247
Lodi, 201, 256
Loeb, John, 233

Logan, 247
Lohr, J., 243
Loiben, 185
Loire wines, 90–94
Lolonis Winery, 238
Lombardy, 114–115
Long Flat Red, 284
Long Island, 264–265
Long Vineyards, 226
Lontué, 275
Loosen, Dr., 165
López de Heredia, 174
L'Ormarins, 293
Los Vascos, 278
Loubère, 334
Loupiac, 61
Loureiro, 179
Lucas Vineyard, 263
Lugana, 118
Lugny, 81
Luna dei Feldi, 124
Lungarotti, 134
Lurton, André, 50
Lurton, Lucien, 48
Lussac-Saint-Emilion, 54
Lustau, Emilio, 318
Lutomer, 190
Lyeth, 230
Lytton Springs, 231

Macabeo, 171
Mâcon, 81
Mâconnais, 81–82
MacRostie, 234
Maculan, Fausto, 118
Madeira, 324–325
Madeira Wine Company, 325
Madera, 324–325
Maderized, maderisé, 17
Madiran, 100
Madrigal, 156
Madrona Vineyards, 254
Magnums, 12
Magoon, 239
Maipo Valley, 275
Maître d'Estournel, 33
Málaga, 325–326
Malbec, 99, 278

Malmsey, 325
Malolactic fermentation, 9
Malvasia, 139
Mancha, La, 177
Manischewitz, 262
Manzanilla, 317
Marc, 334
Maranges, 77
Marches, 135
Marchese di Barolo, 109
Marchesi di Gresy, 109
Marcobrunn (Erbacher), 163
Marcus James, 279
Maréchal Foch, 260
Marey-Monge, 73
Marfil, 177
Margaret River, 288
Margaux, 47–48
Maria Gomes, 180
Maribor, 190
Marietta Cellars, 230
Marino, 136
Mark West Vineyards, 233
Markham Vineyards, 226
Markko Vineyard, 271
Marlborough, 289
Marlstone, 230
Marne Valley, 300
Marqués de Arienzo, 173
Marqués de Cáceres, 174
Marqués de Griñón, 175
Marqués de Murrieta, 174
Marqués de Riscal, 174, 175
Marquis de Caussade, 334
Marquis de Goulaine, 91
Marquis de Montesquiou,
    334
Marsala, 325
Marsannay, 71
Marsanne, 90
Martell, 332
Martha's Vineyard, 224
Martin, Henri, 47
Martin Brothers, 250
Martinez Bujanda, 174
Martini & Rossi, 309
Martini, Louis M., 222
Martinsancho, 175

Marynissen, 295
Marzemino, 115
Mas de Daumas Gassac, 99
Masi, 117
Mascarello, 109
Masia Bach, 176
Maso Poli, 122
Masson, Paul, 207, 243, 244, 247
Mastantuono Winery, 250
Mastroberardino, 138
Mastrojanni, 132
Matanzas Creek, 236
Mataro, 211
Mateus, 178
Mattituck Hills, 265
Maturing wine, see Aging
Matuschka-Greiffenclau, 161
Maule, 275
Mauro, 175
Maury, 99
Mavrodaphne, 188
Mavrud, 189
Maximin Grünhaus, 167, 168
May, Tom and Martha, 224
Mayacamas Mountains, 217, 220
Mayacamas Vineyards, 220
Mazys-Chambertin, 72
Mazoyères-Chambertin, 72
Mazuelo, 171
Mazzocco Vineyards, 231
McDowell Valley, 238
McDowell Valley Vineyards, 238
McLaren Vale, 287
McWilliams, 284
Meador, Doug, 247
Medea, 297
Médoc, 38–48
Meeker Vineyard, 231
Meerlust, 293
Meier's Wine Cellars, 271
Melini, 128
Mellot, Alphonse, 94
Melnik, 189
Melon de Bourgogne, 90
Mendocino, 237–239
Mendoza, 278
Ménétou-Salon, 94
Mentzelopoulos family, 47

Meranese di Collina, 123
Mercurey, 81
Meredyth Vineyards, 271
Meridian, 223, 250
Meritage, 200
Merlot, 34–35, 52, 99, 106, 119,
    209, 265, 273, 291
Merritt Estate, 264
Merritt Island, 256
Merry Vintners, 232
Merryvale Vineyards, 226
Metaireau, Louis, 91
Metodo classico, 309–310
Méthode champenoise, 303, 311
Methuselah, 306
Metric sizes, 12
Meursault, 76
Mezzacorona, 122
Michael, Peter, 231
Michel Lynch, 33
Michel-Schlumberger, 231
Microclimate, 67, 202
Microfiltration, 11
Midi, 28, 98
Milano Winery, 238
Mildara, 284
Mill Creek Vineyards, 231
Millbrook Vineyard, 264
Miller, Mark, 264
Minervois, 99
Minho, 179
Mirabelle, 336
Mirassou, 243
Mis en bouteille au château, 37
Mis en bouteille au domaine, 69
Misket, 189
Mistelle, 326
Mistral, Le, 224
Mitchelton, 288
Moët & Chandon, 306, 307
Mogen David, 264
Molinara, 116
Mommessin, 85
Monastrell, 171
Monbazillac, 99
Monção, 179
Mondavi, Peter, 222
Mondavi, Robert, 223, 256

Monfalletto, 109
Monlezun oak, 324
Monmousseau, 93, 308
Monopole, 38
Monsanto, 128
Monsecco, 111
Montagne-Saint-Emilion, 54
Mont St. John, 219
Montagny, 81
Montalbano, 129
Montalcino, 132
Montana Wine, 289, 290
Montdomaine Cellars, 271
Monte Bello, 244
Monte Real, 174
Monte Vertine, 128
Montefalco, 134
Montefiascone, 137
Montepulciano, 133
Montepulciano (grape), 137
Montepulciano d'Abruzzo, 137
Monterey, 245–249
Monterey Vineyard, 247
Montesodi, 129
Monteviña, 254
Montezemolo, Cordero di, 109
Montgommery, 339
Monthélie, 77
Monticello Cellars, 226
Montilla, 318–319
Montlouis, 93
Montpellier, 256
Montrachet, 77
Montravel, 99
Montrose, 284
Monts du Tessala, 297
Moreau Blanc, 29
Morey-Saint-Denis, 72
Morgan Winery, 247
Morgon, 84
Morio-Muskat, 146
Morningstar Peninsula, 288
Morris, J. W., 230
Morris of Rutherglen, 288
Morton Estate, 290
Mosby Winery, 252
Moscadello di Montalcino, 133
Moscatel de Setúbal, 181

Moscato Canelli, 113
Moscato d'Asti, 113
Mosel-Saar-Ruwer, 164–167
Moselblümchen, 147
Moselle, 164–166
Moss Wood, 289
Moueix, Christian, 56, 225
Moueix, Jean-Pierre, 56
Moulin-à-Vent, 84
Moulin des Carruades, 45
Moulis, 48
Mount Barker, 288
Mount Eden Vineyards, 244
Mount Harlan, 249
Mount Palomar Winery, 253
Mount Pleasant Vineyard, 272
Mount Veeder, 220
Mount Veeder Winery, 220
Mountadam, 287
Mourvèdre, 87, 211
Mousseux, 308
Mouton-Cadet, 33, 45
Mudgee, 285–286
Mulderbosch, 293
Müller, Egon, 167
Müller, Rudolf, 157
Müller-Catoir, 159
Müller-Thurgau, 145–146, 289
Mumm, 306, 307
Mumm Napa Valley, 312
Murfatlar, 190
Murrieta, Marqués de, 174
Murrieta's Well, 241
Murrumbidgee, 284
Muscadelle, 35
Muscadet, 90–91
Muscat, 99, 188, 214, 283–284
Muscat de Beaumes-de-Venise, 89
Muscatel, 257
Musigny, 72
Musigny Blanc, 72
Must, 6

Nahe, 163–164
Nalle Winery, 231
Naoussa, 189
Napa, 216–227

Napa Ridge, 223
Napoléon Cognac, 331
Navalle, 256
Navarra, 178
Navarro Correas, 279
Navarro Vineyards, 238
Nebbiolo, 108–109, 111–112, 212
Neckar, river, 144
Nederburg, 293
Neetlingshof, 293
Négociant, 32
Negri, Nino, 114
Nemea, 188
Nestlé, 223
Neuberger, 184
Neuchâtel, 182
Neusiedlersee, 184
New York State, 259–265, 312
New South Wales, 285–286
New Zealand, 289–290
Newton Vineyard, 221
Neyers Winery, 226
Niagara, 260
Niagara Peninsula, 294–295
Niebaum, Gustav, 222
Niebaum-Coppola Estate, 225
Niederhausen, 164
Niepoort, 323
Nierstein, 160
Nightingale, 223
Nobilo, 290
Noble rot, 58, 186, 206
Nonvintage wine, 363, 368
North Coast counties, 203
North Fork, 265
North Salem Vineyard, 264
Northern Sonoma, 228
Nosiola, 122
Nottage Hill, 284
Nouveau wines, 83
Noval, Quinta do, 324
Novara Hills, 111
Nozzole, 128
Nuits Saint Georges, 73–74
Nuragus, 139
Nussberg, 184

Oak barrels, *see* Aging

Oak Knoll Winery, 268
Oakencroft Vineyards, 271
Oasis Vineyard, 271
Oberemmel, 167
Obester Winery, 239
Ockfen, 167
Oechsle, 149
Oeil de Perdrix, 182
Oestrich, 163
Offley Forrester, 324
Ohio, 271
Oïdium, 324
Ojai Vineyard, 253
Okanagan Valley, 295
Oloroso, 315–315
Oltrepò Pavese, 114
Ontario, 294–295
Oppenheim, 160
Optima, 146
Opus One, 223
Oregon, 268–270
Orfila, 279
Organic farming, 196
Originalabfüllung, 154
Orlando, 284
Ornellaia, 132
Ortega, 146
Ortman, Chuck, 250
Orvieto, 133–134
Osborne, 318
Otard, 332
Ott, Domaines, 97
Oxford Landing, 284
Oxidation, 16, 17

P.X., 315
Paarl, 292
Padthaway, 287
Pahlmeyer, 225
Paicines, 248
Palatinate, 143
Palazzo Altesi, 133
Palette, 98
Palmer Vineyards, 265
Palomino, 315
Palus, 26
Pantelleria, 139
Panther Creek Cellars, 269

Paradiso, Fattoria, 136
Paragon Vineyard, 250
Paraiso Springs, 248
Parducci, 237
Parellada, 171
Parker, Fess, 252
Partager, 29
Paso Robles, 249–250
Passe-Tous-grains, 62
Pasteurization, 11
Paternina, Federico, 174
Patras, 188
Patriarche, 308
Pauillac, 44–46
Paumanock, 265
Pavillon Rouge, 47
Pavillon Blanc, 48
Pays d'Auge, 338
Pays d'Oc, 28, 99
Peconic Bay, 265
Pecota, Robert, 226
Pedrizzetti, 243
Pedro Domecq, see Domecq
Pedro Ximénez, 315
Pedroncelli, 231
Peju Province, 226
Pelee Island, 294, 295
Penafiel, 175
Peñaflor, 279
Pendeli, 188
Penedés, 175–176, 310
Penfolds, 284
Pepi, Robert, 226
Pepperwood Springs, 239
Peppoli, 128
Père Magloire, 339
Père Patriarche, 29
Perez Pascuas, 175
Pergole Torte, Le, 129
Periquita, 181
Perlan, 183
Pernand-Vergelesses, 75
Perrier-Jouët, 306, 307
Pesquera, 175
Pessac-Léognan, 50–51
Petaluma, 287
Pétillant, 93
Petit Chablis, 65

Petit-Verdot, 34
Petite Champagne, 328
Petite Sirah, 211
Petits châteaux, 37
Peynaud, Emile, 47
Pfalz, see Rheinpfalz
Pheasant Ridge, 271
Phelps, Joseph, 224
Philippe Lorraine, 226
Phillips, R. H., 256
Phylloxera, 27, 172, 217, 246, 274
Piave, 118
Picolit, 115, 121
Pièces, 68
Piedmont, 107–111
Piedmont Vineyards, 271
Pieropan, 117
Piesport, 166
Pigato, 115
Pinault, François, 46
Pindar Vineyards, 265
Pine Ridge Winery, 220
Pineau de la Loire, 92
Pineau des Charentes, 326
Pinnacles, 247–248
Pinot Bianco, 116
Pinot Blanc, 95, 214
Pinot Chardonnay, see
          Chardonnay
Pinot Grigio, 115, 118, 120
Pinot Gris, 95, 268
Pinot Meunier, 301
Pinot Noir, 62, 209–210, 268, 301
Pinotage, 291–292
Pio Cesare, 109
Pipe, 321
Piper-Heidsieck, 307, 311
Piper-Sonoma, 232, 311
Pirramimma, 287
Plam Vineyards, 226
Plantaganet, 289
Plavac, 190
Plozner, 120
Po, river, 114
Podere, 107
Poggio alle Gazze, 132
Poggiolo, Il, 131
Poggione, 132

Poire, 336
Pojer & Sandri, 122
Pol Roger, 307
Polignac, 332
Politziano, 133
Pomace, 334
Pomerol, 55–57
Pomino, 129
Pommard, 76
Pommeraie, La, 339
Pommery, 307
Poniatowsky, Prince, 93
Pontallier, Paul, 276
Ponte a Rondolino, 131
Ponzi Vineyards, 268
Pop wines, 208
Port, 319–324
Port of the vintage, 323
Portet, Bernard, 220
Porto, 320
Portugal, 178–182, 319–324
Portugieser, 140
Pouilly-Fuissé, 82
Pouilly-Fumé, 94
Pouilly-Loché, 82
Pouilly-sur-Loire, 93, 94
Pouilly-Vinzelles, 82
Pourriture noble, 58, 148, 206
Poysdorf, 185
Prädikat, 147–148, 149, 184
Pramãggiore, 118
Prats, Bruno, 44, 274
Predicato, 130
Prémeaux, 74
Premiat, 190
Premier cru, 38–39, 52–53, 64,
          67–68
Press wine, 7
Preston Vineyards, 230–231
Preston Wine Cellar, 267
Primitivo, 138, 210
Prince Michel Vineyards, 271
Principessa Gavi, 113
Priorato, 177
Prissé, 81
Procanico, 134
Produttori del Barbaresco, 109
Prohibition, 193–194

Prokupac, 190
Proprietary names, 5, 33, 106,
    129–130, 200
Prosecco, 115, 119, 310
Protos, 175
Provence, 97–98
Prugnolo, 133
Prüm, 165
Prunier, 332
Prunotto, 109
Puerto de Santa María, 315
Pugliese, 265
Puiatti, 120
Puisseguin-Saint-Emilion, 54
Puligny-Montrachet, 76, 77
Pupitres, 304
Putto, 129
Puttonyos, 186

Quady, 324
Quail Ridge Cellars, 226
Quails' Gate Vineyards, 295
Qualitätswein, 147, 184
Qualitätswein mit Prädikat,
    147–148, 184
Quarles Harris, 324
Quarts de Chaume, 92
Querre, Alain, 55
Quetsch, 336
Quilceda Creek, 267
Quincy, 94
Quinta, 321
Quinta da Bacalhôa, 181
Quinta de Bomfim, 323
Quinta de Carmarate, 181
Quinta do Carmo, 182
Quinta do Cotto, 180
Quinta dos Malvedos, 323
Quinta do Noval, 324
Quinta de Pacheca, 180
Quinta da Roeda, 323
Quinta de la Rosa, 180
Quinta de Vargellas, 323
Quintarello, 117
Quivira Vineyards, 231
Qupé, 252

RMS Special Reserve, 336

Raboso, 115, 118
Rabbit Ridge, 233
Racke, 234
Rafanelli, 231
Ragnaud, Marcel, 332
Ragose, Le, 117
Raimat, 176
Rainoldi, 114
Rainwater Madeira, 325
Ramato, 120
Ramisco, 181
Ramos-Pinto, 323
Rancagua, 275
Rancho California, 253
Rancho Sisquoc, 252
Randersacker, 168
Rapazzini, 243
Rapel, 275
Rapidan River Vineyards, 271
Rasmussen, Kent, 219
Ratti, Renato, 109
Rauenthal, 163
Rauli, 276, 277
Ravat, 260
Ravello, 137
Ravenswood, 235
Raventós, 176
Ray, Martin, 244
Raymond Vineyard, 226
Rebello Valente, 324
Recioto, 117
Redde, Michel, 94
Redwood Valley, 237
Refosco, 115
Regaleali, 139
Região Demarcada, 179
Regnié, 84
Rehoboam, 306
Reif Winery, 295
Reinhartshausen, Schloss, 162
Remelluri, 176
Rémueur, 304
Rémy Martin, 332, 336
Rémy-Pannier, 93, 308
Renaissance Vineyards, 254
Reserva, 173, 178
Réserve de la Comtesse, 46
Reserve wines, 200–201

Ress, Balthazar, 162
Restaurants, wine in, 358–361
Retsina, 188
Reuilly, 94
Revere Winery, 226
Rex Hill Vineyards, 269
Rheingau, 160–163
Rheinhessen, 159–160
Rheinpfalz, 158–159
Rheinriesling, 145
Rhine, river, 143–144
Rhône wines, 87–90
Rías Baixas, 177
Ribatejo, 181
Ribeiro, 177
Ribera del Duero, 174–175
Ribolla, 120
Ricasoli, 125
Richebourg, 73
Richmond Grove, 286
Riddling, 304
Ridge, 231, 243–244
Riecine, 128
Riesling, 95–96, 144–145, 213
Rioja, 171–174
Rioja Alta, La, 174
Rioja Vega, 174
Ripasso, 117
Riscal, Marqués de, 174, 175
Riserva, 127, 132
Riserva Ducale, 129
Riunite, 136
Rivella, Ezio, 133
Rivendell, 263
Rivera, 138
Riverland, 287
Riviera del Garda Bresciano, 118
Riverside Farm, 232
Rkatsiteli, 189
Robertson, 323
Rocche, 109
Rocchette, 109
Rochioli, J., 232
Roche aux Moines, 92
Roche Winery, 234
Rocco della Macie, 128
Rodet, Antonin, 81
Roditis, 188

Roederer, 238, 306, 307, 312
Rolin, Nicolas, 75
Roma, 256
Romanée, La, 73
Romanée-Conti, 73
Romanée-Saint-Vivant, 73
Romania, 189–190
Rombauer Vineyards, 226
Ronco del Gnemiz, 121
Rondinella, 116
Rosato, 107
Rosé, 6, 215
Rosemount Estate, 285
Rosenblum Cellars, 241
Rossi, Carlo, 255
Rosso, 107
Rosso Cònero, 135
Rosso di Montalcino, 132
Rosso di Montepulciano, 133
Rosso Piceno, 135
Rotgipfler, 184
Rothbury Estate, 285
Rothschild, Edmond de, 48
Rothschild, Philippe de, 45, 223
Roudon Smith Vineyards, 226
Rouge Homme, 284
Round Hill Cellars, 226
Roussanne, 90
Roussillon, 98–99
Royal Kedem, 264
Rubesco, 134
Rubicon, 225
Ruby Cabernet, 212
Ruby port, 321
Ruchottes-Chambertin, 72
Rudesheim, 163
Rueda, 175
Ruffino, 129, 130, 134
Rufina, 129
Ruinart, 306, 307
Ruländer, 146
Rully, 81
Ruppertsberg, 159
Russia, 190
Russian River Valley, 232–233
Russiz Superiore, 120
Rust, 185
Rustenberg, 293

Rust-en-Verde, 293
Rutherford Hill, 226
Rutherford & Miles, 325
Rutherford Ranch, 226
Rutherglen, 288
Ruwer, river, 167–168

Saale-Unstrut, 143
Saar, river, 166–167
Sachsen, 143
SagPond Vineyards, 265
Sagrantino, 134
Saint-Amour, 84
St. Andrews Winery, 226
Saint-Chinian, 99
St. Clement Vineyards, 226
Saint-Emilion, 52–55
Saint-Emilion (grape), 328
Saint-Estèphe, 44
St. Francis Vineyards, 236
St. George Spirits, 337
Saint-Georges-Saint-Emilion, 54
Saint-Joseph, 90
Saint-Julien, 46–47
Saint-Laurent, 184
Saint Morillon, 278
Saint-Nicolas-de-Bourgueil, 93
St. Nikolaus Hospital, 165
Saint-Péray, 309
St. Raphaël, 326
Saint-Saphorin, 182
St. Supéry, 226
Saint-Véran, 82
Ste. Chapelle Vineyards, 270
Ste. Genevieve Vineyards, 271
Ste. Michelle Vineyards, 267, 312
Saintsbury, 219
Sakonnet Vineyards, 272
Salice Salentino, 138
Salignac, 332
Salinas Valley, 246
Salins, Guigone de, 75
Salm-Dalberg, 164
Salon Le Mesnil, 307
Salvagnin, 183
Samalens, 334
Sammarco, 130
San Benito, 248–249

San Felice, 129
San Gimignano, 131
San Giorgio, 134
San Joaquin Valley, 201–202,
    255–256
San Luis Obispo, 249–251
San Pedro, 278
San Saba, 247
San Sadurní de Noya, 310
Sancerre, 93–94
Sandalford, 288
Sandeman, 318, 323
Sanel Valley, 237
Sanford Winery, 252
Sangiacomo, 219
Sangiovese, 124–1125, 212
Sangiovese di Romagna, 136
Sangre de Toro, 176
Sangría, 169
Sangue di Giuda, 114
Sanlúcar de Barrameda, 315, 317
Santa Barbara, 251–253
Santa Barbara Winery, 252
Santa Clara, 241, 243
Santa Carolina, 278
Santa Cruz Mountains, 243–244
Santa Cruz Mountain Vineyard,
    245
Santa Lucia Mountains, 246, 247
Santa Maddalena, 123
Santa Maria Valley, 251–252
Santa Margherita, 118, 123–124
Santa Monica, 278
Santa Rita, 278
Santa Sofia,
Santa Ynez Valley, 252–252
Santa Ynez Winery, 252
Santenay, 77
Santini, 254
Santorini, 188
Saône, river, 82
Sarah's Vineyard, 243
Sardinia, 139
Sassella, 114
Sassicaia, 131
Saucelito Canyon Vineyard, 251
Saumur, 92
Saumur-Champigny, 92

Sausal, 230
Sauterne, California, 198
Sauternes, 57–61
Sauvignon Blanc, 35, 43, 58, 93, 212, 289–290, 291
Sauvion, Jean, 91
Savennières, 92
Savigny-les-Beaune, 75
Scharffenberger Cellars, 238, 312
Scharzberg, 167
Scharzhofberg, 166–167
Scheurebe, 146
Schiava, 115, 122
Schillerwein, 156
Schiopetto, Mario, 120
Schloss Eltz, 161
Schloss Groenesteyn, 162
Schloss Johannisberg, 161–162
Schloss Reichartshausen, 162
Schloss Rheinhartshausen, 162
Schloss Schönborn, 162
Schloss Schwanburg, 123
Schloss Vollards, 161
Schlossböckelheim, 163–164
Schönborn, Graf von, 162
Schramsberg, 311
Schubert, von, 167
Schug Caneros Estate, 234
Sebastiani, 234
Sebastiani, Sam and Vicki, 234
Scolca, 113
Secco, 107
Sediment in wine, 15, 348–349
Segesta, 139
Seghesio Winery, 231
Segura Viudas, 311
Sekt, 310
Selaks, 290
Selbach-Oster, 165
Select Late Harvest, 206
Sélection de Grains Nobles, 96–97
Sella & Mosca, 139
Sémillon, 35, 58, 213, 283, 285
Sempé, 334
Sendal, 229
Seppelts, 284
Sequoia Grove, 226

Sercial, 325
Serradayres, 181
Serrig, 167
Settesoli, 139
Setúbal, 181
Sèvre-et-Maine, 91
Seyssel, 98, 309
Seyval Blanc, 260
Sfursat, Sforzato, 114
Shafer Vineyards, 220
Shenandoah Valley, 254
Shenandoah Vineyards, 254
Shenandoah Vineyards (Virginia), 271
Sherry, 315–319
Shiraz, 281
Shumen, 189
Sichel, 33, 156
Sichel, Peter Alan, 48
Sicily, 138–139
Sierra Foothills, 253–255
Sierra Madre, 251
Sierra Vista, 254
Siglo, 173
Signorello, 226
Sillery, 301
Silvaner, 145
Silver Oak Cellars, 225
Silverado Trail, 217, 219
Silverado Vineyards, 220
Simi, 229
Simmern, von, 162
Simonini, Attilo, 138
Simonsig, 294
Single *quinta* port, 322–323
Sinskey, Robert, 220
Sion, 183
Sizzano, 111
Skin contact, 194
Sky Vineyards, 226
Slovenia, 190
Smith & Hook, 247
Smith-Madrone Vineyards, 221
Smith Woodehouse, 323
Smoking, 23
Soave, 116
Sobon Estate, 254
Soft wines, 207

Sogrape, 180
Sokol Blosser Winery, 268
Solaia, 130
Solano County, 227
Solera, 316–317, 319
Sommelière, 29
Sommer, Richard, 268
Sonoma, 227–236
Sonoma Coast, 228
Sonoma-Cutrer, 232
Sonoma-Loeb, 233
Sonoma Mountain, 233, 235–236
Sonoma Valley, 233–234
Sorni, 122
Sorì, 109
South Africa, 290–294
South America, 273–279
South Australia, 286–287
Southern Vales, 287
Souverain, Chateau, 222, 229
Soviet Union, 190
Spain:
    table wines, 169–178
    fortified wines, 315–318
    sparkling wines, 310–311
    brandy, 335
Spanna, 111
Spätlese, 147–148
Spätrot, 184
Special natural wines, 208
Splits, 305
Spottswoode, 225
Spring Mountain, 221
Spring Mountain Vineyards, 221
Spumante, 107, 309
Staatsweingüter, 161
Stags Leap District, 219–220
Stag's Leap Wine Cellars, 220
Stags' Leap Winery, 220
Stare, David, 230
Staton Hills, 267
Steele, Jed, 240
Steen, 291
Steinberg, 161
Steinwein, 144
Stellenbosch, 292
Stellenbosch Farmers' Winery, 293

Stellenryk, 293
Steltzner Vineyards, 220
Stemmler, Robert, 234
Sterling Vineyards, 221, 224
Stevenot Winery, 255
Stone Hill Winery, 272
Stonestreet, J., 230, 240
Stoney Ridge, 295
Stony Hill Vineyard, 221
Stony Ridge, 241
Storage of wine, 340–342
Storrs Winery, 245
Story Vineyard, 254
Storybook Mountain, 226
Strong, Rodney, 232
Strozzi, Guicciardini, 131
Südtirol, 122
Styria, 185
Sugar in wine, 6–7, 18–19,
            147–149, 157–158
Suhindol, 189
Suisse Romande, La, 182
Sulfur in wine, 11
Sultana, 281, 291
Sumac Ridge, 295
Summerhill, 295
Summit, 256
Sunny St. Helena, 226
Suntory, 47
Supérieur, 37
Superiore, 104
Sur lie, 91
Sur pointe, 304–305
Süssreserve, 150
Sutter Home Winery, 226, 254
Swan, Joseph, 233
Swan Valley, 288
Swanson Winery, 226
Swedish Hill Vineyards, 263
Switzerland, 182–183
Sycamore Creek, 243
Sylvaner, 145, 213
Symphony, 214
Syrah, 87, 89, 211, 281
Szamorodni, 187
Szürkebarát, 187

T-budding, 195

Tâche, La, 73
Tafelwein, 146–147
Taft Street, 233
Tagus River, 181
Tailles, 301–302
Taittinger, 306, 307, 312
Talbott, Robert, 247
Talley Vineyards, 251
Taltarni, 288
Tamas, Ivan, 241
Tannat, 100
Tannin, 6, 19–20, 35
Tari, 48
Tarra Warra, 287
Tarragona, 177
Tartrates, 15
Tasmania, 289
Tastevin, 16
Tasting wines, 13–23
Taunus Mountains, 161
Taurasi, 138
Taurino, 138
Tavel, 88
Tawny port, 321
Taylor, 262
Taylor California Cellars, 247
Taylor, Walter S., 263
Taylor Fladgate, 323
Tchelistcheff, André, 222
Te Mata, 290
Tedeschi, 117
Temecula, 253
Temperature: storage, 341; serving, 344–345
Tempier, Domaine, 98
Tempranillo, 171, 174
Tenuta, 107
Terlaner, Terlano, 123
Teroldego, 115, 122
Teroldego Rotaliano, 122
Terrabianca, 129
Terras Altas, 180
Terras do Sado, 181
Terre di Tufo, 131
Teruzzi & Puthod, 131
Tesseron, 44
Tête de Cuvée, 67
Texas, 270–271

Thackery, Sean, 241
Thanisch, 165
Thelema, 294
Thompson Seedless, 194
Thunderbird, 208, 255
Ticino, 182
Tinta Negra Mole, 325
Tignanello, 129
Tijsseling Vineyards, 238
Tinscvil, 130
Tio Pepe, 318
Tocai Friulano, 115
Tocai di Lison, 118
Togni, Philip, 221
Tokay, 186–187
Tokay d'Alsace, 95
Tommasi, 117
Torbato di Alghero, 139
Torcolato, 118
Torgiano, 134
Toro, 178
Torre Quarto, 138
Torres, 176, 274, 278
Torres, Marimar, 233
Toso, 279
Tott's, 311
Touraine, 92–93
Tourelles de Pichon, Les, 46
Trakia, 189
Traminer, 96, 122, 146
Transfer process, 308
Trapiche, 279
Travaglini, 111
Travers, Robert and Elinor, 220
Traverso, Sergio, 241
Tre Venezie, 115
Trebbiano, 116, 130
Trebbiano d'Abruzzo, 137
Trebbiano di Romagna, 136
Trefethen, 226
Trentadue, 230
Trentino, 121–122
Trento, 121
Trerose, Tenuta, 133
Trilogy, 226
Trimbach, 97
Trione, 230
Trittenheim, 166

Trocken, 152
Trockenbeerenauslese, 148, 151
Trollinger, 140
Trorçais oak, 329
Truchard, 219
Tualatin Vineyards, 268
Tudal Winery, 225
Turnbull Cellars, 225
Tuscany, 124–133
Twee Jongegezellen, 294
Tyrrells, 285

Ugni Blanc, 328
Uitkyk, 293
Ukiah, 237
Ull de Llebre, 171, 175
Ullage, 359
Umani Ronchi, 135
Umbria, 133–134
Umpqua Valley, 268
Undurraga, 278
Unico, 174
Ürzig, 166

V.D.Q.S., 27
VS Cognac, 330
VSOP Cognac, 330
VSP Cognac, 330
Vacqueyras, 89
Val d'Arbia, 131
Val di Suga, 132
Valais, 183
Valbon, 29
Valbuena, 174
Valckenberg, 156
Valdadige, 122
Valdepeñas, 177–178
Valdivieso, 278
Valdobbiadene, 119
Valgella, 114
Vallana, 111
Valle d'Aosta, 112
Valle Isarco, 123
Vallejo, M.G., 235
Valley of the Moon, 233
Valpantena, 117
Valpolicella, 116–117
Valtellina, 114

Varietal wine names, 4, 199–201
Vaselli, 134
Vasse Felix, 289
Vatting, 6, 35–36, 83
Vaud, 182–183
Vega Sicilia, 174
Vellette, Le, 134
Vendange Tardive, 96–97
Venegazzù, 119
Veneto, 116–119
Ventana Vineyards, 247
Verdejo, 171, 175
Verdelho, 325
Verdicchio, 135
Verduzzo, 115, 118, 121
Vereinigte Hospitien, 165
Vermentino, 115, 139
Vermouth, 326
Vernaccia, 131
Vernatsch, 123
Vesuvio, 137
Veuve Amiot, 308
Veuve Clicquot-Ponsardin, 306, 307
Viader, 225
Viansa Winery, 234
Vichon Winery, 223
Victoria, 287–288
Vidal Blanc, 260, 294
Vidal-Fleury, 90
Vieille Ferme, La, 89
Vigne del Leon, 121
Vignoles, 260
Vietti, 109
Vieux-Château-Certan, 57
Vieux Télégraphe, 88
Vigna, 107
Vila Nova de Gaia, 319
Villa Antinori, see Antinori
Villa Maria, 290
Villa Mt. Eden, 227
Villányi Burgundi, 187
Villiera, 294
Vin aigre, 9
Vin de cuvée, 301
Vin de Pays, 27–28, 99
Vin du pays, 28
Vin de Table, 28–29

Vin jaune, 100
Vin Santo, 131
Viña Cumbrero, 174
Viña Pomal, 173
Viña Real, 173
Viña Sol, 176
Viña Tondonia, 173
Viña Vial, 174
Vinegar, 352
Vineland Estates, 295
Vinho Regional, 179
Vinho Verde, 179
Vinhos, J. P., 181
Vinifera, see *Vitis vinifera*
Vinifera Wine Cellars, 263
Vinification, 5–12, 194–195
Vino da Tavola, 106–107,
    129–130
Vino Nobile di Montepulciano,
    133
Vinòt, 111
Vintage Champagne, 302–303
Vintage charts, 366–367
Vintage Port, 322–323
Vintage Tunina, 120
Vintage year, 302–303, 322, 363
Vintages, 204–205, 362–368
Vintners Quality Alliance, 294,
    295
Vinzelles, 82
Viognier, 89, 214
Viré, 81
Vita Nova, 252
Viticultural areas, 203
Vitis labrusca, 259, 279
Vitis vinifera, 258, 259–260, 264,
    266
Viura, 171, 175
Voerzio, Roberto, 109
Vogüé, Comte de, 72
Vollrads, Schloss, 161
Volnay, 76
Volpe Pasini, 121
Von Strasser, 221
Vörös, 187
Vöslau, 184
Vosne-Romanée, 73
Vougeot, 72

Vouvray, 92–93
Vranac, 190

Wachau, 185
Wachenheim, 159
Wagner, Philip, 272
Wagner Vineyards, 263
Waldrach, 168
Walker Valley Vineyards, 264
Walla Walla Valley, 267, 269
Walnut Crest, 278
Warre, 323
Warwick, 294
Washington, 265–267
Washington Hills, 267
Waterbrook, 267
Weather, *see* Climate
Wegeler-Deinhard, 162, 165
Wehlen, 166
Weibel, 238, 311
Weinbach, Domaine, 97
Weinert, 279
Weingut, 155
Weinstock Cellars, 232
Weissburgunder, 146
Weissherbst, 155–156
Welsch Riesling, 145
Wente, 240–241
West Park, 264
Western Australia, 288–289
Westport Rivers Vineyard, 272
Wetmore, William, 264
Whaler Vineyard, 238
Wheeler, William, 230
White Oaks, 231–232
White Riesling, 145, 213
White Zinfandel, 215
Whitehall Lane, 227
Whole-berry fermentation, 7
Widmer's, 262
Wiederkehr Wine Cellars, 272
Wiemer, Hermann J., 263
Wild Horse Vineyards, 250
Williamette Valley, 268–269
Williams & Humbert, 318
Williams Selyem, 232
Williamsburg Winery, 271
Willm, 97

Wiltingen, 167
Wine:
  buying, 340–341
  glasses, 313, 349–351
  service, 343–352
  and food, 352–356
  see also, Aging, Vinification,
    Tasting
Wine coolers, 208
Wine laws, 2–4
  France, 24–29
  Italy, 103–107
  Germany, 146–155
  California, 201–205
Wine lists, 360–361
Wine racks, 342
Winery Lake, 219
Winiarski, Warren, 220
Winkel, 163
Winzergenossenschaft, 155
Winzerverein, 155
Wirra Wirra, 287
Wisdom & Warter, 318
Woodbridge, 223, 256
Woodburne, Lloyd, 266
Woodbury Vineyards, 264
Woodbury Winery, 26
Woods, Christine, 239
Woodward Canyon, 267
Württemberg, 144, 156
Würzburg, 168
Wyndham Estate, 284
Wynn's, 284

X.O., 331
Xarello, 171, 310

Yakima Valley, 267
Yalumba, 284
Yamhill Valley Vineyards, 269
Yarden, 297
Yarra Valley, 287
Yarra Yering, 287
Yeast, 6
Yellowglen, 284
Yield, 3, 71
York Mountain Winery, 249
Young, Robert, 228
Yquem, 59, 60
Yugoslavia, 190
Yvorne, 183

Z Moore, 232
ZD Wines, 226
Zaca Mesa Winery, 252
Zanella, Maurizio, 115
Zeller Schwarze Katz, 165–166
Zellerbach, James, 235
Zeni, 122
Zeltingen, 166
Zerbina, Fattoria, 136
Zierfandler, 184
Zind-Humbrecht, 97
Zinfandel, 210–211
Zip code wines, 29
Zonin, 118, 136
Zonnebloem, 293
Zweigelt, 184